ECONOMIC COOPERATION IN THE SHADOW OF CONTESTED SOVEREIGNTY

This open access book is the first of its kind to address a question of both theoretical and practical significance: how do countries or entities approach economic cooperation in the face of vexing political concerns and overlapping sovereignty claims?

Built upon three contemporary case studies on North-South Korea, China-Taiwan, and North-South Cyprus – representative pairs of 'divided nations', broadly defined – the book explores from both an empirical and a conceptual perspective the underlying factors, approaches and patterns that influence the economic relationship between the two sides.

The book examines complex dynamics and identifies critical factors across the case studies, making a timely contribution to debates surrounding sovereignty, democracy and legitimacy in the context of international economic laws given the shifting geopolitical landscape. It further informs countries that do not share the same features of divided nations but nonetheless experience diplomatic crises or military conflicts, which render their economic cooperation sensitive and strenuous.

This book is a must-read for researchers, trade lawyers, and students in international law and international relations. It also serves as a valuable asset for negotiators, diplomats and policymakers, providing crucial insights for making decisions that can either escalate or de-escalate geopolitical conflicts.

Studies in International Trade and Investment Law: Volume 33

Studies in International Trade and Investment Law

Series Editors
Gabrielle Marceau
Krista Nadakavukaren Schefer
Federico Ortino
Gregory Shaffer

This series offers a forum for publication of original and scholarly analyses of emerging and significant issues in international trade and investment law – broadly understood to include the whole of the law of the WTO, the public international law of foreign investment, the law of the EU common commercial policy and other regional trade regimes, and any legal or regulatory topic that interacts with global trade and foreign investment. The aim of the series is to produce works which will be readily accessible to trade and investment law scholars and practitioners alike.

Recent titles in this series:

Regional Economic Integration and Dispute Settlement in East Asia: The Evolving Legal Framework
Anna G Tevini

The EU, World Trade Law and the Right to Food: Rethinking Free Trade Agreements with Developing Countries
Giovanni Gruni

Patent Games in the Global South: Pharmaceutical Patent Law Making in Brazil, India and Nigeria
Amaka Vanni

The Nationality of Corporate Investors under International Investment Law
Anil Yilmaz Vastardis

The Regulation of Product Standards in World Trade Law
Ming Du

Investors' International Law
Edited by Jean Ho and Mavluda Sattorova

Rethinking, Repackaging, and Rescuing World Trade Law in the Post-Pandemic Era
Edited by Amrita Bahri, Weihan Zhou and Daria Boklan

Flexible Regional Economic Integration in Africa: Lessons and Implications for the Multilateral Trading System
Timothy Masiko

International Investment Law: An Analysis of the Major Decisions
Edited by Hélène Ruiz Fabri and Edoardo Stoppioni

State Capitalism and International Investment Law
Edited by Panagiotis Delimatsis, Georgios Dimitropoulos and Anastasios Gourgourinis

The European Union and International Investment Law: The Two Dimensions of an Uneasy Relationship
Francesco Montanaro

Financial Market Infrastructure and Economic Integration: A WTO, FTAs, and Competition Law Analysis
George A Papaconstantinou

International Trade Law and Global Data Governance: Aligning Perspectives and Practices
Neha Mishra

Hong Kong as an Actor in International Economic Law: Multilateralism, Bilateralism and Unilateralism
Julien Chaisse

Economic Cooperation in the Shadow of Contested Sovereignty

Chien-Huei Wu
Ching-Fu Lin
and
Han-Wei Liu

•HART•
OXFORD • LONDON • NEW YORK • NEW DELHI • SYDNEY

HART PUBLISHING

Bloomsbury Publishing Plc

Kemp House, Chawley Park, Cumnor Hill, Oxford, OX2 9PH, UK

1385 Broadway, New York, NY 10018, USA

29 Earlsfort Terrace, Dublin 2, Ireland

HART PUBLISHING, the Hart/Stag logo, BLOOMSBURY and the Diana logo are trademarks of Bloomsbury Publishing Plc

First published in Great Britain 2025

A catalogue record for this book is available from the British Library.

A catalogue record for this book is available from the Library of Congress.

ISBN: HB: 978-1-50997-015-5
ePDF: 978-1-50997-017-9
ePub: 978-1-50997-016-2

Typeset by Compuscript Ltd, Shannon

Acknowledgements

THIS COLLABORATIVE WORK originated from a paper presented at the biennial conference of the Society of International Economic Law, held in Washington, DC, in 2018. At the time, none of us – nor anyone else – could have pictured exactly what to write or how to approach the subject. Our initial idea was to explore, from an academic perspective, the reverse side of economic integration among like-minded countries or allies. While the concept of "sovereignty" has long been addressed in the traditional discourse of public international law, it remains relatively less explored when considering how countries or entities with overlapping sovereignty claims engage with each other economically.

When the manuscript of this book was finalised, the world had significantly changed and become much different from the one in which we conceived this idea six years ago. The call for economic security has grown even louder, particularly in the shadow of the Russia–Ukraine and Israel–Hamas conflicts. At the same time, the growing tension between the two sides of the Taiwan Strait and the two Koreas has added complexity to the geopolitical landscape. Such dynamics – alongside the COVID-19 pandemic, which has further complicated not only our writing and research process but also the changing global supply chain and geopolitics – have required the authors to spend more time on this project. Therefore, the two case studies in this book – the Korean Peninsula and the Taiwan Strait – have presented tremendous challenges to our writing. We have made our best efforts to keep this book updated and believe it may offer some valuable lessons in these strange times.

It is crucial to note that while this book stems from academic inquiry, we have found the topic to be inherently political, and different perspectives can be expected. We have strived to remain neutral and present both sides of the ideas to maintain balance, especially considering that all authors are originally from a single country. We acknowledge our limitations – we may not interpret the laws, practices, and politics as precisely as scholars from the jurisdictions this book covers – China, North and South Korea, and North and South Cyprus. Even when discussing Taiwan's laws, policies, and politics, there can be different perspectives as well. Nevertheless, our aim is to contribute to the ongoing discourse surrounding the interplay between sovereignty and economic integration in an increasingly interconnected and complex world.

We are grateful for the help of our talented research assistants, who brought valuable linguistic skills to the project. Chien-Huei Wu would like to express special thanks to Esther Liao for her excellent research assistance and wishes to dedicate this work to lives, stories, and memories, *les êtres chers*, crossing the Line. Ching-Fu Lin is grateful for the support provided by Dae Ho Ha and James Soo. Han-Wei Liu expresses gratitude to Derek Zhang, NG Xin Yu, Peggy Hsu, and Cindy Liu for their valuable research assistance. He also acknowledges the research support received during his tenure at Monash University and subsequently at Singapore Management University. Additionally, he appreciates the support from the Taiwan Study Project.

Last, but not least, we would like to express our gratitude to Jeffrey Cuvilier for meticulously proofreading the manuscript and Tripp Odom for diligently verifying the citations and footnotes. We are also deeply thankful to Roberta Bassi and Verity Stuart from the editorial team at Hart Publishing for their unwavering patience and invaluable support throughout the editing process. Furthermore, we gratefully acknowledge the research grant provided by the Academia Sinica thematic program (AS-TP-110-H01), which has been instrumental in bringing this project to fruition. It is important to note that the views expressed in this book are solely those of the authors and should not be attributed to the institutions they belong to or those mentioned above.

Chien-Huei Wu, Ching-Fu Lin & Han-Wei Liu
2024

Contents

List of Abbreviations

ADB	Asian Development Bank
AKEL	Progressive Party of the Working People (Republic of Cyprus)
APEC	Asia-Pacific Economic Cooperation
APPC	Asia-Pacific Peace Committee of North Korea
ARATS	Association for Relations Across the Taiwan Strait
ASEAN	The Association of Southeast Asian Nations
BDH	Peace and Democracy Movement (Northern Cyprus)
BITs	Bilateral Investment Treaties
CCCI	Cyprus Chamber of Commerce and Industry (CCCI)
CCP	Chinese Communist Party
CEE	Central and Eastern European Countries
CEPA	Closer Economic Partnership Arrangement
CJEU	Court of Justice of the European Union
CODEX	Codex Alimentarius Commission
COVID-19	Coronavirus Disease 2019
CPRK	Committee for the Peaceful Reunification of Korea
CSBIPPA	Cross-Strait Bilateral Investment Protection and Promotion Agreement
CSIS	Center for Strategic and International Studies
CSSTA	Cross-Strait Service Trade Agreement
CTP	Republican Turkish Party (Northern Cyprus)
CYTA	Cyprus Telecommunication Authority
DIKO	Democratic Party (Republic of Cyprus)
DISY	Democratic Rally (Republic of Cyprus)
DMZ	Demilitarized Zone
DPP	Democratic Progressive Party

DPRK	Democratic People's Republic of Korea
ECFA	Cross-Straits Economic Cooperation Framework Agreement
ECJ	European Court of Justice
EDI	United Democrats (Republic of Cyprus)
EEC	European Economic Community
EHP	Early Harvest Program
EOKA	National Organization of Cypriot Struggle
EU	European Union
FAO	Food and Agriculture Organization
FTA	Free Trade Agreements
GATS	General Agreement on Trade in Services
GATT	General Agreement on Tariffs and Trade
ICAO	International Civil Aviation Organization
ICSID Convention	Convention on the Settlement of Investment Disputes between States and Nationals of Other States
ICT	Information and Communication Technology
IPRs	Intellectual Property Rights
KCIA	Korean Central Intelligence Agency
KDZ	Korean Demilitarized Zone
KIC	Kaesong Industrial Complex
KKTCELL	Kibris Mobile Telekomunikasyon Ltd
KMT	Kuomintang (Nationalist Party)
MAC	Mainland Affairs Council (Taiwan)
MEP	Members of the European Parliament
Mercosur	Mercado Común del Sur, Southern Common Market
NATO	North Atlantic Treaty Organization
NUC	National Unification Council
OCRI	One China, Respective Interpretations
OECD	Organization for Economic Co-operation and Development

PACE	Parliamentary Assembly of the Council of Europe
PNTR	Permanent Normal Trade Relations
PRC	People's Republic of China
PRC FIL	Foreign Investment Law of the People's Republic of China
R&D	Research and Development
ROC	Republic of China
ROK	Republic of Korea
SEF	Straits Exchange Foundation
SPS Agreement	The WTO Agreement on the Application of Sanitary and Phytosanitary Measures
SRSG	United Nations Special Representative of the Secretariat General on Cyprus
TAIPEI Act	Taiwan Allies International Protection and Enhancement Initiative Act of 2019
TBT Agreement	Agreement on Technical Barriers to Trade
TCCoC	Turkish Cypriot Chamber of Commerce
TDP	Communal Democracy Party (Northern Cyprus)
TEC	The Treaty Establishment the European Community
TFEU	The Treaty on the Functioning of the European Union
TFSC	Turkish Federated State of Northern Cyprus
THAAD	United States' Terminal High Altitude Area Defense
TIFA	Trade and Investment Framework Agreement
TRIMs Agreement	Agreement on Trade-Related Investment Measures
TRIPs Agreement	Agreement on Trade-Related Aspects of Intellectual Property Rights
TRNC	Turkish Republic of Northern Cyprus
UBP	National Unity Party (Northern Cyprus)
UN	The United Nations

UNDP	United Nations Development Program
UNESCO	United Nations Educational, Scientific and Cultural Organization
UNFICYP	United Nations Peacekeeping Force in Cyprus
VAT	Value-Added Taxes
WHO	World Health Organization
WSAG	Washington Special Actions Group
WTO	World Trade Organization
WWII	World War II

List of Figures

1

Introduction

I. THE IMPORTANCE OF THIS BOOK

IN THE AFTERMATH of the Second World War, trade and investment have been considered one of the most effective tools to avoid armed conflict. Led by the United States and its allies, the Bretton Woods system marked the pre-eminence of multilateralism in addressing economic cooperation across borders. As the World Trade Organization (WTO) has matured into a fully-fledged regime, countries have shifted towards bilateral or regional arrangements to deepen their economic relationships, which is attributable to myriad reasons. Depending on economic, social, and political endowments, bilateral economic arrangements are designed in various ways. For some, the design of arrangements turns on comparative advantages, domestic public policies, and interest group configurations. For others, the motivation is more heavily strategic and geopolitical in nature, driven by the agendas of regional peace and long-term security. A closely related yet often overlooked scenario is how countries or entities approach economic cooperation in the face of vexing political concerns. While trade and investment negotiations may at times have political implications, the conclusion of economic integration arrangements between certain countries or entities may be extremely politically sensitive. This is particularly salient in cases involving certain countries or entities that have contested sovereignty claims over each other or have long argued about state/government recognition, which renders economic cooperation exceptionally strenuous. This work will shed light on our understanding of the concept of sovereignty and the process of economic integration through the exploration of an under-researched question surrounding how countries or entities with conflict sovereignty claims enter economic cooperation, which in turn either exacerbates or diminishes sovereignty concerns.

Conventionally, controversies and concerns over sovereignty during economic cooperation or integration processes are tied to two domains. First, when countries engage in closer economic cooperation or integration, such as the European Union (the EU) and, to a lesser extent, the Association of Southeast Asian Nations (ASEAN), and the Southern Common Market (Mercado Común del Sur, Mercosur), there is a fear of erosion of sovereignty as the regional integration or cooperation organisation gradually becomes the locus of regulatory activities, regardless of whether competence is transferred to the organisation.

Second, as a consequence of economic globalisation, the penetration of global regulatory regimes in economic domains into the domestic legal system, including the WTO and its relevant agreements, such as the Agreement on Technical Barriers to Trade and the WTO Agreement on the Application of Sanitary and Phytosanitary Measures in particular, has also resulted in concerns regarding loss of national sovereignty. Our interest in the sovereignty implications of economic cooperation and integration in these case studies differs from these two observed phenomena. For us, a less explored issue is when a dyad of two countries or entities cooperate economically, whether and how the sovereignty complex implicates and complicates the cooperation processes and eventually exacerbates or diminishes sovereignty concerns. In this light, the issues this work explores differ from European integration or other prototypes of regional integration, such as ASEAN and Mercosur, in that when North-South Korea, North-South Cyprus, and Taiwan/China enter into economic cooperation activities, controversy around the issue of sovereignty already exists. In the context of European integration and other integration processes, sovereignty concerns arise or are exacerbated when integration processes accelerate. In the context of our case studies, sovereign concerns often exist before they enter into economic cooperation and persist when the cooperation process commences.

II. SOVEREIGNTY AND STATES

A. The Concept of Sovereignty

By most accounts, one defining feature of a modern sovereign state is territoriality – the state is an entity exercising "supreme legitimate authority" within a given territory.[1] This concept has its roots in sixteenth- and seventeenth-century Western Europe. Europe in the Middle Ages was ruled under "*Respublica Christiana*," in which "each individual found his definition, identity and purpose, where all lived in common under the same law and morals and where none was severed or independent in his authority or beliefs".[2] At that time, "[e]xclusive territorial sovereignty did not exist,"[3] and "the pope and the emperor intervened regularly in the territorial affairs,"[4] with a complex feudal system composed of various nobles, kings, and clerics at the local levels.[5] A sea change began when, following the end

[1] Daniel Philpott, *Sovereignty: An Introduction and Brief History*, 48 J Int'l Aff 353, 357 (1995).

[2] *Id.*; *see also* Ronald A Brand, *External Sovereignty and International Law*, 18 Fordham Int'l LJ 1685, 1687 (1995).

[3] Mark L Movsesian, *The Persistent Nation State and the Foreign Sovereign Immunities Act* 18 Cardozo L Rev 1083, 1084 (1996).

[4] Philpott *supra* note 1 at 361.

[5] J Samuel Barkin and Bruce Cronin, *The State and the Nation: Changing Norms and the Rules of Sovereignty in International Relations*, 48 Int'l Org 107, 111 (1994).

of the Thirty Years' War in 1648, the Peace of Westphalia greatly curtailed the powers of the Pope and the Emperor.[6]

Underlying the Westphalia order was the notion of decentralisation, comprised of sovereign states. It also established the principles of equality between sovereign states and non-intervention in the internal affairs of other states. As Richard Folk remarks:

> The basic coordinates of the present world order system are contained in the Peace of Westphalia which brought the Thirty Years War to an end in 1648. According to Westphalia logic, the world order system is constituted exclusively by the governments of sovereign states. These governments have complete discretion to rule *national space* (or territory), and can also enter into voluntary arrangements (*e.g.*, treaties) to regulate external relations and interconnections of various sorts. But these governments are *sovereign* and *equal* by juridical fiat, rather than by virtue of some higher authority within the world order system. No one government is entitled to greater formal status than another by reasons of wealth or power or size. In such circumstances, "law and order" rests upon the volition of governments and upon their perception of common interests.[7]

Closely related to the rise of contemporary states is the notion of "sovereignty". This term originated from "*suprema potestas*" – literally translated as "supreme power".[8] Jean Bodin, a French jurist, is widely viewed as the first to lay down a theoretical foundation for the concept of sovereignty.[9] Inspired by French attempts to create a unitary national state following the Hundred Years' War (1350–1450) and emerging English nationhood,[10] Bodin, in his work "Les Six Livres de la République," published in 1576,[11] conceptualised sovereignty as the "absolute and perpetual power of a state," and "subject to no law".[12] Sovereignty is, according to Bodin, the supreme legal and political authority of a state; it can determine how a state treats its people within its boundary.[13] For Bodin, sovereignty would not tolerate any other law-making agent over and above itself – though he acknowledged natural law and rules of divine origin as limitations.[14] Furthermore, sovereignty is indivisible, for the "unity of a legal

[6] *See* Hans Kohn, The Idea of Nationalism: A Study in Its Origins and Background 188 (1944).

[7] Richard A Falk, A Study of Future Worlds 59 (1975).

[8] Jacques Maritain, *The Concept of Sovereignty*, 44 Am Pol Sci Rev 343, 344 (1950).

[9] *See* Francis H Hinsley, *Sovereignty* (2nd edn 1986) p. 71; Ivan Simonovic, *State Sovereignty and Globalization: Are Some States More Equal?*, 28 Ga J Int'l & Compar L 381, 382 (2000).

[10] Johan D van der Vyver, *Sovereignty and Human Rights in Constitutional and International Law*, 5 Emory Int'l L Rev 321, 324 (1991).

[11] "La souverainete est la puissance absolue et perpetuelle d'une République". [Sovereignty is the absolute and perpetual power of a Republic.] Jean Bodin, *On Sovereignty: Four Chapters from The Six Books of the Commonwealth* 1, 11 (Julian Franklin, ed. and trans., Cambridge University Press 1992).

[12] *Id.*

[13] Bodin, supra note 12 ("Sovereignty is the absolute and perpetual power of a commonwealth ... that is, the highest power of command".).

[14] Samantha Besson, *Sovereignty*, Max Planck Encyclopedia of Public International Law (A Peters and R Wolfrum eds, last updated Apr 2011). Others likewise qualified sovereignty with the concept

system seemed logically to require the unification of power in a single ruler or single ruling group".[15]

The concept of sovereignty evolved in the early twentieth century when international law scholars began to draw the line between internal sovereignty, as applied to a state's territory, and external sovereignty, which governs international relations.[16] Notably, Henry Wheaton distinguishes between internal and external sovereignty in the following manner: internal sovereignty is "that which is inherent in the people of any State … by its municipal constitution or fundamental laws," while "[e]xternal sovereignty consists in the independence of one political society, in respect to all other political societies … The law by which it is regulated … may more properly be termed international law".[17] According to Wheaton, the internal sovereignty of a state does not depend upon its recognition by other states, while external sovereignty requires recognition by other states.[18] This shift in focus matched the emergence of modern states and coincided with the development of a classical view of public international law – only an independent sovereign state can engage other sovereign states through its consent to the transfer of rights and the creation of obligations.

B. Statehood and Recognition

"State" is defined by the Montevideo Convention on the Rights and Duties of States as a "person of international law" with the following qualifications: a permanent population, a defined territory, a government, and the capacity to enter into relations with other states.[19] While the Montevideo Convention states that the "political existence of the state is independent of recognition by the other states,"[20] diplomatic recognition is nonetheless often seen as yet another disputable element of statehood. There are two competing views: constitutive theory and declaratory theory. Constitutive theory, supported by positivists like Oppenheim,[21] Kelsen,[22] and Wheaton,[23] perceives recognition as an essential

of natural law. Hugo Grotius for instance, attempted to reconcile the concept of sovereignty with the concept of natural law, arguing that the original sovereignty of the people was transferred to a sovereign government, which had the function and duty to protect the people in exchange. John Locke took this view further by underscoring the social contract between the sovereign government and the people. Hinsley (n 10) at 139; John Locke, *Second Treatise on Government* 309 (1960).

[15] Bodin, *supra* note 12, at 302–03.

[16] *See e.g.*, Jens Bartelson, *The Concept of Sovereignty Revisited*, 17 Eur. J Int'l L 463, 466, 473 (2006).

[17] Henry Wheaton, *Elements of International Law* (4th edn, 1904) p. 34.

[18] *Id.*

[19] *See* Convention on Rights and Duties of States, art 1, Dec 26, 1933, TS No 881, 165 LNTS 3802.

[20] *Id.*, art 3.

[21] Lassa Francis Oppenheim, *International Law: A Treatise* 109 (1905).

[22] Hans Kelsen, *Recognition in International Law: Theoretical Observations*, 35 Am J Int'l L 605 (1941).

[23] Henry Wheaton, *Elements of International Law* 31 (2nd edn, 1880) ("The external sovereignty of any State, on the other hand, may require recognition by other States in order to render it perfect and complete …").

element of statehood. In contrast, for declaratory theorists such as Chen[24] and Brierly,[25] an entity can become a state as long as it possesses the minimal qualifications for statehood – recognition by other states is therefore "declaratory" by nature. The former view is problematic – a state may be recognised by one state but not another, hence "apparently both an 'international person' and not an 'international person' at the same time[.]"[26] Strictly applying the constitutive theory would, as Hersch Lauterpacht admitted, render the citizens of an unrecognised state unprotected under international law.[27]

To date, the accepted view of sovereignty is, according to the late Judge James Crawford of the International Court of Justice, a term "for the totality of international rights and duties recognised by international law as residing in an independent territorial unit – the State".[28] For Crawford, sovereignty is not in itself a right, but is, rather, an attribute of a state.[29] Crawford also explains that the use of the term in a political manner to describe absolute authority and power is problematic. The legal definition, which is that sovereignty refers to the "totality of powers that States may have under international law," proves less problematic. Rejecting sovereignty, in its absolutist sense, as one of the criteria for establishing statehood, Crawford suggests that the concept of sovereignty can be "misleading since it implies a necessary and overriding omnipotence which States do not possess in law or in fact".[30]

Malcom Shaw describes sovereignty as "the capacity of a state to provide for its own well-being and development free from the domination of other states, providing it does not impair or violate their legitimate rights".[31] Shaw opines that "perhaps the outstanding characteristic of a state is its independence, or sovereignty". To Shaw, the principles of sovereignty are "essential in the maintenance of a reasonably stable system of competing states".[32] Such principles include non-intervention, which ensures a sense of stability within the legal order, thus allowing respect for territorial sovereignty to serve as an essential foundational component in international relations.[33] This view taken by Shaw appears to complement Crawford's assertions regarding the relationship between sovereignty and statehood, with sovereignty acting as a characteristic of statehood, rather than a prerequisite for a state to identify itself as such. Shaw underscores the importance of sovereignty as a characteristic of statehood by arguing that sovereignty is essential to the establishment of stability between states.[34]

[24] Ti-Chiang Chen, *The International Law of Recognition* 13 (1951).
[25] Andrew Clapham, *Brierly's Law of Nations* 150–52 (7th edn, 2012).
[26] *Id.*, 151.
[27] Hersch Lauterpacht, *Recognition of States in International Law*, 53 Yale L J 385, 434 (1944).
[28] James Crawford, The Creation of States in International Law 32 (2nd edn, 2007).
[29] *Id.*
[30] *Id.*, 718.
[31] Malcom N Shaw, *International Law* 166 (8th edn 2017).
[32] *Id.* at 168.
[33] *Id.*
[34] *Id.*

The delicate relationship between sovereignty and statehood is best illustrated in the case of divided nations, or "divided states" as some scholars name it, where the parties formerly were part of the same state and may compete for its legitimate representation while struggling for unification or independence. Though some scholarship uses the term "divided states," we apply the term "divided nations" to the same concept. First, the term "nation" reflects our focus on ethnic and cultural identity politics as a key factor in economic cooperation processes. Furthermore, insofar as the term "states" relates to the issue of sovereignty, "divided states" may imply that one or both fractions of a "divided state" cannot separately satisfy the criteria of a "state".[35]

According to Meinhard Hilf, the notion of divided nations ("divided states" in his words) is used to describe the "legal situation of a number of states which previously belonged to a state or to colonial possessions and which, in the period after World War II, found themselves divided into separate states".[36] The notion of divided nations addresses a state of transition, "either between a previous condition of united Statehood and its final dismemberment into two or more independent states, or between a condition of division and eventual unification".[37] Written in 1987, Hilf's definition of the concept is primarily descriptive, with a view toward capturing the anomaly of the state of affairs in the post-war era, frequently resulting from the ideological divide between capitalism and communism during the Cold War. The two Germanies, Koreas, Chinas, and Vietnams were cited as examples of divided nations. Markku Suksi, writing in 2013, offers a slightly different definition: "an existing State with established subjectivity of public international law [that] has been divided *de facto* and later on often also to some extent *de jure* into two parts, each of which claim subjectivity under public international in relation to each other and in relation to other subjects of international law".[38] When Suksi put forward his definition, he cited the two Koreas and two Chinas as examples, with North and South Cyprus identified as another potential case.

In the context of divided nations, questions of sovereignty and statehood surface in inter-se relations between divided nations as well as in their relationships with other subjects of international law in the wider world. Because one part of the divided nation may claim sovereignty over the other and try to prevent third countries or international organisations from entering into official relations with the other part, recognition plays a key role in defining the rules

[35] Also, in the context of the Korean peninsula and China-Taiwan cases, it seems more common to use "divided nations". *See, e.g.*, Johan Galtung, *Divided Nations as a Process: One State, Two States, and In-between: The Case of Korea*, (1972) 9(4) J Peace Rsch 345; John H Herz, *Korea and Germany as Divided Nations: The Systemic Impact* (1975) 15 Asian Surv 957; Weiqun Gu, *Conflicts of Divided Nations: The Cases of China and Korea* (1995).

[36] Meinhard Hilf, *Divided States, in* 10 *Encyclopedia of Public International Law* 126 (Rudolf Bernhardt ed. 1987).

[37] *Id.*

[38] Markku Suksi, *Divided States* para 1, in *Max Planck Encyclopedia of Public International Law* (A Peters and R Wolfrum eds, last updated July 2013).

of conduct for inter-se relations as well as international relations.[39] Therefore, divided nations are normally comprised of partially unrecognised states, either in terms of inter-se relations between the dyad of the divided nations or in terms of external relations with third countries. In some cases, one part of the divided nation may not recognise the other as a state.[40] Externally, third countries or the UN and related agencies may recognise one but not the other. In other cases, both parts of the divided nation may be recognised by the UN or major countries.[41] As a consequence, recognition, or the lack thereof, is a key factor impacting economic cooperation between divided nations and their engagements in international relations. For this reason, when Crawford depicts the phenomenon of divided nations (in his words "divided states") after the Second World War, he refers to a situation in which "certain territorial entities that had previously been either states (Germany, China) or at least distinct territories (Vietnam, Korea) found themselves divided into two or more *separate units of administrations*".[42] Compared to Hilf's reference to "separate states" and Suksi's reference to "*de facto* and later on often to some extent *de jure* two parts," Crawford's description of "separate units of administrations" is rather reserved, incorporating the fact that one part of a divided nation is often not be widely recognised.

Crawford's use of "separate units of administrations" then again links to "unrecognised states," places that do not seem to exist and do not fit into the world after the Second World War, even though they exercise supreme power over a clearly defined territory. Admittedly, in the aftermath of colonialism, and in the wake of self-determination, overlapping sovereignties, colonies, and trusteeships gradually fade away on the stage of international politics, and sovereign states dominate the scene. However, entities governing a given territory seeking independence and struggling for recognition persist and divided nations

[39] This explains why Suksi sees a certain number of countries recognising either of divided nations as an essential feature of such divided nations and thus excludes the case of North–South Cyprus. Nonetheless, the number of countries recognising Taiwan is, in fact, also decreasing significantly. Whereas recognition has important legal significance and normative implication, in this work, we do not see recognition as an indispensable element for the definition of divided nations, in particular because our study focuses on economic cooperation which may still take place with or without the (competition of) recognition.

[40] China does not recognise Taiwan as a sovereignty but sees it as a renegade province of China. Conversely, Taiwan's attitude towards China differs from administration to administration. While the former President Lee Teng-hui defined it as "a special relationship between state and state," the Constitution and Statute Governing the Relationship between Taiwan Area and Mainland Area does not consider China as a foreign state. Similarly, North Cyprus and South Cyprus do not recognise each other. An interesting comparison is North and South Korea. While both Koreas are sovereign states and have a UN seat, they do not see each other as a foreign state. The inter-se relations between two Koreas is not international.

[41] Both Germanies joined the UN on 18 September 1973 under UN General Assembly Resolution 3050, while both Koreas joined the UN on 17 September 1991 under UN General Assembly Resolution 46/1. *See* GA Res 3050, Admission of the German Democratic Republic and the Federal Republic of Germany to membership in the United Nations (1973); GA Res 46/1, Admission of the Democratic People's Republic of Korea and the Republic of Korea to membership in the United Nations (1991).

[42] Crawford, *supra* note 29, at 450 (emphasis added).

are part of this symptom. Ironically, whereas the aim of decolonialisation is to bring an end of these colonies and crown them with sovereignty and statehood, the ideological divide between capitalism and communism during the Cold War after this decolonisation period are the key causes that brought about divided nations which continue to compete for recognition. Due to the lack of international recognition, the statehood of unrecognised states is challenged from time to time. Importantly, the conventional view of international relations endorses greater weight to recognition, which corresponds to the constitutive theory of recognition that a sovereign state cannot exist without international recognition or without external sovereignty, and that, absent sovereignty, statehood does not exist. This is nonetheless challenged by a few international relations scholars who argue that sovereignty is multifaceted, and statehood is a matter of degree.[43]

Stephen Krasner, in his seminal work on sovereignty, identifies four dimensions of sovereignty and argues that they may not necessarily covary. Krasner maintains that sovereignty may be categorised as international legal sovereignty, Westphalian sovereignty, domestic sovereignty, or interdependence sovereignty. International legal sovereignty focuses on mutual recognition, usually between territorial entities with juridical independence, which largely relates to external sovereignty in public international law. Westphalian sovereignty refers to a political organisation that excludes external actors from the authority structure within a given territory, which largely corresponds to internal sovereignty as proposed by public international lawyers. Domestic sovereignty addresses the formal organisation of public authority within the state and its capacity to exercise effective control within its border. This then relates to the government element, as put forward in the Montevideo Convention on the Rights and Duties of States. Interdependence sovereignty relates to the capacity of the public authority in regulating goods, services, persons, capital, and information that crosses the border in the age of globalisation. International legal sovereignty and Westphalian sovereignty concern legitimacy and authority, but not control. Domestic sovereignty relates to authority and control, while interdependence sovereignty exclusively addresses control. The exercise of one form of sovereignty may undermine another. For example, by exercising international legal sovereignty and entering into international agreements, a state may limit its Westphalian sovereignty, the best example being the accession of member states to the EU. A state may also possess one type of sovereignty but not another. Unrecognised states such as Taiwan may have Westphalian sovereignty but not international legal sovereignty.[44] This view of the multifaceted nature of sovereignty and a continuum of statehood corresponds to the declarative theory of recognition in public international law, which we find more convincing and reflective of the reality and complexity of today's international world.

[43] *E.g.*, Nina Caspersen, 'Unrecognized States: The Struggle for Sovereignty in the Modern International System' 3–15 (2011).

[44] Stephen D Krasner, *Sovereignty: Organized Hypocrisy* 3–4 (1999).

III. THE ROLE OF SOVEREIGNTY IN SHAPING ECONOMIC AND POLITICAL RELATIONSHIPS IN THE CONTEXT OF DIVIDED NATIONS

A. Unpacking the Myth of Sovereignty in Divided Nations

The meaning of sovereignty has changed along historical, political, and legal dimensions, and the many facets of what it entails and implies have been continuously contested. Across different contexts and times, sovereignty may be understood as unitary and absolute, or the other way around – divided and relative.[45] More recently, some commentators even argue that sovereignty is no longer a valid concept and approach in the study of global affairs, in light of the advent and growing authority of trans-governmental networks and non-state actors, such as international and supranational organisations, transnational corporations, and civil society groups.[46] Given the essentially open, dynamic, and contestable nature of sovereignty, we cannot and do not aim to exhaust scholarly and practical discourse surrounding this concept. Rather, with regard to the scope and purpose of this book, we examine the relevant modern approaches to sovereignty, which pave the way for our analysis of the three case studies of divided nations and how these entities interact in terms of economic cooperation.

The contemporary shift from absolute and political sovereign authority to legal and relative sovereignty means that sovereignty is seen as both the source of domestic law *and* the subject of its own laws.[47] In terms of international law, a state's actions to calculate interests and give consent to be bound by treaties or other forms of international law, as well as to subsequently implement applicable treaty rights and obligations that create domestic legal effects, are both a demonstration and affirmation of its sovereignty.[48] That is, when a state engages in international actions with legal ramifications, it exercises both its (international) internal and external sovereignty to conduct its internal and external affairs.[49] Externally, a state interacts with other states as an equal in creating

[45] *See generally* Don Herzog, Sovereignty, RIP 50–163 (2020).

[46] *See e.g.* Anne-Marie Slaughter, A *New World Order* (2004); Ramses A Wessel, *Informal International Law-Making as a New Form of World Legislation?*, 8 Int'l Org L Rev 253, 258 (2011); Andreas Fischer-Lescano and Gunther Teubner, *Regime-Collisions: The Vain Search for Legal Unity in the Fragmentation of Global Law*, 25 Mich J Int'l L 999 (2004); and Paul Schiff Berman, *From International Law to Law and Globalization*, 43 Colum J Transnat'l L 485 (2005).

[47] *See e.g.* Richard T Ford, *Law's Territory (A History of Jurisdiction)*, 97 Mich L Rev 843 (1999); Friedrich Kratochwil, *Sovereignty as* Dominium*: Is There a Right of Humanitarian Intervention?*, *in* Beyond Westphalia? National Sovereignty and International Intervention (Gene M Lyons and Michael Mastanduno eds, 1995). *But see* Ben Holland, *Sovereignty as* Dominium*? Reconstructing the Constructivist Roman Law Thesis*, 54 Int'l Stud Q 449 (2010). *See also* Krasner, *supra* note 45.

[48] *See e.g.* Barbara Koremenos et al., *The Rational Design of International Institutions*, 55 Int'l Org 761, 782 (2001); Herald Koh, *The 1994 Roscoe Pound Lecture: Transnational Legal Process*, 75 Neb L Rev 181 (1996); and Andrew T Guzman, How International Law Works: A Rational Choice Theory 119–54 (2008).

[49] *See* Roger P Alford, *International Law as an Interpretive Tool in the Supreme Court, 1901–1945*, *in* International Law in the U.S. Supreme Court: Continuity and Change 257, 257 (David L Sloss

international legal rights and obligations, reflecting its original legal personality, immune from the jurisdiction of others. Internally, a state holds competence and ultimate authority over all people and matters within its territory, which is a prerequisite for the realisation of its international legal rights and obligations. Therefore, the relationship between internal and external sovereignty can be understood as a juncture where domestic constitutional order and international legal order meet.[50] This distinction and interaction between external and internal sovereignty, however, becomes a legally and politically contested area for divided nations, in particular those that fall within the scope of our study – China and Taiwan, North and South Korea, and North and South Cyprus.

Divided nations do not formally recognise one another as a whole and independent state that enjoys full sovereignty distinct from that of theirs, and therefore consider inter-se interactions not as foreign affairs, but, rather, as quasi-foreign affairs (or even quasi-domestic affairs). As such, the negotiation, conclusion, ratification, and implementation of a treaty (or a similar agreement) between divided nations prove exceptionally politically sensitive and legally arduous. To forge an "international" agreement that conditions their future behaviours and creates legal effects on the people and affairs within their territories,[51] divided nations may encounter conundrums surrounding internal and external sovereignty. Externally, while the executive branch normally acts as a sovereign in external affairs with other states (from treaty negotiations to dispute settlements), it may need to pragmatically change hats when engaging with the counterpart in a divided nations relationship to ease political barriers. Internally, depending on how a pair of divided nations defines each other under their respective constitutional and legal frameworks, the review and ratification of an agreement between the two may face special parliamentary procedures,[52] in which the legislative arm exercises sovereignty. More often than not, because of the tricky relationship between divided nations, what has been agreed upon externally may not necessarily be readily welcomed internally.

Such dynamics between divided nations pose a set of theoretically and practically stimulating questions with regard to sovereignty, as well as the interface of domestic constitutional order vis-à-vis international legal order. Arguably, these questions have not been addressed in the existing literature in a systematic manner. To be sure, while internal and external sovereignty function in different dimensions and may be conceptually separate, they cannot be decoupled in

et al. eds, 2011); Wheaton, *supra* note 24, at 34. *See generally* Brad R Roth, *Sovereign Equality and Moral Disagreement: Premises of a Pluralist International Legal Order* (2011).

[50] *See generally* Ernst Ulrich Petersmann, *Multilevel Constitutionalism for Multilevel Governance of Public Goods: Methodology Problems in International Law* (2017).

[51] *See* Guzman, *supra* note 49, at 119–30.

[52] For discussion on parliamentary review of international agreements, *see generally* Mario Mendez, *Constitutional Review of Treaties: Lessons for Comparative Constitutional Design and Practice*, 15 Int'l J Const L 84 (2017); Joanna Harrington, *Scrutiny and Approval: The Role for Westminster-Style Parliaments in Treaty-Making*, 55 Int'l & Comp LQ 121 (2006); and Robert Schütze, *Parliamentary Democracy and International Treaties*, 8 Global Pol'y 7 (6th Supp 2017).

the context of divided nations. How the internal sovereign defines itself against (i.e., distinct from or integral to) its counterpart in a divided nations relationship logically conditions and harnesses whether, to what extent, and how the external sovereign engages with the equal other. How the external sovereign interacts with its counterpart (i.e., recognise, acquiesce, tolerate, or antagonise) in a divided nations relationship in turn shapes relevant oversight, review, and ratification mechanisms. Subject to the changing and multifaceted relationship between a pair of divided nations, how their external sovereigns interact with each other dynamically reflects how their internal sovereigns (which legitimately represent the collective will of the people, at least theoretically[53]) define each other, and vice versa.

This is best exemplified by the case of China and Taiwan. Not long after the conclusion of the Second World War, the Chinese Communists overtook the Republic of China (ROC) government to create the People's Republic of China (PRC). The ROC, under the rule of Chiang Kai-shek, then retreated to Taiwan, otherwise known as Formosa. Since 1949, the ROC and PRC have coexisted, with the PRC occupying Mainland China and the ROC having Taiwan and the outer islands under its effective control. For a long period, however, both sides claimed to be the only legitimate government representing the whole nation.[54] The competition between the ROC and PRC for the representation of China reflected the Cold War standoff between the West and the Soviet bloc. In the post-Cold-War era and, following its democratisation, Taiwan has ceased asserting its representation of China and its competition with the PRC for the Chinese seat in the UN.

The ROC has since gradually lost this zero-sum diplomatic battle. The UN General Assembly in 1971 passed Resolution 2758, making the PRC the representative of China and ousting the ROC.[55] To date, only 12 states recognise the ROC on Taiwan and therefore abstain from official relations with the PRC.[56] The lack of diplomatic recognition has led the ROC to shift its strategies by

[53] The socio-political relationship between the ruling government and its people in China and North Korea certainly merits more in-depth inquiries. However, a complete review and analysis falls beyond the scope of this book. We will address relevant aspects of such socio-political relationship in our case studies in Chapters II, III, and IV, when it plays a role in explaining or elaborating the core theses of this book. Nevertheless, at this moment, a few pieces of literature serve as helpful references. *See generally* David A Lake, *Domination, Authority, and the Forms of Chinese Power*, 10 Chinese J Int'l Pol 357, 378–79 (2017); Susan L Shirk, Fragile Superpower: How China's Internal Politics Could Derail Its Peaceful Rise (2007); Lotus Yang Ruan, *The Chinese Communist Party and Legitimacy: What is the Chinese Communist Party's Official Discourse on Legitimacy?*, The Diplomat (Sept 30, 2015); Han S Park, *North Korean Perceptions of Self and Others: Implications for Policy Choices*, 73 Pac Affs 503 (2001); Justine Guichard, *In the Name of the People: Disagreeing over Peoplehood in the North and South Korean Constitutions*, 4 Asian JL Soc'y 405 (2017).

[54] Y Frank Chiang, *State, Sovereignty, and Taiwan*, 23 Fordham Int'l L J 959, 975 (1999).

[55] GA Res 2758 at 358 (Oct 25, 1971).

[56] *Diplomatic Allies*, Ministry of Foreign Affairs, the Rep of China (Taiwan), https://en.mofa.gov.tw/AlliesIndex.aspx?n=1294&sms=1007 (last visited Mar 10, 2024).

engaging other nations or participating in international organisations under the names such as "Chinese Taipei".[57] From the perspective of public international law, the ROC on Taiwan is often referred to as an "un-recognised state" or "entity sui generis".[58] Crawford remarks that Taiwan is not a state, as it "still has not unequivocally asserted its separation from China and is not recognised as a State distinct from China".[59] Taiwan's inherited ROC constitution defines its territory by reference to "existing national boundaries," adding further complexities in that regard.[60] The unique status of the ROC on Taiwan thus plays a decisive role in shaping its economic ties with the other side of this divided nation.

Compared to China and Taiwan, the relationship between the two Koreas has followed a very different course in both its practical and legal dimensions. Following its liberation from Japanese colonialism at the end of the Second World War in 1945, the Korean peninsula was split along the 38th parallel and occupied by both Soviet and American forces. While local Korean leaders wished for the reunification of the peninsula, reflecting a vision of full and undividable Korean sovereignty, two separate governments were formed: the Republic of Korea in the South, and the Democratic People's Republic of Korea in the North.[61] Both Kim Il-Sung in the North, backed by the Soviet Union and China, and Sygnman Rhee in the South, backed (somewhat reluctantly) by the U.S., decided to go to war, eager to reunify the two Koreas. After much back and forth amid complex geopolitical factors, the division eventually returned to the 38th parallel, and the two Koreas were forced into a ceasefire.[62]

Although both countries initially thrived, with much industrial infrastructure left over from the period of Japanese colonialism, North Korea has experienced continual decline, ultimately relying on foreign aid to survive.[63] These hardships reached a peak in the 1990s, with the country suffering a devastating famine that the government blamed on a flood. North Korea came to rely on humanitarian aid from the U.S., the UN, and even South Korea, although the North Korean government was found to often use this aid for their own political or military interests.[64] The government also turned into a totalitarian dictatorship that

[57] *See, e.g., About Us: Member Economies*, Asia-Pacific Econ Cooperation. Available at: www.apec.org/about-us/about-apec/member-economies (last visited 10 March, 2024).

[58] Shaw, *supra* note 32, at 183–4.

[59] Crawford, *supra* note 29, at 198. Nevertheless, Crawford does acknowledge that "the suppression by force of 23 million people cannot be consistent with the [United Nations] Charter," implying that "to that extent there must be a cross-Strait boundary for the purposes of the use of force". *Id.*

[60] Minguo Xianfa [Constitution] art 4 (Taiwan).

[61] Jongsoo Lee, *The Division of Korea and the Rise of Two Koreas, 1945–1948*, in Routledge Handbook of Modern Korean History 171 (Michael J Seth ed 2016).

[62] Grace J Chae, *The Korean War and its Politics*, *in* Routledge Handbook of Modern Korean History 180 (Michael J Seth ed. 2016).

[63] Andrei Lankov, *A Dynastic Polity in Economic Stagnation and Decline*, *in* Routledge Handbook of Modern Korean History 221 (Michael J Seth ed. 2016).

[64] Marcus Noland, *The North Korean Famine*, *in* Routledge Handbook of Modern Korean History 234 (Michael J Seth ed. 2016).

harshly suppressed any opposition.[65] Conversely, South Korea struggled both economically and politically in the early stages, but eventually rose to be one of the "Four Asian Tigers".[66] After ineffectual democratically elected governments and two military regimes, South Korea eventually developed a strong democracy that has continued to this day.[67] While South Korea, as an open, democratic country, enjoys strong economic and diplomatic ties, North Korea continues to have exceptionally rocky diplomatic relations, largely due to its refusal to consent to nuclear disarmament. Although the South Korean government, especially under President Moon and his "Sunshine Policy," has continued to engage North Korea and has tried to improve relations, the North Korean government has not reciprocated these efforts, often holding diplomatic relations hostage to extract resources and other concessions.

Unlike the Chinese and Korean cases, the North–South Cyprus divide is rooted in ethnic diversity, with the demise of the British Empire after the Second World War its more immediate cause. In the post-war era of decolonisation and self-determination, Cypriots were considering the available paths to independence from the UK. While Greek Cypriots preferred to join Greece and form a Greek union, Turkish Cypriots were suspicious about this idea and, to some degree, cooperated with the British colonial forces to suppress the movement led by Greek Cypriots. After tortuous conflicts and strenuous negotiations, with the agreement of the UK, Turkey, Greece, and Cyprus partisans, the Treaty of Establishment,[68] Treaty of Alliance,[69] and Treaty of Guarantee[70] were signed in Nicosia on 16 August 1960, resulting in the birth of the Republic of Cyprus.

Unfortunately, ethnic conflicts continued to plague the newly formed, ill-fated republic, which was designed in the spirit of power sharing between Greek and Turkish Cypriots. The inter-communal conflicts eventually led to the intervention of the United Nations with the adoption of Security Council Resolution 186 in 1964.[71] A peacekeeping force (UNFICYP) was sent to Cyprus and charged with patrolling the United Nations Buffer Zone (generally known as "Green Line"), established in 1964. The UNFICYP's role was further expanded following a coup on July 14, 1974, which was backed by the Greek junta and led to the invasion of Cyprus by Turkey. The UN Security Council called on all parties to immediately cease fire and demanded an end of foreign military intervention with the adoption of Resolution 353 on 20 July 1974.[72]

[65] Shin Jongdae, *North Korean State-Making: Process and Characteristics*, *in* Routledge Handbook of Modern Korean History 197 (Michael J Seth ed. 2016).

[66] Ingyu Oh and Hannah Jun, *Economic Miracle: From Post-War Reconstruction to Post-Crisis Affluence*, *in* Routledge Handbook of Modern Korean History 295 (Michael J Seth ed. 2016).

[67] Gregg Andrew Brazinsky, *Democratization in South Korea*, *in* Routledge Handbook of Modern Korean History 314 (Michael J Seth ed. 2016).

[68] Treaty concerning the Establishment of the Republic of Cyprus, Cyprus-Greece-Turk-UK, Aug 16, 1960, 382 UNTS 8.

[69] Treaty of Alliance, Cyprus-Greece-Turk, Aug 16, 1960, 397 UNTS 287.

[70] Treaty of Guarantee, Cyprus-Greece-Turk-UK, Aug 16, 1960, 382 UNTS 3.

[71] SC Res 186 (4 Mar, 1964).

[72] SC Res 353 (20 July, 1974).

Though a temporary cease-fire agreement was brokered, it was soon broken by Turkey. Following a series of negotiations, the Third Vienna Agreement was concluded in August 1975, resulting in the relocation of Turkish Cypriots in the South to the North and Greek Cypriots in the North to the South. The separation of Greek Cypriots in the South and Turkish Cypriots in the North was thus institutionalised. In 1983, the Turkish Cypriots in the North declared independence and established the Turkish Republic of Northern Cyprus (TRNC).[73] Turkey immediately recognised the TRNC,[74] while the UN Security Council adopted a resolution calling upon all states not to recognise any Cypriot state other than the Republic of Cyprus.[75] Various efforts to resolve the North–South Cyprus divide, including the Annan Plan referendum in 2004, proved futile. The Republic of Cyprus enjoys UN membership and joined the EU in 2005, while the TRNC continues to suffer from a lack of international recognition but manages to maintain some engagement with the European Commission and the Council of Europe.

B. Economic Cooperation in the Shadow of Sovereignty: Research Questions

The purpose of this book is twofold. First, it aims to unpack how economic ties were and can be shaped between these three sets of divided nations. Second, it seeks to develop an appropriate analytical framework that better explains and predicts the interactions between nations of this sort going forward.

Regarding the former, from a normative perspective, the pattern of interactions between two sides of a divided nation in the shadow of sovereignty can differ from the traditional context. We explore these patterns through three dimensions. *Unilaterally*, how does one side of a divided nation legally perceive the other? In other words, as a matter of domestic law, is there a specific regulatory framework dedicated to economic ties for divided nations caught in a sovereignty controversy? Relatedly, how does one side of a divided nation, as a *bilateral* matter, enter into a trade and investment deal with the other? If so, what do they look like, and to what extent are they similar to, or different from, a typical trade and investment agreement concluded between nations without contested sovereignty? Are these bilateral trade and investment negotiations led by public sectors alone, driven by the private sector, or governed through a public-private hybrid mode because of underlying political concerns? This then brings us to the next issue: What is the role of contested sovereignty, if any,

[73] On the TRNC as a state, *see* Daria Isachenko, The Making of Informal States: Statebuilding in Northern Cyprus and Transdniestria (2012).

[74] Nathalie Tocci, The EU and Conflict Resolution: Promoting Peace in the Backyard 32–33 (2007); James Ker-Lindsay, EU Accession and UN Peacekeeping in Cyprus 16–17 (2005).

[75] SC Res 541 (18 Nov, 1983).

in shaping the behaviour of the selected divided nations at the *regional* and *multilateral* level when it comes to trade and investment?

Exploring the patterns of interactions between divided nations normatively is the first and most crucial step in helping us to reflect upon how economic ties can be shaped in the shadow of contested sovereignty. We must go beyond the surface by identifying the major factors that contribute to the use of legal approaches for these divided nations to engage their respective counterparts. These legal approaches should not be taken at face value. Rather, they touch upon myriad complex issues, including cultural, historical, and (geo)-political considerations. An inquiry into these key factors across the three sets of divided nations could help us deductively map out a theoretical framework to understand, explain, and predict the shaping of economic relationships in the shadow of contested sovereignty.

IV. CONTESTED SOVEREIGNTY AND ECONOMIC COOPERATION

Regardless of its theoretical importance and policy complexity, economic cooperation in the context of divided nations has received little attention in scholarly works. Most scholarly works take the form of journal articles or chapters in edited volumes. Most importantly, these works tend to focus on one single case study, while comparative studies across different divided nations remain outdated, if not missing entirely. Our book is a modest attempt to fill this academic lacuna. Below, we revisit existent academic literature on these three cases and articulate our contributions.

A. China and Taiwan

In *Facing China: Taiwan's Status as a Separate Customs Territory in the World Trade Organization* (2005) Pasha Hsieh wrote about Taiwan's WTO membership, the benefits of that membership to Taiwan, and the conflicts that exist between Taiwan's regulations against China and WTO norms.[76] Hsieh notes that, overall, China and Taiwan's relationship within the WTO appears to provide economic benefits due to deregulation, but politically, the relationship has been stunted by China's refusal to accept Taiwan's status as an independent member of the WTO.

In his 2008 article *China-Taiwan Trade Relations: Implications of the WTO and Asian Regionalism*, Hsieh built on his *Facing China* article, observing in greater depth how the WTO has changed the trade relationship between China

[76] Pasha L Hsieh, *Facing China: Taiwan's Status as a Separate Customs Territory in the World Trade Organization*, 39 J World Trade 1195, 1212 (2005).

and Taiwan. He expands on how the creation of APEC and ASEAN has affected the relationship,[77] with APEC increasing interactions between the two countries, providing a forum for Cross-Strait issues to be addressed. APEC also provides the opportunity for FTAs to be created between members, benefiting Taiwan by ensuring Taiwan is included in such agreements. By contrast, ASEAN's integration with China and the current ASEAN-China FTA represent a potential threat to Taiwan's trade agreements. Hsieh then departs from the benefits of the WTO and ASEAN/APEC to describe the potential benefits of a Cross-Strait Taiwan-China FTA.[78] This is primarily because an FTA would benefit Taiwan by linking Taiwan to the ASEAN Free Trade Area through the ASEAN-China FTA, promoting exports. Hsieh also argues that Taiwan could act as a 'springboard' for China, due to Taiwan's possession of a developed legal regime and better-trained personnel. Finally, Hsieh argues that Taiwan benefits from a "hub and spoke" dynamic as the connection between two major markets: China and the U.S.

In his article *The China–Taiwan ECFA, Geopolitical Dimensions and WTO Law*, Hsieh notes that the trade relationship between China and Taiwan, per his observations in 2011, is very hostile. This is due to China's reluctance to recognise Taiwan as an independent member of the WTO[79] and Taiwan's hostility and economic discrimination towards China as a method of safeguarding its autonomy.[80] This hostility has been touched upon by Hsieh in previous articles. The point of difference here is that Hsieh believes the China-Taiwan Economic Cooperation Framework Agreement (ECFA) will assist in promoting a collaborative trade relationship between China and Taiwan.[81] This is primarily due to the fact that the ECFA is modelled on the ASEAN "framework agreement" model created for its free trade agreements, allowing for the liberalisation of trade in goods and greater discussion on goods that will and will not be included in the trade agreement. These aspects will incentivise both countries to lower their restrictions towards one another and generally liberalise the trade relationship.

In her book *Taiwan's China Dilemma: Contested Identities and Multiple Interests in Taiwan's Cross-Strait Economic Policy*, published in 2016, Syaru Shirley Lin appears to largely agree with Hsieh's sentiments on the Taiwan-China trade relationship.[82] Generally, Lin also agrees that there is economic

[77] Pasha L Hsieh, China-Taiwan Trade Relations: Implications of the WTO and Asian Regionalism, *in Trading Arrangements in the Pacific Rim*: ASEAN and APEC 1, 18 (Paul J Davidson ed., 2008).

[78] *Id.* at 16.

[79] Pasha L Hsieh, *The China–Taiwan ECFA, Geopolitical Dimensions and WTO Law*, 14 J Int'l Econ L 121, 125 (2011).

[80] *Id.* at 126–29.

[81] *Id.* at 137 and 146.

[82] Syaru Shirley Lin, Taiwan's China Dilemma: Contested Identities and Multiple Interests in Taiwan's Cross-Strait Economic Policies (2016).

benefit in Taiwan cooperating with China, yet Taiwan is unwilling to do so due to fear of becoming reliant upon, and intertwined with, China. However, Lin goes into greater depth regarding this relationship and Taiwan's desire to be independent. Lin introduces the argument that "Taiwan's evolving national identity is an important factor in formulating its cross-Strait economic policy because it serves as the foundation for identifying and prioritising the economic interests of purposive actors within a specific international and domestic context".[83] Lin argues that identity is the basis for debating about and creating both domestic and foreign policies and should be taken into account when considering economic relations between Taiwan and China. Lin also disagrees with a pertinent point made by Hsieh: that Taiwan's economic dependence on China would lead to the liberalisation of Taiwan's economic policies. Lin argues that the opposite has occurred. This is evident through Taiwan's Cross-Strait economic policies, which have undergone restrictive, rather than liberal, phases four times in the last 20 years, with heated debate within Taiwan each time.[84] Support among the Taiwanese people for unification fell from 20 percent in 1994 to 9 percent in 2014.[85] Observing such trends, Lin concludes that "the divide between China and Taiwan remains just as hard to bridge, precisely because Taiwan's identity is now based on civic values, such as freedom and democracy, that China is unlikely to adopt in the short run".[86]

Ming-Hua Chiang, in the book *China-Taiwan Rapprochement: The Political Economy of Cross-Straits Relations* published in 2016, takes a slightly different approach to China and Taiwan's economic relationship as compared to Hsieh and Lin. Both Hsieh and Lin appear to touch on the fact that Taiwan is very hostile towards China, with Taiwan ensuring it does not need to rely on China economically by creating harsh regulations of their trade agreements and politically maintaining the country is not linked to China, by, for example, leveraging their WTO membership. Chiang's discussion on China and Taiwan's trade relationship focuses on how Taiwan is becoming economically reliant on China. Chiang provides examples of this reliance, such as how, since the mid-1990s, a large portion of Taiwanese companies have relocated their manufacturing production to China. Further, China has participated in Taiwan's outbound direct investment, while Taiwan's importance in China's foreign direct investment has declined.[87] Chiang also notes that China is Taiwan's largest export and import destination, but Taiwan's share in China's trade has declined over the past decade.[88] Chiang goes on to observe how mainland Chinese tourists

[83] *Id.* at 21.
[84] *Id.* at 207.
[85] *Id.* at 209.
[86] *Id.*
[87] Min-Hua Chiang, *China-Taiwan Rapprochement: The Political Economy of Cross-Straits Relations* 5 & 177 (2016).
[88] *Id.*

have become the largest source of tourism for Taiwan.[89] Additionally, due to the existing low-profit margin in Taiwan's domestic financial sector, many Taiwanese businesses attempt to expand their businesses into China.[90]

Tat Wai Tan, in the article *Comments on the Implication of the US-China Trade War Taiwan* published in 2020, focuses on Hsieh's research on the China-Taiwan economic relationship. Tan opens by putting forward the position that China's economic isolation of Taiwan may initially not appear to be fatal due to Taiwan's apparent economic success.[91] Building on this point, Tan notes that a flaw in Hsieh's study is that he did not document how China's refusal to interact with Taiwan has negatively impacted Taiwan's economic growth. As Hsieh argues that China is hostile towards Taiwan, and vice versa, this may have been a relevant consideration. Tan also argues against Hsieh's characterisation of Taiwan as part of China's supply chain.[92] Tan argues that both China and Taiwan are part of the East and Southeast Asian supply chain, which has been created by American multinational companies over the years, providing Taiwan with a level of autonomy from China. Tan's article is a useful critique of various aspects of Hsieh's arguments.

B. North and South Korea

The divide between the two nations on the Korean peninsula has received considerable scholarly attention from a historical and geopolitical perspective. The mainstream narratives on the historical development and political tensions between the Democratic People's Republic of Korea (hereinafter DPRK or North Korea) and the Republic of Korea (hereinafter ROK or South Korea) orient towards politics surrounding hegemony, ideology, regional security, and sense of national identity and belongingness following the Second World War and the Cold War.[93] Military balance, denuclearisation, domestic political and economic dynamics of the two Koreas, and their changing relationships with major powers, such as the United States, Russia, and China, serve as the major anchors for discourse. In contrast to such mainstream narratives, Theodore Jun Yoo unpacks another historical trajectory post the Second World War and the

[89] *Id.* at 82.

[90] *Id.* at 179.

[91] Tat Wai Tan, *Comments on the Implication of the US–China Trade War Taiwan*, 19(1) Asian Econ Papers 84, 85 (2020).

[92] *Id.* at 88.

[93] *See The Two Koreas and the United States: Issues of Peace, Security, and Economic Cooperation* (Wonmo Dong ed., 2000) (collecting accounts and analyses by experts in the field); *Routledge Handbook of Modern Korean History* (Michael Seth ed., 2016); Yangmo Ku, Inyeop Lee and Jongseok Woo, *Politics in North and South Korea: Political Development, Economy, and Foreign Relations* (2018). Some offer a thorough introduction to and discussion on North Korea, *see, e.g.*, Hazel Smith, North Korea: Markets and Military Rule (2015); *see also* Routledge Handbook of Contemporary North Korea (Adrian Buzo ed., 2021).

Cold War, focusing on popular culture and everyday life instead of national cultural homogeneity, belongingness, and identity. His work sheds important light on the contemporary development and changing relationship of the two remarkably different Koreas today.[94]

In addition to tracing the historical roots of and ideological divide between the two Koreas, Eui-Gak Hwang takes an international perspective on the inter-Korean relationship and compares the possible reunification of South and North Korea with the paths of German and Vietnamese reunification, employing an economic and regime change viewpoint.[95] Hwang's review and analysis of the changes in economic policies in South Korea, from the Sunshine Policy ("Reconciliation and Cooperation Policy") to the Kaesong Industrial Complex, as well as their implications for the paths of reunification, is of significant reference power. While Hwang also examines the influence of international affairs on prospects for stability and possible reunification on the Korean peninsula and emphasises the need for a "multinational body" to oversee a North Korean political transition, the roles and ramifications of trade and investment negotiations and agreements, multilateral institutions (such as the United Nations and World Trade Organization), as well as domestic legal frameworks for the shaping and conditioning of an inter-Korean economic relationship have not been adequately addressed.

C. North and South Cyprus

Scholarly works on the Cyprus issue share the same concern about the future of the island in view of the ethnic conflicts and subsequent divide. Corresponding to their background and training, scholars approach this subject matter from the disciplines of law and political science, with a European or international perspective. EU scholars initially focus on Cyprus' accession negotiations, and later on the impact of EU membership, as well as the application and non-application of EU *acquis* on the island. EU legal scholars' main concern is how to realise fundamental freedoms under EU law[96] on the divided island and how to integrate Cyprus into the Union.[97] For example, Nikos Skoutaris looks at how the EU tackles the *de facto* partial accession of Cyprus, with a special focus on the application of EU laws on the island, where two competing authorities exist.[98] Stéphanie Laulhé Shaelou, taking a socio-legal approach, tries to depict

[94] *See generally* Theodore Jun Yoo, *The Koreas: The Birth of Two Nations Divided* (2020).

[95] *See generally* Eui-Gak Hwang, *The Search for a Unified Korea: Political and Economic Implications* (2010).

[96] *See generally* Nikos Skoutaris, The Cyprus Issue: The Four Freedoms in a Member States under Siege (2011).

[97] *See generally* Stéphanie Laulhé Shaelou, The EU and Cyprus: Principles and Strategies of Full Integration (2010).

[98] *See generally* Skoutaris, *supra* note 97.

Cyprus' integration process into the Union. She argues that disparities arising from geographical, economic, social, and political characteristics between North and South Cyprus should not detour the course of the island's European integration process and proposes a solution promoted by the EU at the transnational level leading to "the enjoyment by the whole island of the benefits of EU membership".[99] For European political scientists, the key issue is to appreciate the impact of Europeanisation and ascertain whether and how the EU can help to resolve the conflict between North and South Cyprus.[100] In this regard, based on international relations theories, Sepos examines how the process of Europeanisation shapes the executive, legislative, and judicial branches of the Cyprus government as well as other areas, including public opinion, the economy, and foreign policy. Furthermore, Diez analyzes the conflicts between the North and South in the context of granting EU membership to Southern Cyprus.[101] Instead of reiterating the conflicts in Cyprus and the role of the EU, contributions in Diez's edited volume add to current debates with the perspectives of contemporary international relations theories and shed light on the potential for the successful and sustainable settlement of the conflicts in Cyprus by identifying the "post-modernisation" of identities and politics in Cyprus and the postmodern characteristics of the EU.

Taking a broad perspective, international relations and international law scholars investigate the role of the UN in mediating the conflicts or resolving the divide.[102] This strand of scholarly works runs across and connects two perspectives, exploring legal issues surrounding Cyprus based on EU law and international law[103] and reflecting on whether and how the EU and UN can help to resolve the North-South Cyprus conflict.[104] Oliver Richmond, for example, investigates the diverse internationals perspectives surrounding North and South Cyprus in terms of their inherent conflicts. He illuminates the views of Cypriot parties on the long-lasting UN peace-making operation on this island and tries to shed light on effective mediation to resolve the conflicts through the UN platform.[105] Frank Hoffmeister, who has worked for the European Commission and served as the UN Special Advisor on Cyprus, systematically assesses the settlement plan for Cyprus proposed by then UN Secretary-General Annan, analysing whether the "Annan Plan" can be accommodated in the EU system from the perspectives of the principles of democracy and the rule of law.

[99] *See generally* Laulhé Shaelou, *supra* note 98.

[100] *See generally* Angelos Sepos, *The Europeanization of Cyprus: Polity, Policies and Politics* (2008).

[101] *See generally* The European Union and the Cyprus Conflict: Modern Conflict, Postmodern Union (Thomas Diez ed., 2002).

[102] *See generally* Oliver P Richmond, Mediating in Cyprus: The Cypriot Communities and the United Nations (1998).

[103] *See generally* Frank Hoffmeister, Legal Aspects of the Cyprus Problem: Annan Plan and EU Accession (2006).

[104] *See generally* James Ker-Lindsay, EU Accession and UN Peacekeeping in Cyprus (2005).

[105] *See generally* Richmond, *supra* note 103.

His work tackles current legal issues arising out of Cyprus' accession to the EU, focusing on the suspension of the *acquis communautaire* in Northern Cyprus.[106] James Ker-Lindsay's research traces the attempts to facilitate the reunification of Cyprus by the UN before Cyprus joined the EU in 2004. He comprehensively narrates the details of discussions between the two sides from 2002 to 2004 and explains why international efforts to resolve the conflict between North and South Cyprus failed, focusing on the UN "Annan Plan" which was eventually rejected in a 2004 referendum held by Southern Cyprus.[107] These scholarly works are attempts to understand the role of international or regional institutions in bridging the North-South divide, efforts whose ultimate aim is the settlement of the Cyprus issue. Insofar as this objective is not attainable in the short term, these scholars suggest possible intermediate measures.

Apart from these two main strands, some scholarly works deserve special attention. In 1968, before the outbreak of communal conflicts and the subsequent North–South divide, Stahis S. Panagides wrote that the appropriation and distribution of economic interests represented the root cause of conflict between Greek and Turkish Cypriots. He therefore explored economic means to resolve these conflicts.[108] By contrast, George C. Georgiou, writing in 2009, reflects on the potential economic consequences of reunification. Building on the economic theories of free trade and economic integration, Georgiou investigates the actors involved in the unification process in Cyprus, including the U.S., the EU, the UK, Russia, and Turkey, and explores its income and wealth distribution effect. Georgiou argues that "there will ultimately be a 'tax dividend' levied on the Greek Cypriots to pay for the much touted 'peace dividend' that will accrue, primarily to Turkish Cypriots".[109] In addition, given the special status of Northern Cyprus in international law, Daria Isacheko explores its state-building process.[110] Isacheko finds that Northern Cyprus, an informal state, actively participates in international politics despite non-recognition. Such an observation is consistent with other unrecognised states or state-like entities.[111] These scholarly works are relevant to our book, as we include Cyprus as one of the case studies in exploring economic integration in divided nations. Panagides and Georgiou offer insights into the economic causes of communal conflicts and the economic consequences of possible unification. Georgiou also raises cautions regarding income and wealth distribution surrounding economic integration between divided nations and points to the role of regional powers in

[106] *See generally* Hoffmeister, *supra* note 104.

[107] *See generally* Ker-Lindsay, *supra* note 105.

[108] *See generally* Stahis S Panagides, *Communal Conflict and Economic Considerations: The Case of Cyprus*, 5(2) J Peace Rsch 133 (1968).

[109] *See generally* George C Georgiou, *Cyprus: Economic Consequences of Reunification*, 20(3) Mediterranean Q 51 (2009).

[110] *See generally* Isacheko, *supra* note 74.

[111] *See generally* Deon Geldenhuys, Contested States in World Politics (2009); *see also* Rowan Nicholson, Statehood and the State-Like in International Law (2019).

the integration process. Isacheko underscores Northern Cyprus' capacity and experience in engaging in international relations.

D. The Contributions of this Book

The intended contribution of this book lies in its ambition to go beyond individual cases and identify those factors affecting the course of economic cooperation in divided nations through a comparative analysis. The book conceptualises a framework that empirically helps to predict both progress and setbacks and normatively assess the pros and cons of economic cooperation.

Several factors determine the scope and shape, as well as the form and substance, of economic cooperation between divided nations. First, the dispute over sovereignty or legitimate representation is of paramount significance and defines the contour of political interactions, which in turn implicate economic ties between these countries or entities. Overlapping claims regarding sovereignty or legitimate representation and the exclusion or inclusion in the UN setting fundamentally anchor inter-se interactions, as well as interactions with the wider world.

Second, cultural, ethnic, and linguistic similarities and diversities play a role in advancing economic exchanges between these countries or entities. Similarities do not necessarily contribute to closer economic cooperation, whereas diversities do not necessarily prevent it. On the one hand, while cultural, ethnic, and linguistic proximity may ease barriers to tighter cooperation between these countries or entities, counterintuitively, it may at the same time foil their interactions, given the fear that deeper and faster integration may lead to ultimate political unification.

Third, public interest and opinion at the domestic level may influence how these countries or entities interact. For instance, different designated agencies, whether public, private, or hybrid, are responsible for managing aspects of political interactions and economic cooperation due to varied domestic demands (or critiques) from the general public and industry stakeholders from the private sector. Similarly, it is not uncommon to see diverse forms in terms of a regulatory framework, legislative oversight, and a review mechanism to moderate concerns about political integration because of ethnic, cultural, and language proximity.

Fourth, fora for economic cooperation vary, and international context matters. Corresponding to their recognition or non-recognition of each other, the format for advancing economic cooperation differs. Often, public authorities are delegated to a specially designed agency or semi-official organisations, such as Straits Exchange Foundation/Associate for Relations Across the Taiwan Strait or the respective Turkish/Greek Cypriot Chambers of Commerce, to satisfy the need for official exchanges arising from economic cooperation. In addition, in these three sets of divided nations, none is entirely isolated and detached from the international community. Rather, all hold memberships in certain multilateral intergovernmental organisations, such as the UN, the WTO, and the EU. In some cases, they coexist; in others, they exclude each other. The roles of these multilateral organisations in stabilising the economic relations or contributing to economic exchange vary.

Finally, yet crucially, geopolitics plays a role, and certain hegemonic powers, such as the U.S., the EU, China, and Russia, have exercised significant influence in various stages of development and play a crucial role in shaping and reshaping the relationships between these countries or entities. By identifying the factors – social, economic, or political – that determine the way in which the selected divided nations engage each other, this book will hopefully provide an analytical framework for policymakers, practitioners, and academics to further appreciate the underlying dynamics, and to predict the patterns of interactions. This might in turn help third parties to optimise their legal and political strategies, rendering them more suitable to their unique situations as they deal with the dilemma involving trade partners in such a complex relationship.

Moreover, as integration between states in one economic sector may create strong incentives for integration in further sectors, and – given the fact that these selected divided nations, especially in the Korea Peninsula and on both sides of the Taiwan Strait, play a decisive role in the global supply chain – the way these countries forge economic ties (or fail to do so) will surely have spillover effects for third-party countries. Of course, there could be a two-way interaction: for some of these third-party countries with high stakes in relevant regions, such as the U.S. and EU, they may have strong incentives and power to shape the patterns of economic integration of these divided nations. On the other hand, less powerful third-party states may have to act more strategically to maximise their interests while dealing with either side of such a divided nation. In this light, by studying these three sets of divided nations in Asia and Europe together, this book will assist policymakers and scholars in developing a more comprehensive and informed view when compared with a standalone study of any of these countries.

V. THE STRUCTURE OF THIS BOOK

At heart, this book aims to systematically address a question of both practical and theoretical significance that is nonetheless under-addressed in the existing literature: How do two political entities comprising a divided nation engage each other in terms of trade, investment, and other economic activities in light of their exceptionally sensitive and even troubled political relationship? Built on three representative case studies of pairs of divided nations – North and South Korea, China and Taiwan, and North and South Cyprus, this book casts a wider net in both an empirical and a conceptual sense by exploring the underlying factors, approaches, and patterns that influence the economic relationships between them. Premised upon the above literature review, which anchors the existing scholarship on contested sovereignty and trade, geopolitics in divided nations and international political economy dynamics, and democratic legitimacy and accountability, the route map for the rest of the book is as follows.

Perhaps the most controversial among the three case studies in this book, China-Taiwan economic relations are considered in Chapter 2. Taiwan-China economic relations operate in a fashion we refer to as a "rollercoaster ride". Domestic issues such as economic development, political climate, and national identity, coupled with geopolitical factors, and in particular Sino-American relations, play a critical role in determining this journey. Chapter II illustrates the dynamics underlying the interactions between both sides of the Taiwan Strait and analyses the complex factors that determine patterns of interaction along the lines of peace, prosperity, sovereignty, and democratic legitimacy. This chapter also contextualises its analyses by considering the more recent role of emerging Sino-American geopolitical tensions.

Chapter 3 deals with the Korean peninsula. Despite a high level of political sensitivity and armed conflicts in the past, North and South Korea have most recently engaged in somewhat positive yet dynamic political interactions to pursue bilateral peace and economic cooperation amid considerable uncertainty. This chapter explores the trajectories and dynamics of inter-Korean relationships and analyses the multifaceted factors therein – including membership status in multilateral organisations, the involvement of hegemonic powers, levels of institutionalisation of bilateral channels, public opinions and industry interests, government support and political risk insurance, and path-dependence effects.

Chapter 4 examines the course of North-South Cyprus economic integration, as it is heavily impacted by ethnological divergence, geopolitics, regional integration championed by the EU, and multilateral institutions underpinned by the UN. As this chapter explains, Cyprus' accession to the EU opened a window of opportunity for further political and economic integration, while Annan's proposal for a comprehensive settlement failed in the Greek Cypriot referendum. Cyprus joined the EU as a divided country, which necessitates the suspension of *acquis* in North Cyprus. Importantly, being a member state of the EU, North–South Cyprus trade is transformed into an issue of the free circulation of the internal market. Among other factors, Chapter 5 underscores the shift in agenda from economic integration to political unification, involvement of the EU and the UN, as well as democratic legitimacy and accountability concerns circling the Cyprus issue.

Premised upon the careful analysis of the three case studies on North and South Korea, China and Taiwan, and North and South Cyprus in the above chapters, this book examines the myriad ways in which the historical backgrounds, economic ties, and internal and external political environments have shaped and reshaped economic cooperation between these divided nations.

Chapter 5 goes one step further by directly addressing the core question of how economic cooperation is configured and reconfigured in the shadow of contested sovereignty. While some multilateral organisations play a role in facilitating economic cooperation and integration in all three case studies, there are limits, since the interactions between each of these countries or entities appear to be moving objects. Despite the underlying dynamics of political economy among these three sets of countries or entities with contested sovereignty, this chapter empirically and conceptually identifies a set of key controlling parameters contributing to, conditioning, and complicating the forms and processes of their economic and political interactions – including competing sovereignty claims, cultural, ethnic, and linguistic proximity and divergence, membership in multilateral settings and organisations, level of economic interdependence, bilateral channels and frameworks, domestic politics and public interest groups, and the influence of regional or global powers. As will be articulated in this chapter, our empirically driven conceptual framework lays the groundwork for future scholarship on the modes of economic cooperation in politically sensitive and strategically strenuous contexts. Chapter 6 concludes.

2

Cross-Strait Economic Relations

I. HISTORICAL BACKGROUND

To understand the economic relations between Taiwan and China, it is useful to review their history. Precisely when Chinese began settling in Taiwan is a matter of debate,[1] but it is generally accepted that Chinese settlers there were well-established by the seventeenth century. In 1624, the Dutch East India Company set up a trading post in Taiwan, taking control from the indigenous inhabitants. However, by the late seventeenth century, Ming General Koxinga had ousted the Dutch and made Taiwan a refuge for Ming Dynasty loyalists. Under Koxinga's brief rule, more Han Chinese migrated to Taiwan, and established a significant population on the island. In 1683, the Qing Empire annexed Taiwan, ruling it indirectly through Fujian until 1885 when the island was officially declared a province.[2] A mere decade later, in 1895,

[1] The narrative discourse about Taiwan history could be different between two sides of the Strait. For the People's Republic of China (PRC) Government, it claims that "Taiwan has belonged to China since ancient times" with the references to Seaboard Geographic Gazetteer compiled in the year 230 by Shen Ying of the State of Wu during the Three Kingdoms Period". *See The Taiwan Question and China's Reunification in the New Era*, the Taiwan Affairs Office of the State Council and the State Council Information Office (China, Aug 2022). Available at: http://gm.china-embassy.gov.cn/eng/sgxw/202208/P020220810850182763063.pdf. On the other side of the Strait, the narrative has gradually shifted over the years. Earlier versions of history textbooks featured stronger cultural, ethnic, and political ties between Taiwan and China. For instance, the version of 1997, published by the National Institute for Compilation and Translation, referred to the troops of the Eastern Wu during the era of Three Kingdoms being sent to Taiwan. Recent years, however, saw the sea change. There is more emphasis on the role of the indigenous people as the Island's owner; Chinese histories are downplayed. This led the textbooks to focus more on the history of Koxinga's settlement in Taiwan and beyond. We have – as far as possible – presented the narrative in a balanced manner for present purposes. In this regard, *see e.g.*, Pei-Fen Sung (宋佩芬) and Wei-His Chang (張韡曦)，臺灣史的詮釋轉變：國族歷史與國家認同教育的省思，《教育科學研究期刊》第55卷3期，2010年9月 [Pei-Fen Sung and Wei-Hsi Chang, *Taiwanese History: Reflections on National History and the Education of National Identity*, 55(3) J Res In Edu Sci (2010)]; Zhaojin Lyu and Haiyan Zhou, *Contesting Master Narratives: Renderings of National History by Mainland China and Taiwan*, China Q (2023).

[2] Hungdah Chiu, The International Legal Status of Taiwan, in The International Status of Taiwan in the New World Order: Legal and Political Considerations 3 (Jean-Marie Henckaerts ed., 1996). But see Lung-chu Chen and W. M. Reisman, Who Owns Taiwan: A Search for International Title, 81 Yale L J 599, 609 (1972) (arguing that for almost two centuries since Taiwan was taken over by Qing-Dynasty China, the government "did virtually nothing to govern or develop Taiwan". This cast doubt on China's effective control of this island).

following the First Sino-Japanese War, China ceded Taiwan to Japan under the Treaty of Shimonoseki.[3]

In 1945, the Republic of China (ROC) government assumed military control of Taiwan, marking the end of a half-century of Japanese colonial rule.[4] That same year witnessed the establishment of the United Nations (UN), with China represented by the ROC government as a founding member.[5] In 1949, the Chinese Communist Party (CCP) defeated the Nationalist Party, or Kuomintang (KMT), and seized control over the entire Mainland. Thereafter, the ROC exercised jurisdiction over Taiwan, the Penghu Islands, Kinmen Islands, Matsu Islands, and a number of smaller islands. Since then, Taiwan-China relations have revolved around two intertwined issues: the representation of China in the UN, and recognition of governments on opposing sides of the Taiwan Strait.[6]

Despite the KMT's defeat and retreat from the Mainland, Chiang Kai-shek vowed to reclaim lost territories from the Communists. The ROC in Taiwan saw itself as the rightful government of all China, and its legitimate representative in the UN. Conversely, the CCP viewed Taiwan as a renegade province. Believing the victory in the civil war made the People's Republic of China (PRC) the ROC's rightful successor, the PRC did not seek new UN membership but maintained that it was entitled to China's seat after the Nationalist retreat.[7] The PRC joined its allies in the Soviet Bloc and others in a diplomatic tug-of-war with the ROC

[3] Government Information Office of the Executive Yuan, The Republic of China Yearbook 2010 52 (Taiwan).

[4] There are different views on when or even whether Taiwan was returned to China. Some argue that, strictly, Japan relinquished its title over Taiwan in 1951 by way of the Treaty of San Francisco. Since nowhere did this Treaty – nor the 1952 Sino-Japan Peace Treaty – specify the beneficiary and the Cairo and Potsdam Declarations were not "legally binding" instruments, the sovereignty over this island was left undetermined. The British Government once took this position. *See e.g.*, 536 Parl Deb HC (5th ser) col 159 (UK) (Referring to the ROC's takeover of Taiwan in 1945, Sir Anthony Eden stated that "arrangements made with Chiang Kai-shek put him there on a basis of military occupation pending further arrangements" and the 1951 Treaty "did not operate as a transfer to Chinese sovereignty … Formosa and the Pescadores are therefore, in the view of H.M. Government, territory the de jure sovereignty over which is uncertain or undetermined".). For similar views, *see e.g.*, Chen and Reisman, *supra* note 2, at 633–47 (arguing that the ROC's "act of securing control of Taiwan in 1945 was a mandate of trust by the Allied Powers"). However, the British Government reversed its position by acknowledging "the position of the Chinese Government that Taiwan is a province of the People's Republic of China" in its 1972 Joint Communique Concerning Upgraded Diplomatic Relations with China. A contrary view is that Taiwan was returned to China by 1949 as a consequence of the ROC's cancellation of the Treaty of Shimonoseki in 1941 and the Cairo and Potsdam Declarations. As per this line of argument, the Treaty of San Francisco served to confirm Japan's relinquishment of its claims. See Claude S. Phillips Jr., *The International Legal Status of Formosa*, 10 Pol Res Q 276 (1957). For a detailed account, see J P Jain, *The Legal Status of Formosa: A Study of British, Chinese and Indian Views*, 57 Am J Int'l L 25 (1963); James Crawford, The Creation of States in International Law 206-–11 (2006); Johnathan I Charney and JRV Prescott, *Resolving Cross-Strait Relations Between China and Taiwan*, 94 Am J Int'l L 453, 460–61 (2000).

[5] UN Charter art 110, ¶3.

[6] Crawford, *supra* note 4, at 199.

[7] Frank Chiang, The One-China Policy: State, Sovereignty, and Taiwan's International Legal Status 147–48 (2017).

for diplomatic recognition.[8] While there were proposals to allow governments on both sides of the Taiwan Strait representation in the UN under the two-China formula,[9] geopolitical shifts eventually culminated in the UN General Assembly adopting Resolution No. 2758 (XXVI), proposed by Albania, which recognised the PRC as "*the only legitimate representative of China to the United Nations*" and led to the expulsion of "the representatives of Chiang Kai-sheik from the place which they unlawfully occupy at the United Nations".[10]

Subsequent years saw further challenges to the ROC's international standing. In 1972, nearly twenty years after the Korean War, escalating Sino-Soviet tensions and shared strategic interests brought about *détente* between the U.S. and China. President Nixon's historic visit to China culminated in the "Sino-U.S. Joint Communique", better known as the Shanghai Communique.[11] For the PRC, this represented a pivotal juncture in its extensive expansion of international relations over the last fifty years, influencing its approach to defining relations with Taiwan.[12] In the relevant part, Beijing asserted that:

> The Government of the People's Republic of China is the sole legal government of China; Taiwan is a province of China which has long been returned to the motherland;

[8] See Eric Ting-Lun Huang, *Taiwan's Status in a Changing World: United Nations Representation and Membership for Taiwan*, 9 Ann Surv Int'l & Com. L. 55, 80–81 (2003); Pasha L Hsieh, *The Taiwan Question and the One-China Policy: Legal Challenges with Renewed Momentum*, 84(3) Die Friedens-Warte 59, 61 (2009) [hereinafter Hsieh, *The Taiwan Question*].

[9] Parris Chang and Kok-Ui Lim, *Taiwan's Case for United Nations Membership*, 1 UCLA J Int'l L & Foreign Aff 393, 394 (1996); Y Frank Chiang, *One-China Policy and Taiwan*, 28 Fordham Int'l LJ 1 (2004) [hereinafter Chiang, *One-China Policy and Taiwan*] (noting that Japan and the U.S, sought to help create "two Chinas": the old one ruled by the PRC, and the other one having the ROC as its government in Taiwan.).

[10] GA Res 2758 at 2 (Oct 25, 1971) (emphasis added). In fact, knowing that the adoption of this Resolution was unavoidable, Chiang Kai-shek ordered his delegation to walk out of the UN in advance to prevent humiliation. Dennis V Hickey, Foreign Policy Making in Taiwan: From Principle to Pragmatism 11 (2007). It should be noted, however, that interpreting the 2758 Resolution has been rather political and complicated. While the PRC maintained that Taiwan is an "inalienable part of China's territory" and that the PRC is "the sole legal government representing the whole of China" by referring to Resolution 2758, some would instead interpret this Resolution as not addressing the Taiwan issue. The PRC reaffirms its position in a more recent document. See *The Taiwan Question and China's Reunification in the New Era*, *supra* note 1. *Cf.* Madoka Fukuda, *China Is Using a UN Resolution to Further Its Claim Over Taiwan*, The Diplomat (Aug 26, 2022). Available at: https://thediplomat.com/2022/08/china-is-using-a-un-resolution-to-further-its-claim-over-taiwan/ (last visited Jan 24, 2024) (arguing that this Resolution recognised the PRC as the sole lawful representative of China and a permanent member of the Security Council, expelling Chiang Kai-shek's representatives; however, it did not mention Taiwan or affirm the PRC's "One China" principle, which includes Taiwan as part of the PRC). Hsieh, *The Taiwan Question*, *supra* note 8, at 62 (observing that "Neither UN Resolution 2758 nor the ROC's loss of recognition from major states resolved the Taiwan question. These decisions clarified that the PRC is now the legitimate government of China, but they left it ambiguous as to whether Taiwan is part of the 'China' that the PRC claims to represent".) The resurgence of this debate in recent times, influenced by the evolving geopolitical landscape, is discussed in detail in Chapter 5.

[11] 17 Foreign Relations of the United States (1969–1976) at v, Foreign Service Institute Office of the Historian (2006).

[12] Yu-Jie Chen, *"One China" Contention in China-Taiwan Relations: Law, Politics and Identity*, 252 China Q 1025, 1025 (2022).

> the liberation of Taiwan is China's internal affair in which no other country has the right to interfere; and all U.S. forces and military installations must be withdrawn from Taiwan. The Chinese government firmly opposes any activities which aim at the creation of "one China, one Taiwan", "one China, two governments", "two Chinas", an "independent Taiwan", or advocate that "the status of Taiwan remains to be determined".[13]

Washington emphasised its interest in the "peaceful settlement of the Taiwan question by the Chinese themselves", while leaving its position on this question vague by merely "acknowledge[ing] the Chinese position that there is but one China and Taiwan is part of China" in the subsequent 1979 Normalisation Communique.[14] Despite the ambiguity surrounding the concept of "One China",[15] numerous countries subsequently severed diplomatic relations with the ROC in favour of the PRC – following Beijing's assumption of China's seat in the UN and the establishment of diplomatic ties between the U.S. and China under the Communist Party. At the time of this writing, only twelve countries recognise the ROC government.[16]

[13] Foreign Relations of the United States (1969–1976), *supra* note 11, at 569.

[14] Joint Communique of the United States of America and the People's Republic of China (Normalisation Communique), Jan 1, 1979, 1 Foreign Relations of the United States (1977–1980) at 505. This led commentators to argue that while the US had no trouble in accepting the notion of "One China", the text revealed that President Nixon was hesitant to accept the claim that the PRC was the sole legitimate government of China. Chiang, *One-China Policy and Taiwan*, *supra* note 9, at 49 Jacques deLisle, too, pointed out that the US and China "have had different understandings of these fundamental texts". Per deLisle, "[w]here China sees U.S. acceptance of China's position that Taiwan is part of China, the U.S. insists that it merely acknowledges the existence of a view ostensibly shared on both sides of the Strait. From the U.S. perspective, the U.S.'s Taiwan Relations Act (TRA) and – less securely – President Ronald Reagan's Six Assurances stand alongside the Three Communiques as authoritative statements of U.S. policy". Jacques deLisle, *Trump, Tsai, and the Three Communiques: Prospects for Stability in US-China-Taiwan Relations*, Foreign Pol'y Res Inst (Mar 9, 2017). Available at: www.fpri.org/2017/03/trump-tsai-three-communiques-prospects-stability-us-china-taiwan-relations/.

[15] Similar to the US, other countries have adopted the "One China" policy using the term "acknowledge" while establishing diplomatic ties with the PRC. Australia, for instance, "recognises the government of the [PRC] as the sole legal Government of China [and] acknowledges the position of the Chinese Government that Taiwan is a province of the People's Republic of China" through its 1972 Joint Communique. Joint Communiqué of the Australian Government and the Government of the People's Republic of China Concerning the Establishment of Diplomatic Relations Between Australia and China, Dec 21, 1972, PM Transcripts. Available at: https://pmtranscripts.pmc.gov.au/release/transcript-3119. Using both "recognises" and "acknowledges" in the same document has led some to argue that the "Communique introduced a deliberate ambiguity that alludes to a broader understanding of the meaning of China than just the People's Republic of China", thereby creating "a flexible, secure and enduring basis for relations with both Beijing and Taipei that has aligned with shifts in cross-straits relations". Mark Harrison, *Australia's One-China Policy and Why It Matters*, The Interpreter (Oct 11, 2017). Available at: www.lowyinstitute.org/the-interpreter/australia-s-one-china-policy-why-it-matters; *see also* Benjamin Herscovitch and Mark Harrison, *Enhancing Australia's Taiwan Ties*, Lowy Inst (Dec 6, 2023). Available at: www.lowyinstitute.org/publications/enhancing-australia-s-taiwan-ties.

[16] *Diplomatic Allies*, Ministry of Foreign Affairs, the Rep of China (Taiwan). Available at: https://en.mofa.gov.tw/AlliesIndex.aspx?n=1294&sms=1007 (last visited Mar 10, 2024).

PRC pressure to acknowledge its One-China principle[17] has diminished the number of nations recognising the ROC and restricted Taiwan's freedom to participate in international organisations, most of which require sovereignty for membership.[18] There are but a few exceptions. Notably, in addition to a "Fishing Entity" that is eligible to participate in Regional Fisheries Management Organizations,[19] Taiwan is permitted to participate in the Asian Development Bank (ADB), the Asia-Pacific Economic Cooperation (APEC), and the World Trade Organization (WTO). The membership of the latter two institutions is not limited to statehood: APEC allows "economies" to participate,[20] while the WTO is open not only to a "State" but also to "a separate customs territory possessing full autonomy in the conduct of its external commercial relations".[21] The ADB represents an even more interesting case. Although the ADB's membership is restricted to "members and associate members of the United Nations Economic Commission for Asia and the Far East" and "other regional countries and non-regional developed countries which are members of the United Nations or of any of its specialised agencies",[22] the ROC retained its seat without being ousted after the PRC's admission.[23]

While the ADB, APEC, and WTO are crucial venues for managing various issues concerning international economic affairs, Taiwan's participation in them is exceptional. Even within these institutions, Taiwan's interactions with other members, including Mainland China, are overshadowed by the "One-China" policy.[24] Taiwan's application for membership in the General Agreement on Tariffs and Trade (GATT) in the early 1990s – to which the ROC government was

[17] Note, however, that the "One China" policy of the US is not the same as the "One China" principle referred to by the Chinese government. It contains other elements, such as resolving the Cross-Strait disputes peacefully.

[18] In what follows, we use "Taiwan", "ROC", and "ROC in Taiwan" interchangeably to refer to the government exercising jurisdiction over this island. Admittedly, however, each term may involve different political connotations.

[19] See generally Andrew Serdy, *Bringing Taiwan into the International Fisheries Fold: The Legal Personality of a Fishing Entity*, 75(1) British YB Int'l L 183 (2005).

[20] How APEC Operates, Asia-Pacific Economic Cooperation. Available at: www.apec.org/About-Us/How-APEC-Operates. See also Merit E Janow, *Assessing APEC's Role in Economic Integration in the Asia-Pacific Region*, 17 Nw J Int'l L & Bus 947, 956 (1997) (noting that because of the efforts of South Korea, the 1991 Seoul meeting included the PRC, Hong Kong, and Taiwan as members of APEC, which made itself the "first international governmental forum at which all three entities were included as participants".).

[21] Marrakesh Agreement Establishing the World Trade Organization, Apr 15, 1994, 1867 UNTS 154, art XII [hereinafter Marrakesh Agreement].

[22] Agreement Establishing the Asian Development Bank, Dec 4, 1965 art 3, 571 UNTS 123 (effective Aug 22, 1966).

[23] Hungdah Chiu, *The International Legal Status of the Republic of China (Revised Version)*, 5 Occasional Papers/Reprints Series in Contemporary Asian Studies 1, 23 (1992) (reporting that Deng Xiaoping seemed to reconsider their policy of isolating Taiwan from the international community, and on one occasion, informed Professor Winston LY Yang of Seton Hall University that Taiwan can retain its seat under the name "Taipei, China".).

[24] For a recount of the notion of "One China", see, e.g., Chong Ja Ian, *The Many "One Chinas": Multiple Approaches to Taiwan and China*, Carnegie Endowment for Int'l Peace (Feb 9, 2023). Available at: https://carnegieendowment.org/2023/02/09/many-one-chinas-multiple-approaches-to-taiwan-and-china-pub-89003 (observing that there are ten types of positions on the "One China" issue).

one of the original contracting parties – was vehemently opposed by the PRC, which described the application as "utterly illegal" and meriting no discussion.[25] After Taiwan lodged its application, the PRC maintained that membership for Taiwan in the GATT might be possible only after the PRC was "restored" to China's seat therein.[26] Later, in the mid-2000s, China attempted to require the WTO to categorise Taiwan as a "Separate Customs Territory of China", but the U.S. shot down the proposal.[27] The uneasy relationship persisted even after both sides joined the WTO. It is observed that Chinese officials have been, as a general practice, "unwilling to make contact with Taiwan officials, let alone hold formal talks on any subject", as the PRC has been concerned that formal talks may "create an impression that Taiwan is on par with China and may be used by Taiwan to boost its image or even expand its diplomatic space".[28] For Beijing, "contacts between the two sides are internal matters not to be conducted under the WTO auspices".[29]

As detailed below, the absence of recognition and the PRC's exclusionary practices have, on the one hand, impaired Taiwan's participation in international economic organisations[30] and, on the other, have limited the way governments on both sides of the Taiwan Strait engage each other in multilateral settings. Nevertheless, this zero-sum political game does not necessarily reflect the demand for closer economic ties on both sides of the Taiwan Strait. We consider this below.

II. CROSS-STRAIT ECONOMIC RELATIONS: SETTING THE STAGE

Historically, Taiwan and China have maintained robust economic relations. During the Japanese colonial era, trade between Taiwan and Mainland China accounted for a significant portion of Taiwan's external trade with countries other than Japan.[31] However, these ties were disrupted when the Nationalist government relocated to Taiwan in 1949.[32] Economic relations only resumed in the late 1970s under Deng Xiaoping's "Open-Door" policy.

[25] Susanna Chan, *Taiwan's Application to the GATT: A New Urgency with the Conclusion of the Uruguay Round*, 2 Ind J Global Legal Stud 275, 285–86 (1994); Pasha Hsieh, Facing China: Taiwan's Status as a Separate Customs Territory in the World Trade Organization, 39 J World Trade 1195, 1199–1200 (2005) [hereinafter Hsieh, Facing China].

[26] Chan, *supra* note 25, at 285.

[27] Qingjiang Kong, Cross-Taiwan Strait Relations: What Are the Legitimate Expectations from the WTO?, 14 Minn J Global Trade 91, 98 (2005).

[28] *Id.* at 99–100.

[29] *Id.* at 100.

[30] See, e.g., Steve Charnovitz, *Taiwan's WTO Membership and Its International Implications*, 1 Asian J WTO & Int'l Health L & Pol'y 401, 424 (2006).

[31] Robert F Ash and YY Kueh, *Economic Integration within Greater China: Trade and Investment Flows Between China, Hong Kong and Taiwan*, 136 China Quarterly 711, 716 (1993).

[32] *Id.*

Quantifying Cross-Strait trade is challenging due to politicised trade regimes and differing statistical methodologies in Taiwan and China.[33] Taiwan's unilateral restrictions on trade with Mainland China in certain economic sectors, and the fact that Taiwan plays a critical role in supplying intermediate goods assembled and re-exported to the rest of the world, could further complicate matters.[34] One should also note, however, that there is a discrepancy between the trade statistics issued by authorities of Taiwan and China due to using different methodologies.[35]

In the first few years after the two sides resumed economic ties, recorded exports and imports were virtually zero, as trade was indirectly administered through Hong Kong due to restrictions on direct shipments to Mainland China. However, as Figure 2.1 demonstrates, trade between Taiwan and the Chinese Mainland gradually increased after 2002 once both had joined the WTO.

Figure 2.1 Cross-Strait Trade Volume

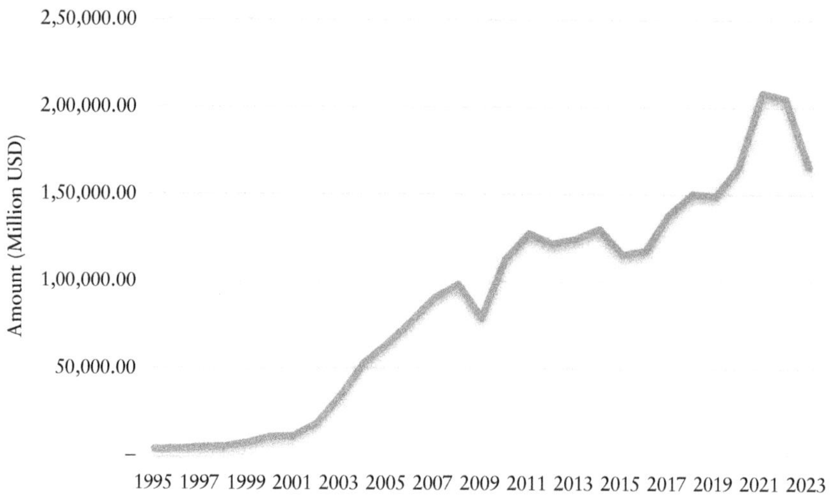

Source: International Trade Administration Trade Statistics Database.

Over the past two decades, globalisation has drawn both sides of the Taiwan Strait increasingly closer – a dynamic that extends beyond trade. Since the 1978 reforms, Taiwanese companies and capital have been crucial in shaping China's manufacturing capacities in coastal areas.[36] As Figure 2.1 shows, although initial investments from Taiwan were small – reflecting the cautiousness and restrictions of its policymakers – new rounds of reforms in China's foreign investment

[33] Daniel Rosen and Zhi Whang, The Implications of China-Taiwan Economic Liberalization 6 (2010).

[34] *Id.*

[35] *Id.* at 9 (noting that Taiwan's data does not capture the real volume of export to China because indirect flows are omitted).

[36] *Id.* at 5.

regime coupled with its participation in the global trading system allowed Taiwanese investors to play a more significant role. New dynamics driven by geopolitics in the post-Covid era, however, are redefining Cross-Strait economic ties, as further elaborated below.

Figure 2.2 Taiwan Outbound Investment in Chinese Mainland from 1991 to November 2022 (1,000 USD)

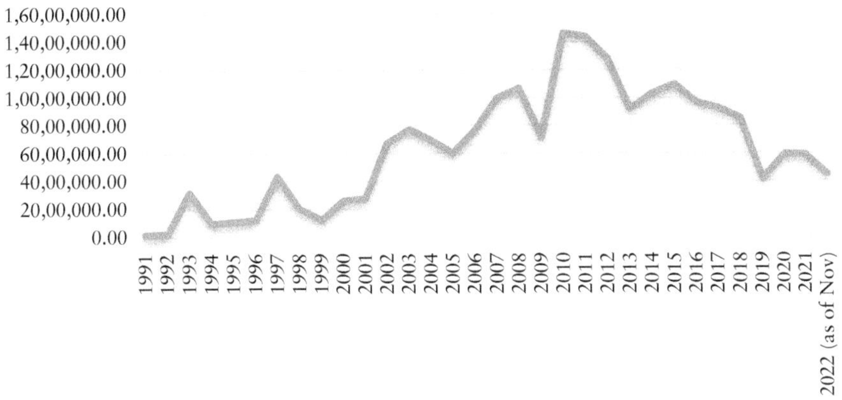

Despite political ups and downs, Cross-Strait trade and investment have constantly increased. This two-way economic relationship is imbalanced, however. Per one account (Figure 2.3), in 2021, China (including Hong Kong) is the trading partner with which Taiwan has the greatest trade surplus. This, in fact, has been a consistent trend rather than a one-off phenomenon: China has been running a large trade deficit with Taiwan for years (Figure 2.4).

Figure 2.3 Trade balance between Taiwan and its main trade partners 2023 Trade surplus or deficit of Taiwan in 2023, by leading trade partner (in billion U.S. dollars)

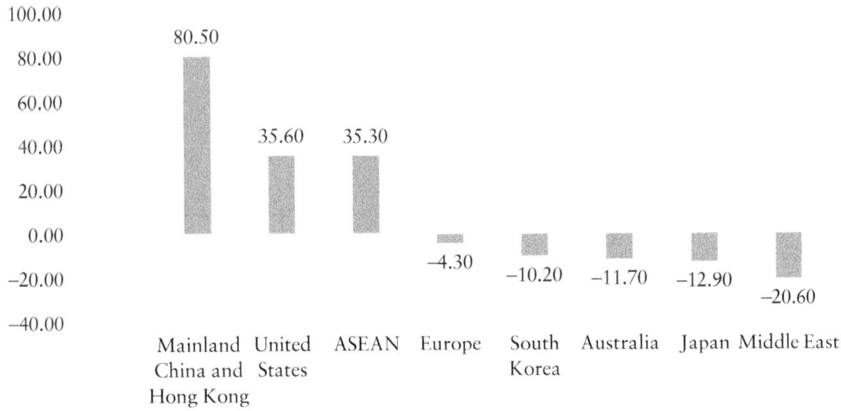

Source: Statista Data Service.

Such surpluses have several legal and political implications. China's trade deficits, in part, reflect Taiwan's restrictive measures towards Mainland China. However, the legality of Taiwan's China-specific measures under the WTO framework is questionable.[37] This is particularly true as neither side of the Taiwan Strait has invoked the non-application clause of Article XIII of the World Trade Organization Agreement – the Marrakesh Agreement – to exclude the obligations of the WTO that applied to this bilateral relationship before they joined the organisation.[38] Nor did Taiwan explicitly rely upon national security or other exceptions as it imposed such restrictions on its trade with China.

Intriguingly, until recently, the PRC Government hesitated to challenge Taiwan's measures within the WTO framework as doing so might inadvertently grant Taiwan a degree of international recognition as a distinct entity and thereby undermine the "One China" principle. More importantly, even after both sides integrated into the global trading system, China continued to reject the applicability of WTO laws to their bilateral relations, viewing them as applicable among "nations". Professor Kong Qingjian of the China University of Political Science and Law highlighted:

> The current arrangement permits different interpretations of the relationship between China and Taiwan within the WTO. Taiwan's status as "Separate Customs Territory" under the name of "Chinese Taipei" allows China to interpret Taiwan's status in the WTO as a separate customs territory of China similar to Hong Kong or Macau … In principle, both are bound by the WTO Agreement, as special international law, in their trade relations with each other. *In practice, however, as international law is by nature law among nations, it would not be accepted as binding norms on cross-strait relations by China as long as Taiwan is seen as a renegade province.*[39]

Beyond the potential for legal action under the WTO, Taiwan's trade surplus with China has deeper implications. Firstly, the PRC government could arguably leverage these deficits for political ends.[40] For example, China imposed bans on Taiwanese agricultural imports, including pineapples and fishery products, in 2021 and 2022, citing biosafety concerns.[41] Similar bans were applied

[37] Julian Chang and Steven M Goldstein, *Introduction: the WTO and Cross-Strait Economic Relations*, *in* Economic Reform and Cross-Strait Relations: Taiwan and China in the WTO 1, 36–37 (Julian Chang and Steven M Goldstein eds, 2007).

[38] Marrakesh Agreement, *supra* note 21, art XIII.

[39] Kong, *supra* note 27, 94–5 (emphasis added).

[40] Yuh-Jiun Lin, *Taiwan's Trade Imbalance with China: The Factors and the Trend*, 12 Am J Chinese Stud 139 (2005).

[41] Xinhua She (新华社)，国台办：大陆暂停进口台湾菠萝是正常生物安全防范举措 (Guo tai ban: Dalu zanting jinkou Taiwan boluo shi zhengchang shengwu anquan fangfan jucuo) [Xinhua News Agency, *The Taiwan Affairs Office of the State Council: The mainland's suspension of imports of Taiwan pineapples is a normal biosecurity precaution*]. Available at: https://tinyurl.com/2v82c6w2 (last visited Mar 15, 2023); Zhonghua Renmin Gongheguo Haiguan Zongshu (中华人民共和国海关总署), 海关总署动植物检疫司关于暂停台湾番荔枝和莲雾输入大陆的通知 (Haiguan zong shu dong zhiwu jianyi si guanyu zanting Taiwan fan lizhi he lian wu shuru dalu de tongzhi) [General Administration of Customs of the People's Republic of China, *Notice of the*

to fishery products in June 2022, with Taiwanese citrus and frozen fish later added onto the blacklist in August of the same year.[42] Indeed, these bans may be justified by WTO regulations and may not necessarily have significant political implications.[43] However, while these bans might align with WTO regulations, some, including Taiwanese trade officials, perceive them as politically motivated measures by the PRC to counter the pro-independence Democratic Progressive Party (DPP).[44] In essence, these actions can be seen as economic coercion tactics employed by the PRC to suppress dissent and further its political objectives.[45]

However, such trade surpluses also pose a dilemma for China. In fact, the agricultural sector constitutes a relatively small portion of Taiwan's economy – approximately 2 per cent of its gross domestic product (GDP).[46] A major

Department of Supervision on Animal and Plant Quarantine of the General Administration of Customs on Suspending the Import of Taiwan Sugar Apples and Wax Apples to the Mainland]. Available at: www.gwytb.gov.cn/bmst/202109/t20210919_12379638.htm (last visited Mar 15, 2023).

[42] Zhonghua Renmin Gongheguo Haiguan Zongshu (中华人民共和国海关总署), 海关总署动植物检疫司关于暂停台湾石斑鱼输入大陆的通知 (Haiguan zong shu dong zhiwu jianyi si guanyu zanting Taiwan shi ban yu shuru dalu de tongzhi) [General Administration of Customs of the People's Republic of China, *Notice of the Department of Supervision on Animal and Plant Quarantine of the General Administration of Customs on Suspending the Import of Taiwan Grouper to the Mainland*]. Available at: www.gwytb.gov.cn/bmst/202206/t20220610_12443211.htm (last visited Mar 15, 2023); Xinhua She (新华社), 海关总署：3日起暂停台湾地区柑橘类水果、冰鲜白带鱼、冻竹荚鱼输入大陆 (Haiguan zong shu: 3 ri qi zanting Taiwan diqu ganju lei shuiguo, bing xian bai daiyu, dong zhu jia yu shuru dalu) [Xinhua News Agency, *General Administration of Customs: Suspension of imports of citrus fruits, chilled beltfish, and frozen bamboo pod fish from the Taiwan region to the mainland starting from the 3rd day* [of August 2022]]. Available at: www.gwytb.gov.cn/bmst/202208/t20220803_12457969.htm.

[43] China's Taiwan Affairs Office of the State Council spokesperson, Zhu Fenglian, stated that the decision was made to protect agricultural production and ecological security. Xinhua She (新华社), 国台办：暂停输入台湾地区番荔枝和莲雾科学合理、完全正当 (Guo tai ban: Zanting shuru Taiwan diqu fan lizhi he lian wu kexue heli, wanquan zhengdang) [Xinhua News Agency, *Taiwan Affairs Office of the State Council: The Suspension of the Import of Custard Apples and Lotus Mist from Taiwan is Scientifically Reasonable and Completely Justified*]. Available at: www.gov.cn/xinwen/2021-09/22/content_5638743.htm (last visited Apr 5, 2023). Likely, news media often interpret China's recent restrictions on Australian exports as economic coercion; however, alternative perspectives have attempted to demystify the underlying legal and political dynamics. Some reports suggesting China's tariff increase on Australian cotton from 1 to 40 per cent was a retaliatory action have been misconstrued according to Weihuan Zhou and James Laurenceson, since the China-Australia Free Trade Agreement (ChAFTA) does not provide Australian cotton with any additional market access outside of China's WTO concessions. Under the WTO, China has agreed to a tariff-rate quota (TRQ) under which imports up to 894,000 tons are subject to a 1 per cent tariff whereas out-of-quota imports face a 40 per cent tariff. Weihuan Zhou and James Laurenceson, *Demystifying Australia-China Trade Tensions*, 56 J World Trade 51, 78–79 (2022).

[44] Abigail Ng, *China Has Banned Taiwan's Pineapples. Taiwan Says It's Not Fair Play*, CNBC (Mar 4, 2021). Available at: www.cnbc.com/2021/03/04/taiwan-chinas-ban-on-pineapples-not-in-line-with-global-trade-rules.html.

[45] *How China Uses Economic Coercion to Silence Critics and Achieve its Political Aims Globally: Hearing Before the Congressional-Executive Committee on China*, 117th Cong 6 (2021) (statement of Bonnie S Glaser, Asia Program Director, German Marshall Fund of the United States). Available at: www.govinfo.gov/app/details/CHRG-117jhrg46272/CHRG-117jhrg46272.

[46] Breakdown of the Gross domestic product (GDP) of Taiwan from 2013 to 2023, by economic sector (Feb 2024). Available at: www.statista.com/statistics/321366/taiwan-gdp-breakdown-by-sector/ (last visited May 8, 2024).

portion of Taiwan's exports to China are electrical machinery, particularly semiconductor products.[47] Such a trade concentration can work as a double-edged sword that is not necessarily in China's favour.[48] Although decades of economic integration has enabled China to lock Taiwan into a state of economic dependence, China finds itself heavily reliant on sophisticated intermediate products from the other side of the Strait – especially high-ended semiconductors, which it cannot self-manufacture.[49] Such co-dependence makes China vulnerable to the changing political economy; for example, the U.S. imposed export controls to impede the Chinese efforts to become self-sufficient in the production of advanced semiconductors.[50] These external factors could, in turn, affect the way in which Taiwan regulates its economic relations with Mainland China, as discussed below.

Figure 2.4 Trade Balance Between Mainland China and Taiwan from 2015 to 2021 (in billion U.S. dollars)

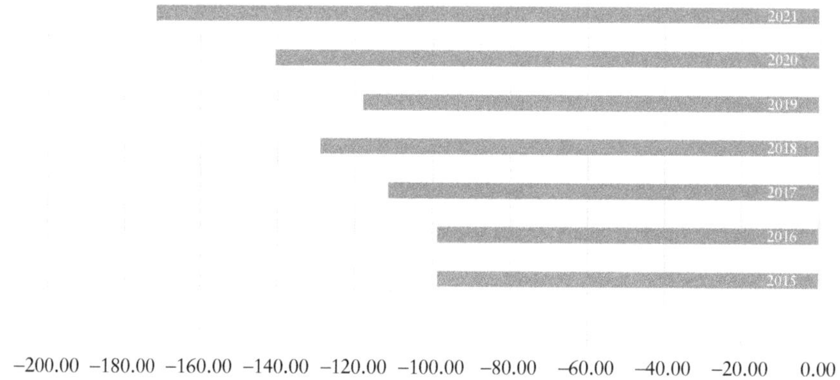

Source: Statista; MOFCOM, PRC.

[47] According to one account, China's imports of semiconductors totalled more than US$430 billion in 2021, 36% of which came from Taiwan. Taiwan Semiconductor Manufacturing Company (TSMC), the biggest foundry in the world, is a key supplier of cutting-edge semiconductors to China's consumer electronics sector. Bo-Jiun Jing, et al., *Taiwan Holds All the Chips in US-China Tech Showdown*, East Asia Forum (Dec 3, 2022). Available at: www.eastasiaforum.org/2022/12/03/taiwan-holds-all-the-chips-in-us-china-tech-showdown/#:~:text=China's%20trade%20flow%20data%20for,of%20which%20came%20from%20Taiwan.

[48] Roy Lee, *Taiwan's China Dependency is a Double-Edged Sword*, East Asia Forum (July 6, 2021). Available at: www.eastasiaforum.org/2021/07/06/taiwans-china-dependency-is-a-double-edged-sword/(arguing that the pressure to diversify supply chain will increase for companies located in China with major clients in the US).

[49] Bonnie S Glaser and Jeremy Mark, *Taiwan and China are Locked in Economic Co-Dependence: Both Sides Have Leverage but Have Been Reluctant to Use It*, Foreign Pol'y (Apr 14, 2021). Available at: https://foreignpolicy.com/2021/04/14/taiwan-china-econonomic-codependence/.

[50] *See* Bureau of Industry Security, Commerce Implements New Export Controls on Advanced Computing and Semiconductor Manufacturing Items to the People's Republic of China (PRC) (Oct 7, 2022). Available at: www.bis.doc.gov/index.php/documents/about-bis/newsroom/press-releases/3158-2022-10-07-bis-press-release-advanced-computing-and-semiconductor-manufacturing-controls-final/file.

III. COOPERATION'S FORM AND SUBSTANCE: HOW DO THEY INTERACT, AND WHY?

A decade of turmoil following the Cultural Revolution allowed Deng Xiaoping to introduce a pragmatic leadership program, prioritizing economic revival over ideological orthodoxy.[51] Alongside the "Open Door" policy, Deng's PRC advocated for "Three Links" (direct mail, trade, and transportation) with Taiwan.[52] The ROC, however, initially responded tepidly, adhering to the "Three-Nos Policy": no contact, no compromise, no negotiation. It was not until the 1980s, under the KMT leadership of Chiang Ching-Kuo and amidst Taiwan's democratisation, that trade, investment, and travel to China began to liberalise.[53] Since then, Cross-Strait economic relations have steadily grown,[54] with trade and investment accelerating after WTO accession in the early 2000s.[55] From being Taiwan's 26th-largest trade partner in the early 1990s, China now accounts for approximately 40 per cent of Taiwan's exports.[56] As this bilateral economic relationship has evolved, Taiwan has become China's eighth-largest export

[51] Guocang Huan, *China's Open-Door Policy, 1978-1984*, 39(2) J Int'l Affs 1, 1–2 (1986).

[52] Wen Qing, *"One Country, Two Systems": The Best Way to Peaceful Reunification*, 33 Beijing Rev (1990). Available at: www.bjreview.com.cn/nation/txt/2009-05/26/content_197568.htm.

[53] Richard N Watanabe, Foreign Exchange and Capital Movement Controls in Taiwan, 16 UCLA Pac Basin L J 1, 33–36 (1997); Charng Kao (高長), 兩岸經貿交流 30 週年之回顧與前瞻，《展望與指南》，第十五卷第十一期 [Charng Kao, *Retrospect and Prospect on the 30th Anniversary of Cross-Strait Economic Exchanges*, 15(11) Prospect & Exploration (2017)]; Jianmin Wang (王建民), 30年两岸交流与两岸关系发展回望(上), 《统一论坛》杂志 (30 nian liangan jiaoliu yu liangan guanxi fazhan huiwang (shang), tongyiluntan zazhi) 2017年12月26日)[Jianmin Wang. *Looking Back at 30 years of Cross-Strait Exchanges and the Development of Cross-Strait Relations* (Part 1) "Unity Forum" Magazine (Dec 26, 2017)].

[54] Initially, both sides engaged each other in a more direct way through Hong Kong. See, eg, Jianming Shan, *Cross-Strait Trade and Investment and the Role of Hong Kong*, 16 Wis Int'l L J 661 (1998).

[55] Total trade volume has grown from US$546 million in 1980 to $82.62 billion in 2002. Zhonghua minguo dalu weiyuanhui (中華民國大陸委員會), 兩岸經貿統計數據 (liangan jingmao tongji shuju), 2016年11月20日 [Mainland Affairs Council Republic of China (Taiwan), *Data on Cross-Strait Economic Relations*), Ministry of Commerce of the People's Rep. of China] (Nov 20, 2016). Available at: http://aetats.mofcom.gov.cn/article/f/200611/20061103792147.shtml. Note, however, that trade volume across Taiwan Strait provided by the ROC were not identical. Liangan jingji jiaoliu tongji subao jiushiyi nian shier yuefen, see Zhonghua minguo dalu weiyuanhui (中華民國大陸委員會), 兩岸經濟交流統計速報九十一年十二月份 (liangan jingji jiaoliu tongji subao jiushiyi nian shier yuefen)[Mainland Affairs Council Republic of China (Taiwan), *Brief of Cross-strait Economic Exchanges*], Mainland Affairs Council, Rep of China] (12 2002). Available at: https://ws.mac.gov.tw/001/Upload/OldFile/public/data/97116484171.gif.

[56] Ying-Ru Yin (殷英洳) and Tsung-Hsien Tsai (蔡宗顯), 111 年我國出進口貿易概況 (111 Nian woguo chu jinkou maoyi gaikuang)[Overview of the Nation's Import and Export Trade for 2022]. Available at: https://service.mof.gov.tw/public/Data/statistic/bulletin/112/111%E5%B9%B4%E6%88%91%E5%9C%8B%E5%87%BA%E9%80%B2%E5%8F%A3%E8%B2%BF%E6%98%93%E6%A6%82%E6%B3%81.pdf.

Jin chukou maoyi liang (進出口貿易量) [Export and Import Trade Volumes], Executive Yuan of the Rep. of China. Available at: www.ey.gov.tw/state/6A206590076F7EF/8b5032af-1a67-4c02-bd16-8791aa459cd2.

partner[57] and third-largest source of imports.[58] Taiwan has also become the Mainland's primary source of investment from the 1970s to 2023.[59] Despite these advancements, cross-Strait economic ties are increasingly strained. We delve into the dynamics of this engagement in the sections below.

A. The Chinese Approach to Cross-Strait Economic Ties: Internalising Everything

Joining the WTO was a pivotal moment for both sides of the Taiwan Strait. Joining allowed Taiwan to navigate the PRC's exclusionary practices and regularised Cross-Strait trade relations under multilateral trade norms. However, China's trade and investment policies towards Taiwan have always been anchored against its steadfast assertion of the "One China" principle, as articulated in the PRC Constitution.[60] The Preamble of the Constitution states that:

> Taiwan is part of the sacred territory of the People's Republic of China. It is the sacred duty of all the Chinese people, including our fellow Chinese in Taiwan, to achieve the great reunification of the motherland.[61]

As a result, this mandate becomes the keystone that guides the PRC's policy toward Taiwan in economic exchanges. While China and Taiwan (under the name "Separate Customs Territory of Taiwan, Penghu, Kinmen and Matsu", otherwise known as "Chinese Taipei") are both WTO Members, the PRC government has, from time to time, taken unilateral measures to portray the island as a breakaway province and avoid giving the impression that Taiwan is a separate sovereign nation. Trade and investment arrangements between the two sides reflect this tense relationship. The following section will examine China's multilateral and bilateral interactions with Taiwan to offer a better understanding of this.

[57] Distribution of Chinese Exports in 2022, by Trade Partner, Statista (Feb 2024). Available at: www.statista.com/statistics/270326/main-export-partners-for-china/ (last visited Apr 17, 2023).

[58] *China's Leading Import Partners in 2022, by import value*, Statista (Feb 2024). Available at: www.statista.com/statistics/257042/chinas-main-import-partners-by-import-value/ (last visited Apr 17, 2023).

[59] *Share of Taiwan's exports in 2023, by major trade partner*, STATISTA (Feb 2024). Available at: www.statista.com/statistics/1266748/main-export-partners-for-taiwan/ (last visited May 8, 2024).

[60] Zhonghua renmin gonghegou xianfa (中华人民共和国宪法) [Constitution] preamble (1982, as latest amended in 2018) (PRC).

[61] *Id.* preamble. Article 52 likewise provides that "Citizens of the People's Republic of China shall have the obligation to safeguard national unity and the solidarity of all the country's ethnic groups".

(i) Taiwan's "Special Treatment" under the Multilateral Framework

Trade in Goods

Anticipating its WTO accession, in December 2000, China passed the "Measures for the Administration of Trade with Taiwan Region".[62] These Measures were created to "develop the trade between Mainland China and the Taiwan Region, to maintain the regular trade order and facilitate the economic development of both sides of the Taiwan Strait".[63] Hence, while China's Foreign Trade Law, as amended in 2004, laid the foundation for trade with other countries, this Law does not apply to Taiwan – the island that the PRC government sees as a part of China itself. A good example is Article 6 of the Measures, which prohibits words and symbols inconsistent with the "One China" Principle from being used in contracts and goods involved in trade with Taiwan.[64]

For the PRC, its "One China" principle manifests itself in a matrix of unilateral measures that work against the spirit of the WTO. Not long after its WTO accession, the PRC launched its first anti-dumping investigation on cold-rolled steel products from Russia, South Korea, Ukraine, Kazakhstan, and Taiwan.[65] The PRC notified all but Taiwan of the investigations, treating the issue as an "internal matter" through the steel industry associations of both sides of the Taiwan Strait. As a matter of international law, China's failure to notify the Taiwan government could be challenged for violating the Anti-dumping Agreement – short for the Agreement on the Implementation of Article VI

[62] Dui Taiwan diqu maoyi guanli banfa (对台湾地区贸易管理办法) [Measures for the Administration of Trade with Taiwan Region] (promulgated by the Ministry of Foreign Trade and Economic Cooperation, the People's Rep of China, Dec 29, 2000, effective Dec 29, 2000). In fact, as early as 1993, the PRC adopted the "Procedures for the Administration of Small-Volume Exchange of Goods Between the Mainland and Taiwan". Duiwai maoyi jingji hezuo bu (对外贸易经济合作部) and Haiguan zongshu (海关总署), 对外贸易经济合作部、海关总署关于发布《对台湾地区小额贸易的管理办法》的通知 (Duiwai maoyi jingji hezuo bu, haiguan zong shu guanyu fabu "dui Taiwan diqu xiao e maoyi de guanli banfa" de tongzhi) [Notice by the Ministry of Foreign Trade and Economic Cooperation of Procedures for the Administration of Small-Volume Exchange of Goods Between the Mainland and Taiwan] (issued by Ministry of Foreign Trade & Economic Cooperation (incl former Ministry of Foreign Economy & Trade) (now renamed as the Ministry of Commerce, MOFCOM) and General Administration of Customs, Sep 25, 1993).

[63] Measures for the Administration of Trade with Taiwan Region, *supra* note 62, art 1.

[64] *Id.* art 6.

[65] Shangwubu chanye diaochaju (商务部产业损害调查局), 我国对原产于俄罗斯、韩国、乌克兰、哈萨克斯坦、台湾地区的冷轧板卷进行反倾销立案调查, 商务部产业调查局 (Woguo dui yuanchanyu eluosi, hanguo, wukelan, hasakesitan, taiwan diqu de lengyabanjuan jinxing fanqingxiao lian tiaocha), 2002年3月20日[*China's Anti-Dumping Investigation Against Cold-Rolled Coils Originating in Russia, South Korea, Ukraine, Kazakhstan and Taiwan, Industrial Investigation Bureau of the Ministry of Commerce*] (Mar 20, 2002, 3:59PM). Available at: http://dcj.mofcom.gov.cn/article/date/ckzcfg/200507/20050700199760.shtml. Notably, the PRC employed the term "Taiwan region" in its announcement to emphasise its perspective that Taiwan is a part of it.

of the GATT 1994.[66] For China, however, this was a clear and logical decision aligned with its "One China" Principle – Taiwan is not a separate sovereign State and so did not need to be addressed differently – as Taiwan is excluded from the scope of China's Foreign Trade Law.

In subsequent anti-dumping investigations and safeguard measures relating to polyvinyl and certain steel products from Taiwan, such practices were replicated, thus raising concerns under both the Anti-dumping Agreement and the Safeguard Agreement.[67] As part of its efforts to minimise controversy, the PRC made its first official contact with its Taiwanese counterparts within the framework of the WTO. It is apparent, however, that the use of the Chinese language rather than any of the official languages of the WTO indicates that the PRC is uncomfortable dealing with the "Separate Customs Territory of Taiwan, Penghu, Kinmen, and Matsu", which is referred to as "Chinese Taipei" within the multilateral trade system.[68]

The PRC government has, on the other hand, engaged Taiwan strategically by granting Taiwan more favourable treatment that seems inconsistent with its WTO commitments – in particular, some of these measures were implemented even before the bilateral trade agreement with Taiwan was signed in 2010, as indicated below.[69] A prime example is its "fruit diplomacy". By giving tariff-free status to 15 Taiwanese fruit items, China attempted to temper "Taiwan's negative reaction" to its passage of the Anti-Separation Law with fruit farmers from Southern Taiwan, major supporters of Taiwan's independence.[70] Policies of this kind have a dual function: they can serve as a way for Beijing to "win over the hearts of Taiwan compatriots",[71] but they can also be used as punitive measures to exert pressure on Taiwan, as noted in Part II above. Depending on the specific policy in question and its circumstances, either function may be more prominent.

[66] Agreement on Implementation of Article VI of the General Agreement on Tariffs and Trade 1994, Apr 15, 1994, 33 ILM 15, art 6 (requiring notification to interested parties, including the government of the exporting Member). Some Chinese scholars also admitted that the political issues complicated the way Beijing addressed this matter. Kong, *supra* note 27, at 109–10 ("Indeed Beijing, against its WTO obligation, did not inform the Taiwanese government, but rather informed only the Taiwanese companies or industry concerned in such investigations".).

[67] Agreement on Safeguards, April 15, 1994, Marrakesh Agreement Establishing the World Trade Organization, Annex 1A, art 12. Available at: https://eur-lex.europa.eu/EN/legal-content/summary/wto-agreement.html. For a critique of China's failure to notifications, see Hsieh, Facing China, *supra* note 25, at 1219–20.

[68] MAN-JUNG CHAN et al. (詹滿容等), WTO架構下兩岸互動之研究68, 2003 (WTO Jiagou xia liangan hudong zhi yanjiu) [Studies on the Cross-Strait Interaction under the WTO Framework] 68, (2003).

[69] Xinhua she (新华社)，15种台湾水果8月1日起正式实施零关税措施(15 zhong Taiwan shuiguo 8 yue 1 ri qi zhengshi shishi lingguanshui cuoshi) 2005年8月2日[Xinhua News Agency, *15 Types of Taiwan Fruits Formally Implement Zero-Tariff Measures from August 1st*] 2 August 2005. Available at: www.gov.cn/jrzg/2005-08/02/content_19516.htm.

[70] Rachel Brown, *The Fruits of Diplomacy*, Foreign Policy (Aug 15, 2011). Available at: https://foreignpolicy.com/2011/08/15/the-fruits-of-diplomacy/.

[71] Pasha Hsieh, *The China-Taiwan ECFA, Geopolitical Dimensions and WTO Law*, 14 J Int'l Econ L 121, 127 (2011) [hereinafter Hsieh, *China-Taiwan ECFA*].

Trade in Services

The trade in services is also characterised by an uneasy relationship. Consider the legal services sector. Under the General Agreement on Trade in Services (GATS), China has agreed to allow foreign law firms to provide certain legal services in the form of representative offices in selected cities.[72] To accomplish this, the State Council, as per the "Lawyers Law of the People's Republic of China", passed the "Administrative Regulations for Foreign Law Firms' Representative Organisations in China", effective January 1, 2002.[73] However, the Administrative Regulations, along with other rules for implementation, do not apply to Taiwanese law firms – despite Taiwan's WTO Membership. Article 34 of this Regulations specifically reads as follows:

> The administrative measures for the establishment of a Representative Organisation in Mainland China by a law firm in China's separate Customs territory shall be separately formulated by the judicial administrative department of the State Council according to the principles of these Regulations.[74]

Under the PRC's "One China" principle, therefore, lawyers qualified to practice in Taiwan are by no means considered "foreign" lawyers. Taiwanese lawyers who plan to establish their representative offices in China are subject to the approval of relevant authorities at the provincial level, as per the "Notice of the Ministry of Justice on Matters concerning Delegating to Lower Levels Approval of the License for the Establishment of Representative Offices of the Law Firms of Hong Kong, Macao, and Taiwan in the Mainland of China and the Practicing License of Representatives of Such Representative Offices".[75]

Taiwanese lawyers do not fall within the category of "foreign lawyers;" they are subject to separate rules from those governing Hong Kong and Macau lawyers. The "Administrative Measures for the Representative Offices of the Law Firms of Hong Kong Special Administrative Region and Macao Special

[72] China has opened legal services under Mode 3 with conditions. Among others, foreign law firms can offer legal services only in the form of "representative offices" in designated cities, including Beijing, Shanghai, Guangzhou, Shenzhen, Haikou, Dalian, Qingdao, Ningbo, Yantai, Tianjin, Suzhou, Xiamen, Zhuhai, Hanghou, Fuzhou, Wuhan, Chengdu, Shenyang and Kunming. Moreover, the scope of business of these representative offices is also limited to specific activities such as "provid[ing] clients with consultancy on the legislation of the country/region where the lawyers of the law firm are permitted to engage in lawyer's professional work, and on international conventions and practices". China-Schedule of Specific Commitments for Trade in Services, Feb 14, 2002, GATS/SC/135.

[73] Waiguo lushi shiwu suo zhu hua daibiao jigou guanli tiaoli (外国律师事务所驻华代表机构管理条例) [Administrative Regulations for Foreign Law Firms' Representative Organisations in China] (promulgated by State Council, Dec. 22, 2001, effective Jan 1, 2002).

[74] *Id.* art 34.

[75] Sifa bu guanyu xiafang gangao tai lushi shiwu suo zhu neidi huo dalu daibiao jigou he paizhu daibiao zhiye xuke shenpi youguan shixiang de tongzhi (司法部关于下放港澳台律师事务所驻内地或大陆代表机构和派驻代表执业许可审批有关事项的通知) [Notice of the Ministry of Justice on Matters concerning Delegating to Lower Levels Approval of the License for the Establishment of Representative Offices of the Law Firms of Hong Kong, Macao, and Taiwan in the Mainland of China and the Practicing License of Representatives of Such Representative Offices].

Administrative Region Stationed in the Mainland", as amended in 2015, apply to Hong Kong and Macau lawyers, and contain no specific limitations on office locations.[76] In contrast, Taiwanese lawyers were initially restricted to establishing their representative offices only in Fuzhou and Xiamen in Fujian Province. This restriction was not lifted until 2017, after which they were allowed to operate in the entire Fujian Province and other regions including Shanghai, Jiangsu Province, Zhejiang Province, and Guangdong Province.[77] The geographical restrictions imposed on Taiwanese lawyers could potentially be challenged by Taiwan or other WTO members for their inconsistency with China's GATS commitments.[78] However, to date, no such case has been brought.

China introduced a dedicated regime for what it refers to as "Taiwan residents" – those "Chinese citizens residing in Taiwan" as defined under the Measures for the Administration of Chinese Citizens Travelling to or from Taiwan Region – to sit the bar exam to be qualified as a PRC lawyer.[79] In 2008,

[76] Xianggang, Aomen tebie xingzhengqu lushi shiwu suo zhu neidi daibia jigou guanli banfa (香港、澳门特别行政区律师事务所驻内地代表机构管理办法) [Administrative Measures for the Representative Offices of the Law Firms of Hong Kong Special Administrative Region and Macao Special Administrative Region Stationed in the Mainland] (promulgated on Mar 13, 2002, latest amended on Apr 27, 2015).

[77] Sifabu (司法部), 司法部关于放宽扩大台湾地区律师事务所在大陆设立代表处地域范围等三项开放措施的通知 (Sifa bu guanyu fangkuan kuoda Taiwan diqu lushi shiwu suo zai dalu sheli daibiao chu diyu fanwei deng san iang kaifang cuoshi de tongzhi), 2017年7月31日[Notice of the Ministry of Justice on Three Opening-up Measures including Expanding the Territorial Scope of Representative Offices Formed in the Mainland by Law Firms in Taiwan] (promulgated by the Ministry of Justice, July 31, 2017). Apart from the geographical differences, there are other distinctions as well. For example, Taiwanese law firms are mandated to establish a representative office in specific areas by teaming up with local Chinese law firms through a joint venture. On the other hand, Hong Kong law firms have the option, but not the obligation, to form a joint venture with a local counterpart unless they intend to provide legal services related to Chinese laws.

[78] For example, the fact that Taiwanese lawyers are not allowed to establish their representative offices in cities like Beijing, Tianjin, and Wuhan, which are specified under China's GATS commitments, may give rise to legal challenges. On the other hand, other WTO members could express concerns about the cities or provinces that are open to Taiwanese lawyers only.

[79] Zhongguo gongmin wanglai Taiwan diqu guanli banfa (中国公民往来台湾地区管理办法) [Measures for the Administration of Chinese Citizens Travelling to or from Taiwan Region (2015 Amendment). From as far back as the 1990s, the term "Taiwan resident" has been employed by the PRC to refer to individuals living in the ROC (Taiwan). This can be evidenced by a 1992 normative document from the Ministry of Civil Affairs regarding family issues, which explicitly states: "Taiwan is a province of China. When we refer to Taiwanese residents, we are referring to individuals who currently reside in the Taiwan region, including Taiwan Island, the Penghu Islands, Kinmen, and Matsu Islands". (「台湾是中国的一个省，我们所称台湾居民是指目前仍居住在台湾地区（包括台湾岛、澎湖列岛、金门、马祖岛）的居民). *See* Minzheng bu hunyin si tan gangao tongbao, Taiwan jumin ji huaqiao shouyang zinu de tiaojian he dengji chengxu(民政部婚姻司谈港澳同胞、台湾居民及华侨收养子女的条件和登记程序) [The Marriage Department of the Ministry of Civil Affairs discusses the conditions and registration procedures for the adoption of children by Hong Kong and Macau compatriots, Taiwanese residents, and overseas Chinese] (Apr 1, 1992). In various normative documents spanning different domains, Taiwanese individuals are regarded and treated as "Chinese citizens", akin to the residents of Hong Kong and Macau. *See e.g.*, Xianggang aomen Taiwan jumin zai neidi (dalu) canjia shehui baoxian zhanxing banfa (香港澳门台湾居民在内地（大陆）参加社会保险暂行办法) [Interim Measures for Participation in Social Insurance by Hong Kong, Macao and Taiwan Residents in the Mainland], art. 2 (states that "Hong Kong, Macao and Taiwan residents engaged in individual industrial and commercial

the Ministry of Justice adopted the "Measures for the Administration of Legal Practice in the Mainland by Taiwan Residents who have Obtained the National Legal Professional Qualification", which, along with "Some Provisions on Taiwan Residents' Taking the National Judicial Examination", detailed the process governing Taiwan residents' legal practice in Mainland China.[80] In 2017, citing the need for "promoting cross-strait exchanges … deepening cross-strait economic and social integration and development, and safeguarding the legitimate rights and interests of compatriots on both sides of the Taiwan Strait", the Ministry of Justice issued the "Number 176 Notice", allowing Taiwan residents with the PRC qualification to "engage in Mainland non-litigation legal matters in the capacity" and appear before the courts in relation to Taiwan-related civil cases.[81]

Despite some additional limitations, Taiwan residents who have qualified as PRC lawyers are generally treated similarly to Chinese citizens. The "One China" principle is not only reflected in this; it also serves a deeper purpose. The PRC government sees the bar exam as an opportunity for political indoctrination – rather than a validation of expertise.[82] Through the use of nuanced and politically charged test questions, test-takers will be compelled to consider what the Party-State expects of them, which reinforces social and political control.[83] Treating Taiwanese residents separately from foreign lawyers demonstrates a very subtle method by which the PRC seeks to impact

business operation in the mainland may, according to the relevant provisions of the registration places, participate in basic pension insurance and basic medical insurance for employees; and Hong Kong, Macao and Taiwan residents flexibly employed in the mainland and having obtained the residence permits for Hong Kong, Macao and Taiwan residents may, according to the relevant provisions of the residence places, participate in basic pension insurance and basic medical insurance for employees".).

[80] Qude guojia falu zhiye zige de taiwan jumin zai dalu cengshi lushi zhiye guanli banfa (取得国家法律职业资格的台湾居民在大陆从事律师职业管理办法) [Measures for the Administration of Legal Practice in the Mainland by Taiwan Residents who have Obtained the National Legal Professional Qualification] (promulgated by the Ministry of Justice, Dec 21, 2008; effective Jan 1, 2009, as amended in 2017). Taiwan jumin canjia guoja sifa kaoshi ruogan guiding (台湾居民参加国家司法考试若干规定) [Some Provisions on Taiwan Residents' Taking the National Judicial Examination] (promulgated by Ministry of Justice of the People's Rep of China, June 4, 2008; effective June 4, 2008).

[81] Sifa bu guanyu xiugai "qude guojia falu zhiye zige de taiwan jumin zai dalu congshi lushi zhiye guanli banfa" de jueding (司法部关于修改《取得国家法律职业资格的台湾居民在大陆从事律师职业管理办法》的决定) [Decision of the Ministry of Justice on Revising the "Administrative Measures for Residents of Taiwan Region Who Have Obtained the National Legal Professional Qualifications to Practice as Lawyers in the Mainland] (promulgated by Ministry of Justice of the People's Rep of China, Sep 21, 2017, effective Nov 1, 2017).

[82] For instance, in the 2023 bar exam, President Xi Jinping's thoughts on the rule of law are part of the subjects. *See* 2023 Nian guojia tongyi falu zhiye zige kaoshi gonggao (2023年国家统一法律职业资格考试公告) [Announcement of the 2023 National Unified Legal Professional Qualification Examination]. Available at: www.moj.gov.cn/pub/sfbgw/zwxxgk/fdzdgknr/fdzdgknrtzwj/202306/t20230609_480443.html (last visited June 22, 2023).

[83] Rachel E Stern, *Political Reliability and the Chinese Bar Exam*, 43 J L & Soc'y 506, 515–16 (2016); Rachel E Stern and Lawrence J Liu, *The Good Lawyer: State-Led Professional Socialization in Contemporary China*, 45 L & Social Inq 226 (2020).

the Taiwanese in a broad sense, not just by influencing their economic and professional activities but also by interfering with their thoughts and actions on a wider scale.

Intellectual Property Rights (IPRs)

China's stance on the IPRs of the Taiwanese people provides yet another salient example. For years preceding the conclusion of the Cross-Strait Agreement on Intellectual Property Right Protection and Cooperation in 2010,[84] the PRC denied Taiwanese applicants' the right of priority in terms of patents vested under Article 2 of the Agreement on the Trade-Related Aspects of Intellectual Property Rights (TRIPs Agreement). This provision requires all WTO Members to comply with Article 4 of the Paris Convention for the Protection of Industrial Property (Paris Convention) by having claimants file a subsequent patent application in another country for the same invention and be treated as if they had been filed on the same day as the first application.[85]

For China, there are good reasons for this measure. First, the Paris Convention is a state-to-state agreement to which Taiwan is not a party.[86] Refusing to accord the right of priority could avoid the impression that it recognises Taiwan's statehood. Second, an IPR is territorial and is granted based on domestic laws. In Beijing's view, giving effect to the right of priority can hardly be a sovereignty-neutral matter. Further, the right of priority provisions under the Chinese Patent Law contains explicit references to "foreign applicant" and "foreign country", which, in and of themselves, should not apply to Taiwan, either in a legal or a political sense. Driven by political considerations since the 1980s, the PRC has had a separate regime governing patent filing for Taiwanese residents – the "Specific Requirements on the Patent Applications Filed by Taiwan Compatriots" – which operates in parallel with its Patent Law as generally applicable to foreigners. It grants Taiwanese residents "equal rights as the people in Mainland while filing an application to the China Patent Office for an invention patent and obtaining the patent protection".[87] As for the right of priority, said Requirements allowed Taiwanese residents to rely on their first filing with China's Patent Office to claim the right of priority in other Paris Convention signatories, and vice versa.[88] Despite several subsequent amendments, the fundamental tone remains

[84] [Haixia Liang'an Zhihui Caichanquan Baohu Hezuo Xieyi] [Cross-Strait Agreement on Intellectual Property Right Protection and Cooperation], China-Taiwan, June 29, 2010. Available at: https://law.moj.gov.tw/LawClass/LawAll.aspx?PCODE=Q0070023.

[85] Agreement on Trade-Related Aspects of Intellectual Property Rights, Art 2, Apr 15, 1994, 1869 UNTS 299, 33 ILM 1197 [hereinafter TRIPs Agreement].

[86] Paris Convention for the Protection of Industrial Property as last revised at the Stockholm Revision Conference, July 14, 1967, 21 UST 1583, 828 UNTS 305 [hereinafter Paris Convention].

[87] Taiwan tongbao lai dalu shenqing zhuanli de juti guidìng (台湾同胞来大陆申请专利的具体规定) [Specific Requirements on the Patent Applications Filed by Taiwan Compatriots] (promulgated by Chinese Patent Office, Jan 8, 1988; effective Jan 8, 1988) [hereinafter 1988 Specific Requirements].

[88] *Id.* art 3.

unchanged: the right of priority provisions under the Patent Law applies to all but Taiwan, regardless of its inconsistency with the WTO.[89]

Investment

Except for the WTO Agreement on Trade-Related Investment Measures (TRIMs Agreement), for political reasons, Taiwan is not a party to any of the major international investment treaties. These exclusions encompass the Convention on the Settlement of Investment Disputes between States and Nationals of Other States (ICSID Convention) and the Energy Charter Treaty.[90] Thus, the Taiwanese government has little space to engage its Chinese counterpart at this level in terms of investment protection. Taiwan's absence from the international investment community perfectly matches the PRC's "One China" principle, which internalises the Cross-Strait investment issues.

Since the 1980s,[91] China has introduced several rules for Taiwan, notably, "Special Preferential Policies of the State Council for Taiwan Compatriots' Investment in Economic Special Zones",[92] the "Provisions of the State Council of the People's Republic of China for Encouraging Taiwan Compatriots to Invest in the Mainland",[93] "Law of the People's Republic of China on the Protection of Investments of Taiwan Compatriots",[94] and its implementations

[89] *See e.g.*, Guanyu shouli tai bao zhuanlì shenqing de guiding (关于受理台胞专利申请的规定) [Provisions on the Acceptance of Patent Applications Filed by Taiwan Compatriots], art 1 [hereinafter 1993 Patent Provisions on Taiwan Compatriots]. For a recount, see generally Ping-Hsun Chen, *A Fake Right of Priority under the Cross-Strait Agreement on Intellectual Property Right Protection and Cooperation*, 20 Marq Intell Prop L Rev 213, 232-34 (2016) (arguing that "2010 Patent Rule indicate that a right of priority claimed by a Taiwanese applicant is different from a right of priority claimed by a normal applicant. In other words, China shows that it has never granted to a Taiwan applicant a right of priority mandated by the Paris Convention".).

[90] Han-Wei Liu, *A Missing Part in International Investment Law: The Effectiveness of Investment Protection of Taiwan's Bits vis-à-vis ASEAN States*, 16 UC Davis J Int'l L & Pol'y 131, 134 (2009).

[91] These instruments were driven by both political and economic motivations. Mao's autarkic economic policies caused the nation to miss out on East Asia's explosive growth during the 1960s and 1970s. Thus, China "desperately lacked the capital, technology, and managerial expertise" it could have obtained from Taiwan to put its economy back on track. Later, another wave of strong demand among investors from Taiwan was driven by a series of economic and diplomatic sanctions imposed by the US and its allies following the Tiananmen Square tragedy in 1989. Murray Scot Tanner, Chinese Economic Coercion Against Taiwan: A Tricky Weapon to Use 37 (2007); Harry Harding, *The Impact of Tiananmen on China's Foreign Policy*, 1(3) NBR Analysis (1990) (noting that direct foreign investment dropped by 22 per cent in the first half of 1990 and there was a 20 per cent decline in tourism revenue in 1989).

[92] Guowuyuan guanyu Taiwan tongbao dao jingji tequ touzi de tebie youhui banfa (国务院关于台湾同胞到经济特区投资的特别优惠办法) [Special Preferential Policies of the State Council for Taiwanese Compatriots' Investment in Economic Special Zones] (promulgated by the State Council, Apr 5, 1983).

[93] Guowuyuanguanyugulitaiwantongbaotouzideguiding(国务院关于鼓励台湾同胞投资的规定) [Provisions of the State Council of the People's Republic of China for Encouraging Taiwan Compatriots to Invest in the Mainland] (promulgated by the State Council of the People's Rep of China, July 3, 1988).

[94] Zhonghua renmin gongheguo Taiwan tongbao touzi baohu fa (中华人民共和国台湾同胞投资保护法) [Law of the People's Republic of China on the Protection of Investments of Taiwan

rules, namely, "Detailed Rules for the Implementation of the Law of the People's Republic of China on the Protection of Investments of Taiwan Compatriots" (Implementation Rules for Taiwan Compatriots' Investment Protection Law).[95] Furthermore, as Taiwanese investors may opt to invest in China through intermediaries in a third country for tax or other reasons – including Taiwan government restrictions on Chinese mainland investments, as noted in Part III. 2 B (2) – in 2013 China introduced "Interim Measures for Recognising Taiwan Investor Trans-Investment Through a Third Place" to provide further protection to these investors.[96]

While Taiwanese investors are, per the Implementation Rules for Taiwan Compatriots' Investment Protection Law,[97] also subject to "negative list" and other restrictions as applied to foreigner investors under the "Foreign Investment Law of the People's Republic of China" (PRC FIL)[98] and the "Regulation for the Implementation of the Foreign Investment Law",[99] China does not place Taiwan

Compatriots] (promulgated by the National People's Congress, Mar 5, 1994; effective Mar 5, 1994; latest amended Dec 28, 2019, effective Jan 1, 2020).

[95] Zhonghua renmin gongheguo Taiwān tongbao touzi baohu fa shishi xize (中华人民共和国台湾同胞投资保护法实施细则) [Detailed Rules for the Implementation of the Law of the People's Republic of China on the Protection of Investments of Taiwan Compatriots] (promulgated by the State Council of the People's Rep of China, Dec 7, 1999, as latest amended Nov 29, 2020, effective Nov 29, 2020) [hereinafter Implementation Rules for Taiwan Compatriots' Investment Protection Law].

[96] Taiwan touzi zhe jing di san di zhuan touzi rending zhanxing banfa (台湾投资者经第三地转投资认定暂行办) [Interim Measures for Recognition of the Trans-investment of Taiwan Investors through a Third Place] (promulgated by the Ministry of Commerce and Taiwan Affairs Office of the State Council, Feb 20, 2013, as amended Dec 31, 2019, effective Jan 1, 2020). The purpose of these measures is to set up standards and requirements for acknowledging investments made through a third country, and to guarantee that Taiwanese investors receive equal protections to those investing directly in China. It is important to note that participation in these measures is voluntary, and it is up to Taiwanese investors to decide if they wish to be recognised as such when investing in China.

[97] Implementation Rules for Taiwan Compatriots' Investment Protection Law, *supra* note 95, art 5 (stating that "Investments of Taiwan compatriots shall be governed by the Law of the People's Republic of China on the Protection of Investments of Taiwan Compatriots and these Implementing Rules; in case of whatever is not stipulated in the Law of the People's Republic of China on the Protection of Investments of Taiwan Compatriots and these Implementing Rules, reference shall be made to relevant foreign-related economic laws and administrative regulations of the State".).

[98] Zhonghua renmin gongheguo waishang touzi fa (中华人民共和国外商投资法) [Foreign Investment Law of the People's Republic of China] (promulgated by the People's Congress of the People's Rep of China, Mar 15, 2019, effective Jan 1, 2020) [hereinafter PRC FIL].

[99] Zhonghua renmin gongheguo waishang touzi fa shishi tiaoli (中华人民共和国外商投资法实施条例) [The Regulation for Implementing the Foreign Investment Law of the People's Republic of China] (adopted by the State Council, Dec 12, 2019, effective Jan 1, 2020) [FIL Implementation Regulation]. The new regime adopts pre-establishment national treatment – the treatment accorded to foreign investors and their investments at the initial stage of their investment that is no less favourable than that accorded to Chinese domestic investors and their investments. Unless certain conditions are met, foreign investors are not permitted to invest in fields where a "negative list" prohibits foreign investment. PRC FIL, *supra* note 98, art 4 and art 28. China's National Development and Reform Commission (NDRC) and Ministry of Commerce (MOFCOM) therefore released the "2021 Negative List" on December 27, 2021. The 2021 Negative List reduces the number of prohibited and restricted industries from 33 to 31. New sectors open to foreign investors are automobile manufacturing and satellite television broadcast ground receiving facilities. Overall, a less

on a par with other foreigners. A few examples should suffice to illustrate this. While delineating the FIL, the Spokesperson for the National People's Congress, Zhang Yesui, has openly remarked that:

> Hong Kong Special Administrative Region, Macau Special Administrative Region, and Taiwan are "all part of China". At the same time, Hong Kong, Macau, and Taiwan belong to separate customs territories, and investments from Hong Kong, Macau, and Taiwan are "neither the same as foreign investment, nor entirely the same as domestic investment", and have "a certain special characteristic".[100]

Moreover, under the Implementation Rules for Taiwan Compatriots' Investment Protection Law, Taiwan compatriots' investment "shall enjoy preferential treatment according to the provisions of relevant laws, administrative regulations of the State and these Implementing Rules",[101] while FIL requires foreign investors to "abide by the laws and regulations of China".[102] The nuanced difference reflected in the lack of reference to "China" in the said Implementation Rules suggests that Taiwan is viewed as part of the nation.

There are other special arrangements to help Taiwanese investors settle down in China. This can be exemplified by reference to Article 15 of the Implementation Rules which states that:

> Children of Taiwan compatriot investors themselves and children of Taiwan compatriot employees in enterprises with investment by Taiwan compatriots may enter primary schools, middle schools or higher-learning institutions on the Mainland to receive education in accordance with the relevant provisions of the State.[103]

Similarly, Article 17 of the Implementation Rules stipulates that Taiwanese investors are entitled to the same treatment as Mainland enterprises when purchasing equipment, raw materials, and other materials, as well as when accessing services like water, electricity, transportation, labour, advertising, and communication. Furthermore, they should be treated equally with Mainland Chinese citizens in areas such as transportation, communication, tourism, and accommodation.[104] The aim of these special arrangements is to foster greater

burdensome mechanism was introduced to further liberalise the market for foreign investors. For the evolution of the foreign investment law regime in China, *see e.g.*, Yawen Zheng, *China's New Foreign Investment Law and Its Contribution Towards the Country's Development Goal*, 22 J World Inv & Trade 388 (2021).

[100] ZHANG Yesui (张业遂),进一步为港澳台投资提供更加开放、便利的营商和发展环境(Jinyibu wei gangao tai touzi tigong gengjia kaifang, bianli de ying shang he fazhan huanjing) 2019年3月4日 [ZHANG Yesui, *Further provide a more open and convenient business and development environment for investment in Hong Kong, Macao and Taiwan], Xinhua Net* (Mar 4, 2019) (the original Chinese text reads: 「香港特别行政区、澳门特别行政区和台湾地区『都是中国的一部分』」。同时，港澳台属于单独关税区，来自港澳台的投资「既不同于外资，也不完全等同于内资」，具有「一定的特殊性」. Available at: www.xinhuanet.com/politics/2019lh/2019-03/04/c_1210072714.htm.

[101] PRC FIL, *supra* note 98, art 6.

[102] Implementation Rules for Taiwan Compatriots' Investment Protection Law, *supra* note 95, art 4.

[103] *Id.* art 15.

[104] *Id.* art 17.

economic and social cooperation between Taiwan and the Chinese Mainland. These policies go beyond mere economic activities and are part of the PRC's efforts to strengthen ties between the two regions in various spheres of activity. To this end, the PRC also – through the Taiwan Affairs Office of the State Council, rather than the Ministry of Foreign Affairs – rolled out policies offering preferential treatments – notably, "31 Measures" to further economic and cultural exchanges via investment. However, these measures were not institutionalised by way of legislation.[105]

Overall, despite certain pitfalls in these laws and regulations[106] and, of course, the underlying political implications, the PRC nevertheless made itself one of the most popular destinations for Taiwanese investors through unilateral measures. Some of these laws and regulations were introduced or amended, as a result of the conclusion of the Economic Cooperation Framework Agreement.

(ii) China's Engagement with Taiwan Through the Bilateral Framework

Besides treating Taiwan differently from other WTO Members unilaterally, China engages its Taiwanese counterpart via bilateral arrangements. Thus, on June 29, 2010, both sides of the Strait signed a landmark trade pact, the Cross-Straits Economic Cooperation Framework Agreement (ECFA),[107] which in its preamble identifies the agreement as "in line with the basic principles" of the WTO.[108] Nonetheless, this trade deal is often understood in Chinese discourse as an internal matter – another arrangement akin to the Closer Economic Partnership Arrangement (CEPA) concluded between Mainland China and Hong Kong and Macau, respectively, under the "One China, two systems" model.[109]

[105] Guowuyuan Taiwan shiwu bangongshi, guojia fazhan he gaige weiyuanhui guanyu yinfa "guanyu cujin liangan jingji wenhua jiaoliu hezuo de ruogan cuoshi" de tongzhi (国务院台湾事务办公室、国家发展和改革委员会关于印发《关于促进两岸经济文化交流合作的若干措施》的通知) 2018年2月28日[Notice by the Taiwan Affairs Office of the State Council and the National Development and Reform Commission of Issuing the Several Measures for Promoting the Cross-Strait Economic and Cultural Exchanges and Cooperation] (Issued by Taiwan Affairs Office of the State Council National Development & Reform Commission (incl former State Development Planning Commission), Feb 28, 2018, effective Feb 28, 2018). Under 31 Measures, for instance, Taiwanese enterprises may participate in the construction of infrastructure (*e.g.*, energy, transportation, water conservancy, and public utilities) and Taiwanese financial institutions may cooperate with China UnionPay and non-bank payment institutions in China per relevant laws to provide convenient micropayment services for Taiwan compatriots. Similar initiatives can be found at local levels too. *See e.g.*, Mingya Qian (钱明雅), Guangzhou 60 tiao huiji tai bao cuoshi (广州60条惠及台胞措施) [Guangzhou releases 60 measures benefiting Taiwan compatriots; Taiwanese enterprises recognised as "high-tech enterprises" can receive millions in subsidies], 南方日報 [Nanfang Daily] (Feb 8, 2023). Available at: https://news.southcn.com/node_54a44f01a2/cb0c90e606.shtml.

[106] Jie Huang, *Negotiating the First Bilateral Investment Agreement Between Mainland China and Taiwan: Difficulties and Solutions*, 42 Hong Kong L J 971, 974–75 (2012).

[107] Cross-Straits Economic Cooperation Framework Agreement, June 29, 2010. Available at: www.ecfa.org.tw/EcfaAttachment/ECFADoc/ECFA.pdf [hereinafter ECFA].

[108] *Id.* preamble.

[109] *See e.g.*, Tsai-Lung Hong and Chih-Hai Yang, *The Economic Cooperation Framework Agreement between China and Taiwan: Understanding Its Economics and Politics*, 10(3) Asian Econ

For Beijing, the CEPAs seem to offer a promising model to engage Taiwan economically, thus showing the "supremacy of the [PRC] central government over its separate customs territories".[110] Recognising its political implications, the Taiwanese government has acted carefully during negotiations, as discussed below.

At this juncture, it is useful to outline the key features of the ECFA. First, China and Taiwan compromised by not calling this pact a "free trade agreement", which could have suggested inter-state relations under international law.[111] Second, the ECFA is not a fully-fledged free trade agreement. Built upon the experience of the ASEAN-China Framework Agreement, the ECFA is an "interim agreement" necessary for the creation of a free trade area under Article XXIV:5 of the GATT.[112] Thus, the ECFA is neither like other FTAs nor CEPAs, as it does not abolish tariffs for "substantially all the trade".[113] As a framework agreement, it contains five chapters, with sixteen articles addressing trade in goods, trade in services, investment, economic cooperation, and other arrangements, including dispute resolutions.[114]

Despite its tentative nature, in Chapter 4, the ECFA laid down the "Early Harvest Program" (EHP), which was set to axe tariffs and restrictions in select Cross-Strait goods and service sectors. EHP is supplemented by Annexes I–V. Annexes I and IV identify the product and service sectors that fall within the EHP, while Annexes II, III, and V provide more detailed rules addressing issues such as the rules of origin, safeguard measures for trade in goods, and definitions and other measures applicable to trade in services. The PRC has acted accordingly by adopting implementation measures such as the "Measures of the General Administration of Customs of the People's Republic of China for the Administration of the Place of Origin for Imported and Exported Goods

Papers (2011) (noting that "China has said that it will make 'proper and reasonable' arrangements for Taiwan to strengthen its international position under the 'One China' principle after the ECFA is in place") *See also* Hui-Ping Chen (陈辉萍)，ECFA 框架下海峡两岸投资协议的法律思考，時代法学，第10卷第3期，2012年6月，第43-44頁[Hui-Ping Chen, *Some Legal Reflections on the Investment Agreement Between Mainland China and Taiwan under the ECFA Framework*, 10 (3) Present-day L Sci 43 (2012)] (arguing that ECFA is a special arrangement between two administrative areas under the "One-China" principle.); XIAO Ping (肖平) and ZENG Liling (曾丽凌)，论《海峡两岸经济合作框架协议》之法律性质与效果，《海峡法学》，2011年3月，第32頁[XIAO Ping and ZENG Liling, *On the Legal Nature and Effects of the Economic Cooperation Framework Agreement*, 1 Cross-Strait Legal Science 30, 32 (2011).

[110] Hsieh, *China-Taiwan ECFA*, *supra* note 71 at 139.

[111] *Id.*

[112] *Id.* at 140.

[113] Mainland and Hong Kong Closer Economic Partnership Arrangement, China-H.K., June 29, 2003, art. 19.3.3. Available at: www.tid.gov.hk/english/cepa/files/main_e.pdf [hereinafter PRC-HK CEPA]. CEPAs were already full PTAs as they were signed, though they also allowed for further liberalisation. For a comparison between CEPAs and ECFA, *see generally*, Yun-Wing Sung, *A Comparison Between the CEPA and the ECFA*, *in* Economic Integration Across the Taiwan Strait: Global Perspectives 30 (Peter C.Y. Chow ed., 2013).

[114] These five chapters are Chapter 1 (General Principles), Chapter 2 (Trade and Investment), Chapter 3 (Economic Cooperation), Chapter 4 (Early Harvest), and Chapter 5 (Other Provisions).

under the Cross-Strait Economic Cooperation Framework Agreement"[115] and the "Notice of the General Administration of Customs on Relevant Issues Concerning the Implementation of the Early Harvest Program for Trade in Goods under the Cross-Straits Economic Cooperation Framework Agreement".[116] It was not until January 1, 2013 that EHP products' tariffs were eliminated.[117]

Various follow-up arrangements under the ECFA[118] aimed for even more comprehensive economic ties between the two sides of the Strait. Two of these were particularly noteworthy. The "Cross-Strait Bilateral Investment Protection and Promotion Agreement" (CSBIPPA) was signed on August 9, 2012, and took effect in February 2013.[119] Political considerations, however, have made the CSBIPPA different from the ususal bilateral investment treaties (BITs). For instance, it avoids using terms like "national", but rather, attempts to depoliticalise by using more neutral references. The term "investor", for instance, is defined as "a natural person or an enterprise of a Party that makes an investment in the other party". "Natural person" and "enterprise of a Party" refer to "*a natural person holding the identification document of that Party*" and "an entity constituted in a Party under the laws and regulations of that Party", respectively.[120] In the same vein, while the CSBIPPA maintains the "non-discriminatory" principle,[121] it avoids terminology – notably, "national treatment" – that might imply the existence of two separate sovereign States.

[115] Zhonghua renmin gongheguo haiguan "haixia liangan jīngji hezuo kuangjia xieyi" xiang xia jin chukou huowu yuan chandi guanli banfa (中华人民共和国海关《海峡两岸经济合作框架协议》项下进出口货物原产地管理办法) [Measures of the General Administration of Customs of the People's Republic of China for the Administration of the Place of Origin for Imported and Exported Goods under the Cross-strait Economic Cooperation Framework Agreement] (promulgated by the General Administration of Customs, Dec. 29, 2010, Order of the General Administration of Customs No. 200).

[116] Haiguan zong shu guanyu "haixia liang'an jingji hezuo kuangjia xieyi" huowu maoyi zaoqi shouhuo jihua shishi youguan wenti de tongzhi (海关总署关于《海峡两岸经济合作框架协议》货物贸易早期收获计划实施有关问题的通知) [Notice of the General Administration of Customs on Relevant Issues Concerning the Implementation of the Early Harvest Program for Trade in Goods under the Cross-Straits Economic Cooperation Framework Agreement] (promulgated by the General Administration of Customs, August 1, 2011, No. 281 [2011] of the General Administration of Customs).

[117] Haixia liangan jingji hezuo jiagou xieyi (ECFA) zhi hang qingxing (海峽兩岸經濟合作架構協議(ECFA)執行情形) [Implementation of the Economic Cooperation Framework Agreement (ECFA) Across the Taiwan Strait]. Available at: www.ecfa.org.tw/ShowDetail.aspx?nid=1121&pid=1044. There are several memorandums of understandings to facilitate the bilateral economic exchanges. A prime example is the MoU in the financial sector.

See e.g., Haixia liangan yinhang ye jiandu guanli hezuo liaojie beiwanglu (海峽兩岸銀行業監督管理合作瞭解備忘錄) [Memorandum of Understanding on Cooperation in Supervision and Management of the Banking Industry Across the Straits] (Nov. 16, 2009).

[118] According to Article 13 of ECFA, the annexes and the follow-up agreements signed as per the ECFA "shall be parts of this Agreement". ECFA, *supra* note 107, art. 13.

[119] Haixia liangan touzi baohu he cujin xieyi (海峡两岸投资保护和促进协议)[Cross-Strait Bilateral Investment Protection and Promotion Agreement] [hereinafter CSBIPPA] (Aug. 9, 2012).

[120] *Id*. art. 1.2 (1) and (2).

[121] *Id*. art. 3.

This observation is supported by a comparison of the text between the CSBIPPA and the "Investment Agreement" signed on June 28, 2017, under the framework of the CEPA.[122] Article 5(1) of the Investment Agreement between Hong Kong and the Chinese Mainland is named a "National Treatment" which reads:

> One side shall accord to investors of the other side treatment no less favourable than that it accords, in like circumstances, to its own investors with respect to the establishment, acquisition, expansion, management, conduct, operation, and sale or other disposition of investments in its area.[123]

By contrast, while the CSBIPPA features a similar clause, it is included alongside other typical BIT investment protection clauses under the heading "Treatment of Investment". In relevant part, it reads:

> Treatment accorded by a Party to investors of the other Party with respect to the operation, management, maintenance, enjoyment, use, sale, or other disposition of their investments shall not be less favorable than that accorded by such Party, in like circumstances, to its own investors and their investments.[124]

Likely, the designs of the dispute resolution under the CSBIPPA is, as detailed below, different from the general practice of a typical inter-state BIT. Another, more controversial case is the bilateral agreement concerning trade in services. The "Cross-Strait Service Trade Agreement" (CSSTA) was signed in June 2013, but it did not secure legislative approval due to the shifting political landscape. The CSSTA, which encompassed market access for a broad spectrum of service sectors, such as construction, health, transportation, and financial services, touched on the cross-border mobility of service providers and inward investment. The intricate dynamics of implementing this agreement, compounded by political factors, made it highly controversial, and it failed to achieve the endorsement of the regulators. For similar reasons, two subsequent agreements, one on dispute resolutions[125] and another on trade in goods,[126] never came to fruition.

[122] The Investment Agreement of the Mainland and Hong Kong Closer Economic Partnership Arrangement, China-HK, June 28, 2017 (effective from Jan. 1, 2018) [hereinafter PRC-HK Investment Agreement].

[123] Interestingly, this agreement did omit the term "nation" by using the phrase "most favourable treatment" under Article 6 – deviating from the usual language of "most favoured nation treatment" widely found in standard BITs. *Id.* arts 5 (1) and 6.

[124] *CSBIPPA*, *supra* note 119, art. 3(3).

[125] ECFA Article 10 provides that "The two Parties shall engage in consultations on the establishment of appropriate dispute settlement procedures no later than six months after the entry into force of this Agreement, and expeditiously reach an agreement in order to settle any dispute arising from the interpretation, implementation and application of this Agreement".

[126] ECFA Article 3(1) provides that "The two Parties have agreed, on the basis of the Early Harvest for Trade in Goods as stipulated in Article 7 of this Agreement, to conduct consultations on an agreement on trade in goods no later than six months after the entry into force of this Agreement, and expeditiously conclude such consultations".

B. Taiwan's Approach Towards Trade and Investment with China

(i) The Concept of "China" as a Matter of Law

The Chinese mode of engaging its counterpart on the other side of the Strait is detailed above. In short, China views Taiwan as its breakaway province and thus treats Cross-Strait economic ties as an internal affair. On the other side of the Strait, it is a subject of debate that Taiwan regards its relations with the PRC in a manner that differs from typical international interactions, as one may observe from a legal perspective.

This unique stance is largely shaped by Taiwan's progression towards democratisation, which significantly influences how the island's Constitution is interpreted. Despite these evolving internal political dynamics, Taiwan continues to retain its official name as the "Republic of China", a factor that adds complexity to its international and Cross-Strait relations. This juxtaposition of democratisation and constitutional interpretation under the official state nomenclature presents a nuanced and debated aspect of Taiwan's political identity and its external engagements.[127] Before we consider Taiwan's strategies and dilemma in the shaping of its economic relations with the PRC, it is useful to first set the stage, illustrating how Taiwan sees its counterpart as a matter of law.

The ROC Constitution, originally passed in 1946 and effective from December 25, 1947, was established while the Nationalist government was engaged in a civil war with the Chinese Communist Party (CCP).[128] Despite the Nationalist government's defeat and retreat to Taiwan, the Constitution remained unaltered for a significant period, creating a discrepancy between the constitutional framework and the political reality of the time. This incongruity is exemplified by references to several provisions in the main text of the Constitution. Article 26, for instance, provides that the "National Assembly" shall include delegates from Tibet and Mongolia,[129] while the Legislative Yuan, the major legislator under the ROC Constitutional framework, shall also have delegates from "Mongolian Leagues and Banners" and "those to be elected from Tibet", in addition to those elected by each province and municipality.[130]

[127] For a recount of the evolution of Taiwan's constitutional law, *see e.g.*, Jiunn-rong Yeh, The Constitution of Taiwan: A Contextual Analysis 24 (2016). Yeh suggests that, through seven rounds of amendments in the late 1990s and early 2000s, the ROC's constitution has been dramatically revised. *Inter alia*, the relationship between central and local governments in Taiwan has been realigned to reflect political realities, notably regarding the legal status of Taiwan Province. This adjustment addresses whether Taiwan is an independent country or simply a province of the "Republic of China". Such constitutional transformations have not only contributed to the "Taiwanisation" of the constitution but also heightened public awareness of these issues. *See also* Chien-Chih Lin (林建志)，〈給臺灣制憲的備忘錄〉，《中研院法學期刊》，第三十三期，頁 145、154 [Chien-Chih Lin, *Memorandum to Taiwan's Constitution Makers*, 33 Academia Sinica L. J. 145, 154 (2023) (arguing that while the Taiwanisation of the Constitution is evident, "One China" persists in Taiwan's constitutional framework) [hereinafter Lin, *Memorandum to Taiwan's Constitution Makers*].

[128] For a brief introduction, *see* Tay-sheng Wang and I-Hsun Sandy Chou, *The Emergence of Modern Constitutional Culture in Taiwan*, 5(1) N.T.U. L. Rev. 1, 13–15 (2010).

[129] Minguo Xianfa [The Constitutional Law of the ROC] (Taiwan), art. 26 (1947).

[130] *Id*. art. 64.

It was not until 1991, with the repeal of the "Temporary Provisions against the Communist Rebellion", that constitutional reforms began to reflect the political realities. The 1991 amendment redefined the ROC's territory as comprising the "Free Area", effectively controlled by the ROC, and the Chinese Mainland, under the jurisdiction of the PRC after 1949.[131] This amendment acknowledged the distinct governance of the two areas and allowed for the specification of Cross-Strait interactions through legislation.[132] A more recent amendment to the ROC Constitution, effective June, underscored in the preamble that it shall apply to "meet the requisites of the nation prior to national unification".[133] The Amendment stipulates, *inter alia*, that electors of the Free Area of the ROC are entitled to vote for a referendum concerning the change of territory of nation,[134] and "[t]he president and the vice president shall be directly elected by the entire populace of the free area" of the ROC.[135]

In line with these constitutional mandates, legislation – most notably, the "Act Governing Relations between the People of the Taiwan Area and the Mainland Area", last amended in June 2023. This law, widely known as the "Law Governing Cross-Strait Relations", has become the enabling legislation for a wide range of issues concerning interactions between the two sides. Although the Law Governing Cross-Strait Relations is primarily administered by the Mainland Affairs Council (MAC), the ROC government established the Straits Exchange Foundation (SEF) as a semi-official proxy – which is authorised to exercise public authority[136] – to engage its Chinese counterpart, the Association for Relations Across the Taiwan Strait (ARATS).[137]

From 2008 to 2015, when the Nationalist Party was in power, a series of SEF-ARATS negotiations resulted in 23 agreements between both sides,

[131] The 1991 Amendment, Minguo Xianfa [The Constitutional Law of the ROC] (Taiwan).

[132] *Id.* art. 11.

[133] The 2005 Amendment, Minguo Xianfa [The Constitutional Law of the ROC] (Taiwan) [hereinafter 2005 Amendment]. The preamble and main text of the amendments to the ROC's Constitution illustrate a nuanced stance on national unification. From its text, it distinguishes between the "Free Area of the Republic of China" and the "Mainland Area", suggesting a "One-China" that anticipates future unification with mainland China. Yet, this has been a matter of debate, and interpretations vary. Some see this as a non-binding goal without a fixed timeline. Others view it as a mere policy statement, while some believe it indicates a constitutional obligation toward unification. Yet, there is also a perspective that these texts are political expediencies, keeping open the possibilities of both unification and independence. For a recount, *see* Lin, *Memorandum to Taiwan's Constitution Makers*, *supra* note 127, at 152–53.

[134] 2005 Amendment, *supra* note 133, art 1.

[135] *Id.* art 2.

[136] Lu wei hui yu hai ji hui guanxi (陸委會與海基會關係) [The relationship between the Mainland Affairs Council and the SEF]. Available at: www.mac.gov.tw/cp.aspx?n=0984A85A3A9A6677 (stating that the SEF is essentially a non-governmental organisation. In terms of business execution, it is mainly commissioned by the government to handle negotiations, exchanges, and services involving public authority in cross-strait interactions).

[137] Taiwan Diqu yu Dalu Diqü Renmen Guanxi Tiaoli (臺灣地區與大陸地區人民關係條例) [The Law Governing Relations between the People of the Taiwan Area and the Mainland Area] (promulgated by the Legislative Yuan, July 31, 1992, effective Sept 18, 1992, last amended June 8, 2023) [hereinafter The Law Governing Cross-Strait Relations].

including the ECFA discussed above.[138] While these semi-official proxies served as a handy tool to "make cooperation on an equal footing possible between two governments that refuse to recognise each other",[139] these bilateral agreements – and the way in which the Taiwanese government interacted with the Chinese government – have relied on the controversial "1992 Consensus". This mirrors debates over the ROC Constitution's interpretation. While the text upholds a "One (Republic of) China", implying potential reunification, some would argue that this perspective often overlooks Taiwan's unwritten "small-C" constitution, shaped by its evolving political and social landscape, which represents a significant departure from the original constitutional narrative.[140] The changing dynamics outlined below have shaped Taiwan's engagement strategy with the other side, reflecting its evolving political and social landscape in these interactions.

(ii) Cross-Strait Economic Ties: Between Economic Dependence and Political Divergence

From a strictly legal perspective, under the ROC laws, its territory is comprised of two parts: the "Free Area" and the "Mainland area" – the former consists of the island groups of Taiwan, Penghu, Kinmen, Matsu, and some minor islands, while the latter refers to, essentially, the territory controlled by the PRC. References to these two terms can be found in the Constitutional Law and the Law Governing Cross-Strait Relations. Article 11 of the ROC's Constitution, as amended in 2005, provides that:

> Rights and obligations between the people of the Chinese mainland area and those of the free area, and the disposition of other related affairs may be specified by law.[141]

Article 2 of the Law Governing Cross-Strait Relations further provides that:

> "Taiwan Area" refers to Taiwan, Penghu, Kinmen, Matsu, and any other area under the effective control of the Government. 2. "Mainland Area" refers to the territory of the Republic of China outside the Taiwan Area. 3. "People of the Taiwan Area" refers to the people who have household registrations in the Taiwan Area. 4. "People

[138] For a list of the Cross-Strait agreements, *see* the website of the ROC Mainland Affairs Council, Liangan Xieyi (兩岸協議), Mainland Aff Council of the Executive Yuan (Taiwan). Available at: www.mac.gov.tw/cp.aspx?n=1494D59CE74DF095.

[139] Yu-Jie Chen and Jerome A Cohen, *China-Taiwan Relations Re-Examined: The "1992 Consensus" and Cross-Strait Agreements*, 14 U PA Asian L Rev 1, 2 (2019). For a detailed analysis of these proxies, *see* Pasha L Hsieh, *Legitimacy of Taiwan's Trade Negotiation with China: Demystifying Political Challenges*, 68 Poli Sci 3 (2016).

[140] Chien-Chi Lin and Yen-Tu Su, *The Constitutional Law and Politics in Taiwan, in* Oxford Handbook of Constitutional Law in Asia (David Law et al., eds, forthcoming 2024, on file with the authors).

[141] Zhonghua minguo xianfa zeng xiu tiaowen (中華民國憲法增修條文) [The Additional Articles of the Constitution of the Republic of China] (as amended June 10, 1995) (hereinafter the *Amendment to the ROC Const*).

of the Mainland Area" refers to the people who have household registrations in the Mainland Area.[142]

The aforementioned provisions appear to be in harmony with the references found in the amendment to the ROC's Constitution, which declares that the amended clauses were designed to "meet the needs of the nation prior to national unification".[143] While these laws were passed or amended during a period when there might have been some political inclination towards unification, they may not encapsulate the evolving dynamics, given the progression of Taiwan's national identity and democratisation process over the years. This is also reflected in the shifting patterns of the Cross-Strait trade and investment, as the Taiwanese government has been struggling with striking an optimal balance between economic dependence and political divergence. A "catch-22" situation is the defining characteristic of Taiwan's approach. In what follows, we unfold the push-and-pull forces that shape this shifting landscape.

Cross-Strait Ties as Taiwan's Strategy of Economic Transformation

As noted above, since both sides have resumed economic relations, the PRC has experienced a large trade deficit with Taiwan. In 1986, for instance, Taiwan enjoyed a US$0.67 billion surplus, but by 1993 that had risen to US$12.89 billion.[144] For the past 10 years or so, Beijing has constantly run a trade deficit of above US$60 billion with Taiwan.[145] These trade volumes reflect not only China's changing policies, but Taiwan's struggle in transforming itself into a more advanced economy over decades.

Notwithstanding the stunning "Taiwan miracle" of the period from the 1960s through to the 1980s, Taiwan's development resulted in increasing pressures. While Taiwan emerged as one of the "Four Asian Tigers", it faced various structural challenges. Internally, an immediate result of its economic growth was rising living standards, and hence, rising labour costs, with the nominal wage rate increasing at 13.7 per cent per annum between 1975 and 1985.[146] Further, years of wealth creation came hand in hand with social and distributive

[142] *The Law Governing Cross-Strait Relations*, *supra* note 137, art 2.

[143] *Amendment to the ROC Const supra* note 141 (the original Chinese text reads: 「為因應國家統一前之需要，依照憲法第二十七條第一項第三款及第一百七十四條第一款之規定，增修本憲法條文如左：」("To meet the requisites of the nation prior to national unification, the following articles of the ROC Constitution are added or amended to the ROC Constitution in accordance with Article 27, Paragraph 1, Item 3; and Article 174, Item 1:").

[144] Suisheng Zhao, *Economic Interdependence and Political Divergence: The Emerging Pattern of Relations across the Taiwan Strait*, 6 J Contemp China 177, 180 (1997).

[145] National Bureau of Statistics of China, *Merchandise Trade Balance of Taiwan with Mainland China and Hong Kong from 2013 to 2023* (in billion US dollars), STATISTA (Feb 2024). Available at: www.statista.com/statistics/320608/taiwan-trade-balance-with-china-and-hong-kong/ (last visited May 8, 2024).

[146] Barry Naughton, Economic Policy Reform in the PRC and Taiwan, in The China Circle: Economics and Technology in the PRC, Taiwan, and Hong Kong 87 (Barry Naughton ed., 1997).

injustices, labour welfare, and environmental problems. Taiwan's exceptional growth based on labour-intensive goods began to slow in the late 1980s.

The increase in production costs reflected not only a labour shortage, but also an adjustment of the undervalued New Taiwan Dollar under U.S. pressure to reduce American trade deficits.[147] Further, the rise of emerging economies in Southeast Asian resulted in a drop in Taiwan's competitiveness as an export-oriented economy.[148] These and other factors changed Taiwan's economic dynamics, incentivising policymakers to reorganise the island's economy around the information and communication technology (ICT) sector.[149] Indeed, many government-funded research and development (R&D) initiatives focused on their collaboration with U.S. firms, modelled on American experience to build up the ICT industry.[150] However, China's formidable market, plentiful cheap labour, tax shelters and investment incentives specifically tailored to Taiwan, made it a popular destination for Taiwanese investors – especially traditional, labour-intensive investors.[151]

In the 1980s, a sea change began. In July 1985, the ROC's Nationalist government, after a three-decade ban, authorised Cross-Strait trade via Hong Kong and Macau.[152] In August 1987, not long after the lifting of Martial Law, Taiwan further liberalised the indirect import of 27 products from China,[153] followed by the adoption of the "Handling Principles of Indirect Import of Goods from Mainland China",[154] the "Rules Governing the Products of Mainland China",[155] and "Measures for the Administration of Indirect Exports of Goods to Mainland China",[156] among others. Meanwhile, the ruling Nationalist Party relaxed restrictions on Taiwanese businesses' indirect investment in and technical cooperation with China.[157] To better understand this transition, which saw

[147] *Id.* at 88–91.

[148] Philippe Chevalérias, *The Taiwanese Economy After the Miracle: An Industry in Restructuration, Structural Weaknesses and the Challenge of China*, 83 China Persps 35 (2010).

[149] *Id.* at 36.

[150] *Id.* at 37.

[151] Dick K Nanto and Emma Chanlett-Avery, Congressional Research Service, The Rise of China and Its Effect on Taiwan, Japan, and South Korea: US Policy Choices 1, 29 (2006). Available at: https://sgp.fas.org/crs/row/RL32882.pdf ("While the U.S. market will always be a major export destination, Japan, South Korea, and Taiwan have progressively turned toward China for imports and exports, and their companies increasingly are dividing their manufacturing processes to take advantage of lower costs in China").

[152] Dui gangao diqu zhuankou maoyi san xiang jiben yuanze (對港澳地區轉口貿易三項基本原則) [Three Basic Principles for Indirect Trade via Hong Kong and Macau].

[153] William Tsai (蔡學儀)，兩岸三通之發展與分析，展望與探索，第2卷第2期，2004年2月，第34、42頁[William Tsai, *The Dynamics and Analyses of Direct Trading Relationships between Taiwan and China*, 2 (2) Prospect & Exploration 34, 42 (2004).

[154] Dalu chanpin jianjie shuru chuli yuanze (大陸產品間接輸入處理原則) [Handling Principles of Indirect Import of Goods from Mainland China].

[155] Dalu diqu wupin guanli banfa(大陸地區物品管理辦法) [Rules Governing the Products of Mainland China].

[156] Dui dalu diqu jianjie shuchu huopin guanli banfa (對大陸地區間接輸出貨品管理辦法) [Measures for the Administration of Indirect Exports of Goods to Mainland China].

[157] Dui dalu diqu congshi jianjie touzi huo jishu hezuo guanli banfa (對大陸地區從事間接投資或技術合作管理辦法).

Taiwan resumed economic interactions with China, one must consider how the political climate of the island had changed over the four decades. These political factors have played, and continue to play, a decisive role in shaping economic relations with the PRC government. As detailed below, democratization and rising national identity have been particularly influential in slowing Taiwan's economic integration with China.

The Role of Democratisation in Shaping Cross-Strait Economic Relations

For Taiwan, 1987 was a watershed year, with major political reforms having since taken place. Taiwan's democratisation and localisation process began when former President Chiang Ching-Kuo, the son of Chiang Kai-shek, lifted Martial Law on July 15, 1987.[158] The death of Chiang in 1998 marked a new era for the ROC. Taiwan's first popularly elected president – Lee Teng-Hui – also the first ROC leader to have been borne on the island, began to fundamentally reconsider the question of whether Taiwan would ever truly seek unification with Mainland China, despite the official name of the nation being the "Republic of China". President Lee, as a gesture of conciliation to Beijing when he first assumed the presidency, reiterated the notion of "One China" on various occasions and created agencies to work towards reunification, most notably, the National Unification Council (NUC), an advisory body that initiated the "Guidelines for National Unification".[159]

The Guidelines provided, among other matters, that "[b]oth the Mainland and Taiwan are parts of Chinese territory. Helping to bring about national unification should be the common responsibility of all Chinese people".[160] To this end, however, it underscored that the timing and manner of such a unification must "first respect the rights and interests of the people in the Taiwan area, and protect their security and welfare".[161] The Guidelines and the NUC ceased to function 2006 under former President Chen.[162]

The notion of a "1992 Consensus" has been a source of controversy.[163] This term was first coined by Su Chi in 2000, who at the time was the chairperson

[158] For a history, see, e.g., Denny Roy, Taiwan: A Political History 76–104 (2003).

[159] Chien-min Chao and Bruce J Dickson, Introduction: Assessing the Lee Teng-Hui Legacy, in Assessing the Lee Teng-Hui Legacy in Taiwan's Politics: Democratic Consolidation and External Relations 1, 10–11 (Bruce J Dickson and Chien-Min Chao eds, 2002).

[160] Guidelines for National Unification (adopted by the Nat'l Unification Council on Feb 23, 1991 and by the Executive Yuan on Mar 14, 1991; repealed on Feb 28, 2006).

[161] *Id.*

[162] Office of the President, Rep of China, President Chen's Concluding Remarks at National Security Conference (Feb 27, 2006, Taiwan). Available at: https://english.president.gov.tw/NEWS/2180. Although the pro-independence Chen Administration abolished the Guidelines and the NUC, President Ma, despite his differing stance on China, did not reinstate them.

[163] 蘇起 & 鄭安國編，「一個中國，各自表述」共識的史實 Chi Su & An-kuo Cheng eds, "Yige Zhongguo, Gezi Biaoshu" Gongshi de Shishi ["One China, with Respective Interpretations" – A Historical Account of the Consensus of 1992] (2003). Chi Su, Taiwan's Relations with Mainland China: A Tail Wagging Two Dogs 12–15 (2009).

of the MAC While the KMT was in power. This concept emerged from the formula: "One China, Respective Interpretations" (OCRI), without specifying which side was the legitimate representative of China. For the KMT, "China" referred to an entity that included Taiwan, but there was disagreement with the CCP over which government legitimately and exclusively represented this "China".[164] After a 2005 meeting in Beijing between the leaders of both sides of the Strait, Hu Jintao and Lien Chan, the PRC began to officially and consistently employ the "1992 Consensus" terminology.[165] According to the PRC's interpretation, however, the "One-China principle", under which Taiwan is part of China, is the subject of consensus, not the "respective interpretations".[166] As noted below, the concept of consensus, and whether this one even existed,[167] have been matters of controversy affecting both sides of the Taiwan Strait as they engage in deeper economic exchanges.

The Cross-Strait exchanges were halted after President Lee visited the U.S and characterised Taiwan-China relations as a "special state-to-state relationship".[168] The KMT under Lee adopted "a more pragmatic, more flexible and more forward-looking approach to upgrade Taiwan's external relations", which amounted, in the eyes of the PRC, to "a de facto two China policy without articulating that political reality".[169] Meanwhile, given Taiwan's declining political leverage as a result of its growing economic reliance on Beijing and the "hollowing-out" effects resulting from the rapid growth of capital outflows to China, in 1996 President Lee launched his "No Haste, Be Patient" policy.[170] This capped outbound investment to China at US$50 million and imposed restrictions on investment in high-tech and infrastructure projects through implementation rules adopted under the mandate of the aforementioned Law Governing Cross-Strait Relations.[171] To diversify Taiwan's economy in order to be less reliant on China, Lee then rolled out the "Southbound Policy", redirecting the island's trade and investment

[164] Yu-Jie Chen, *supra* note 12, at 1034–35.

[165] *Id.* at 1034.

[166] Chen and Cohen, *supra* note 135, at 11.

[167] Former President LEE Teng-Hui, for instance, denied the existence of the so-called "1992 Consensus". *See* Vincent Y. Chao, *So-Called '1992 Consensus' a Fabrication: Lee Teng-Hui*, Taipei Times (Dec 28, 2010). Available at: www.taipeitimes.com/News/front/archives/2010/12/28/2003492047.

[168] Bruce Jacobs and I-Hao Ben Liu, *Lee Teng-Hui and the Idea of Taiwan*, 190 China Q 375, 385 (2007).

[169] Michael Leifer, *Taiwan and South-East Asia: The Limits to Pragmatic Diplomacy*, 165 China Quarterly 173, 181 (2001).

[170] Lee Teng-Hui, President of the Republic of China, Inaugural Address, May 20, 1996, unofficial translation available at New Congress. Available at: http://newcongress.yam.org.tw/taiwan_sino/leespeec.html; TY Wang, *Lifting the "No Haste, Be Patient" Policy: Implications for Cross-Strait Relations*, 15 Cambridge Rev Int'l Aff 131, 132 (2002).

[171] Douglas B Fuller, *The Cross-Strait Economic Relationship's Impact on Development in Taiwan and China: Adversaries and Partners*, 48 Asian Surv 239, 241 (2008).

to emerging economies in Southeast Asia.[172] There are mixed views towards the "No Haste, Be Patient" policy and its effectiveness. High-tech firms, for instance, reportedly worked around restrictions by investing in China via vehicles in the Cayman Islands, the British Virgin Islands, and the U.S.[173]

Taiwan's transformation under Lee from authoritarianism to democracy had a significant impact on Cross-Strait economic exchanges. As its democratisation process continued to evolve, Taiwan witnessed the "first peaceful transition of power from one political party to another in Taiwanese history and probably in all of Chinese history",[174] as the DPP, led by Chen Shui-bian, came to power in 2000. The transition of political power, as per Leifer, served to "reiterate a de facto independence" of Taiwan, and did not lead to any substantial alterations in the conditions under which Taiwan is allowed buy limited participation in the international community.[175]

Amid the evolving political climate and economic conditions following the September 11 attacks and implosion of the dotcom bubble, and in preparation for Taiwan's WTO accession, President Chen, known for his pro-independence stance, adopted a more conciliatory approach by implementing the "Active Openness, Effective Management" policy,[176] and undertaking various reforms. One conspicuous example is the amendment to the *Regulations Governing the Approval of Investment or Technical Cooperation in Mainland China*, lifting the $50 million cap on investment and abolishing the complicated categories of investment restrictions – "prohibited", "permitted", and "subject to approval" were replaced with a simplified scheme containing two categories, "prohibited" and "general".[177] Another salient example is the "Mini Three Links" program, which legalised economic interactions between Taiwan's offshore islands and adjacent ports of the Mainland, and contained interim measures oriented

[172] Throughout the 1990s, the Taiwanese government, as part of its "Go South" policy, concluded bilateral investment treaties with many Association of Southeast Asian Nations (ASEAN) countries; its capital flows to this region also increased. See Han-Wei Liu, *A Missing Part in International Investment Law: The Effectiveness of Investment Protection of Taiwan's Bits vis-à-vis ASEAN States*, 16 UC Davis J Int'l L & Pol'y 131, 138–40 (2009).

[173] See Chang-Hsien Tsai, *Exit, Voice and International Jurisdictional Competition: A Case Study of the Evolution of Taiwan's Regulatory Regime for Outward Investment in Mainland China, 1997–2008*, 39 Syracuse J Int'l L 303 (2012).

[174] Erik Eckholm, *Taiwan's New Leader Ends Decades of Nationalist Rule*, NY Times (May 20, 2020), www.nytimes.com/2000/05/20/world/taiwan-s-new-leader-ends-decades-of-nationalist-rule.html (quoting Wu Yu-Shan, a political scientist of National Taiwan University).

[175] Leifer, *supra* note 169, at 174.

[176] Editorial, *Change Course Now on Strait Policy*, Taipei Times (Sep 12, 2004), www.taipeitimes.com/News/editorials/print/2004/09/12/2003202613.

[177] "Jīji kaifang, youxiao guanli" zhengce shuoming (「積極開放、有效管理」政策說明) [Explanations of "Active Openness, Effective Management" Policy], Mainland Affairs Council, Republic of China (Taiwan). Available at: www.mac.gov.tw/News_Content.aspx?n=AE7D888EFB4A10BA&sms=7BBB02645A537D41&s=34A141D5C0E1EF90.

towards direct transportation (*e.g.*, chartered direct flights), signalling Chen's policy shift.[178]

Notwithstanding reforms under the Chen administration, there were no bilateral negotiations on Cross-Strait trade and investment, given the wide gap between the two sides. President Chen's proposal of "One Country on Each Side" – evidenced in his abolishment of the NUC and the said Guidelines – asserting Taiwan's status as an independent "sovereign state", clashed with Beijing's One-China principle and further complicated the political stalemate.[179] President Chen remained vigilant about the need to preserve Taiwan's competitiveness via various restrictions. The hollowing-out effects, demonstrated by China overtaking Taiwan as the world's third largest manufacturer of ICT hardware in 2000,[180] rendered the relocation of certain sectors of strategic importance, notably semiconductors, both sensitive and subject to stringent restrictions on outbound investment in China.[181] On the other hand, President Chen implemented initiatives aimed at fostering Taiwan's economic development and safeguarding national security to create a conducive environment for Chinese investors. For instance, an outright ban on Chinese investors' purchase of real property in Taiwan was replaced with an approval system through an amendment to the Law Governing Cross-Strait Relations.[182] The Regulations Governing Permission of Trade between Taiwan Area and Mainland Area was likewise amended to allow direct trade between two sides of the Taiwan Strait.[183]

[178] *See, e.g*, Overview of the Provisional Implementation of "Mini-three-links" between the Offshore Islands of Kinmen and Matsu and Mainland China, Mainland Affairs Council (Dec 18, 2000) (Taiwan). Available at: www.mac.gov.tw/en/News_Content.aspx?n=AEC54CE1BB842CD0&sms=7C0CA8982E163402&s=E0EB95D7DBB072B0.

[179] *See, e.g., Presidents since 1947: Chen Shui-Bian (10–11th terms)*, Office of the President. Available at: https://english.president.gov.tw/Page/87 (last visited May 3, 2024) (Taiwan) (noting that Chen Shui-Bian "[p]ropose[d] the 'One Country on Each Side' formula in 2002 that emphasises Taiwan as a sovereign state, whereas mainland China passe[d] the Anti-Separation Law in 2005"). In an interview with the Associated Press on December 10, 2007, former President Chen Shui-bian used Singapore as an example to argue that a country can be heavily influenced by Chinese culture without being part of China. He drew a parallel to Taiwan, suggesting it has its own distinct identity and culture. Additionally, Chen discussed his efforts to apply for UN membership under the name "Taiwan" to avoid competing with the PRC over the "One China" principle. *Associated Press Interview with President Chen Shui-bian*, Office of the President (Dec 10, 2007) (Taiwan). Available at: www.mac.gov.tw/en/News_Content.aspx?n=8A319E37A32E01EA&sms=2413CFE1BCE87E0E&s=657A9108427E73AE.

[180] Chyan Yang and Shiu-Wan Hung, *Taiwan's Dilemma Across the Strait: Lifting the Ban on Semiconductor Investment in China*, 43 Asian Survey 681, 682 (2003).

[181] *See e.g.*, *id.* at 687–96; Syaru Shirley Lin, *Taiwan's China Dilemma: Contested Identities and Multiple Interests* in Taiwan's Cross-Strait Economic Policy 114-22 (2016).

[182] Dalu zhengce yu gongzuo (大陸政策與工作) [Mainland China Policy and Work], the Mainland Affairs Council (ROC). Available at: www.mac.gov.tw/News_Content.aspx?n=9223A12B5B31CB37&sms=35FA2C4073CF4DFB&s=1EBF54814FF20ABD (last visited: July 15, 2023).

[183] Taiwan diqu yu dalu diqu maoyi xuke banfa (臺灣地區與大陸地區貿易許可辦法) [Regulations Governing Permission of Trade between Taiwan Area and Mainland Area] (promulgated Apr 26, 1993, as last amended Mar 16, 2022). Zì woguo kaifang liangan maoyi shang zhijie jiaoyi yilai, zhijie shenbao dui zhongguo dalu chukou huo zhi bizhong jie jie shangsheng (自我國開放兩岸貿易商直接交易以來，直接申報對中國大陸出口貨值比重節節上升) [Since our country opened

Notwithstanding Chen's relaxation in some areas, Taiwan maintained a separate set of rules governing its economic exchanges with the other side of the Strait – which are often more burdensome than those dealing with other trading partners.[184] These restrictions have received harsh criticism for their discriminatory effects, which may run afoul of Taiwan's WTO commitments. The WTO Secretariat, for instance, observed that although "all of Chinese Taipei's trade is on an MFN basis", it prohibited "inbound Cross-Strait trade involving some 2,200 tariff lines".[185] Taiwan's restrictions specifically applied to the Chinese Mainland have also been on the agenda of industry stakeholders – the European Chamber of Commerce in Taipei, for instance, had urged Taiwan to normalise its economic relations with China.[186] Cross-Strait economic relations worsened after President Chen shifted to the "Active Management, Effective Openness" policy in response to China's lukewarm welcome of his "Active Openness, Effective Management" initiative and the promulgation of the Anti-Secession Law in 2005.[187] The stalemate was finally broken in 2008 when President Ma Ying-jeou took office and began to reinvent the Cross-Strait economic ties.

Deeper Economic Integration in the Shadow of Annexation

As noted above, Taiwan has had to engage in a balancing act to pursue politically acceptable economic relations with China while acting in the shadow of the "One-China" principle. Despite the disagreement about what "China" means in the controversial 1992 Consensus, Ma Ying-jeou's election in 2008 saw both the KMT and the CPP display a renewed eagerness to cooperate. The "1992 Consensus" thus became a convenient tool – with neither side willing to publicly challenge the other's reading of the term.[188] On this basis, President Ma took a fresh approach, adopting various new measures unilaterally or via bilateral frameworks.

up direct transactions between cross-strait traders, the proportion of directly declared exports to mainland China has steadily increased], Mainland Aff Council (ROC). Available at: www.mac.gov.tw/cn/News_Content.aspx?n=DED5DAB0D6C7BED6&sms=8E0A247A631E0960&s=805AFE14CA596CD3 (last visited: July 15, 2023) (noting that "In the past, the cross-strait trade management system used indirect methods. When our manufacturers exported goods to mainland China, most of their export declaration documents used Hong Kong and other third places as the declared export areas. This phenomenon has improved, and the proportion of directly declaring export destinations in mainland China has increased significantly".).

[184] For a recount of Taiwan's WTO-inconsistent measures vis-à-vis China, see Hsieh, *China-Taiwan ECFA*, *supra* note 71.

[185] Secretariat Report, Trade Policy Review: Separate Customs Territory of Taiwan, Penghu, Kinmen and Matsu, WTO Doc WT/TPR/S/165, para 8 (May 16, 2006).

[186] *EU Chamber's Position Papers Push Direct Links Agenda*, Taiwan Today (Nov 3, 2006). Available at: https://taiwantoday.tw/news.php?unit=6,23,45,6,6&post=8119.

[187] See generally Mainland Aff Council et al., Supporting Mechanisms for "Active Management, Effective Opening" in Cross-Strait Economic and Trade Relations (Mar 22, 2006). Available at: https://ws.mac.gov.tw/001/Upload/OldFile/public/data/97716221671.pdf.

[188] Yu-Jie Chen, *supra* note 12, at 1035.

Unilaterally, the Ma administration, as a gesture of goodwill, relaxed the ceiling on Mainland-bound capital investment and streamlined the investment review process in August 2008, three months after he assumed the presidency. An amendment to the *Regulations Governing the Approval of Investment or Technical Cooperation in Mainland China* raised the cap on individual investment in the Mainland to $5 million per year, while allowing small and medium-sized enterprises (SMEs) and non-SMEs to invest up to 60% of their net worth or the consolidated net worth of the affiliated enterprises involved.[189] Other notable measures included expanding the scope of manufacturing and service sectors open to Chinese inbound investment,[190] facilitating the entry of Chinese professionals into Taiwan,[191] strengthening the Mini Three Links,[192] authorising the exchange of Renminbi (RMB) by amending Articles 38 and 92 of the Law Governing Cross-Strait Relations,[193] and the relaxation of bans on investment from the PRC in the Taiwan Stock Exchange.[194]

These measures should be considered against the broader context in which President Ma attempted to engage with the PRC to institutionalise economic links bilaterally. In tandem with Ma's unilateral measures, the two sides resumed official dialogues through their respective proxies, SEF and ARATS. Acting based on the "1992 Consensus", with the Nationalist Party's own OCRI formula,[195] there were 21 agreements concluded between 2008 and 2016, including the above-mentioned landmark ECFA.[196] Broadly, the conclusion of the

[189] For an overview, see Mainland Aff Council, *The Government's Mainland Policy and Related Important Measures Since May 20*. Available at: www.mac.gov.tw/en/News_Content.aspx?n=C62A6E4BD490D38E&sms=F56AA93EEC16ECD5&s=C0DAD6AE6B654676.

[190] Under President Ma, Taiwan also adopted a set of rules and procedures on the Chinese investment in Taiwan. *See e.g.*, Dalu diqu renmin lai tai touzi xuke banfa (大陸地區人民來臺投資許可辦法) [Measures Governing Investment Permit to the People of Mainland Area] (promulgated on June 30, 2009, as last amended Dec 30, 2020); Dalu diqu zhi yingli shiye huo qi yu di san diqu touzi zhi yingli shiye zai tai sheli fen gongsi huo banshi chu xuke banfa (大陸地區之營利事業或其於第三地區投資之營利事業在臺設立分公司或辦事處許可辦法) [Measures for Permitting the Establishment of Branches or Offices in Taiwan by Profit-seeking Enterprises in the Mainland Area or Profit-Profit Enterprises Investing in a Third Area] (formerly known as 「大陸地區之營利事業在臺設立分公司或辦事處許可辦法」 (Measures for Permitting Profit-seeking Enterprises in the Mainland Area to Establish Branches or Offices in Taiwan) (promulgated on June 30, 2009, as last amended Nov 17, 2022).

[191] Mainland Aff Council, Major Measures of the Government's Mainland Policy: Facilitating visits by Mainland professionals to Taiwan (July 31, 2008). Available at: https://www.mac.gov.tw/en/cp.aspx?n=7EAA16F21B02FD43&s=670812630439EA8C.

[192] Mainland Aff Council, Major Measures of the Government's Mainland Policy: Expanding the "Mini-Three-Links" (June 19, 2008). Available at: www.mac.gov.tw/en/cp.aspx?n=7EAA16F21B02FD43&s=EE6922E9CFA19138.

[193] Mainland Aff Council, Major Measures of the Government's Mainland Policy: Allowing RMB-NTD Conversion Business to Be Implemented in the Taiwan Area. Available at: www.mac.gov.tw/en/cp.aspx?n=7EAA16F21B02FD43&s=7A3354652CAE6AEA.

[194] See Tsai, *supra* note 173, at 318–20.

[195] Maeve Whelan-Wuest, Commentary, *Former Taiwan President Ma on One China, the 1992 Consensus, and Taiwan's Future*, Brookings (Mar 16, 2017). Available at: www.brookings.edu/articles/former-taiwan-president-ma-on-one-china-the-1992-consensus-and-taiwans-future/; JM Norton, *'One China,' 5 Interpretations*, The Diplomat (July 27 2016).

[196] ECFA, *supra* note 107.

ECFA has two-fold political implications. First, this trade deal was seen as the most significant – yet controversial – breakthrough since the Chinese Civil War divided the two sides in 1949.[197] Second, the ECFA is the first ever FTA-type trade pact between WTO Members "with long-lasting sovereign disputes".[198]

While the KMT touted the ECFA as a purely economic agreement to revive Taiwan's economy, the lack of transparency and underlying political implications – the fear of being annexed by China – raised enormous concerns about the legitimacy of the ECFA and the subsequent talks on Cross-Strait trade in services.[199] Ma's attempt to conclude the CSSTA with China in 2014 was the straw that broke the camel's back. While some argued that Taiwan would benefit most from the CSSTA,[200] and despite the fact that the Ma administration reiterated that this pact would be delinked from Chinese citizens' employment and immigration issues,[201] it could not overcome popular fear that the arrangement would further deepen Taiwan's economic dependence on the Mainland and ultimately lead to unification.[202] Such suspicions, coupled with dissatisfaction over weak legislative oversight, translated into a vivid oppositional political and social movement during March and April of 2014, known as the "Sunflower Movement" which featured protesters occupying the legislature.[203] The public uproar led to legislators suspending the controversial deal.

[197] *See e.g.*, Lucy Hornby, *Taiwan and China Sign Trade Pact*, Reuters (June 29, 2010). Available at: www.reuters.com/article/us-china-taiwan-signing/taiwan-and-china-sign-trade-pact-idUSTRE65S17Z20100629; Historic Taiwan-China Trade Deal Takes Effect, BBC News (Sep 12, 2010). Available at: www.bbc.com/news/world-asia-pacific-11275274.

[198] Hsieh, *China-Taiwan ECFA*, supra note 71, at 122.

[199] JoAnn Fan, Opinion, *The Economics of the Cross-Strait Service Agreement*, Brookings (Apr 18, 2014). Available at: www.brookings.edu/articles/the-economics-of-the-cross-strait-services-agreement/.

[200] Liangan qia qian fuwu maoyi xieyi dui wo zongti jingji ji chanye zhi yingxiang pinggu (兩岸洽簽服務貿易協議對我總體經濟及產業之影響評估) 2013年7月17日 [Cross-strait Negotiation for Service Trade Agreement Impact on the Overall Economic and Industrial Impact Assessment, Ministry of Econ Aff (July 17, 2013). Available at: www.ecfa.org.tw/Download.aspx?No=40&strT=ECFADoc.

[201] The CSSTA has explicitly followed the Annex on Movement of Natural Persons Supplying Services under the GATS/WTO by carving out "measures affecting natural persons seeking access to the employment market" and "measures regarding citizenship, residence or employment on a permanent basis".

[202] Joel Atkinson, *Taiwan's Sunflower Movement Chooses Democracy Over China Trade Pact*, World Pol Rev (Apr 9, 2014). Available at: www.worldpoliticsreview.com/taiwan-s-sunflower-movement-chooses-democracy-over-china-trade-pact/; Ming-sho Ho, *Occupy Congress in Taiwan: Political Opportunity, Threat, and the Sunflower Movement*, 15 J. East Asian Studies 6, 80 (2015) (noting that "Taiwanese people appeared more concerned about the political consequences of tightened economic relations than the Ma Ying-jeou government, whose promotion of CSSTA stressed mostly the economic benefits without reassuring the public regarding popular anxieties about losing political liberties".).

[203] For additional background, see generally Glenn Smith, *Taiwan's Sunflower Movement*, Foreign Pol'y in Focus (May 29, 2014). Available at: https://fpif.org/taiwans-sunflower-movement/. For legal analysis, see, e.g., Brian Christopher Jones and Yen-Tu Su, *The Sunflower Movement and Its Aftermath*, in Law & Politics of Taiwan Sunflower and Hong Kong Umbrella Movements 15 (Brian Christopher Jones ed., 2017); Chien Huei Wu, *Dance with the Dragon: Closer Economic Integration with China and Deteriorating Democracy and Rule of Law in Taiwan and Hong Kong?*, 45 Hong Kong LJ 275 (2015).

The CSSTA saga hinges on two inter-related factors: the rise of Taiwanese national identity and democratisation. The presidency of Lee Teng-hui, the first Taiwan-born president of the ROC, marked a significant shift in Taiwan's political landscape. Not long after he took power, President Lee began using alternative terms to draw a clear line between Taiwan and China, indicating the ROC's effective control as limited to Taiwan and the offshore islands.[204] In 1998, Lee coined the term, "New Taiwanese", underscoring the existence of a Taiwanese identity separate from the Chinese Mainland.[205] At the same time, while the ROC's Constitutional framework has references to the "Free Area" and the "Mainland area", and despite the amendments featuring the phrase "prior to national unification", from a legal perspective, there is no definitive timeline for achieving ultimate unification. This lack of specificity gave President Lee some flexibility to reinterpret the narrative by introducing a new term – "the ROC on Taiwan" – in the 1990s.[206] This marked a shift from the traditional KMT proposition that stressed a unified Chinese identity.[207]

Under Lee, the ROC government rolled out policies that facilitated the formation of a distinct identity for Taiwan's citizens. According to Shih-shan Tsai, Taiwan's identity has become progressively stronger and more discernible over the decades.[208] This strengthening of identity has been driven by a combination of factors. Taiwan's democratisation, expanding freedoms, and economic success have played a significant role.[209] On the other hand, the unfortunate

[204] Shiho Maehara, *Lee Teng-hui and the Formation of Taiwanese Identity*, *in* Changing Taiwanese Identities 87, 88 (J Bruce Jacobs and Peter Kang eds, 2017).

[205] Office of the President, Republic of China (Taiwan), President Lee Addresses National Assembly (Dec 8, 1998). Available at: https://english.president.gov.tw/NEWS/1205 ("He said that the 'New Taiwanese' concept represents the aspiration, identity and wish shared by many people in this society, and that he is only bringing to light this common understanding of the people. The President pointed out that the idea was raised not only to win the elections, but more so, for promoting ethnic integration as well as social and national development. In other words, its introduction aims to brighten the future for the coming generations, he said".).

[206] Yu-Jie Chen, *supra* note 12, at 1033. Some leading Taiwanese legal academics, notably, Professor Hsu Tzong-Li, who is currently serving as a justice of Taiwan's Constitutional Court, see the Cross-Strait relations as "special state-to-state relations", akin to the one between West and East Germany before reunification. Hsu Zhong-Li (許宗力), 兩岸關係法律定位百年來的演變與最新發展, 月旦法學雜誌第 12期, 39–47 [HSU Zhong-Li, *The Latest Developments – From the Perspective of Taiwan, Yuedan faxue*, 12, 39–47]. These dynamics over the years also led some constitutional law scholars to focus on "small-C", living constitution.

[207] *See, e.g.*, Yun-Han Chu, *Taiwan's National Identity Politics and the Prospect of Cross-Strait Relations*, 44 Asian Survey 484 (2004) (noting that the power struggle after Lee took over the KMT-led Taiwan was not just about the "redistribution of power between the mainlander and Taiwanese elites but was, more fundamentally, a clash between two seemingly irreconcilable emotional claims about Taiwan's statehood and the national identity of the people of Taiwan").

[208] Shih-shan Henry Tsai, Lee Teng-hui and Taiwan's Quest for Identity at xii (2005).

[209] A critical moment in this democratisation process was the 1990 student-led "Wild Lily Movement" (野百合學運). The students demanded the end of martial law, the implementation of democratic reforms, and the creation of a new constitution, while calling for direct presidential elections and the establishment of a multi-party system. Lee responded positively to the students by promising to implement democratic reforms. The Wild Lily Movement is often contrasted with the 1989 crackdown of student-led protests in Beijing's Tiananmen Square by the Chinese Communist

record of human rights violations on the other side of the Strait, along with China's persistent threats to "liberate" Taiwan by force, have also contributed to this development.

Therefore, while Taiwan has long enjoyed a trade surplus with China, these benefits have failed to translate into the political capital Beijing envisaged – at least not in terms of Taiwan's national identity. According to one survey, while in 1992 approximately one in four respondents identified themselves as Chinese, this number fell dramatically to less than 10 per cent after 2002.[210] During the years in which the CCSTA was being negotiated, the percentage of individuals declaring a Chinese identity remained somewhere between 3.9 to 3.8 per cent, while over 50 per cent proclaimed themselves to be Taiwanese.[211] Despite Taiwan's economic dependence on China, alongside its cultural, historical, linguistic, and geographic proximity, the sea change in national identity amid democratisation rendered problematic President Ma's efforts to take Cross-Strait economic ties to the next level.

The fact that the DPP's Tsai Ing-wen won the Presidential Election in 2016 may be seen as reflective of such a shift. In 2019, Beijing's heavy-handed crackdown on Hong Kong's pro-democracy protests further intensified the Taiwanese people's fear of annexation by China.[212] While President Tsai, in her first presidential inaugural address, referred to the "historical fact" of the 1992 SEF-ARATS meeting and called for peaceful cooperation with the Chinese government, she refused to concede that entering into negotiations was contingent on acceptance of the "One-China" principle, "one country, two systems", or the "1992 Consensus".[213] This was especially so given that President Xi Jinping had expressly linked the 1992 Consensus with "one country, two systems", leaving little, if any, space for interpretation.[214] Even for the

Party (CCP) just nine months earlier, which highlighted the different paths adopted by the governments on both sides of the Strait. *See e.g.*, John Liu, *In Taiwan, the Tiananmen Tragedy Has a Special Resonance*, The Diplomat (June 8, 2019). Available at: https://thediplomat.com/2019/06/in-taiwan-the-tiananmen-tragedy-has-a-special-resonance/.

[210] Election Study Centre, Nat'l Chengchi Uni, Taiwanese/Chinese Identity(1992/06-2023/12) (Feb 2, 2024). Available at: https://esc.nccu.edu.tw/PageDoc/Detail?fid=7800&id=6961.

[211] *Id.*

[212] Yu-Jie Chen, *supra* note 12, at 1025.

[213] In contrast to President Ma, President Tsai did not accept the existence of the 1992 Consensus. During her initial presidential inauguration speech, Tsai alluded to the "historical fact" of the 1992 SEF-ARATS meeting and the mutual understanding of finding common ground between the two sides. However, in her second term's inaugural address, Tsai made no reference to the 1992 Consensus. Instead, she reiterated her stance on pursuing "peaceful and stable Cross-Strait relations" and firmly rejected the concept of "One country, two systems". Office of the President, Republic of China (Taiwan), Inaugural address of the ROC 14th-term President Tsai Ing-wen (May 20, 2016). Available at: https://english.president.gov.tw/News/4893; Office of the President, Republic of China (Taiwan), Inaugural address of the ROC 15th-term President Tsai Ing-wen (May 20, 2020). Available at: https://english.president.gov.tw/NEWS/6004; Lindsay Maizland, *Why China-Taiwan Relations Are So Tense*, Council on Foreign Rel. (Feb 8, 2024). Available at: www.cfr.org/backgrounder/china-taiwan-relations.

[214] Xijinping chuxi "gao taiwan tongbao shu" fabiao 40 zhounian jinian hui bing fabiao zhongyao jianghua (习近平出席《告台湾同胞书》发表40周年纪念会并发表重要讲话) [Xi Jinping Attends

KMT, Xi's reading of the 1992 Consensus was not consistent with that originally intended.[215]

In contrast with Xi's position, Tsai's DPP has long followed its "Resolution on Taiwan's Future", which was incorporated into the party charter in 1999.[216] Central to this Resolution is that Taiwan is an "independent sovereign state whose jurisdiction lies only in the territories of Taiwan, Penghu, Kinmen and Matsu and its affiliated islands" and while "Taiwan is called the Republic of China under the current Constitution, it does not belong to the PRC, and nor does the PRC belong to Taiwan".[217] Notably, Tsai's 2019 National Day speech used a new political terminology, "the Republic of China (Taiwan)", which is, as Yu-Jie Chen observed, is a step forward compared from Lee Teng-Hui's "Republic of China on Taiwan".[218]

It came as no surprise when Beijing cut off contact with Taipei following Tsai's election to the presidency.[219] While the ECFA remains in force, no bilateral agreements have been reached under the Tsai administration. Worse still, the Chinese government has used various coercive tactics – diplomatic, military, and economic – to pressure Taiwan to accept its One-China principle. Recent examples include its import ban on selected agricultural products.[220] The tension escalated to an unprecedented level following U.S. House Speaker Nancy Pelosi's visit to Taiwan in August 2022, triggering a series of extraordinary war games by the People's Liberation Army (PLA) surrounding Taiwan.[221]

the 40th Anniversary Commemoration of the "Message to Compatriots in Taiwan" and Delivers an Important Speech] www.gov.cn/xinwen/2019-01/02/content_5354209.htm; Yu-Jie Chen, *supra* note 12, at 1037.

[215] The Statement of the KMT (Jan 3, 2019). Available at: www.kmt.org.tw/2019/01/blog-post_3.html (last visited: July 15, 2023) (「1992年11月兩岸海基、海協兩會在雙方政府各自授權下，歷經協商及函電達成『九二共識』，亦即『兩岸都堅持一個中國的原則，但是對於它的涵義，雙方同意用口頭聲明方式各自表達』，顯示兩岸關係求同存異的性質，既符合客觀事實，也符合雙方規定，更能暫時擱置分歧，此即本黨吳主席一再重申『一中各表』的『九二共識』("In November 1992, under the respective authorizations of their governments, SEF and the ARATS reached the '1992 Consensus' through consultations and correspondence. This consensus is that 'both sides of the strait adhere to the principle of "One China" but agree to express their interpretations of it through oral statements.' This demonstrates the nature of seeking common ground while preserving differences in cross-strait relations. It not only conforms to objective facts and the regulations of both sides, but also allows for the temporary shelving of disagreements. This is the '1992 Consensus' of 'one China, respective interpretations' that Chairman Wu of our party has repeatedly reiterated.).

[216] Democratic Progressive Party, Resolution on Taiwan's Future (ratified at the 2nd Session of the 8th DPP National Congress on May 8 and 9, 1999). Available at: www.dpp.org.tw/en/upload/download/Resolutions.pdf.

[217] *Id*. at 64.

[218] Yu-Jie Chen, *supra* note 12, at 1037.

[219] Javier C Hernández, *China Suspends Diplomatic Contact with Taiwan*, NY Times (June 25, 2016). Available at: www.nytimes.com/2016/06/26/world/asia/china-suspends-diplomatic-contact-with-taiwan.html.

[220] Tim McDonald, *China and Taiwan Face Off in Pineapple War*, BBC News (Mar 20, 2021). Available at: www.bbc.com/news/business-56353963.

[221] Dave Sharma, Opinion, *Taiwan Has Lost Ground Because of Pelosi's Visit: Chinese Military Exercises Have Changed the Status Quo in Its Favor*, Nikkei Asia (Aug 14, 2022). Available at: https://asia.nikkei.com/Opinion/Taiwan-has-lost-ground-because-of-Pelosi-s-visit.

The changing geopolitical climate further complicated the matter – Taiwan has put in place more restrictions on trade and investment concerning high-tech sector – especially in relation to semi-conductors.[222] Amid the changing dynamics, notably, Taiwan also began raising trade barrier concerns multilaterally through the WTO.[223]

Although no Cross-Strait agreements have been negotiated since Tsai took office in 2016, the controversy surrounding the CCSTA has placed the supervisory mechanism governing the way in which the Taiwanese government engages China bilaterally in the spotlight to ensure Taiwan's sovereignty and democracy. We now consider these issues below.

Figure 2.5 Changing National Identity in Taiwan (1992–June 2023)

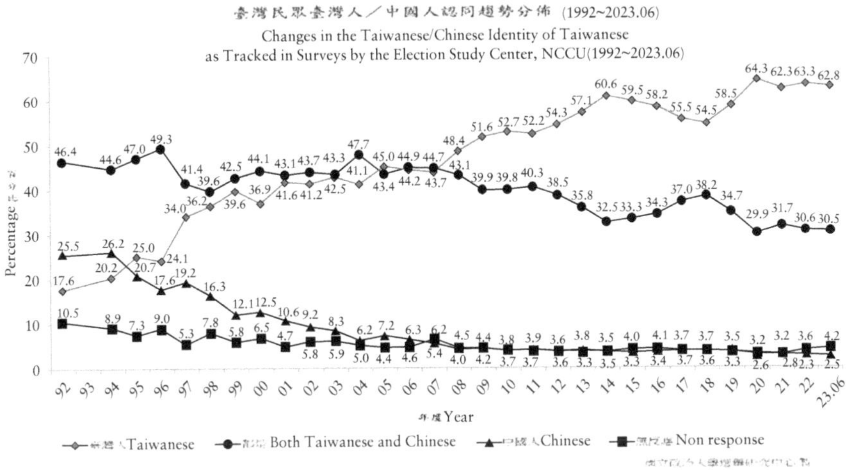

Source: Election Study Centre, NCCU (Taiwan).

IV TREATY-MAKING AND SUPERVISORY MECHANISMS

The changing social and political climate has increased demand for transparency and legitimacy when the Taiwanese government has attempted to engage with China in ways that would have broader long-term political implications. For decades, Cross-Strait dialogues have been undertaken via two proxies,

[222] Xiuzheng zhanlue xing gao keji huopin zhonglei, teding zhanlue xing gao keji huopin zhonglei ji shuchu guanzhi diquzhi shu wang eluosi ji baieluosi gao keji huopin qingdan'(ru fujian), bing zi jiri shengxiao (修正「戰略性高科技貨品種類、特定戰略性高科技貨品種類及輸出管制地區」之「輸往俄羅斯及白俄羅斯高科技貨品清單」(如附件)，並自即日生效) [The "List of High-Tech Goods for Export to Russia and Belarus" under the "Types of Strategic High-Tech Goods, Specific Types of Strategic High-Tech Goods, and Export Control Areas" has been amended (as attached) and is effective immediately], Ministry of Econ Aff Rep of China. Available at: www.trade.gov.tw/Pages/Detail.aspx?nodeID=39&pid=755244 (last visited July 15, 2023).

[223] Taiwan in 2021 raised specific trade concerns in the SPS Committee meeting. Comm. on Sanitary and Phytosanitary Measures, *Summary of the Meeting of 3-5 November 2021*, WTO Doc G/SPS/R/104 Para 3.13 (Dec 17, 2021).

Taiwan's SEF and China's ARATS. The SEF is a semi-official institution primarily funded by the government;[224] it negotiates with its Chinese counterpart under the government mandate and supervision. While such a "White Glove" model has yielded more than 20 single-issue agreements since the 1990s, the mistrust of official checks and balances in the shadow of "One China", as seen in the Sunflower Movement, underscored the need for a full-fledged oversight mechanism.

In Taiwan, the "Conclusion of Treaties Act", passed after the Sunflower Movement, is the primary statute governing the "procedure for concluding treaties and agreements" and their effects, as concluded between "the ROC and *other countries*".[225] Yet, as previously noted, the constitutional amendment recognises both Taiwan and the Mainland as two areas of the ROC. This leaves this Act with no oversight role with respect to China, as the Act applies only to agreements signed between the ROC government and its authorised agencies or institutions and "foreign governments", "international organisations", or "agencies and institutions entrusted by foreign governments".[226]

Consequently, there were various proposals to develop the legal framework governing agreements concluded by, and between, both sides of the Taiwan Strait. As of this writing, however, none of these proposals has been crystalised into a law given the underlying complexity around the Cross-Strait politics. This can be exemplified by the disagreement over even the title of the law. For instance, the pro-independence New Power Party's proposal contained explicit references to "our nation" and "PRC", making clear that the law applies to agreements signed by and between two states, while KMT's proposals followed the framework of the constitutional amendment and the Law Governing Cross-Strait Relations, referring to the draft bill as the law overseeing the conclusion of agreements between "Taiwan Area" and "Mainland Area".[227] Somewhere in between are the DPP's proposals, which used the neutral term "Cross-Strait Agreements".[228]

More recently, the Law Governing Cross-Strait Relations has been amended to include Article 5-3, which subjects "negotiation of an agreement involving political issues" to parliamentary control.[229] While the new provision was passed

[224] The Law Governing Cross-Strait Relations, *supra* note 137, art 4.1.

[225] Tiaoyue dijie fa (條約締結法) [Conclusion of Treaties Act] (promulgated on July 1, 2015) (emphasis added).

[226] *Id*. art 2.

[227] Liangan xieyi jiandu tiaoli lifayuan di jiu jie ji di shi jie xiangguan banben caoan（兩岸協議監督條例，立法院第九屆及第十屆相關版本草案[Statute on the Supervision of Cross-Strait Agreements – Draft Bill of Relevant Versions of the Ninth and Tenth Legislators, Legislative Yuan]. Available at: www.mac.gov.tw/CSASR/News.aspx?n=31D80F602BE78F77&sms=77196D4469ABAD63.

[228] *Id*.

[229] The Law Governing Cross-Strait Relations, *supra* note 137, art 5-3. The Executive Yuan is required to submit a plan and an evaluation report on the potential constitutional or major political impact to the Legislative Yuan 90 days before negotiations begin and the negotiation can only start after the plan is approved by three-quarters of the attending members of the Legislative Yuan at a session attended by three-quarters of all members.

to "set up a high-standard, high-threshold democratic supervision mechanism" to protect "national sovereignty and Taiwan's freedom and democracy",[230] it seems still a matter of debate whether an arrangement regarding Cross-Strait economic exchanges would fall under the scope of "negotiation of an agreement involving political issues".[231]

Although the supervisory mechanism has not yet seen the light of day, institutionalising Cross-Strait economic relations through bilateral agreements has been and continues to be politically sensitive – a unique feature that has not been seen in a normal, inter-state trade agreement.

V. DISPUTE RESOLUTIONS

Both sides of the Strait may, as a matter of law, resolve their trade and investment disputes through either a bilateral agreement or a multilateral framework. Bilaterally, Article 10 of the ECFA sets out the dispute settlement process as follows:

1. The two Parties shall engage in consultations on the establishment of appropriate dispute settlement procedures no later than six months after the entry into force of this Agreement, and expeditiously reach an agreement in order to settle any dispute arising from the interpretation, implementation and application of this Agreement.
2. Any dispute over the interpretation, implementation and application of this Agreement prior to the date the dispute settlement agreement mentioned in paragraph 1 of this Article enters into force shall be resolved through consultations by the two Parties or in an appropriate manner by the Cross-Straits Economic Cooperation Committee to be established in accordance with Article 11 of this Agreement.

Like the CEPA between Hong Kong and China, the ECFA maintains the "power-oriented" approach to dispute resolution. Disputes arising from the

[230] Xingzheng yuan yuan hui tongguo Taiwan diqu yu dalu diqu renmin guanxi tiaoli di wu tiao zhi sanxiuzheng caoan (行政院院會通過「臺灣地區與大陸地區人民關係條例第五條之三」修正草案) [The Executive Yuan Council approves the amendment draft of "Article 5-3 of the Act Governing Relations between the People of the Taiwan Area and the Mainland Area.] Newsletter of the Mainland Aff Council (Mar 28, 2019). Available at: www.mac.gov.tw/News_Content.aspx?n=B383123AEADAEE52&s=912E9F6266E55408.

[231] As Taiwan's presidential election is set to be held in 2024, there are voices calling for resuming the negotiations of CCSTA. Tsai Administration expressed that there is no urgent need to re-reopen the CCSTA negotiations and Article 5-3 of the said law is in a good shape to address the relevant issues. *See e.g.*, Kewenzhe han chongqi fu mao qiang luying bu zuo liangan jiandu tiaoli (柯文哲喊重啟服貿　嗆綠營不做兩岸監督條例) [Ko Wen-je Called for the Restart of Trade in Services, Choking the Green Camp and Not Implementing Cross-Strait Supervision Regulations], Radio Taiwan Int'l (June 20, 2023). Available at: www.rti.org.tw/news/view/id/2171289 (last visited: July 15, 2023); 王照坤 (WANG Chao-Kun). Shikong beijing butong lu wei hui: Xian wu tanpan fu mao xuqiu (時空背景不同　陸委會：現無談判服貿需求) [Different Contexts, Mainland Affairs Council: There is Currently No Need to Negotiate the Service Trade Agreement], Radio Taiwan Int'l (June 29, 2023). Available at: www.rti.org.tw/news/view/id/2172118 (last visited July 15, 2023).

implementation of the CEPA are resolved through the "Steering Committee",[232] while under the ECFA, the Cross-Strait Economic Cooperation Committee is in charge of similar tasks before establishing the dispute settlement mechanism.[233] Unlike CEPA, however, the ECFA was established to create a "rule-oriented" dispute resolution process within six months after its entry into force. On its face, the ECFA adopts a rule-based, rather than power-based, dispute settlement system to address disputes arising from it. In essence, however, this may be seen as a political compromise for both sides. For Taiwan, such an institutional design could arguably moderate its concern that the island would be considered on par with Hong Kong and, thus, part of China.[234] On the other hand, the establishment of the dispute settlement regime relies on China's cooperation – without which disputes would still be subject to the power-ruled system in the shadow of politics. To date, such a rule-based system has not been created to depoliticise conflict resolution.

This, in turn, affects the way in which both sides resolve investment-related conflicts under the aforementioned CSBIPPA: Under this agreement, "[d]isputes between the Parties concerning the interpretation, implementation or application of this Agreement shall be dealt with in accordance with Article 10" of the ECFA.[235] Unless and until dispute settlement procedures under ECFA Article 10 are successfully negotiated, there will be no "state-state" dispute settlement under CSBIPPA, as is often seen in a normal bilateral investment treaty context. While CSBIPPA does set out five channels for investors to resolve their disputes directly with the host party, there is no reference to international arbitration mechanisms such as the ICSID Convention.[236]

Another salient feature of the ECFA's dispute settlement mechanism is the lack of reference to the WTO. While it is common for trade negotiators to include the "choice of forum" clause in the FTAs, allowing parties to select the mechanisms – including the WTO – to resolve the disputes,[237] the ECFA has no such references. Indeed, either party is still entitled to bring cases to the global trade system wherever the WTO laws apply, regardless of the wording. However, the deliberate omittance of such references can only serve to demonstrate the complexity of Cross-Strait politics – and the uneasy relationship between Taiwan and China when it comes to the internationalisation of conflicts.

[232] PRC-Hong Kong CEPA.

[233] ECFA, *supra* note 107, arts 10 and 11.1.5.

[234] SUN Guoping(孙国平)，论ECFA争端解决机制模式之构建，《国际经济法学刊》，2011年，第18卷第3期，頁239、243 [SUN Guoping, *The Construction of DSM Mode of ECFA*, 18 (3) J Int'l Econ L 239, 243 (China, 2011)].

[235] CSBIPPA, *supra* note 119, art 12.

[236] *Id*. art 13.1.

[237] *See e.g.*, Comprehensive and Progressive Agreement for Transpacific Partnership, Mar 8, 2018, UNTC 56101, art 28.4. [hereinafter CPTPP]. Such a clause can also be seen in China's FTAs. *See e.g.*, China-Austl Free Trade Agreement, June 17, 2015, ATS 15, art 15.14.

Such a pattern echoes the manner in which Taiwan and China have engaged with each other under the WTO. Over the past two decades, although either side may occasionally join the proceedings as a third party,[238] China has not brought a single WTO dispute against Taiwan as a complaint, and vice versa.[239] However, as Cross-Strait tensions have intensified in recent years, the DPP government did react to China's coercive tactics by raising concerns about the fruit ban before the WTO Sanitary and Phytosanitary Committee (SPS Committee) in November 2021.[240] Although it remains too early to tell if this case will escalate as a formal complaint against China, such a move marks a critical step for Taiwan in internationalising Cross-Strait trade conflicts through the global trade system.

VI Summary and Conclusion

Several observations can be drawn from our analysis thus far. First, the concept of "China" is a decisive factor in shaping Cross-Strait economic relations. As a matter of constitutional law, the ROC and PRC both claim that they are "China", although there are different interpretations of what this means. These conflicting positions have then been implemented into various laws, regulations, and other measures when each side engages the other. For its part, the rigid "One-China" principle guides the PRC government to internalise its interactions with Taiwan. Such a pattern can be seen elsewhere, be it unilateral, bilateral, or multilateral. While Taiwan sees its territory as covering both the "Free Area" and the "Mainland Area" while retaining the official name "Republic of China", its evolving national identity goes hand-in-hand with two decades of democratisation and has led the Taiwanese people to be vigilant as they forge economic relations with China. Despite their cultural and historical ties, as well as their geographic proximity, the way in which the Taiwanese government engages its Chinese counterpart has revealed the underlying tensions. Although the Nationalist government attempted to institutionalise Cross-Strait trade and investment through bilateral agreements between 2008 and 2016, these efforts were halted before the island was pushed down the path of no return in its dependence on China. As democratisation continues, and given the lessons from Hong Kong, concerns over annexation by China have continued to grow.

It remains to be seen how Taiwan's DPP-led government will navigate its relationship with the PRC under the new presidency of William Lai, who was

[238] Taiwan, for instance, has joined *US-Steel Safeguards* and *China-Rare Earths* as a third party. *See* Appellate Body Report, *United States-Definitive Safeguard Measures on Imports of Certain Steel Products*, WTO Doc WT/DS252/AB/R 1 (Nov 10, 2003) (listing China as "Appellant" and Taiwan as "Third Participant"); Appellate Body Report, *China – Measures Related to the Exportation of Rare Earths, Tungsten and Molybdenum*, WTO Doc WT/DS431/AB/R 16 (Aug 7, 2014) (same). As Taiwan has not yet been a respondent since it joined the WTO, there is no case where China acts as a third party against Taiwan.

[239] *Disputes by Member*, World Trade Org. Available at: www.wto.org/english/tratop_e/dispu_e/dispu_by_country_e.htm.

[240] Comm on Sanitary and Phytosanitary Measures, *Summary of the Meeting of 3–5 November 2021*, WTO Doc G/SPS/R/104 Para 3.13 (Dec 17, 2021).

elected in early 2024. Lai's perceived pro-independence stance has been a point of contention for Beijing, adding complexity to Cross-Strait relations. Recent actions such as the PRC's decision to end tariff concessions for twelve Taiwanese products, citing violations of the ECFA,[241] highlight the economic aspects of this tension. Furthermore, the diplomatic landscape is shifting, as evidenced by Nauru, one of Taiwan's last diplomatic allies, switching allegiance to Beijing shortly after Lai's election.[242] This development further accentuates Taiwan's ongoing challenge in striking a delicate balance between economic interdependence and political divergence with the other side of the Strait.[243] Suffice it to say that these deep concerns have translated into Taiwan's laws and policies towards China – at least in terms of economic activities – which demonstrate Taiwan's struggle for an optimal balance between economic (inter)dependence and political divergence in the long run.

[241] Shangwu bu guanyu jiu Taiwan diqu dui Dalu maoyi xianzhi cuoshi jinxing maoyi bilei diaocha zuizhong jielun de gonggao (商务部关于就台湾地区对大陆贸易限制措施进行贸易壁垒调查最终结论的公告) 2023年12月15日[Ministry of Commerce, Announcement on the Final Conclusion of the Trade Barrier Investigation Regarding Trade Restriction Measures by the Taiwan Region Against the Mainland, Announcement No 54 of 2023] (Dec 15, 2023); *Chinese Mainland to End Tariff Concessions for 12 Taiwan-produced Products*, Global Times (Dec 21, 2023). Available at: www.globaltimes.cn/page/202312/1304048.shtml.

[242] *China and Nauru Resume Diplomatic Relations*, Ministry of Foreign Affairs of the People's Republic of China (Jan 24, 2024). Available at: www.mfa.gov.cn/eng/zxxx_662805/202401/t20240124_11232061.html; Kelly Ng, *Nauru Cuts Diplomatic Ties with Taiwan in Favour of China*, BBC (Jan 15, 2024). Available at: www.bbc.com/news/world-asia-67978185.

[243] William Lai has been considered even more outspoken than President Tsai in terms of Taiwan's independence. During the campaign, however, he promised to follow Tsai's path of moderation. In his victory speech on election night, Lai stated that: "[t]he election has shown the world the commitment of the Taiwanese people to democracy, which I hope China can understand". Eric Cheung et al., *Taiwan Voters Dismiss China Warnings and Hand Ruling Party a Historic Third Consecutive Presidential Win*, CNN (Jan 13, 2024). Available at: https://edition.cnn.com/2024/01/13/asia/taiwan-presidential-election-results-intl-hnk/index.html. Following the election, the spokesperson of the Ministry of Foreign Affairs of the PRC replied that no matter "whatever changes take place in Taiwan, the basic fact that there is only one China in the world and Taiwan is part of China will not change". *Id*. The "One China" principle, as per the spokesperson, "is the solid anchor for peace and stability in the Taiwan Strait". *Id*. Some anticipate a more assertive approach from Beijing prior to Lai's inauguration in May, with the goal of testing "how much [Beijing] can get Lai to concede and then to hold him to their interpretations of those concessions". Helen Davidson and Amy Hawkins, *China's Muted Reaction to Taiwan's Election Result May Signal a Waiting Game*, The Guardian (Jan 18, 2024). Available at: www.theguardian.com/world/2024/jan/18/china-response-taiwan-election-democratic-progressive-party?ref=upstract.com (quoting Ja-Ian Chong, professor of political science at National University of Singapore). On the PRC's response, *see e.g.*, Xinhua she (新华社), 国台办：台湾地区两项选举结果改变不了两岸关系基本格局和发展方向 (Guo tai ban: Taiwan diqu liangxiang xuanju jieguo gaibian bu liao liangan guanxi jiben geju he fazhan fangxiang) [Xinhua News Agency, *Taiwan Affairs Office of the State Council, The Results of Two Elections in the Taiwan Region Cannot Change the Basic Pattern and Development Direction of Cross-Strait Relations*] (Jan 17, 2024). Available at: www.gwytb.gov.cn/xwdt/xwfb/wyly/202401/t20240117_12594378.htm (last visited: Jan 27, 2024).

Chronology of the Cross-Strait Interaction in the Latest Century

1911	• The Republic of China (ROC) was officially established in 1912 and based on the Chinese Mainland until 1949, when the Nationalist Party (Kuomintang) retreated to Taiwan.
1945	• The ROC government assumed military control of Taiwan and ended the Japanese colonial rule.
1946	• The ROC passed its constitution while the Nationalist government was at war with the Chinese Communist Party (CCP).
1949	• The Chinese Civil War ended with the CCP's victory over the KMT, leading to the CCP's control over mainland China. • Meanwhile, the KMT retreated to Taiwan, establishing ROC jurisdiction on nearby islands. The People's Republic of China (PRC) was founded in the same year. • MAO Zedong assumed the role of Chairman within the Central People's Government of the PRC.
1950	• On June 25, 1950, North Korea invaded South Korea, marking the start of the Korean War. • On June 27, 1950, US President Harry Truman ordered the 7th Fleet to sail into the Taiwan Strait to prevent any attack on Taiwan by the PRC.
1954	• MAO Zedong was elected as President of the PRC at the First National People's Congress (NPC). • The Korean War solidified the US' commitment to defending Taiwan. In December 1954, the US and ROC signed the "Mutual Defense Treaty between the United States and the Republic of China," formalizing American's commitment to Taiwan's defence.
1971	• The ROC lost its United Nations seat to the PRC. • The United Nations General Assembly passed Resolution 2758 on October 25, 1971. This resolution recognized the PRC as "the only legitimate representative of China to the United Nations."
1972	• The Joint Communique of the United States of America and the People's Republic of China, known as the "Shanghai Communique," was issued on February 28, 1972, during President Richard Nixon's visit to China. The Shanghai Communique laid a new foundation for Cross-Strait relations, and bilateral Sino-U.S. relations.
1975	• CHIANG Kai-shek, former President of the ROC (Taiwan) passed away.
1976	• Former Chairman of CCP, MAO Zedong passed away.
1978	• Resumption of economic relations between China and Taiwan under Deng Xiaoping's "Open Door" policy.
1979	• The Joint Communique on the Establishment of Diplomatic Relations between the United States of America and the People's Republic of China, known as "the Normalization Communique," was issued on December 15, 1978, and took effect on January 1, 1979. • The U.S. established diplomatic relations with the PRC and enacted the Taiwan Relations Act, which continued informal relations with Taiwan and committed the U.S. to assisting Taiwan in maintaining its self-defence capability.

(continued)

(Continued)

1982	• The Joint Communique of the United States of America and the People's Republic of China, known as the "August 17 Communique," was issued on August 17, 1982, under the Reagan administration. "Six Assurances" were communicated by US President Ronald Reagan to Taiwan government.
1985	• The ROC's Nationalist government authorized Cross-Strait trade via Hong Kong and Macau.
1987	• Taiwan's democratization and localization process began when former President CHIANG Ching-Kuo lifted Martial Law. • Taiwan liberalized the indirect import of 27 products from China, followed by the adoption of the "Handling Principles of Indirect Import of Goods from Mainland China," the "Rules Governing the Products of Mainland China," and "Measures for the Administration of Indirect Exports of Goods to Mainland China."
1988	• Former President of the ROC (Taiwan), CHIANG Ching-Kuo, passed away.
1991	• The Straits Exchange Foundation (SEF) was established by the ROC government as a semi-official organization to handle cross-strait matters due to the complex political and legal status of cross-strait relations. The PRC also set up the Association for Relations Across the Taiwan Straits (ARATS) for handling technical and business matters with Taiwan. • The amendments to the ROC's Constitution ("The Additional Articles of the Constitution of the Republic of China") were passed to alter the original constitution to meet the requisites of the nation and the political status of Taiwan "prior to national unification." The notions of "Mainland Area" and "Free Area" were introduced. The ROC's Constitution underwent seven rounds of amendment from 1991 to 2005. • The "Temporary Provisions against the Communist Rebellion" was repealed.
1992	• The year that saw the emergence of the disputed "1992 Consensus." • Taiwan passed the "Act Governing Relations between the People of the Taiwan Area and the Mainland Area," last amended in 2023. • The second constitutional amendment was passed with major changes, such as Presidents and Vice Presidents being elected by the ROC's "Free Area" population for four-year terms and the introduction of direct elections for provincial and municipal heads.
1993	• The Wang–Koo summit in 1993 marked the first significant attempt at cross-strait dialogue since 1949 between ARATS Chairman WANG Daohan and SEF Chairman KOO Chen-fu. This meeting in Singapore, along with follow-ups until 1998, focused on enhancing trade and people-to-people exchanges, signing four agreements to this effect. • JIANG Zemin was elected as President of the PRC at the Eighth NPC.
1996	• The newly elected president of the ROC (Taiwan), Lee Teng-Hui, launched his "No Haste, Be Patient" policy. • The 1996 constitutional amendment, based on KMT-DPP consensus, aimed to strengthen the presidency by allowing the direct appointment of the Premier, effectively reducing the Taiwan Provincial Government's role.

(continued)

(Continued)

1997	• DENG Xiaoping, the Paramount Leader of the CCP, passed away.
1998	• JIANG Zemin was reelected as President of the PRC at the Ninth NPC.
2000	• China passed the "Measures for the Administration of Trade with Taiwan Region." • In 2000, CHEN Shui-bian of the Democratic Progressive Party (DPP) was elected Taiwan's President. His election signified a pivotal shift towards a stronger assertion of Taiwan's identity, departing from previous Cross-Strait policies.
2001	• PRC joined the WTO as the 143rd member.
2002	• Taiwan became the 144th member of the WTO under the name "Separate Customs Territory of Taiwan, Penghu, Kinmen, and Matsu." • State Council of the PRC passed the "Administrative Regulations for Foreign Law Firms' Representative Organizations in China."
2003	• HU Jintao was elected as President of the PRC at the Tenth NPC.
2004	• The first direct flights between Taiwan and China began in 1949, marking a significant step toward improving cross-strait relations.
2005	• The seventh amendment to ROC's Constitution was passed. It stipulates that any change to the territory of the ROC requires a proposal by one-quarter of all legislators, approval of the proposal by three-quarters of those present at the vote, and valid votes cast by half of the total electorate in the free areas of the ROC through a referendum six months after the announcement. • The Cross-Strait economic relationship worsened after former President CHEN Shui-bian shifted to the "Active Management, Effective Openness" policy in response to China's lukewarm welcome of his "Active Openness, Effective Management" initiative and the promulgation of the Anti-Secession Law.
2007	• Taiwanese lawyers were allowed to operate in the entire Fujian Province and other regions, including Shanghai, Jiangsu Province, Zhejiang Province, and Guangdong Province.
2008	• KMT's MA Ying-jeou was elected as the 12th-term President of ROC (Taiwan). Ma initiated reforms in 2008 to strengthen Cross Strait economic ties, notably easing investment restrictions into mainland China and simplifying the investment approval process. • HU Jintao was reelected as President of the PRC at the Eleventh NPC. • In China, the Ministry of Justice adopted the "Measures for the Administration of Legal Practice in the Mainland by Taiwan Residents who have Obtained the National Legal Professional Qualification," which, along with the "Some Provisions on Taiwan Residents' Taking the National Judicial Examination," details the process governing Taiwan residents' legal practice in Mainland China.
2010	• PRC and ROC (Taiwan) signed the Economic Cooperation Framework Agreement (ECFA). • PRC and ROC (Taiwan) signed the Cross-Strait Agreement on Intellectual Property Rights Protection and Cooperation. • PRC and ROC (Taiwan) signed the Cross-Strait Economic Cooperation Framework Agreement.

(continued)

(Continued)

2013	• The Cross-Strait Bilateral Investment Protection and Promotion Agreement came into effect. • XI Jinping was elected as President of the PRC at the Twelfth NPC.
2014	• The Sunflower Student Movement in Taiwan protested against the Cross-Strait Service Trade Agreement, demonstrating public concern over increasing Chinese influence and the lack of transparency in Cross-Strait negotiations.
2016	• In 2016, President Tsai Ing-wen of the DPP was elected as the first female president of the ROC (Taiwan), marking a significant shift in Taiwan's approach to cross-strait relations. Tsai's administration adopted a more cautious stance towards China, departing from the previous KMT government's China-friendly policies. Notably, she refused to explicitly acknowledge the so-called "1992 Consensus," which had been a cornerstone of the KMT's China policy. This policy shift led to increased tensions with Beijing and a reduction in official cross-strait dialogues. • The 114th Congress passed both H.Con.Res. 88 and S.Con.Res. 38 reaffirming the Taiwan Relations Act and the Six Assurances as foundational elements of U.S.-Taiwan relations. These resolutions called on the US President and the State Department to publicly and consistently affirm the Six Assurances as a cornerstone of the relationship between the U.S. and Taiwan.
2019	• PRC's heavy-handed crackdown on Hong Kong's pro-democracy protests intensified the Taiwanese people's fear of annexation by China. • Incumbent PRC President XI Jinping discusses the prospect of reunification as necessary and inevitable, in addition to the "One Country, Two Systems" approach, at the fortieth anniversary of the issuance of the "Letter to Compatriots in Taiwan."
2020	• LEE Tung Hui, the former President of ROC (Taiwan) passed away.
2022	• US House Speaker Nancy Pelosi visited ROC (Taiwan), intensifying U.S.-China tensions. China strongly objected, citing sovereignty concerns, and conducted military drills around Taiwan. • JIANG Zemin, the former President of the PRC and General Secretary of CCP, passed away.
2023	• Former Premier of the PRC, LI Keqiang passed away. • China resumed importing grouper fish from Taiwan, lifting a previous ban – imposed in June 2022 – in the weeks leading up to Taiwan's general elections. The PRC announced that it would cease tariff cuts under the Economic Cooperation Framework Agreement for 12 chemical products in December 2023, effective January 1. 2024.
2024	• In the Taiwan presidential election, William Lai of the DPP won, signaling continued support for democracy and a firm stance against the PRC's sovereignty claims. Beijing reacted by emphasizing its unwavering commitment to "reunification" and opposing Taiwan independence. • During "Two Sessions" of 2024, incumbent PRC President XI Jinping reiterates peaceful reunification at the National Committee of the Chinese People's Political Consultative Conference.

3

Inter-Korean Economic Relations

THIS CHAPTER DISCUSSES the historical trajectory of the inter-Korean dispute over sovereignty or legitimate representation that defines the contours of bilateral political interactions, which in turn implicate the economic ties between the two Koreas. Despite a high level of political sensitivity and previous armed conflicts, the Democratic People's Republic of Korea (hereinafter DPRK or North Korea) and the Republic of Korea (hereinafter ROK or South Korea) have recently engaged in dynamic political interactions to pursue bilateral peace and economic cooperation amid considerable uncertainty. Importantly, both North and South Korea consider themselves as belonging to the same country, although both occupy UN seats under the "two Koreas model". At the same time, North and South Korea have preferred to avoid official contact, resulting in few formal agreements or arrangements. Years ago, the ultimate goal of unification between the two Koreas seemed certain, albeit with no consensus on the timeline and approaches to achieving it. However, given recent rather dramatic developments, this goal no longer seems possible.

Sharing the same identity does not necessarily contribute to closer economic exchanges. Therefore, in terms of real-world trade and investment, the two Koreas have reaped very limited benefits from the development of inter-Korean economic activities on any meaningful scale, other than the Kaesong Industrial Complex and the Mount Kumgang Tourist Resort. This chapter unpacks such multifaceted interactions and identifies a series of factors – such as membership in multilateral organisations, roles played by hegemonic powers like the United States and China, levels of institutionalisation of bilateral channels, public opinions and industry interests, government support for key infrastructure and political risk insurance, and the historical legacies and path dependence effects – which are crucial in the case of North and South Korea.

I. HISTORICAL BACKGROUND

A. Post-Second World War Korean Peninsula and the 1953 Armistice Agreement

The troubled relationship between North Korea and South Korea may be largely characterised by the political economy post the Second World War and the conclusion of the 1953 Military Armistice in Korea and related Temporary Supplementary Agreement[1] (hereinafter the 1953 Armistice Agreement). The defeat of Japan at the end of the Second World War freed the Korean peninsula from decades-long Japanese colonial rule, but Korea was soon divided by an international power struggle between the United States and the Soviet Union.[2] The 38th parallel divides the Korean peninsula into two separate zones: the United States selected Syngman Rhee to head the provisional government in the South, and the Soviet Union chose Kim Il Sung to rule the North.[3] Backed by the People's Republic of China and the Soviet Union, in June 1950, Kim Il Sung announced his intention to invade and liberate the South, which was defended principally by the United States.[4] The Korean War ended on July 27, 1953, with the restoration of the 38th parallel as the Korean Demilitarised Zone (KDZ), separating today's DPRK and ROK.[5]

The 1953 Armistice Agreement, marking the end of the Korean War, was signed between the Commander-in-Chief of the United Nations Command and the Supreme Commander of the Korean People's Army, as well as the Commander of the Chinese People's Volunteer Army, to reach "a complete cessation of hostilities and of all acts of armed force in Korea until a final peaceful settlement is achieved".[6] However, 75 years later, such a peaceful settlement has yet to be realised.[7] Notably, the fact that representatives of the United States and China were signatories to the 1953 Armistice Agreement regarding the separation of the two Koreas reflects the "multilateralisation" of inter-Korean affairs (in particular, the significant influence of the United States and China).[8] In terms of institutionalisation, the Agreement established the Military Armistice Commission to supervise the implementation work and the Neutral Nations Supervisory Commission to examine illicit military actions within the KDZ.[9]

[1] The Korean War Armistice Agreement, July 27, 1953, 4 UST 234 [hereinafter 1953 Armistice Agreement]. Available at: www.usfk.mil/Portals/105/Documents/SOFA/G_Armistice_Agreement.pdf.

[2] *See* Brian Bridges, Japan and Korea in the 1990s: From Antagonism to Adjustment 163 (1993).

[3] *See* Eunice Lee, *Operation "Denucleunification": A Proposal for the Reunification and Denuclearization of the Korean Peninsula*, 33 Hastings Int'l & Comp L Rev 245, 284 (2010).

[4] Paul Stewart Kim, Comment, *Who's Preparing for the Pecuniary Downside of the Merger? Economy: The Imperative in the Reunification of North and South Korea*, 9 J Bus Entrepreneurship & L 295, 297 (2016).

[5] *Id.* at 297–98; *see also* Louise I Gerdes, North and South Korea 14–15 (2007).

[6] 1953 Armistice Agreement, pmbl. It should be noted that ROK was not a signatory to the 1953 Armistice Agreement, because President Syngman Rhee disagreed with dividing the Korean peninsula at the 38th parallel and refused to sign the document. *See* Balbina Y Hwang, *Reviving the Korean Armistice: Building Future Peace on Historical Precedents*, 6(6) Korea Economic Institute Academic Paper Series, at 3–5 (2011).

[7] Jeong-ho Roh, *The Legal and Institutional Approach to Inter-Korean Relations*, *in* Inter-Korean Relations: Problems and Prospects 159, 159–61 (Samuel S Kim ed., 2004).

[8] *See* Adam de Bear, Comment, *From Sunshine to Storm Clouds: An Examination of South Korea's Policy on North Korea*, 23 Mich St Int'l L Rev 823, 829 (2015).

[9] 1953 Armistice Agreement, art II, paras 24 and 41. Another crucial defect of the Agreement pointed out by a commentator is the lack of a maritime demarcation line, which has bred plenty serious conflicts until the United Nations Command set up a de facto Northern Limit Line. *See* Hwang, *supra* note 6, at 5.

While fruitful in ending serious armed conflicts resulting from the Korean War, the 1953 Armistice Agreement has helped shape the inter-Korean relationship over the ensuing decades, characterised by the absence of a final, peaceful settlement, sharply polarised ideologies, symbolic interactions, and unstable institutionalisation across the 38th parallel.[10]

After the Korean War, the two nations embarked on different paths in terms of economic and social development. While local Korean leaders sought the peninsula's reunification, envisioning a fully sovereign and undivided Korea, two different governmental structures and ideologies emerged.[11] The ROK implied a democratic system with a quick transition to industrialisation that relied on high prices and imported commodities, ideas, and culture from the United States. Conversely, the DPRK relied on a self-contained government system to manage the economy and oversee social development of the country.[12] Post-war, the ROK lacked educational facilities, a skilled workforce, and educated teachers, which led ROK to request aid from the United States. Between 1950 and 1966, the United States recruited professionals to train ROK educators, provide supplies, and offer scholarships to ROK students.[13] Over the long-term, the United States government deployed education as a tool to integrate American political norms and ideologies into ROK culture. While the ROK was busy developing its educational infrastructure, the DPRK concentrated on post-war reconstruction. In 1953, Kim Il-sung visited Moscow seeking the cancelation of North Korea's debt to the Soviets, and in 1958, he visited Beijing to request the cancellation of the country's debt to China. Within a few years, the DPRK was free of its high wartime debt, and initiated the Three-Year Economic Reconstruction Plan,[14] aiming to rebuild war-damaged factories, public areas, and hydroelectric dams, and commence trading with other communist countries. Although Kim Il-sung's regime was debt free, he needed DPRK citizens to share in the same goals, which led to the Cheollima movement – a campaign to increase the labour force and transform the DPRK into an industrial nation.

On August 13, 1960, Yun Boseon was elected President of the ROK under a new parliamentary system. Under President Yun, Prime Minister Chang Myon served as head of state. President Yun and Prime Minister Chang aimed to establish a strong democratic government and create the first five-year economic

[10] *See* de Bear, *supra* note 8, at 830–31. The lack of stabilising effect of the 1953 Armistice Agreement is best illustrated by the fact that North Korea has unilaterally declared the Agreement "null and void" many times. *See, e.g., Important Measures to Defend Nation's Sovereignty, Dignity and Country's Supreme Interests: CPRK*, KCNA (Mar 8, 2013). Available at: www.kcna.co.jp/item/2013/201303/news08/20130308-01ee.html.

[11] Jongsoo Lee, *The Division of Korea and the Rise of Two Koreas, 1945–1948*, *in* Routledge Handbook of Modern Korean History 171 (Michael J Seth ed., 2016).

[12] Theodore Jun Yoo, The Koreas: The Birth of Two Nations Divided 30 (2020).

[13] Spending $12.6 billion U.S. dollars from 1946 to 1976, the United States Operations Mission sent 6,700 Koreans to the United States for educational training, and the United States Information Service (USIS) provided scholarships for 950 students to study in the United States. *Id.* at 34.

[14] *Id.* at 46.

development plan. However, on May 16, 1961 military groups, led by Major General Park Chung-hee, launched a coup and seized power. The new regime sought to justify this to the public with the slogan: "the elimination of social [injustice], corruption and the vicious [cycle] of poverty".[15] The Supreme Court fell in line, compelling President Yun to resign and empowering Park Chung-hee to act as president. Park aimed to rebuild the foundation of ROK's economy by mobilising the population and investing in trade with democratic countries. Park's economic program established essential industrial centres in major metropolitan centres, including Seoul, Busan, and Daegu, which significantly boosted in rapid transformation of ROK into an industrial nation. The nation was rapidly urbanising and an immense number of jobs were being created, but the ROK also faced numerous challenges. The sudden growth of the economy led to an unexpected baby boom and residential overcrowding. The ROK government therefore supported citizens' emigration as part of its national development strategy to ensure foreign remittances and reduce pressure on ROK's economy.[16] In 1970, ROK was committed to participating in the international economy as both an exporter and importer; meanwhile, the DPRK was self-isolating aside from maintaining its relationships with the Soviet Union and China.

B. The 1972 Joint Communiqué and the No Talks Period Until 1989

The two Koreas rarely engaged in constructive talks or interactions between the conclusion of the 1953 Armistice Agreement and 1989. One of the very few occasions when they did interact resulted in the July 4 South–North Joint Communiqué in 1972 (hereinafter the 1972 Joint Communiqué), signed by the Director of the Central Intelligence Agency in ROK (Hu-rak Lee) and the Director of the Organisation and Guidance Department in DPRK (Young-joo Kim).[17] The 1972 Joint Communiqué was the result of inter-Korean meetings between high-ranking officials, as proposed by the Red Cross Societies from both sides in 1971.[18] The 1972 Joint Communiqué set the tone for future relations between ROK and DPRK, setting forth three basic principles to achieve reunification: "First, unification shall be achieved independently, without depending on foreign powers and without foreign interference;" "Second, unification shall be achieved through peaceful means, without resorting to the use of force against each other;" and "Third, a great national unity as one people shall be sought first, transcending differences in ideas, ideologies, and systems".[19] The Communiqué's orientation towards reunification was also reflected in the

[15] Eui-Gak Hwang, The Search for a Unified Korea 4 (2010).

[16] Yoo, *supra* note 12, at 88.

[17] July 4th North–South Joint Communiqué, N Kor-S Kor, July 4, 1972 [hereinafter the 1972 Joint Communiqué]. Available at: https://peacemaker.un.org/korea-4july-communique72.

[18] Don Oberdorfer and Robert Carlin, The Two Koreas: A Contemporary History 18–20 (2013).

[19] 1972 Joint Communiqué, Point 1.

Yushin Constitution (the Fourth Republic) of ROK, which was amended immediately following the joint statement.[20] Additionally, such principles indicated the two Koreas' intention to define their relationship as strictly bilateral, without undue "multilateral" influence from countries like the United States and China.[21] Furthermore, ROK and DPRK agreed in the Communiqué to "carry out numerous exchanges in various fields", and to "install a direct telephone line" to "prevent the outbreak of unexpected military incidents".[22] The relationship between the two Koreas remained dormant (known as the No Talks Period) until the conclusion of the Agreement on Reconciliation, Non-Aggression, and Exchanges and Cooperation between South and North Korea[23] in 1991 (hereinafter the 1991 Basic Agreement). Nonetheless, the 1972 Joint Communiqué served as a constructive first step towards further confidence building, political dialogue, and economic cooperation in the ensuing decades.[24]

As negotiations between the United States and China progressed, the ROK and DPRK began to engage in a peaceful conversation, vowing in 1972 to explore a route to reunification. At the beginning of the conversation, the DPRK made mention of positive aspects of the ROK, such as the Inter-Korean Red Cross, but then moved on to rural underdevelopment in the South, and the gap between rich and poor. Ignoring criticism from DPRK, President Park's authoritarian regime launched an industrial program targeted at expanding heavy machinery and chemical industries with a limited number of corporations. President Park also announced the Rural Revitalisation Program, which was not about improving rural areas, but instead focused on large conglomerates such as Hyundai, LG, Samsung, and Daewoo.[25] As these large conglomerates grew, the companies and politicians exchanged bribes for political favours.

In ROK, the lack of democratic legitimacy and increasing corruption caused mass protests against the dictatorship of President Park. On October 26, 1979, President Park Chung-hee's eighteen-year military dictatorship came to an end when Kim Jaegyu (1926–1980), a former South Korean Army lieutenant general, and Director of the Korean Central Intelligence Agency (KCIA), assassinated Park inside the Blue House.[26] The end of Park's eighteen years of authoritarian rule gave rise to much anxiety concerning constitutional procedures.

[20] *See* de Bear, *supra* note 8, at 833–34 (referencing 1972 Daehanminkuk Hunbeob [Hunbeob] [Constitution] (Dec 27, 1972) (S Kor), pmbl, arts 37–43, 46).

[21] *Id.*, at 829; *see also* Roh, *supra* note 7, at 163.

[22] 1972 Joint Communiqué, Points 3 & 5.

[23] Agreement on Reconciliation, Non-Aggression, and Exchanges and Cooperation between South and North Korea, Dec 13, 1991 [hereinafter the 1991 Basic Agreement]. Available at: https://peacemaker.un.org/korea-reconciliation-nonaggression91. The original agreement was signed in English and French.

[24] Sabine Burghart and Rudiger Frank, *Inter-Korean Cooperation 2000–2008: Commercial and Non-Commercial Transactions and Human Exchanges* 8 (Vienna Working Papers on East Asian Economy and Society, Working Paper 1(1), 2008).

[25] Yoo, *supra* note 12, at 119.

[26] *Id.* at 122.

Chun Doo-hwan, a major general of the ROK army, soon declared himself President of ROK on the strength of his military position. As word circulated throughout the country, protests broke out with university students and ordinary citizens in Gwangju breaking into police stations and armouries to steal firearms. Within a few weeks, there were tens of thousands of protesters, and President Chun deployed the military to crush the revolt, resulting in approximately 600 deaths, including both soldiers and citizens.[27] The Gwangju Uprising helped to shift the country to a democratic form of government. Finally, in 1985, the ROK constitution was modified to allow for direct presidential elections, paving the way for General Roh Tae-woo to become ROK's 13th president. President Roh guaranteed a greater scope of political liberalisation, initiated an anti-corruption campaign, and spearheaded the ROK joining the United Nations.[28]

C. United Nations Membership, 1991 Basic Agreement, and Kaesong Industrial Complex

Each of the two Koreas have long claimed to be the sole legitimate government and representative of Korea, and have opposed either of them joining the United Nations alone because of the adverse implications for reunification.[29] In addition, the influence and veto power of China and the Soviet Union stymied the ROK's multiple attempts to apply to the United Nations for membership on its own after obtaining observer status in 1949.[30] Against the backdrop of the dramatically changed global political landscape following the collapse of the Soviet Union, the United States' removal of its nuclear weapons from the ROK, and the successful economic development and democratisation of the ROK, the DPRK may have come to realise that it would have to accept the dual membership proposal and coexist alongside the ROK in the United Nations.[31] The General Assembly, at its first plenary meeting on September 17, 1991, considered separate applications for membership from the ROK and DPRK and, based on the recommendations of the Security Council, admitted both countries to the United Nations.[32] Despite their uneven political, economic, and military voice at the international level, the two Koreas have had equal legal status in front of the United Nations since the adoption of 1991 General Assembly Resolution 46/1.

Three months after the passage of Resolution 46/1, the 1991 Basic Agreement was concluded between the ROK and DPRK, serving as the first concrete step

[27] *Id.* at 125.

[28] SC Res 702 (Aug 8, 1991).

[29] Chi Young Pak, Korea and the United Nations 63 (2000).

[30] *Id.* at 64.

[31] *See* Burghart and Frank, *supra* note 24, at 8–9; David E Sanger, *North Korea Reluctantly Seeks U.N. Seat*, New York Times (May 29, 1991). Available at: www.nytimes.com/1991/05/29/world/north-korea-reluctantly-seeks-un-seat.html.

[32] GA Res 46/1 (Sep 17, 1991).

to institutionalise inter-Korean trade. The 1991 Basic Agreement reaffirmed the three principles established by the 1972 Joint Communiqué, as well as emphasising the determination to "remove the state of political and military confrontation and achieve national reconciliation", and to "realise multi-faceted exchanges and cooperation to advance common national interests and prosperity".[33] It was also noted by the ROK and DPRK in the 1991 Basic Agreement that their relations are "not … a relationship between states", but, rather, "a special interim relationship stemming from the process towards reunification".[34] The 1991 Basic Agreement required both the ROK and DPRK to respect one another's political regimes, not to interfere in each other's internal affairs, and to cease mutual competition and confrontation in international organisations.[35] Importantly, the 1991 Basic Agreement established a South-North Political Committee between high-level officials and a South-North Liaison Office in Panmunjon to ensure the effective implementation of the Agreement.[36] In terms of economic cooperation, the Agreement required the two Koreas to "engage in economic exchanges and cooperation, including the joint development of resources, the trade of goods *as domestic commerce* [emphasis added] and joint ventures", in addition to cooperation in areas such as science and technology, education, health, the environment, and the arts.[37] The ROK and DPRK were further required to promote – on an "intra-Korean" basis – travel and contact, correspondence and reunion visits, railroad reconnection, postal and telecommunications services, and joint efforts in relevant international organisations.[38] To effectively implement economic cooperation and exchanges, the Agreement established a Joint South–North Economic Exchange and Cooperation Commission among high-level officials.[39] While there were certain weaknesses in the 1991 Agreement,[40] this marked the first time that the two Koreas had both called for the institutionalisation of economic cooperation.

Another important development in relation to inter-Korean economic cooperation during the Kim Dae-jung administration was the establishment of the Kaesong Industrial Complex (KIC) framework, which was initially a private endeavour led by the Hyundai Group in 1998 but was quickly adopted by the ROK government.[41] Since its establishment in 2000, the KIC has been a focal

[33] 1991 Basic Agreement, pmbl.
[34] *Id.*
[35] *Id.*, arts 1–3, 6.
[36] *Id.*, arts 7 and 8.
[37] *Id.*, arts 15 and 16.
[38] *Id.*, arts 17–21.
[39] *Id.*, arts 22 and 23.
[40] For instance, some commentators have highlighted the lack of safeguard agreement in relation to DPRK's nuclear weapons program, which seemed troublesome to the international community. *See* de Bear, *supra* note 8, at 843–44. For relevant discussion about the 1991 Basic Agreement, *see also* Hyug-Baeg Im and Yu-Jeong Choi, *Inter-Korean and Cross-Strait Relations through the Window of Regional Integration Theories*, 51 Asian Surv 785 (2011); and Roh, *supra* note 7, at 161–62.
[41] *See* de Bear, *supra* note 8, at 856–57 (referring to examples such as Gaeseong Gongeop Jigu Jiweonae Gwanhan Beopyul [Kaesong Industrial Zone Support Act], Act No 8484, May 25, 2007).

point and primary site for economic cooperation (allowing ROK businesses to manufacture products by using DPRK labour resources), with the aims of alleviating tensions across the KDZ and providing a channel for the DPRK to reform its economy.[42] As elaborated below, the KIC has been very important to North Korea in economic terms and has played a crucial role in inter-Korean trade.[43]

D. Sunshine Policy, Inter-Korean Summits, and June 15 Joint Declaration

After the 1991 Basic Agreement, the two Koreas have slowly worked towards more stable relations based on the Agreement's institutionalisation premises, but they have yet to agree upon the optimal approach to reunification.[44] In 1998, in the context of the growing gap between the two Koreas in terms of economic development, ROK President Kim Dae-jung adopted the Sunshine Policy (officially titled "Reconciliation and Cooperation Policy") to address its relationship with the DPRK and soften the latter's hostile attitude.[45] The Sunshine Policy aimed to provide economic assistance to the North and maintain a high level of security and reconciliation with the North, and indeed contributed to a few high-profile investments from the South and increased political interactions between the two sides, including the two Korean Summits (held in June 2000 and October 2007, see discussion *infra*).[46]

Against this backdrop, the first inter-Korean Summit between Kim Dae-jung and Kim Jung-il – "the largest and most monumental development between the two Koreas since the end of the Korean War"[47] – was held on June 13–15, 2000 in Pyongyang, despite multiple scandals concerning money and politics surrounding North–South relations.[48] On June 15, 2000, the two Korean leaders issued the North–South Joint Declaration (hereinafter the June 15 Joint Declaration) in

[42] *See* Mark E Manyin and Dick K Nanto, Cong Research Serv, RL34093, The Kaesong North–South Korean Industrial Complex 5 (2011). Available at: www.fas.org/sgp/crs/row/RL34093.pdf.

[43] *See* Pierce Lee, *Rules of Origin and the Kaesong Industrial Complex: South Korea's Uphill Battle Against the Principle of Territoriality*, 39 NC J Int'l L 1, 7–8 (2013).

[44] Im and Choi, *supra* note 40, at 795.

[45] Making a reference to the Greek fable "The North Wind and the Sun", President Kim stated that "sunshine is more effective than strong wind in making North Korea come out of isolation and confrontation". Burghart and Frank, *supra* note 24, at 9.

[46] For more discussion on the implementation and criticisms of the Sunshine Policy, *see generally* Key-Young Son, South Korean Engagement Policies and North Korea: Identities, Norms and the Sunshine Policy (2006); Hyun-key Kim Hogarth, *South Korea's Sunshine Policy, Reciprocity and Nationhood*, 11 Persp Glob Dev & Tech 99 (2012).

[47] De Bear, *supra* note 8, at 855.

[48] There were allegations and public critique towards the Kim Dae-jung administration for having paid the North millions of dollars to have a summit meeting with Kim Jung-il. The involvement of the state-owned Korea Development Bank and the Hyundai group in transferring a huge amount of money to the North resulted in bribery charges against high-level government officials and company leaders. *See* Don Kirk, *South Korean Leader Assailed on* Funds Transfer to North, New York Times (Jan. 31, 2003). Available at: www.nytimes.com/2003/01/31/international/asia/south-korean-leader-assailed-on-funds-transfer-to-north.html.

the names of the President of the ROK and the National Defence Commission Chairman of the DPRK, concluding the "historical meeting and summit talks".[49] The two Koreas agreed in the June 15 Joint Declaration to address the issue of reunification (wherein ROK supported a confederation model and the DPRK backed a loose form of the federation) as well as humanitarian matters, and to facilitate the "balanced development of the national economy through economic cooperation" and "cooperation and exchanges in civic, cultural, sports, health, environmental and all other fields".[50] The June 15 Joint Declaration yet again emphasised in its text that both sides had to further reinforce economic cooperation and exchanges to promote economic growth on the peninsula.

After 2003, President Roh Moo-hyun received a great deal of criticism from the United States and conservative groups from South Korea for following in his predecessor's footsteps and continuing the Sunshine Policy under a different name: the "Peace and Prosperity Policy".[51] The renewed Sunshine Policy emphasised the importance of addressing the nuclear crisis in the short-term, achieving peaceful relations in the mid-term, and becoming an economic hub in North-eastern Asia in the long term.[52] Nevertheless, in that same year, the DPRK announced its withdrawal from the Nuclear Non-proliferation Treaty and freed itself from the multilateral monitoring mechanisms attached to its Safeguards Agreement with the International Atomic Energy Agency.[53] In the midst of such a negative atmosphere and heightened international tensions (especially with regard to the roles played by the United States during this period)[54] resulting from the nuclear crisis, the second inter-Korean summit between Roh Moo-hyun and Kim Jung-il was held in 2007.[55] The 2007 Summit resulted in an eight-point agreement signed by both leaders that aims to achieve permanent peace, pledging that the "highest authorities" from both sides "will meet frequently for the advancement of relations between the two sides".[56] Albeit under different policy flags, both administrations under Presidents Kim Dae-jung and Roh Moo-hyun

[49] South-North Joint Declaration, N. Kor. S. Kor., June 15, 2000 [hereinafter June 15 Joint Declaration]. Available at: https://peacemaker.un.org/koreadprk-southnorthdeclaration.

[50] *Id.*

[51] Choong Nam Kim, *The Roh Moo Hyun Government's Policy Toward North Korea* 7, E-W Ctr, Working Paper No 11 (2005).

[52] *Id.* at 14.

[53] *Id.* at 13. *See also North Korea Withdraws from Nuclear Treaty*, The Guardian (Jan 10, 2003). Available at: www.theguardian.com/world/2003/jan/10/northkorea1.

[54] During this period, the United States urged ROK to leverage its Sunshine Policy/Peace and Prosperity Policy (or, engagement policies) and toughen its communications and negotiations with DPRK, which effectively caused some frictions between the United States and ROK. In this regard, President Roh Moo-hyun stated that the United States (and Japan) stopped being a positive force in inter-Korean relations and claimed that it was crucial to establish its own independent foreign policy from the United States (referring to China as a potential alternative) and strengthen its military capacity to build a self-reliant military. *See* Kim, *supra* note 51, at 15, 23–24.

[55] Adian Foster-Carter, *North Korea-South Korea Relations: Summit Success?*, 9(3) Compar Connections 93, 93–94 (2007).

[56] Declaration on the Advancement of South-North Korean Relations Peace and Prosperity, N Kor-S Kor, Oct 4, 2007. Available at: https://peacemaker.un.org/node/1659.

proactively engaged and provided aid to the DPRK to facilitate a constructive environment, build mutual trust, foster economic interactions, and pave the way to peaceful reunification.[57]

E. Lee Myung-bak and Park Geun-hye Administration

President Lee Myung-bak, an ROK politician and businessman, opposed the Sunshine Policy during his term, from 2008 to 2013.[58] Breaking with past precedent, President Lee announced that he would not recklessly invest money in North Korea. President Lee Myung-bak argued that the previous administration's engagement policies ignored the DPRK's human rights violations and expanding nuclear program, and that continuing an "aid-economic relationship" would be nothing more than an exercise in rhetoric without fruitful result.[59] A policy called "Vision 3000: Denuclearisation and Openness" – through which the ROK promised to assist the DPRK in increasing its per capita income to $3,000 in the coming decade if the latter agreed to open its economy and cease its nuclear program – was proposed by the Lee administration to the DPRK.[60] Additionally, if the DPRK showed a willingness to reduce its inordinate nuclear programs, President Lee of ROK offered to help improve the DPRK's economy, education, infrastructure, finances, and living conditions within five years. Such an aggressive proposal was quickly rejected by the DPRK, and subsequently, South-North talks froze and the termination of the KIC was once again discussed.[61] Inter-Korean relations became increasingly troubled after the Cheonan ship and Yeonpyeong Island incidents in 2010,[62] and President Lee Myung-bak changed his conditional engagement policy to a disengagement policy, "turn[ing] 'the clock of reunification' back to the Cold War era".[63] The Sunshine Policy (or, more generally, engagement policies) was officially declared a failure by the ROK's Ministry of Unification in November 2010.[64]

[57] Burghart and Frank, *supra* note 24, at 9–10. It was estimated that the two administrations together provided North Korea with nearly $3 billion in aid. Alisher Khamidov, *The Lee Myung-bak Revolution: Explaining Continuity and Change in South Korea's Foreign Policy*, SAIS U.S.-Kor YB 23, 26 (2008).

[58] *Id.*

[59] *Id.* at 26–27. *See also* de Bear, *supra* note 8, at 863–64.

[60] Im and Choi, *supra* note 40, at 798–99.

[61] *Id.*

[62] *See* de Bear, *supra* note 8, at 866–71.

[63] Im and Choi, *supra* note 40, at 799.

[64] *See South Korea Formally Declares End to Sunshine Policy*, Voice of America (Nov 17, 2010). Available at: www.voanews.com/a/south-korea-formally-declares-end-to-sunshine-policy--108904544/130750.html; for more discussion on the policies adopted during the period, *see* Ministry of Unification of South Korea, 2010 White Paper On Reunification. Available at: www.unikorea.go.kr/eng_unikorea/news/Publications/whitepaper/.

Park Geun-hye began her term as the first female president of ROK in 2012, but did not complete her term of office as she was impeached in 2017.[65] Park Geun-hye was sentenced to 25 years in jail after being found guilty of abuse of power and coercion.[66] In addition to the jail term, Park Geun-hye was fined 18 billion won.[67] In general, President Park adopted a policy that fell between the engagement policies of Presidents Kim Dae-jung Roh and Moo-hyun, and the disengagement policy of President Lee Myung-bak, while noting that "[a] lack of trust has long undermined attempts at genuine reconciliation between North and South Korea".[68] Based on the constitutional mandate to seek peaceful unification, President Park argued that ROK "should adopt a policy of 'trustpolitik,' establishing mutually binding expectations based on global norms", also contending that "steps should not be taken for mere political expediency".[69] Furthermore, two coexisting guidelines were to be kept in mind by the ROK when dealing with the North: "First, North Korea must keep its agreements made with South Korea and the international community to establish a minimum level of trust, and second, there must be assured consequences for actions that breach the peace".[70] Therefore, as President Park adopted a trustpolitik policy falling between proactive engagement and aggressive disengagement, she focused on denuclearisation, as well as the necessity of requiring affirmative actions to be taken by the DPRK, especially regarding its commitment under the 1953 Armistice Agreement and the June 15 Joint Declarations.[71]

F. Moon Administration, and the United States' Influence under Trump and Biden

Following the impeachment of Park Geun-hye, Moon Jae-in was elected as the nineteenth President of the ROK. Since taking office, President Moon Jae-in has

[65] *Park Geun-hye. South Korea's First Female President*, BBC News (Apr 6, 2018). Available at: www.bbc.com/news/world-asia-20787271.

[66] Choe Sang-Hun, *Park Geun-hye, Ex-South Korean Leader, Gets 25 Years in Prison*, New York Times (Aug 24, 2018). Available at: www.nytimes.com/2018/08/24/world/asia/park-geun-hye-sentenced-south-korea.html?smid=url-share.

[67] South Korean court rejects former president Park Geun-hye's appeal against corruption conviction, ABC News (Jan 14, 2021). Available at: www.abc.net.au/news/2021-01-14/former-south-korea-president-park-guen-hye-final-appeal-fails/13058974.

[68] Park Geun-Hye, *A New Kind of Korea: Building Trust Between Pyongyang and Seoul*, 90(5) Foreign Affs (2011). Available at: www.foreignaffairs.com/articles/68136/park-geun-hye/a-new-kind-of-korea. *See also* de Bear, *supra* note 8, at 873–75; Gi-Wook Shin and David Straub, *Jang Song-taek Purge Further Undermines North Korea's Foreign Relations*, East Asia Forum (Feb 12, 2014). Available at: https://eastasiaforum.org/2014/02/12/jang-song-taek-purge-further-undermines-north-koreas-foreign-relations/.

[69] *Id.*

[70] *Id.*

[71] For instance, DPRK has withdrawn from the Armistice Agreement in 1994, 1996, 2003, 2006, 2009, and 2013. *See Chronology of Major North Korean Statements on the Korean War Armistice*, Yonhap News (May 28, 2009). Available at: https://en.yna.co.kr/view/AEN20090528004200315.

received positive ratings for engagement with DPRK. President Moon created various political policies regarding the relationship with DPRK, which have resulted in inter-Korean summits, agreements, family reunions, and military confidence-building measures. As an open, democratic country, the ROK enjoys substantial economic and diplomatic ties with other nations, while the DPRK has more complicated diplomatic relations due to its unwillingness to relinquish its nuclear weapons.[72] Under President Moon and his "Sunshine Policy", the ROK administration remained engaged with North Korea and has attempted to repair relations.[73] For instance, the Kaesong Industrial Complex (KIC) involved extensive cooperation between the DPRK and ROK governments, as well as associated private companies. However, in several instances, DPRK leadership has demonstrated a lack of concern towards the development of inter-Korean ties, often holding diplomatic relations hostage to obtain what it desires and liberate resources. Despite this hardship, President Moon did not stop, but insisted that major government agencies responsible for inter-Korean relationships continue to develop the relationship with North Korea. Major government agencies responsible for inter-Korean relationships include the Ministry of Unification for ROK and the Committee for the Peaceful Reunification of Korea (CPRK) for DPRK.[74]

Prior to Donald Trump's election, the U.S. had made numerous attempts to address problems posed by North Korea's nuclear weapons, including increased military cooperation with regional partners, broad sanctions, and non-proliferation measures such as export limits. The U.S. also pursued substantial diplomatic endeavours to persuade North Korea to stop its nuclear weapons program in exchange for economic assistance from the United States. None of these measures proved successful. President Trump attempted to depart from past administrations' diplomatic techniques by cultivating a personal rapport with North Korean Supreme Leader Kim Jong Un, ostensibly to cultivate mutual trust in the talks. However, President Trump's approach did not rethink the U.S. negotiating position in the discussions, instead maintaining the existing strategy, which did not enable North Korea to engage in a phased denuclearisation process. President Trump's policy framework was similar to previous U.S. administrations: complete and verifiable denuclearisation as the first step, followed by peace, reconciliation, sanctions reductions, and stability.[75]

[72] Amanda Macias, *North Korea says it won't restart nuclear discussions until U.S. drops its 'hostile policies'*, CNBC (March 17, 2021). Available at: www.cnbc.com/2021/03/17/north-korea-says-wont-restart-talks-until-us-drops-its-hostile-policies.html.

[73] Eui-Gak Hwang, The Search for a Unified Korea 119 (2010).

[74] *Weekly Report on North Korea from March 27 to April 2, 2021 (No 1563)*, Ministry of Unification (S Kor) (Apr 2, 2021). Available at: www.unikorea.go.kr/eng_unikorea/relations/infoNK/weekly/?boardId=bbs_0000000000000040&mode=view&cntId=54352&category=&pageIdx=10.

[75] Daniel Wertz, National Committee on North Korea, The U.S., North Korea, and Nuclear Diplomacy (Oct 2018). Available at: www.ncnk.org/resources/briefing-papers/all-briefing-papers/history-u.s.-dprk-relations.

Following the election of Joe Biden on November 3, 2020, the U.S. government supported diplomacy between North and South Korea to achieve denuclearisation with limited willingness. Joe Biden's administration decided to continue supporting South Korea's defence by providing 30,000 U.S. soldiers, stationed throughout South Korea. In the future, President Joe Biden will also seek to pursue South Korea's Pyongyang peace initiative to have a significant impact on the inter-Korean relationship, where the U.S. government supported President Moon's longstanding peace with Pyongyang as a primary policy goal.[76] In the midst of the COVID-19 pandemic, on January 17, 2022, North Korea launched two suspected ballistic missiles, marking the country's fourth missile test in January 2022, and seventh since September 2021. This spate of tests is seen by many as a way to pressure the Biden administration into easing sanctions under its policy toward Pyongyang, which is limited to engagement and is not working.[77]

When the Biden administration concluded its review of its North Korea policy in April 2021, it announced that it would pursue a middle ground between the Obama administration's "strategic patience" and a mixture of "maximum pressure" and personal engagement with North Korea's leader Kim Jong Un.[78] During the same month, Jen Psaki, the White House press secretary, stated that President Biden seeks a "calibrated, practical approach that is open to and will explore diplomacy with the DPRK". Indeed, the United States has reached out to North Korea, both publicly and privately, in pursuit of the goal of denuclearisation, with the incentive of reducing economic sanctions. However, North Korea did not accept this offer and continued its ballistic missile and nuclear weapons programs. In response to the nuclear weapons actions threatening the region, the Biden administration imposed the first sanctions on North Koreans tied to the ballistic missile program on Wednesday, January 12, 2022. To address their support of, or linkages to, North Korea's ballistic missile programs, the U.S. has placed sanctions on North Korean and Russian people and businesses tied to the recent North Korean ballistic missile program.[79] Needless to say, the United States has been concentrating on recovering from the pandemic challenges, settling the Russia-Ukraine war, and dealing with China. Meanwhile, the U.S.

[76] Tobias Harris, Abigail Bard, and Haneul Lee, Center for American Progress, Prospects for Diplomacy with North Korea (Nov 3, 2021). Available at: www.americanprogress.org/article/prospects-diplomacy-north-korea/.

[77] *US and Allies Condemn North Korea over Missile Test "Provocations"*, The Guardian (Feb 13, 2022). Available at: www.theguardian.com/world/2022/feb/13/us-and-allies-condemn-north-korea-over-missile-test-provocations.

[78] Anthony Ruggiero and Matthew Zweiz, *Biden's North Korea Policy Needs Rebooting*, Foreign Policy (Jan 24, 2022). Available at: https://foreignpolicy.com/2022/01/24/biden-north-korea-missiles-sanctions/.

[79] Amanda Macias, *U.S. Sanctions 8 People and Entities following North Korean Missile Launches*, CNBC (Jan 12, 2022). Available at: www.cnbc.com/2022/01/12/us-sanctions-5-north-koreans-over-weapons-programs-following-missile-launches.html.

has consistently, publicly stated that it is prepared to negotiate denuclearisation and human rights with the DPRK at any time. Pyongyang, on the other hand, has indicated that it will not engage in discussions with Washington unless the sanctions against the North are abandoned.[80]

G. Yoon Administration: Old Wine in Old Bottles?

After five years in the presidency, Moon's presidency ended and Yoon Suk-yeol, candidate of the conservative People Power Party, won the election on March 9 and assumed office as president on May 10, 2022.[81] Yoon came to office promising an "audacious plan" to enhance North Korea's economy in exchange for denuclearisation in his inauguration speech.[82] President Yoon, the country's former top prosecutor, came to office expecting to usher in a period of conservative party dominance that would dramatically alter the country's policies in the face of North Korea's nuclear aspirations. Before becoming the President of South Korea, President Yoon was a political newcomer who ascended through the ranks of various prosecutor's offices and, most notably, assisted in the conviction of former President Park Geun-hye in her impeachment trial.[83]

President Yoon has urged increased collaboration with Washington in dealing with North Korea's growing nuclear threat and believes that international sanctions are necessary to pressure North Korea to give up its nuclear weapons. Unlike President Moon's administration, which sought fewer international sanctions, Yoon's administration will likely align its goals with those of the U.S. on denuclearisation.[84] During the electoral campaign, Inter-Korean relations were a vital issue, particularly with tensions increasing due to North Korea's missile testing. Indeed, North Korea demonstrated a new type of hypersonic missile with the ability to operate at very high speed. Yoon responded in the conventional manner, stating that the opportunity for diplomacy and dialogue will "always be left open" and "based on strong national defense posture, not of submission" to protect the citizens and safeguard the country. Nonetheless,

[80] Hyun-wook Kim, *A Korean Perspective on the Biden Administration's North Korea Policy*, The Stimson Center (Feb 28, 2022). Available at: www.stimson.org/2022/a-korean-perspective-on-the-biden-administrations-north-korea-policy/.

[81] Mitch Shin, *Yoon Suk-yeol Becomes South Korea's President-Elect*, The Diplomat (Mar 10, 2022). Available at: https://thediplomat.com/2022/03/yoon-suk-yeol-becomes-south-koreas-president-elect/.

[82] Jessie Yeung and Gawon Bae, *South Korea's new President Yoon Suk Yeol Urges North Korean Denuclearization in Inauguration Address*, CNN (May 10, 2022). Available at: https://edition.cnn.com/2022/05/10/asia/yoon-suk-yeol-south-korea-president-inauguration-intl-hnk/index.html.

[83] Michelle Ye Hee Lee and Min Joo Kim, *What You Need to Know about South Korea's President-Elect, Yoon Suk-yeol*, Washington Post (Mar 9, 2022). Available at: www.washingtonpost.com/world/2022/03/09/south-korea-yoon-suk-yeol-president/.

[84] *Id.*

many worried a sudden change in South Korea's behaviour might trigger heightened military tensions.[85]

Soon after assuming office, the Yoon administration released an initial policy blueprint for foreign and national security, which laid out Yoon's perspectives on the relationship with North Korea, a strong national security and defence stance, and South Korea's global and regional diplomatic interests.[86] Yoon's North Korean policy platform encompasses three goals – complete denuclearisation, reciprocity, and human rights. Unlike Moon's administration, Yoon's foreign policy explores prioritising deterrence of North Korea within South Korea's defence and global defence priorities.[87]

Alongside broader geopolitical unrest in the region, the inter-Korean relationship worsened during the first years of the Yoon administration. North Korea arguably took advantage of Russia's invasion of Ukraine and the heightening of cross-Strait tensions and attempted to advance its military aggression in Northern Asia. Supporting the United States' Indo-pacific strategy and regional security, President Yoon recently restated the importance of regional peace and emphasised that any cooperation (by China or Russia) with North Korea on military affairs should halt right away.[88] During his 2023 New Year's address, Yoon vowed to "completely block" North Korea's nuclear threat and to strengthen the ROK's military preparedness in hopes of achieving "a true and lasting peace based on strength".[89] Around the same time, Kim Jong Un declared that North Korea will no longer seek reunification with South Korea, and that it will further boost its military power, including spy satellites and nuclear materials, so as to counter what he called "US-led confrontation" and "South Korea provocation"[90] Kim Jong Un also exchanged messages with China's Xi Jinping on forging closer ties and cooperation between the two countries, posing further risks of instability in the region.[91]

[85] Jessie Yeung et al., *How South Korea's New President Could Shake up the Region*, CNN (Mar 11, 2022). Available at: https://edition.cnn.com/2022/03/10/asia/yoon-suk-yeol-new-south-korean-president-stance-intl-hnk/index.html.

[86] Scott Snyder, *South Korean President-Elect Yoon Suk-Yeol's Early Foreign Policy Challenges*, Forbes (Mar 24, 2022). Available at: www.forbes.com/sites/scottasnyder/2022/03/24/south-korean-president-elect-yoon-suk-yeols-early-foreign-policy-challenges/?sh=6ff57658656d.

[87] *Id.*

[88] Jack Kim, *South Korea's Yoon Says any Military Cooperation with North Korea Must Stop*, Reuters (Sep 6, 2023). Available at: www.reuters.com/world/asia-pacific/south-koreas-yoon-says-any-attempt-cooperate-militarily-with-north-korea-must-2023-09-06/.

[89] Steven Borowiec, *South Korea's Yoon Vows to "Completely Block" North's Nuclear Threat*, Nikkei Asia (Jan 1, 2024). Available at: https://asia.nikkei.com/Politics/Defense/South-Korea-s-Yoon-vows-to-completely-block-North-s-nuclear-threat.

[90] Hyung-Jin Kim, *North Korea's Kim Vows to Launch 3 More Spy Satellites and Produce More Nuclear Materials in 2024*, AP (Jan 1, 2024). Available at: https://apnews.com/article/north-korea-kim-spy-satellites-nuclear-party-meeting-236fcaee8927d8f69359b45aaa88e2c0.

[91] Jack Kim, *North Korea Kim Jong Un, China's Xi Exchange Message Vowing Closer Ties, Yonhap Reports*, Reuters (Jan 1, 2024). Available at: www.reuters.com/world/asia-pacific/north-korea-kim-jong-un-chinas-xi-exchange-message-vowing-closer-ties-yonhap-2023-12-31/.

II. INTER-KOREA ECONOMIC RELATIONS: FORM AND SUBSTANCE OF COOPERATION

This section provides a detailed discussion of projects established by North and South Korean governments to foster an inter-Korean economic relationship. It outlines two projects on which both governments have worked for years to improve both political relations and economic trade cooperation. This section dives deeper into the development of inter-Korean economic relations since the late 1980s and provides a detailed analysis of each project.

A. Existing Economic Cooperation between North and South Korea: An Overview

Inter-Korean economic cooperation has developed from general trade flow, production orders from the South (in specific sectors such as food, textiles, and television), and KIC projects to large-scale investments initiated by Hyundai at Mount Geumgang (or Mount Geumkang).[92] Besides the KIC and Mount Geumgang investment programs – the focal points of South-North trade – economic cooperation between the two Koreas has been extremely limited due to enormous ideological and political differences.[93] In addition, as noted by Burghart and Frank:

> [T]he South Korean economy becomes increasingly dependent on China but would not be able to exist without the decades-old close economic cooperation with the United States and Japan. On the other hand, South Koreans regard improved relations with the North as vital for their future, a certain decrease in unification enthusiasm notwithstanding. Analysts in Seoul have understood that unification will be very costly, and that it would be wise to pay these costs gradually in advance. They want to do so by raising the status of transportation and communication networks, industry and services closer to the South Korean level in a controlled fashion, rather than being faced with the herculean task of accomplishing all this within a limited period of time in order to avoid unrest, destabilization and massive migration after a possible collapse of North Korea.[94]

Drawn from the most recent data and statistics published by the Ministry of Unification of South Korea, Figure 3.1 presents the status of inter-Korean

[92] For more discussion on the three early stages (1989–1997, 1998–2002, and 2003–2007) of inter-Korean economic development, *see generally* Soo-Ho Lim, *The Future of Inter-Korean Economic Cooperation*, Samsung Economic Research Institute – Korea Economic Trends (12 Nov, 2007). Available at: www.samsungsgr.com (enter title into "search"); *see also* Hyo-Won Lee, *The Current State and Required Modifications of the Inter-Korean Exchange and Cooperation Act*, 11 J. Korean L. 55, 56 (2011).

[93] Burghart and Frank, *supra* note 24, at 9.

[94] *Id*, at 7.

exchange and cooperation from the South's perspective. The total volume of economic exchange between the South Korean and North Korean governments from 1989 to 2020 was 24,860 million USD. Inter-Korean trade was extremely limited in the years 1989 to 2002, worth only 642 million USD in total.[95] Since 2003, following a series of engagement policies, such as the Sunshine policy adopted by the Kim Dae-jung and Roh Moo-hyun administrations, inter-Korean trade and dialogue gradually grew (with trade reaching 724 million USD in 2003 alone).[96] The main cooperative business developments the North and South created during this stage were the railroad system and the Mount Geumgang Tourist Region. Nevertheless, given the discontinuation of engagement policies and the passive strategy of President Lee Myung-bak, inter-Korean trade refroze in the context of the cold and troubled relationship between ROK and DPRK (a remarkable drop in inter-Korean trade can be seen in 2013, as shown in Figures 3.1 and 3.2 below).

Tensions between the two Koreas grew, leading to a decrease in dialogue and fluctuating Inter-Korean trade volumes.[97] However, from 2013 to 2015, inter-Korean exchange and cooperation rapidly increased from 1,136 million USD to 2,714 million USD due to critical new trade policies announced by the North Korean government. The North Korean government crafted new policies advocating for diversification of trade channels between North and South Korea, and wanted to diversify export commodities, develop light industries, and reduce its reliance on natural resource exports. Indeed, to attract foreign investment, 'institutional and policy support' was developed.[98] While inter-Korean trade was rapidly increasing, political and military tensions were unstable due to the North Korean government conducting a third nuclear test in February 2013. Despite the rapid increase in inter-Korean economic trade from 2013 to 2015, the North Korean government then conducted a fourth nuclear test in January 2016, and inter-Korean economic cooperation took a step backward. On 10 February 2016, in response to the North Korean government's ongoing nuclear and missile tests, South Korean President Park Geun-hye announced, via the Ministry of Unification of South Korea, the closure of the Kaesong Industrial Complex (KIC). As shown in Figures 3.1 and 3.2, this caused inter-Korean economic trade to decrease to 333 million USD from 2,714 million USD.

[95] *See Inter-Korean Exchanges & Cooperation* [*Data and Statistics*], Ministry of Unification, Republic of Korea. Available at: www.unikorea.go.kr/eng_unikorea/relations/statistics/exchanges/ (last accessed Apr 26, 2024) [hereinafter *Inter-Korean Statistics*].

[96] *Id.*

[97] *Id.*

[98] Jong-kyu Lee and Jin-wook Nam, *North Korea's External Trade Relations*, *in* Outside Looking In: A View into the North Korean Economy 96 (J. James Kim and Han Minjeong eds, 2014).

Figure 3.1 Volume of South Korean Trade Entering and Exiting North Korea[99]

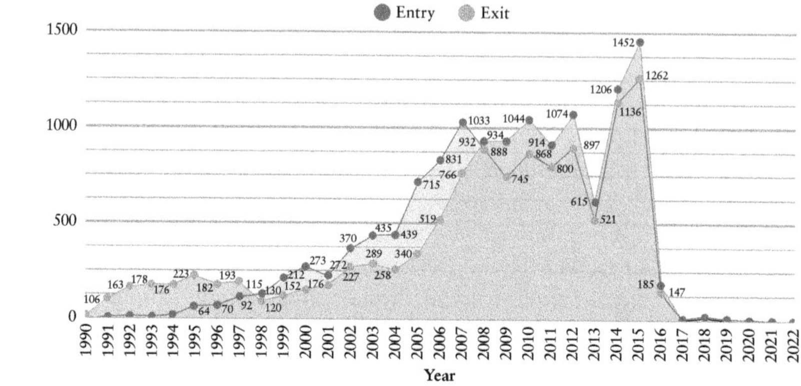

Year	1989	1990	1991	1992	1993	1994	1995	1996	1997	1998	1999	2000
Entry	19	12	106	163	178	176	223	182	193	92	122	152
Exit	0	1	6	11	8	18	64	70	115	130	212	273
Total	19	13	112	174	186	194	287	252	308	222	334	425

Year	2001	2002	2003	2004	2005	2006	2007	2008	2009	2010	2011	2012
Entry	176	272	289	258	340	519	766	932	934	1,044	914	1,074
Exit	227	370	435	439	715	831	1,033	888	745	868	800	897
Total	403	642	724	697	1,055	1,350	1,799	1,820	1,679	1,912	1,714	1,971

Year	2013	2014	2015	2016	2017	2018	2019	2020	2021	2022	Total
Entry	615	1,206	1,452	185	0	11	0	0	0	0	**12,605**
Exit	521	1,136	1,262	147	1	21	7	4	1	0	**12,256**
Total	1,136	2,342	2,714	332	1	32	7	4	1	0	**24,861**

Since the numbers were rounded off, the 'subtotal' of entries/exits for each year may be diffrent from the 'total'. A trade amount below one million dollars is marked by '0'. (Unit: Million Dollars)

Figure 3.2 Trade Volume by Type[100]

Class	Entry				Exit			(Unit: Million USD)
	General trade. Consignment processing	Economic cooperation (Gaeseong Industrial Complex. Mt. Geumgang Tourism. Other cooperation in light industry	Non-commercial trade (Governmental. Private support/ Social and cultural cooperation/ Light-water reactor (LWR) project)	Total	General trade. Consignment processing	Economic cooperation (Gaeseong Industrial Complex. Mt. Geumgang Tourism. Other cooperation in light	Non-commercial trade (Governmental. Private support/ Social and cultural cooperation/ Light-water reactor (LWR)	Total
2006	441	77	1	519	116	294	421	831
2007	646	120	–	766	146	520	367	1033
2008	624	308	–	932	184	596	108	888
2009	499	435	–	934	167	541	37	745
2010	334	710	–	1044	101	744	23	868
2011	4	909	1	914	–	789	11	800
2012	1	1073	–	1074	–	888	9	897
2013	1	615	–	616	–	518	3	521
2014	–	1206	–	1206	–	1132	4	1136
2015	–	1452	–	1452	–	1252	10	1262
2016	–	185	–	185	–	145	2	147
2017	–	–	–	–	–	–	1	1
2018	–	–	11	11	–	–	21	21
2019	–	–	–	–	–	–	7	7
2020	–	–	–	–	–	–	4	4
2021	–	–	–	–	–	–	1	1
2022	–	–	–	–	–	–	–	–
Total	2550	7090	13	9653	713	7420	1029	9162

[99] Ministry of Unification of South Korea, 2021 White Paper On Reunification 314, and Ministry of Unification of South Korea, 2023 White Paper On Reunification 266.

[100] Ministry of Unification of South Korea, 2023 White Paper on Reunification 268.

B. Kaesong Industrial Complex

As noted above, the KIC was operated by the Hyundai Group from 1998 against the backdrop of President Kim Dae-jung's Sunshine Policy and improved South-North relations.[101] In 2000, several months before the first inter-Korean summit meeting, President Kim Dae-jung announced his policy goal of establishing an inter-Korean economic community, which paved the way for the Hyundai Group to obtain Kim Jong-il's approval to secure exclusive KIC development rights.[102] Two months after the first inter-Korean summit meeting, Hyundai Asan subsequently signed an agreement with the Asia-Pacific Peace Committee of North Korea (APPC) regarding the construction and operation of the KIC.[103] Despite a few difficulties in the process, the DPRK announced the Kaesong Industrial District Act in November 2002 pursuant to the order of the Permanent Commission of the Supreme People's Assembly, which designated the KIC area a special economic zone.[104] A month later, the DPRK issued a certificate to Hyundai Asan, authorising the use of 16,000 acres of land for KIC development for up to 50 years; by the end of June 2003, the construction of KIC was in process.[105] It should be noted that to obtain such rights to the KIC, Hyundai Asan paid USD 12 million to the DPRK.[106] As rightly pointed out by Soo-hyun Lee:

> At its core, the KIC is a joint business venture between North and South Korea … Though its origin and composition are unconventional, the mechanics of the KIC are quite simple: South Korean firms ship raw materials to their subsidiaries based at the KIC; under South Korean managerial leadership, North Korean workers manufacture those raw materials into consumer goods; thereafter, those labour-intensive products are shipped back to South Korea for retail sale domestically or export abroad.[107]

In this sense, the ROK actually worked through a pseudo-private party, Hyundai Asan, to provide raw materials and management services (including

[101] *See* Eul-Chul Lim, Kaesong Industrial Complex: History, Pending Issues, and Outlook 4–7 (2007).

[102] *Id.* at 14.

[103] Gong-eobjigu geonseol-unyeong-e and wanhan hab-uiseo [Agreement on the Construction and Operation of the Industrial District], Hyundai Asan-Asia-Pacific Peace Committee of North Korea (Aug 22, 2000).

[104] JoseonminjuJu-ui-in Mingonghwagug Gaeseong Gong-eobjigubeob [Kaesong Industrial District Act] (promulgated by the Permanent Comm. of the Sup. People's Assemb, Nov 27, 2002); International Crisis Group, The Case for Kaesong: Fostering Korean Peace through Economic Ties (2019).

[105] *See* Ho Cheol Kim, *Does Annex 22-B of the Proposed United States-Korea Free Trade Agreement Contemplate and Allow for Trade with Respect to North Korea*, 40 Geo. J. Int'l L. 67, 70–73 (2008); *see also* Lim, *supra* note 101, at 31.

[106] Manyin and Nanto, *supra* note 42, at 11.

[107] Soo-hyun Lee, *Dispute Settlement in Cross-Border Public-Private Partnerships with Diplomatic Agendas: Learning from the Kaesong Industrial Complex*, 23(2) J Int'l & Area Stud 61, 62–63 (2016).

electricity, water, waste disposal, transportation, etc.) at KIC facilities, while the DPRK offered the land and labour.[108] The DPRK government received considerable foreign exchange from the wages paid by ROK firms, as well as leasing fees and insurance taxes (around USD 100 million annually), and the ROK benefited from the cheap labour (KIC workers from the DPRK earned around USD 63 monthly).[109] Furthermore, under its general engagement policies, the ROK government – with coordination by the Inter-Korean Cooperation District Policy Planning Division under the Ministry of Unification – has supplied South Korean companies with low-interest loans, tax exemptions and favourable tax rates, and even political risk insurance to facilitate the KIC investment.[110] Apart from the foreign exchange input, the DPRK has also benefited from various forms of commercial infrastructure constructed by ROK companies (for instance, the ROK's Korea Electric Power Corporation established power-transmission line to send high-voltage electricity to KIC). These have enabled the DPRK to attract foreign investment from countries other than the ROK. Additionally, the ROK has secured a relatively stable channel through which to engage with the DPRK.[111] Importantly, as can be seen from the description above, a notably defining feature of the KIC is the high level of government involvement and, hence, a high level of politicisation in establishing and operating the project.

Remarkably, the KIC business constituted a gigantic portion of inter-Korean trade during its operations. As shown in Figure 3.3 below, beginning in 2005, the number of Kaesong Industrial Complex Companies and associated production levels increased gradually until 2015. KIC projects came to an end due to the comprehensive suspension of the KIC project on February 10, 2016. Over ten years of operations, the North and South Korean governments were able to establish seven types of industries in the KIC, which generated 323,305 million USD over the decade.

The KIC operations were subject to many complicating influences, including political factors involving the ROK and DPRK governments, resulting in numerous problems. For instance, after President Lee Myung-bak discontinued the previous administration's engagement policies and announced an aggressive disengagement policy, the downturn in the inter-Korean relationship was

[108] *See* Pierce Lee, *supra* note 43, at 7.

[109] *See* Marcus Noland, Interview, *Are North and South Korea Back in Business?*, Council on Foreign Relations (Aug 14, 2013). Available at: www.cfr.org/interview/are-north-and-south-korea-back-business.

[110] Manyin and Nanto, *supra* note 42, at 6 and 12.

[111] *Id*, at 7.

Figure 3.3 Kaesong Industrial Complex Projects[112]

The Number of Kaesong Industrial Complex Companies

Year	2005	2006	2007	2008	2009	2010	2011	2012	2013	2014	2015
The Number of Companies	18	30	65	93	117	121	123	123	123	125	125

*The statistics for the Kaesong Industrial Complex were prepared as of the end of 2015, due to the comprehensive suspension of the Kaesong Industrial Complex on Feb. 10, 2016.

Number of Companies in the Complex (Total:125)

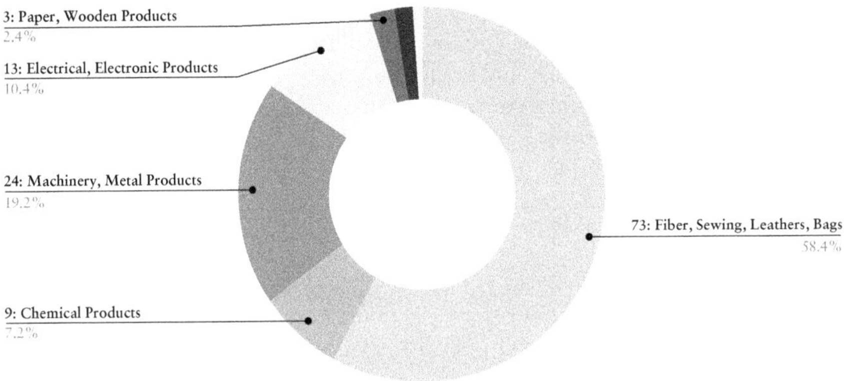

Year	2005	2006	2007	2008	2009	2010	2011	2012	2013	2014	2015	Total
The Number of Companies	1,491	7,373	18,478	25,142	25,648	32,332	40,185	46,950	22,379	46,997	56,330	323,305

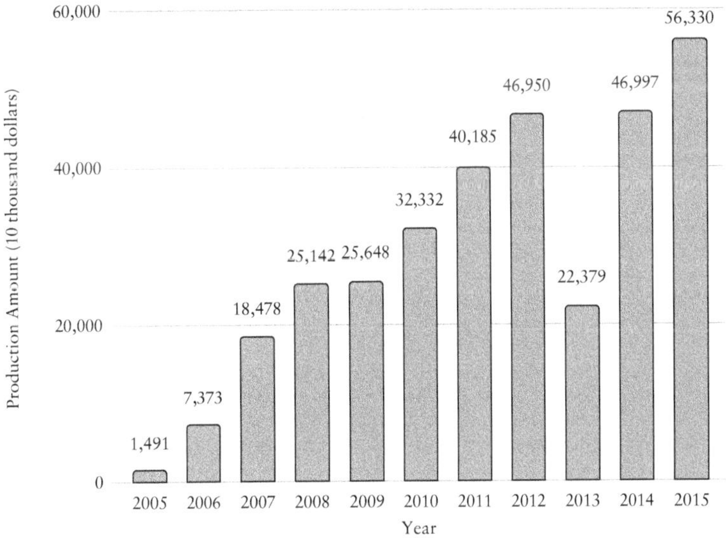

[112] Ministry of Unification of South Korea, 2021 White Paper on Reunification 317; and Ministry of Unification of South Korea, 2023 White Paper on Reunification 269.

followed by complications in terms of economic cooperation.[113] The suspension of the KIC was seen as a "war of pride" between the two Koreas, as the DPRK utilised the KIC as a political tool against the ROK who then demanded that the DPRK provide guarantees that would protect its KIC investment.[114] In addition to the "war of pride", there have been other controversies surrounding the operations of the KIC, including, *inter alia*, (1) regional security concerns over the risk of the DPRK using billions in foreign exchange garnered from the KIC to fund its nuclear weapons program and armed aggression,[115] (2) considerable uncertainty and instability regarding economic performance (such as sudden increases in wages for employees unilaterally imposed by the DPRK government) due to political and social factors,[116] (3) inadequate investment protection, enforcement mechanisms, and dispute settlement,[117] and (4) determination of origin of product rules under the WTO for KIC products (ordered by the ROK, but manufactured in the DPRK) – the DPRK is not a WTO Member and products deemed to originate there are subject to high tariffs.[118]

[113] *See* Bongchul Kim and Ho Kim, *Analysis and Proposals to the Laws in the Kaesong Industrial Complex: For Better Regulations under New Environments on the Korean Peninsula*, 54(4) Korea J 80, 84 (2014); and Hyung-Jin Kim, *North Korea Recalls 53,000 Workers, Suspends Operations at North-South Factory Complex*, Toronto Star (Apr 8, 2013). Available at: www.thestar.com/news/world/north-korea-recalls-53-000-workers-suspends-operations-at-north-south-factory-complex/article_a64904a0-53bb-5779-83c5-a85162295fb2.html.

[114] *See* Justin McCurry, *South Korea to Withdraw Last Workers from Kaesong Joint-Venture with North*, The Guardian (Apr 29, 2013). Available at: www.theguardian.com/world/2013/apr/29/south-korea-workers-venture-north; Yi Seul Kim, *Building a Two-Fold Structure in Resolving Political Disputes on the Korean Peninsula: Case Study on the Kaesong Industrial Complex*, 21 Sw. J. Int'l L. 375, 378–79 (2014); Kim and Kim, *supra* note 113, at 86; *North and South Korea Hold Fifth Round of Kaesong Industrial Zone Talks*, The Telegraph (July 22, 2013). Available at: www.telegraph.co.uk/news/worldnews/asia/northkorea/10194327/North-and-South-Korea-hold-fifth-round-of-Kaesong-industrial-zone-talks.html.

[115] *See* Manyin and Nanto, *supra* note 42, at 18; *see also* Scott Snyder and See-won Byung, *Cheonan and Yeonpyeong: The Northeast Asian Response to North Korea's Provocations*, 156(2) The Rusi J. 74 (2011).

[116] Soo-hyun Lee, *supra* note 107, at 68–69. For more general discussion, *see* Ivar Alvik, Contracting with Sovereignty: State Contracts and International Arbitration 16 (2011).

[117] Soo-Hyun Lee, *supra* note 107, at 70–71. There are a few agreements relevant to investment protection, enforcement mechanisms, and dispute settlement between ROK and DPRK, but have been of limited use in practice, largely due to the special (and troubled) relationship between the two countries or entities. Such agreements include, e.g. the Agreement on Investment Protection Between the South and the North (signed on Dec.16, 2000), the Agreement on Clearing Settlement Between the South and the North (signed on Dec 16, 2000), the Agreement on Procedures for Resolution of Commercial Disputes Between the South and the North (signed on Dec 16, 2000), and the Agreement on Prevention of Double Taxation Between the South and the North (signed on Dec 16, 2000). *See Major Agreements*, Ministry of Unification, Republic of Korea, https://web.archive.org/web/20170114072650/http://eng.unikorea.go.kr/content.do?cmsid=1889 (archived Oct. 8, 2014).

[118] *See generally* Lee, *supra* note 43. Because ROK law defines inter-Korean trade as internal trade within a nation, but DPRK is not a WTO Member, various rule of origin issues with respect to the KIC products may occur and raise practical questions relevant not only to the two Koreas but also other WTO Members. The ROK government has tried to address this issue by incorporating some "outward processing provisions" in some of its FTAs. *See also* Dukgeun Ahn, *Legal Issues for Korea's "Internal Trade" in the WTO System*, *in* Multilateral and Regional Frameworks for Globalization: WTO and Free Trade Agreements 362, 362–76 (Wonhyuk Lim and Ramon Torrent eds, 2005).

Besides the "war of pride", North Korea's third nuclear test in February 2013 and its fourth nuclear test in February 2016 prompted the South Korean government to shut down KIC because of intense political pressure from Washington and Beijing.[119] The KIC had been running for over a decade, offering many substantial opportunities for individuals from the DPRK and ROK to engage in cooperative activities. South Korean firms benefited from lower labour costs, while North Korea benefited from earning vital hard currency and the opportunity to begin restructuring its economy. As of 2024, the KIC remains closed and stands as one of the primary, though currently unused, keys to the inter-Korean economic relationship.[120]

C. Thin Economic Exchange in Mount Geumgang Resort

In addition to the KIC, the Mount Geumgang Resort has also provided a point of economic exchange between the two Koreas, albeit of a very limited nature. The Mount Geumgang Resort, which constituted another source of foreign exchange for DPRK, was also operated by Hyundai Asan following a decision to develop the area into a tourist destination in 1998.[121] As shown in Figure 3.4 below, as an inter-Korean tourism project, the Mount Geumgang Resort attracted 371,637 tourists from 1998 to 2000. The number of tourists increased exponentially reaching a total of nearly 2 million by 2008,[122] the year the resort closed.[123] In order to operate Mountain Geumgang Resort, the North and South Korean governments made two primary promises. The first occurred during the Inter-Korean economic cooperation system working-level contact in January 2004, when both governments entered into an agreement on access to, and the right to remain, in the Gaeseong Industrial Zone and the Geumgang Mountain Tourist Zone. The second occurred during the second contact between authorities to promote Geumgang Mountain tourism in February 2008. Both governments entered into an agreement to promote tourism in the Geumgang Mountain Tourist Zone. However, the Geumgang Resort has remained closed since a shooting incident in 2008. For South Korean citizens it is now a mere memory of a glimpse of life in the DPRK.[124]

[119] International Crisis Group, The Case for Kaesong: Fostering Korean Peace through Economic Ties (2019). Available at: www.crisisgroup.org/asia/north-east-asia/korean-peninsula/300-case-kaesong-fostering-korean-peace-through-economic-ties.

[120] Grant Wyeth, *Time to Reopen the Kaesong Industrial Complex? A Conversation with Jin-hyang Kim*, The Diplomat (Feb. 27, 2020). Available at: https://thediplomat.com/2020/02/time-to-reopen-the-kaesong-industrial-complex-a-conversation-with-jin-hyang-kim/.

[121] Burghart and Frank, *supra* note 24, at 15.

[122] *Id.*

[123] Burghart and Frank, *supra* note 24, at 15. On July 11, 2008, a ROK woman entered a military zone at the resort and was shot and killed by a DPRK soldier. *See* Jonathan Watts, *South Korean Tourist Shot Dead in North Korea*, The Guardian (July 11, 2008). Available at: www.theguardian.com/world/2008/jul/11/korea.

[124] Burghart and Frank, *supra* note 24, at 15.

Figure 3.4 Mountain Geumgang/Kaeseong Tour/Pyongyang Tour[125]

Year		1998	1999	2000	2001	2002	2003	2004	2005	2006	2007	2008	2009–2022	Total
Mt Geumgang Tour	Sea Route	10,544	148,074	213,009	57,879	84,727	38,306	449	–	–	–	–	–	552,988
	Land Route	–	–	–	–	–	36,028	267,971	298,247	234,446	345,006	199,966	–	1,381,664
	Total	10,544	148,074	213,009	57,879	84,727	74,334	268,420	298,247	234,446	345,006	199,966	–	1,934,662
Gaeseong Tour		–	–	–	–	–	–	–	1,484	–	7,427	103,122	–	112,033
Pyongyang Tour		–	–	–	–	–	1,109	–	1,280	–	–	–	–	2,299

III. LEGAL FRAMEWORK FOR INTER-KOREAN ECONOMIC COOPERATION

As neither the ROK nor the DPRK recognise the other as the sole sovereign nation-state legitimately representing Korea, they do not interact through conventional channels consisting of diplomats and foreign affairs agencies.[126] This is reflected in the constitutions of the ROK and the DPRK, both of which reference unification.[127] Commentators have argued that due to the lack of mutual legal recognition of one another's sovereignty, "international" (or inter-Korean) agreements concluded between the ROK and DPRK should be regarded as, at best, informal treaties.[128]

[125] Ministry of Unification of South Korea, 2021 White Paper on Reunification 311, and Ministry of Unification of South Korea, 2023 White Paper on Reunification 263.

[126] *See generally* Samuel S Kim, *The Rivalry Between the Two Koreas, in* Asian Rivalries: Conflict, Escalation, and Limitations on Two-Level Games 145 (Sumit Ganguly and: William R Thompson eds, 2011).

[127] The ROK Constitution preamble states that "[w]e, the people of Korea, … upholding the cause of the Provisional Republic of Korea Government … having assumed the mission of … peaceful unification of our homeland and having determined to consolidate national unity with justice, humanitarianism and brotherly love". Daehanminkuk Hunbeob [Hunbeob] [Constitution], pmbl (S Kor). It also makes the mission of peaceful unification mandatory and affirmative in Article 4: "The Republic of Korea shall seek unification and shall formulate and carry out a policy of peaceful unification based on the principles of freedom and democracy". *Id.* art 4. Likewise, the Socialist Constitution of the Democratic People's Republic of Korea, which was adopted on December 27, 1972 by the Supreme People's Assembly and subsequently amended many times (the latest amendment was in 2016), states that "The great Comrades Kim Il Sung and Kim Jong Il are the sun of the nation and the lodestar of national reunification … the reunification of the country as the supreme national task", "developed the movement for national reunification into a nationwide movement … through the united efforts of the whole nation". In addition, "[t]he [DPRK] shall strive to achieve the complete victory of socialism in the northern half of Korea by … vigorously performing the three revolutions –ideological, technological and cultural – and reunify the country on the principle of independence, peaceful reunification and great national unity". Socialist Constitution of the Democratic People's Republic of Korea, pmbl & art 9, official English translation archived at www.ncnk.org/resources/publications/dprk-constitution-2019.pdf/file_view.

[128] *See e.g.* Yi Seul Kim, *supra* note 114, at 381–82.

While the two Koreas have interacted through their respective government agencies, no diplomats and foreign affairs agencies have been officially involved. Rather, considering each side to be a part of the same sovereign nation-state, the ROK has designated the Minister of Unification to work with its DPRK counterpart, the Committee for the Peaceful Reunification of the Fatherland (CPRF). More specifically, the CPRF was set up by the United Front Department of Worker's Party of Korea in 1961 to attract "patriotic Koreans in the ROK and abroad to work for the reunification of Korea along the communist lines proposed by Kim Il-Sung" under its broader view that the ROK government lacks political legitimacy.[129] On the other side, the ROK government established the Ministry of Unification in 1969 as an agency in charge of "all issues pertaining to inter-Korean relations and unification ... reflect[ing] the unique reality of the Korean peninsula, which still remains divided since the end of the Korean War".[130]

Under the Ministry of Unification, a few other government agencies work towards improving the inter-Korean relationship: the Office of Inter-Korean Dialogue, National Institute for Unification Education, Settlement Support Centre for North Korean Defectors (Hanawon), Settlement Support Centre for North Korean Defectors, Hwacheon Branch (Hanawon Hwacheon Branch), Inter-Korea Transit Office, Secretariat of Inter-Korea Joint Liaison Office, Secretariat of South-North Joint Committee for Gaeseong Industrial Complex, North Korean Human Rights Records Centre, and the Centre for Unified Korean Future. With the Ministry of Unification and a few other government agencies, the North and South Korean governments concluded 77 agreements related to inter-Korean economic cooperation, 35 agreements related to inter-Korean political agreements, and ten military-related agreements. The first economic cooperation agreement between North and South Korea was signed on September 26, 2000, and the most recent economic cooperation agreement was signed on September 11, 2013. An economic cooperation agreement consists of various policies about private sectors and how the government will cooperate with the private sector to improve the inter-Korean economy. Additionally, the two Koreas concluded dozens of agreements concerning transportation necessary for both countries to facilitate trade: provision of materials and equipment for the inter-Korean railroad, construction of connecting roads, and connecting routes in the Kaesong Industrial Zone. Generally, inter-Korean economic cooperation agreements are specific and focused on solving economic problems that arising during inter-Korean economic development.

[129] *See Glossary – Committee for the Peaceful Reunification of the Fatherland*, Korea Briefing 2000–2001: First Steps Toward Reconciliation and Reunification 265 (Kongdan Oh and Ralph C Hassig eds, 2002); *see also The Committee for the Peaceful Reunification of the Fatherland*, National Archives & Records Services (N Kor) [in Korean]. Available at: https://web.archive.org/web/20111123120534/http://contents.archives.go.kr/next/content/listSubjectDescription.do?id=007131 (archived Nov 23, 2011).

[130] *See About MOU*, Ministry of Unification, Republic of Korea. Available at: www.unikorea.go.kr/eng_unikorea/about/aboutmou/infomation/.

To develop the inter-Korean relationship, the countries needed a political agreement to serve as a baseline for cooperation. The first political agreement between North and South Korea addressed the formation and operation of the Inter-Korean Coordination Committee, which was established on January 1, 1972. This agreement assisted the North and South to establish smoother communication which, in turn, led to other projects and agreements. The most recent agreement was conducted during the 2018 third Inter-Korean Summit. During the third Inter-Korean Summit, Moon Jae-in, President of South Korea, and Kim Jong Un, Supreme Leader of North Korea, assessed progress made since the historic Panmunjeom Declaration, including close conversations and communication between the two sides' administrations, civilian exchanges and cooperation across a variety of fields, and unprecedented measures to decrease military tension.[131] However, in contrast to both economic cooperation and political agreements, the North and South did not sign many military agreements. To date, only ten military agreements have been reached. This is due to the high degree of risk both countries must account for, which ultimately affects neighbouring and allied countries, as well.

In terms of domestic law, both the ROK and DPRK have passed legislation and regulations to address different aspects of inter-Korean relations, including economic cooperation and exchange. The ROK's interactions with the DPRK are regulated by several laws and regulations including, inter alia, the Development of Inter-Korean Relations Act,[132] the Inter-Korean Exchange and Cooperation Act[133] and its Enforcement Decree,[134] the Inter-Korean Cooperation Fund Act[135] and its Enforcement Decree,[136] and the National Security Act.[137] As characterised by Hyo-Won Lee, in light of the special relationship between the ROK and DPRK, the National Security Act will apply

[131] Pyongyang Joint Declaration of September 2018, N Kor-S Kor, Sept 19, 2018. Available at: www.ncnk.org/node/1633.

[132] Nambukgwangye baljeone gwanhan beomnyul [Development of Inter-Korean Relations Act], Act No 7763, Dec 29, 2005, *amended by* Act No 12584, May 20, 2014 (S Kor). Available at: https://elaw.klri.re.kr/kor_service/lawView.do?hseq=32776&lang=ENG.

[133] Nambukgyoryuhyeomnyeoge gwanhan beomnyul [Inter-Korean Exchange and Cooperation Act], Act No 4239, Aug 1, 1990, *most recently amended by* Act No 12396, Mar 11, 2014 (S Kor). Available at: https://elaw.klri.re.kr/kor_service/lawView.do?hseq=32217&lang=ENG.

[134] Nambukgyoryuhyeomnyeoge gwanhan beomnyul sihaengnyeong [Enforcement Decree of the Inter-Korean Exchange and Cooperation Act], Presidential Decree No 21648, Jul 30, 2009, *most recently amended by* Presidential Decree No 27751, Dec 30, 2016 (S Kor). Available at: https://elaw.klri.re.kr/kor_service/lawView.do?hseq=43057&lang=ENG.

[135] Nambukyeomnyeokgigeumbeop [Inter-Korean Cooperation Fund Act], Act No 4240, Aug 1, 1990, *most recently amended by* Act No 10303, May 17, 2010 (S Kor). Available at: https://elaw.klri.re.kr/kor_service/lawView.do?hseq=18314&lang=ENG.

[136] Enforcement Decree of the Inter-Korean Cooperation Fund Act (adopted by Presidential Decree No 13237, Dec 31, 1990; most recently amended by Presidential Decree No 22405, Sep 27, 2010). Available at: https://elaw.klri.re.kr/kor_service/lawView.do?hseq=21972&lang=ENG.

[137] National Security Act (wholly Amended by Act No 3318, Dec 31, 1980; most recently amended by Act No 13722, Jan 6, 2016). Available at: https://elaw.klri.re.kr/kor_service/lawView.do?hseq=39798&lang=ENG.

where the DPRK works as an illegal group of anti-state movements, and the Inter-Korean Exchange and Cooperation Act will apply where the DPRK works towards conversation and cooperation related to peaceful unification with the ROK.[138] Among these domestic laws and regulations, the ROK's Inter-Korean Exchange and Cooperation Act and Development of Inter-Korean Relations Act are crucially relevant and of great importance to economic exchanges and cooperation between the two Koreas.

The Inter-Korean Exchange and Cooperation Act was passed in 1990 to animate interactions between the two sides towards ultimate reunification; prior to 2018, it was revised sixteen times.[139] Administered by the Ministry of Unification, the Act has thirty Articles covering its purpose, definitions, and institutions, visits, trade in goods, cooperative projects, payment systems, transportation, communication and quarantine affairs, etc. The purpose of the Act is "to contribute to the peace and unification of the Korean Peninsula by prescribing matters necessary to promote reciprocal exchange and cooperation between the south and north of the Military Demarcation Line".[140] Pursuant to the Act, the Ministry of Unification is authorised to issue executive orders in relation to certain inter-Korean trade matters.[141] The Act also established the "Inter-Korean Exchange and Cooperation Promotion Council" as an institutional framework to "consult on and coordinate policies for inter-Korean exchange and cooperation and to deliberate upon and resolve important matters", to "establish basic principles and policies", "approve and authorise important affairs", and to "determine the scope of goods to trade".[142] Most importantly, while the Act does not define the inter-Korean trade relationship as international – namely, transactions between ROK and DPRK "shall be deemed internal transactions between the same people, not those between nations"[143] – it imposes a number of limitations, which are common in the conventional practice of international trade, such as quarantine inspection requirements on transportation equipment, cargo, and persons coming from DPRK.[144] Last but not least, the Act authorises the ROK government to "subsidise or provide other necessary support to those executing the projects for inter-Korean exchange and cooperation" when necessary.[145] While the Inter-Korean Exchange and Cooperation Act has been revised and improved against the background of a changing ROK–DPRK relationship, it appears to have done more to limit, rather than facilitate, economic and trade cooperation.

[138] Soo-Hyun Lee, *supra* note 107, at 61–62.

[139] Inter-Korean Exchange and Cooperation Act, art 1. *See generally* Jong-Dae Shin and Eun-Suk Choi, *Bukhanui Chejejeonhwangwa Nambukgwangyebaljeone Gwanhan Beopjedo [Legal System for the System Transition of North Korea and for the Development of North-South Relations]*, 36 gongbeobyeongu [Pub L] 145 (2008) [in Korean].

[140] Inter-Korean Exchange and Cooperation Act, art 1.

[141] *See e.g.* Inter-Korean Exchange and Cooperation Act, arts 9, 10, 13, and 15.

[142] Inter-Korean Exchange and Cooperation Act, art 4.

[143] *Id*, art 12.

[144] *Id*, art 23.

[145] *Id*, art 24.

Another highly relevant law is the Development of Inter-Korean Relations Act, enacted in 2015 to impose discipline on specific areas of exchange and development. To set the key tone for the ROK–DPRK relationship, Article 3 of the Act explicitly stipulates that "Inter-Korean relations are not relations between nations, but special relations established temporarily in the course of pursuing unification" and that "Inter-Korean trade shall not be regarded as international trade, but, rather, as intranational trade".[146] Again, the Act is highly institutionalised and reflects the underlying ideological basis of Korean peninsula politics, as it creates the "Inter-Korean Relations Development Committee" under the Ministry of Unification (with the Minister serving as the Chairperson of the Committee) to "deliberate on a master plan and other important matters for the development of inter-Korean relations".[147] The Act also provides some level of transparency and accountability by stipulating rules for the appointment of Representatives of the South-North Korean Summit and the dispatch of public officials.[148] Moreover, the Act provides rules and procedures for conclusion, ratification, and termination of South-North Korean agreements, as well as their default legal status under ROK law. Article 21 specifically gives the President the power to conclude and ratify agreements between the ROK and DPRK with the Minister's assistance after a formal deliberation by the State Council.[149] The National Assembly, pursuant to the same Article, "shall have a right to consent to the conclusion and ratification of South–North Korean agreements which place heavy financial burdens on the State or nationals, or South–North Korean agreements concerning legislative matters", but not when such agreements only "determine simple technical or procedural matters concerning the implementation of South–North Korean agreements already concluded or ratified by the President".[150] Beyond developing exchanges and relationships between the two Koreas, the Development of Inter-Korean Relations Act was updated in March 2020 to ensure more accessible and comfortable access to Panmunjom. With the update, the South Korean government has opened the Panmunjom Tour Support Centre and the "DMZ Peace Trail" in November 2020 to create new tourist sites and improve infrastructure. The South Korean government believes this Act will help protect the lives and security of people who live near the border area.[151] Finally, the Act allows for the suspension or termination of any South–North agreements upon a significant change in circumstances between the two sides.[152]

[146] Development of Inter-Korean Relations Act, art 3.
[147] *Id*, art 14.
[148] *Id*, arts 15 and 16.
[149] *Id*, art 21.
[150] *Id*. Upon the completion of the due procedure set by art 21, "South-North Koran agreements, which have been ratified by the National Assembly or have undergone deliberation by the State Council under Article 21 shall be promulgated by the President under the Act on the Promulgation of Statutes". *Id*. art 22.
[151] Ministry of Unification of South Korea, 2021 White Paper on Reunification 4.
[152] Development of inter-Korean Relations Act, art 23.

The Inter-Korean Exchange and Cooperation Act and the Development of Inter-Korean Relations Act did not merely expand the relationship between the two Koreas. The South Korean government also signed several Memorandums of Understanding (MOUs) with various international organisations and companies in furtherance of creating a peaceful inter-Korean relationship. On January 30, 2020, North Korea halted inter-Korean cross-border travel as a precautionary measure in response to COVID-19. Following that, on June 9, 2020, the North Korean government cut off military contact links and, on June 16, 2020, it dismantled the inter-Korean joint liaison office in Gaeseong. Despite the continued suspension of cross-border passage, the Inter-Korean Transit Office conducted thirty-five simulations of cross-border transportation with necessary agencies to create a stable inter-Korean transit system. After dozens of meetings with the Inter-Korean Transit Office management council, the Ministry of Unification of South Korea signed an MOU with the Korea Railroad Corporation and the Gangwon-do Office of Education to rebuild a sustainable inter-Korean transit system.[153] In addition, to addressing the health issues of North Korean defectors, in 2020, the South Korean government signed MOUs on medical assistance for North Korean defectors with Life House and the National Cancer Centre. This resulted in the creation of sixty-five hospitals nationwide to create a stable life for both North and South Koreans.[154]

While we have limited access to North Korea's legal framework for inter-Korean economic cooperation, there are some specific laws and regulations worth noting. The Socialist Constitution of the DPRK (the DPRK Constitution) basically codifies the Juche-oriented ideas of Kim Il Sung and the Kim Jong Il and covers general sections of Politics, Economy, Culture, National Defence, State Organs (Supreme People's Assembly), the Chairman of the State Affairs Commission of the DPRK, the State Affairs Commission, the Presidium of the Supreme People's Assembly, the Cabinet, the Local People's Assembly, the Local People's Committee, the Public Prosecutors Office and the Court, Emblem, Flag, Anthem, and Capital.[155] It describes all the specific regulations to which the government and the citizens of North Korea should adhere, with the immortal Juche mindset. The ultimate goal of reunification is explicitly spelled out in the preamble, which reads "the great leader Comrade Kim Il Sung and the great leader Comrade Kim Jong Il are saviours of the nation who performed immortal exploits for achieving the cause of national reunification". The "reunification of the country" is upheld as the "supreme national task" and requires "all their efforts … for its realization". Article 9 of the Constitution also enshrines the objective of the DPRK to "strive to achieve the complete victory of socialism in

[153] Ministry of Unification of South Korea, 2021 White Paper on Reunification 103.
[154] *Id.* at 74.
[155] Socialist Constitution of the Democratic People's Republic of Korea, official English translation. Archived at: www.ncnk.org/resources/publications/dprk-constitution-2019.pdf/file_view (last visited Apr 26, 2024).

the northern half of Korea ... peaceful reunification and great national unity". However, the legal status of the South and how the bilateral relationship shall be governed are not made clear in the Constitution.

An essential legal framework in North Korea that aims to cope with inter-Korean economic cooperation is the North–South Economic Cooperation Law enacted in July 2005. This was passed to establish the legal framework of North Korea's contribution to develop the national economy by "strictly establishing systems and conducting economic cooperation with the South",[156] covering areas of construction, tourism, corporate management, toll processing, technology exchanges and banks, insurance, telecommunications, transportation, volunteer work, and exchanges of goods between the two Koreas.[157] Article 3 stipulates to which organisations the law applies: institutions, businesses, and organisations that cooperate with the South in economic cooperation. It also applies to corporations and individuals in the South who cooperate economically with the North.[158] As both countries need a primary government agency that will manage the economic cooperation, in Article 5, the North Korean government stated that the Central National Economic Cooperation Guidance Agency would be the government agency in charge.[159] In contrast, the Ministry of Unification will be the primary government agency that will hold the management authority for South Korea. To maintain fair cooperation, the North Korean government added Article 4 to guarantee a balanced development of the national economy with the interests of the entire nation at the forefront and proceeds from the principle of respect, trust, and presence or absence.[160]

Under the North-South Economic Cooperation Law, any inter-Korean economic cooperation that may undermine the "safety of society", the "development of the national economy", the "health and environmental protection of residents", and the "flow of the people" shall be prohibited.[161] All the plans of inter-Korean economic cooperation shall go through an application and approval process managed by the Central National Economic Cooperation Guidance Agency, as nothing can be proceeded without prior formal approval.[162]

Two important aspects should be noted here. First, according to Article 19 of the North-South Economic Cooperation Law, tariffs are not imposed on any suppliers involved in inter-Korea economic cooperation.[163] Second, the supervisory control over inter-Korean economic cooperation is not to be

[156] North-South Economic Cooperation Law, [Korean title] (promulgated [promulgation date]) (no longer publicly accessible; archival copy and official English translation on file with author).
[157] *Id*, art. 2.
[158] *Id*, art. 3.
[159] *Id*, art. 5.
[160] *Id*, art. 4.
[161] *Id*, art. 8.
[162] *Id*, arts 10–12.
[163] *Id*, art. 19.

carried out by a foreign affairs or reunification agency, but a central agency for economic cooperation.[164] Overall, the North-South Economic Cooperation Law provides highly restrictive rules for inter-Korean economic cooperation that allows for only *ad hoc* and pre-approved projects, subject to special payment bank arrangements and confidentiality requirements.[165] Having said that, the Law has a light touch on dispute resolution (through consultation, or commercial dispute resolution procedures agreed between the two Koreas), perhaps due to the already highly restricted rules applied on a limited pre-approved cooperation projects. In light of the North-South Economic Cooperation Law, there is no room for North Korea to allow for systematic and cross-cutting inter-Korean economic cooperation, and only case-by-case pre-approved cooperation projects are allowed.

IV. CONCLUSION

Beginning with the first political agreement on January 1, 1972, both the North and South Korean governments have invested many years and much effort to establish inter-Korean economic cooperation. Despite the time and financial investment involved in their economic cooperation, both countries have not yet found a perfect alliance that suits their legal frameworks. Due to North Korea's missile launches and nuclear tests, North and South Korea simultaneously faced the downfall of various projects that led to economic cooperation. Indeed, the main projects between the two countries, such as the Kaesong Industrial Complex and the Mount Kumgang Resort, are now closed, and there is no discussion of how these two projects will be re-established. Most importantly, after 50 years of economic cooperation and the investment of both countries and given North Korea's current nuclear status, it is highly unlikely that both countries will create any new projects. While President Yoon Suk-yeol's administration has not created a different path for inter-Korea economic cooperation, it remains to be seen how his stand (likely a middle ground between Park and Moon) and policies will shape inter-Korean relationships, particularly in the turbulent geopolitical landscape globally. Yet again, given all the agreements and the legal framework the governments have established to date, it seems unrealistic that any significant changes in economic cooperation will be realised unless the North Korean government drastically alters its nuclear weapons status. We will reflect on these factors in Chapter V, along with other findings in other case studies, as we move towards a close.

[164] *Id*, art. 25.
[165] *Id*, arts 21 and 23.

Chronology of South and North Korea History in the Latest Century

1945	• After the Second World War, the Japanese occupation of Korea ends with Soviet troops occupying the North, and US troops in the South.
1946	• North Korea's Communist Party, the Korean Workers' Party, inaugurated. Soviet-backed leadership installed, including Red Army-trained Kim Il-sung.
1948	• The Republic of Korea proclaimed. • The Democratic People's Republic of Korea proclaimed, with Kim Il-sung installed as leader. • Soviet troops withdraw.
1950	• South sustained by crucial US military, economic and political support. • South declares independence, sparking North Korean invasion
1953	• End of Korean War • Signing of the Armistice Agreement • Armistice ends Korean War, which has cost two million lives.
1960	• President Syngman Ree steps down after student protests against electoral fraud. A new constitution forms the Second Republic, but political freedom remains limited. • Rapid industrial growth in North Korea
1961	• Coup d'état in South Korea; military coup puts General Park Chung-hee in power.
1963	• In South Korea, General Park restores political freedom and proclaims the Third Republic. A major program of industrial development begins.
1968	• North Korea captures the USS Pueblo, a US naval intelligence ship.
1972	• North and South Korea issue joint statement on peaceful reunification. • In South Korea, Park increases his powers with constitutional changes. • The first meeting of the South-North Coordinating Committee
1974	• Kim Il-sung designates the eldest son, Kim Jong-il as his successor.
1979	• In South Korea, Park is assassinated. General Chun Doo-hwan seizes power the following year.
1980	• In South Korea, increasing shift towards the high-tech computer industry. • The Kwangju Uprising in May 1980 saw 250,000 people protest the South Korean military government in Kwangju city. Despite brutal suppression, it marked a pivotal moment in South Korea's struggle for democracy.
1981	• Chun Doo-hwan indirectly elected to a seven-year term. • The Fifth republic established in March 1981 by Chun Doo-hwan, the 11th and 12th President of South Korea.
1985	• North Korea joins the international Nuclear Non-Proliferation Treaty, barring the country from producing nuclear weapons. • The first reunion of dispersed family members due to Korean War.

(continued)

(Continued)

1986	• In North Korea, research nuclear reactor in Yongbyon becomes operational. • In South Korea, the constitution has changed to allow direct election of the president.
1987	• In South Korea, President Chun Doo-hwan is pushed out of office by student unrest and international pressure in the build-up to the Sixth Constitution. General Roh Tae-woo succeeds President Chun, grants a greater degree of political liberalisation, and launches an anti-corruption drive.
1988	• Olympic games in Seoul with first free parliamentary elections.
1990	• South Korea established diplomatic ties with Russia.
1991	• North and South Korea join United Nations.
1992	• South Korea established diplomatic ties with China
1993	• President Roh succeeded by Kim Young Sam, a former opponent of the regime and the first freely elected civilian president.
1994	• North Korea test-fires a medium-range Rodong ballistic missile into the Sea of Japan. Kim Il Sung's death. • North Korea and the US sign an Agreed Framework under which Pyongyang commits to freezing its nuclear program in return for heavy fuel oil and two light-water nuclear reactors.
1996	• South Korea admitted to Organisation for Economic Cooperation and Development • North Korea announces it will no longer abide by the armistice that ended the Korean War and sends thousands of troops into the demilitarised zone. • A North Korean submarine with 26 commandos and crew on board runs aground near the South Korean town of Gangneung. All but one on board is killed along with 17 South Koreans following several skirmishes.
1998	• Development of Sunshine Policy. • Kim Dae-Jung sworn in as president and pursues a "sunshine policy" of offering unconditional economic and humanitarian aid to North Korea. • Commencement of South Korea's visit to Geumgangsan Mountain. • North Korea fires a multistage long-range rocket that flies over Japan and lands in the Pacific Ocean, well beyond North Korea's known capability.
2000	• Inter-Korean Summit: June 15 South-North Joint Declaration
2001	• Opening of Incheon International Airport, built on tidal land off the port of Incheon.
2002	• North Korea Launched economic reforms • US President George W Bush labels North Korea, Iraq and Iran an "axis of evil" for continuing to build "weapons of mass destruction." • Naval Battle: Battle between South Korean and North Korean naval vessels along their disputed sea border leaves four South Koreans dead and nineteen wounded. Thirty North Koreans are thought to have been killed.

(continued)

(Continued)

2003	• North Korea withdraws from the 1992 agreement with South Korea to keep the Korean Peninsula free of nuclear weapons. • Pyongyang declares it has completed the reprocessing of 8,000 spent nuclear fuel rods.
2004	• Opening of the Kaesong Industrial Complex
2006	• North Korea conduct first nuclear test.
2007	• South and North Korea agree to restart high-level talks suspended since July 2006 in wake of the North's nuclear test. • Nuclear Declaration: Second inter-Korean summit held in Pyongyang. President Roh Moo-hyun becomes the first South Korean leader to walk across the Demilitarised Zone separating North and South. • Inter-Korean Summit: Adoption of the "Declaration on the Advancement of South-North Relations Peace and Prosperity."
2008	• North–South relations deteriorate sharply after new South Korean President Lee Myung-bak promises to take a harder line on North Korea. • North agrees to provide full access to Yongbyon nuclear site after the US removes it from terrorism blacklist.
2009	• North Korea says it is scrapping all military and political deals with the South. • North Korea launches a long-range rocket, carrying what it says is a communications satellite; its neighbours accuse it of testing long-range missile technology. Condemnation from the UN Security Council prompts North Korea to walk out of six-party talks and restart its nuclear facilities. • North Korea frees American journalists Laura Ling and Euna Lee after former US President Bill Clinton facilitates their release. The pair had been sentenced to 12 years of hard labour for allegedly crossing the border illegally. • North Korea conducts a second nuclear test.
2010	• North Korean Torpedo sank a South Korean navy ship causing the loss of 46 sailors for South Korea. • North Korea attacks South Korea's Yeonpyeong Island causing the deaths of two civilians and two marines.
2011	• North Korean's leader Kim Jong-il dies and Kim Jong Un succeeds to his office.
2013	• North Korea successfully conducts a third underground nuclear weapons test.
2015	• Both North and South Korea trade fire across the border.
2016	• North Korea conducts its fourth nuclear test.
2017	• Kim Jong-nam, the half-brother of Kim Jong-un, is assassinated in Malaysia; North Korea is widely suspected to be responsible. North Korea conducts its fifth nuclear test.

(continued)

(Continued)

2018	• South Korea and North Korea marched together at the opening ceremony of PyeongChang Winter Olympics. • 2018 Inter-Korean Summit: Signing of the Panmunjom Declaration by the two Koreas. • 2018 Inter-Korean Summit: Reaffirmation of the pledge to implement the Panmunjom Declaration by both Korean leaders. • 2018 Inter-Korean Summit: Announcement of the Pyongyang Joint Declaration of September 2018 by both Korean leaders.
2019	• US–North Korea summit with President Donald Trump and Kim Jong Un. • North Korea fires several short-range projectiles into its eastern coast sea.
2020	• North Korea declares emergency over suspected COVID-19 case and locks down its borders.
2023	• North Korea fired two ballistic missiles off its east coast which violation of Security Council resolutions. • South Korea submarine missile launch. • US and South Korea agreed key nuclear weapons deal.
2024	• North Korea continued to advance military ties with Russia, pushing forward key advanced weapons programs. • South Korea establishes Relations with Cuba (a close ally of North Korea). • North Korea ends economic cooperation: North Korea's parliament votes to abolish all remaining economic cooperation agreements with South Korea. This includes joint ventures in the Kaesong Industrial Complex. • Kim Jong Un abandons unification goal with South and vows to dismantle father's unification arch as he declares South Korea "principal enemy". • Increased Military Drills: Both North and South Korea conduct large-scale military exercises throughout March. • North Korea dismantles unification agencies: North Korea disbands government agencies previously dedicated to promoting inter-Korean dialogue and reunification efforts.

4

Northern and Southern Cyprus

I. HISTORICAL BACKGROUND

THE CONFLICT OVER Cyprus may be traced back to 1571 when the Ottoman Empire conquered the island but has its recent roots in the devastating wars of the late Ottoman era, ranging from the Anglo-Turkish War (1807–1809) to the Russo-Turkish War (1877–1878).[1] After the Berlin Congress (1884–1885), Cyprus was transferred to the British in 1878 and became a British protectorate. By virtue of the 1923 Treaty of Lausanne,[2] the Republic of Turkey, established in 1922 by Mustafa Kemal Atatürk with the dissolution of the Ottoman Empire after the First World War, recognised the annexation of the island by the British in 1914.[3] From 1925 to 1960, Cyprus was a Crown colony. While the first few decades of British colonial rule remained largely peaceful, both Greek Cypriots and Turkish Cypriots became more attached to their respective motherlands, Greece and Turkey, and the demand for independence from the British, surged under the wave of self-determination after the Second World War. Importantly, the pursuit of independence was set against a backdrop of decolonisation, but was nonetheless overshadowed by the Cold War, struggle for power and regional rivalry.

Divergences nonetheless existed as to the prospective paths after claiming independence.[4] Two words played a critical role in Cypriot's pursuit for independence: *enosis* (union) and *taksim* (partition) and Creek Cypriots and

[1] See generally Angelos Sepos, The Europeanization of Cyprus: Polity, Policies and Politics 15–33 (2008); Oliver P Richmond, Mediating in Cyprus: the Cypriot Communities and the United Nations (1998); Marilena Varnava, Cyprus before 1974: the Prelude to Crisis (2020); Salahi R Sonyel, Cyprus: The Destruction of a Republic and its Aftermath (2003); John Burke, Britain and the Cyprus Crisis of 1974: Conflict, Colonialism and the Politics of Remembrance in Greek Cypriot Society (2018); Clement Dodd, The History and Politics of the Cyprus Conflict (2010); Joseph S Joseph, Cyprus: Ethnic Conflict and International Politics (1997).

[2] Treaty of Peace with Turkey, July 24, 1923, 28 LNTS 11 [hereinafter Treaty of Lausanne].

[3] *Id.* art 20 ("Turkey hereby recognizes the annexation of Cyprus proclaimed by the British Government on the 5th November, 1914.").

[4] Neophytos Loizides, Design Peace: Cyprus and Institutional Innovations in Divided Societies 22 (2016).

Turkish Cypriots have different narratives of their history. In the 1950s, Greek Cypriots established the anti-British, pro-Greek EOKA (National Organisation of Cypriot Struggle)[5] with the leader of the political wing being Archbishop Makarios and that of the military wing Georgios Grivas – a Cyprus-born colonel in the Greek Army. Turkish Cypriots were more or less suspicious about this attempt and the end goal the EOKA aimed to achieve. By contrast, the Turkish Cypriots, led by Rauf Denktash, who later became the President of the Turkish Republic of Northern Cyprus (TRNC), established a paramilitary organisation (the Turkish Resistance Organisation, or Türk Mükavemet Teşkilatı) which cooperated with British colonial forces to suppress the *enosis* movement and articulated their own agenda of *taksim*, partition of the island into Turkish-Cypriot and Greek-Cypriot zones.[6] The clashes manifested when British colonial rulers hired Turkish Cypriots as auxiliary policemen during the EOKA struggle. Greek-Cypriot demonstrators witnessed the enmity from Turkish Cypriots tasked with policing the demonstrations.[7]

The struggle for independence between Greek Cypriots and Turkish Cypriots finally yielded progress after torturous military conflicts and diplomatic negotiations. In addition to Cyprus, three parties – the UK, Turkey and Greece – were involved and this led to the Zurich and London agreements in February 1959. Based on the results of the Zurich and London Conferences, three formal international instruments, the Treaty of Establishment,[8] Treaty of Alliance[9] and Treaty of Guarantee,[10] were signed in Nicosia on August 16, 1960. The Treaty of Establishment established the Republic of Cyprus with consociational characteristics aiming to accommodate and bridge the diversity and allowed for two British sovereign bases on the island. The Treaty of Alliance forged the alliance, in particular the security cooperation, between Cyprus on the one hand and Greece and Turkey on the other. The Treaty of Alliance even provides for the stationing of troops from the latter two countries in Cyprus for the preservation of peace. The Treaty of Guarantee established Britain, Greece and Turkey's recognition and guarantee of the independence of Cyprus, its

[5] Christalla Yakinthou, *The EU's Role in the Cyprus Conflict: System Failure or Structural Metamorphosis?*, *in* EU Conflict Management 32, 33 (James Hughes ed., 2010); *see generally* David French, Fighting EOKA: the British Counter-Insurgency Campaign on Cyprus, 1955–1959 (2015); Andrew R Novo, The EOKA Cause: Nationalism and the Failure of Cypriot Enosis (2021).

[6] Sepos, *supra* note 1, at 18–19.

[7] Olga Demetriou, *Catalysis, Catachresis: the EU's Impact on the Cyprus Conflict*, *in* The European Union and Border Conflicts: the Power of Integration and Association 64, 68 (Thomas Diez et al. eds, 2008).

[8] Treaty concerning the Establishment of the Republic of Cyprus, Cyprus-Greece-Turk-UK, Aug 16, 1960, 382 UNTS 8.

[9] Treaty of Alliance, Cyprus-Greece-Turk, Aug 16, 1960, 397 UNTS 287.

[10] Treaty of Guarantee, Cyprus-Greece-Turkey-UK, Aug 16, 1960, 382 UNTS 3.

constitutional order, and its territorial integrity.[11] These treaties, together with the Constitution of the Republic of Cyprus, all entered into force on the same day, August 16, 1960.[12] At this point, it is clear that geopolitics, the struggle for power and regional rivalry, play a critical role in the Cypriot struggle for independence. Importantly, the two Cypriot motherlands, Greece and Turkey, were key Mediterranean allies of the United States (the US) in in containing communism, but the Republic of Cyprus was a non-aligned country and the communist party has had strong domestic support in the Republic of Cyprus since its inception.

The joy at the birth of new Republic did not last very long. The Constitution was said to be too generous to Turkish Cypriots who were, it was claimed, over-represented by 3 to 7 (Greek Cypriots) in the organisation of the administration. The separation majority voting system also prevented the new administration from functioning well. Partly aiming to break the deadlock and partly wishing to appease the Greek Cypriots against his domestic opponents, President Makarios presented a plan for constitutional reform, which was rejected by the Turkish-Cypriot leadership and led to a crisis of constitutional order arising from the withdrawal of all Turkish-Cypriot members from the government.[13] Inter-communal conflicts ensued, resulting in many deaths and the forced displacement of Turkish Cypriots. The weak Makarios government finally collapsed after a *coup d'état* on July 15, 1974, backed by a Greek junta in close conjunction with EOKA-B, which had been secretly established by Georgios Grivas in 1971 and proscribed by Makarios in April 1974. The coup resulted in the ousting of Makarios and established a Greek junta puppet regime.

In response to this coup, Turkey, asserting its right as guarantor to intervene with a view to restore the constitutional order, landed 40,000 troops in the north of Cyprus and captured a small strip of land. A ceasefire agreement was brokered by the United Nations (the UN) and negotiations were held between the three guarantors and the two communities. During the negotiation, Turkey and the leaders of the Turkish Cypriots demanded the formation of a bi-zonal federal system with 34 per cent of the land reserved for Turkish Cypriots. While the acting President of the Republic of Cyprus, Glafcos Clerides, asked for an

[11] Sepos, *supra* note 1, at 19. This guarantor status is controversial and arguably laid the groundwork for Turkey's subsequent invasion: as a guarantor, Turkey has the right, either collectively or individually, to restore the constitutional order and state unity of Cyprus. Of course, Turkey did not, in fact, pursue this objective during its invasion. Kıvanç Ulusoy, *Europeanization's Time Constraint: the Case of Cyprus*, *in* Turkey's Accession to the European Union: Political and Economic Challenges 277, 281 (Belgin Akçay and Bahri Yilmaz ed., 2012).

[12] Nikos Skoutaris, *The Application of the Acquis Communautaire in the Areas Not Under the Effective Control of the Republic of Cyprus: The Green Line Regulation*, 45 Common Mkt L Rev 727, 729 (2008).

[13] Nathalie Tocci, The EU and Conflict Resolution: Promoting Peace in the Backyard 32 (2007); Sepos, *supra* note 1, at 23; Richmond, *supra* note 1, at 90; James Ker-Lindsay, EU Accession and UN Peacekeeping in Cyprus 10 (2005).

adjournment for 36–48 hours to allow consultation, but, a few hours later, Turkey attacked for the second time and occupied 37 percent of the island.[14] The Turkish troops remain in northern Cyprus and the 1960 constitutional order has never been restored.[15] Up to this point, the Greek-Cypriots' aspiration of *enosis* was dead and Turkish-Cypriots, in the name of self-administration aiming for self-determination, announced the establishment of the Turkish Federated State of Cyprus (TFSC) in February 1975.[16]

In response to the deteriorating situation in Cyprus, the UN intensified its condemnation of Turkey. With UN Security Council Resolution 186 in 1964,[17] a peacekeeping force (UNFICYP) was sent to Cyprus, this was originally planned to last for three months, but turned out to be much longer than envisaged.[18] The UNFICYP is in charge of patrolling the UN Buffer Zone (generally known as "Green Line") first established in 1964 and extended in 1974 after the ceasefire agreement of August 16, 1974. However, intense diplomatic relations led to the Third Vienna Agreement in August 1975 in the form of communiqué, which provided for the relocation of Turkish-Cypriots in the South to the North and Creek-Cypriots in the North to the South. This agreement thus institutionalised the separation between Greek Cypriots in the South and Turkish Cypriots in the North. In 1983, the Turkish Cypriots in the North declared independence and established the Turkish Republic of Northern Cyprus (TRNC),[19] which was soon condemned by the international community, except Turkey, which recognises it.[20] The UN Security Council adopted a resolution calling upon all states not to recognise any Cypriot state other than the Republic of Cyprus.[21] Therefore, North Cyprus, or the "TRNC", is not recognised and, for this reason,[22] has suffered from economic isolation from the international community. Southern Cyprus, by contrast, as the only legitimate government of Cyprus, following Greece's example, concluded an Association Agreement with the European Union (then, the European Economic Community, EEC) in 1973 with an accompanying protocol on Rule of Origin (Origin Protocol).[23] It applied for accession to the EU in 1990 and finalised its accession process

[14] Sepos, *supra* note 1, at 23–24.

[15] Tocci, *supra* note 13, at 32.

[16] Ker-Lindsay, *supra* note 13, at 14–15. The Turkish Federated State of Cyprus was succeeded by Turkish Republic of Northern Cyprus in 1983.

[17] SC Res 186, ¶ 4 (Mar 4, 1964).

[18] Richmond, *supra* note 1, at 94–95.

[19] On the TRNC as a state, see Daria Isachenko, The Making of Informal States: Statebuilding in Northern Cyprus and Transdniestria (2012).

[20] Tocci, *supra* note 13 at 32–33; Ker-Lindsay, *supra* note 13, at 16–17.

[21] SC Res 541 (Nov 18, 1983).

[22] On this recognition saga, *see generally* Costas M Constantinou and Yiannis Papadakis, *The Cypriot State(s)* in situ*: Cross-Ethnic Contact and the Discourse of Recognition*, *in* The European Union and the Cyprus Conflict: Modern Conflict, Postmodern Union 73 (Thomas Diez ed., 2002).

[23] Agreement establishing an Association between the European Economic Community and the Republic of Cyprus, 1973 OJ (L 133) 2.

in the 2004 enlargement wave.[24] The Greek-Turkish divide had been a thorny issue for the accession negotiations;[25] economic relations between Northern and Southern parts of Cyprus had been almost been non-existent for decades prior to accession.

II. POLITICAL AND ECONOMIC RELATIONS BETWEEN NORTHERN AND SOUTHERN CYPRUS

A. The Internal Political and Economic Development of the Republic of Cyprus, the Turkish Federated State of Cyprus (1974–1983), and the Turkish Republic of Northern Cyprus (1983)

When the Ottoman Empire invaded Cyprus, the population on the island was around 200,000 people, who were predominantly Greek. At the end of the seventeenth century, under the rule of the Ottoman Empire, around 30,000 Turks settled in Cyprus, accounting for 20 percent of the population.[26] When the TFSC was established in 1974, and even after 1983 when the TRNC was established, Turkish immigrants continued to "settle" in Northern Cyprus and are called "Turkish settlers". The composition of the population of Northern Cyprus can thus be distinguished into two main categories: with or without the nationality of the TRNC. Those with TRNC nationality may be those who are originally from Northern Cyprus, who have emigrated from Turkey and those who have emigrated from third countries. Those without TRNC nationality may come from Turkey or other third countries. The most controversial categories here are Turkish settlers, in particular those with TRNC nationality.

In 1960, when the new Republic of Cyprus was established, the official data indicates that the whole population on the island was around 578,207, with 104,942 being Turkish.[27] Turkish Cypriots accounted for 18 percent of the entire population. In 1996, according to the statistics of the TRNC and Turkey, the population in Northern Cyprus had reached 200,857 with 164,460 possessing TRNC nationality and 30,702 possessing Turkish nationality; around one-fourth or one-third of the population in Northern Cyprus originated from Turkey.[28]

[24] See Neill Nugent, *EU Enlargement and 'the Cyprus Problem'*, 38 J Common Mkt Stud 131 (2000); Helen Xanthaki, *The Route to EU Accession, in* Cyprus and the EU: the Road to Accession 11 (Constantin Stefanou ed., 2005); Frank Hoffmeister, Legal Aspects of the Cyprus Problem: Annan Plan and EU Accession 83–96 (2006).

[25] See Neophytos G Loizides, *Greek-Turkish Dilemmas and the Cyprus EU Accession Process*, 33 Sec Dialogue 429 (2002).

[26] Muzaffer Ercan Yilmaz, *The Cyprus Conflict and the Question of Identity*, 4 Uluslararası Hukuk ve Politika [Rev Int'l L & Pol] 74, 76 (2005).

[27] Select Committee on Foreign Affairs, Written Evidence: How Many Turkish Cypriots Remain in Cyprus, 2004–5, HC, ¶ 1.1 (UK). Available at: https://publications.parliament.uk/pa/cm200405/cmselect/cmfaff/113/113we33.htm.

[28] *Id.*

The population of the whole island was around 880,058 in 1996.[29] In 2021, the population under the effective control of the Republic of Cyprus was 918,100,[30] with that of the whole island being 1,244,000.[31] Between 81,475 to 100,574 originated from Turkey and have settled in Northern Cyprus.

The status of Turkish settlers is ambivalent not only in the Republic of Cyprus but also in the TRNC. While the Republic of Cyprus considers that Northern Cyprus is illegally occupied and recognises Turkish Cypriots in the North as its nationals, this policy does not extend to Turkish settlers or second-generation settlers whose parents, either one or both, originated from Turkey. The legal as well as social status of Turkish settlers is also delicate in the TRNC as Northern Cyprus has mixed feelings toward Turkey. While some consider Turkey as their motherland, others identify themselves as Turkish Cypriots and complain about Turkish influence on or interference with the TRNC's politics.

Currently, the major parties dominating the Republic of Cyprus are: the Progressive Party of the Working People (AKEL), and the Democratic Rally (DISY) Democratic Party (DIKO). AKEL is moderate on the issue of Northern Cyprus even though it was opposed to the Annan Plan during the 2004 referendum. It was believed that AKEL's position was due to its intention to avoid conflict with the ruling party, DIKO.[32] DISY is a right-wing party that favoured the Annan Plan in 2004.[33] Notably, the former president, Glafkos Clerides, was in favour of the Annan plan and Nicos Anastasiades resumed negotiations after he was elected in 2013. DIKO is a centre-right party whose representative figure is former president Tassos Papadopoulos; considered a hard-liner,[34] he called for a rejection of the plan on the eve of the referendum.[35] Since its independence in 1960, except for Makarios who has no party affiliation, George Vasiliou belongs to the United Democrats (EDI), Glafkos Clerides belongs to DISY, Tassos Papadopoulos belongs to DIKO, Demetris Christofias belongs to AKEL, Nicos Anastasiades belongs to DISY. The current president, Nikos Christodoulides, used to be affiliated with DISY but last ran as an independent candidate.

In contrast, the active parties in the TRNC are the National Unity Party (UBP), the Republican Turkish Party (CTP) and the Communal Democracy Party (TDP). There are other smaller parties. The UBP is a conservative party,

[29] *Population Total – Cyprus*, World Bank. Available at: https://data.worldbank.org/indicator/SP.POP.TOTL?locations=CY (last visited Apr 3, 2024).

[30] Census of Population and Housing 2021, Preliminary Results by District, Municipality/Community, Cystat (2022). Available at: www.cystat.gov.cy/en/PressRelease?id=66208.

[31] United Nations Department of Economic and Social Affairs, World Population Prospects 2022 ("Complete" data table in group "Standard Projections", subgroup "Demographic Indicators"). Available at: https://population.un.org/wpp/Download/.

[32] James Ker-Lindsay and Keith Webb, *Cyprus*, 43 Eur J Pol Rsch 969, 976 (2004) [hereinafter *Cyprus 2004*]. *See also* James Ker-Lindsay and Keith Webb, *Cyprus*, 44 Eur J Pol Rsch 975, 979 (2005) [hereinafter *Cyprus 2005*].

[33] *Cyprus 2005*, *supra* note 32, at 975.

[34] *Id.* 975–76.

[35] Dinko Dinkov and Stoyan Stoyanov, *The Cyprus Problem: International Politics Simulation*, 47 Managerial L 171, 189 (2005).

whose representative figure is the former president Rauf Denktash, who is against compromise in the future or final resolution of Cyprus island.[36] CTP is a centre-left party that enthusiastically seeks a solution for the Cyprus question and obtained the majority of seats in parliament during the 2004 referendum.[37] TDP is a centre-left party, with the former president Mustafa Akinci being the representative figure.[38] Since the division of the island in 1974, except for Rauf Denktash, who served as the president until 2005, all the other presidents served only one term. Mehmet Ali belongs to CTP, Derviş Eroğlu belongs to UBP, Mustafa Akinci belongs to TDP and the current president, Ersin Tatar, belongs to UBP.

Soon after the inception of the Republic of Cyprus in 1960, the constitutional order was disrupted by the withdrawal of Turkish Cypriots from the institutions of the state. This was remedied by Law No. 33/64 and justified by the doctrine of necessity in the *Mustafa Ibrahim* case in 1964.[39] When Turkish Cypriots established the TRNC in 1983, their representatives also unanimously approved the Constitution for the TRNC. Both the constitutions of the Republic of Cyprus and the TRNC assign executive powers, notably diplomatic powers, to the President, powers which, to varying degrees, may be checked or overseen by the legislature (house of representatives or assembly).[40]

In the past two decades, the political orientations of the leaders of the Republic of Cyprus and the TRNC shape the pace and direction of economic cooperation, unification or not, across the island of Cyprus. In February 2003, Tassos Papadopoulos, a hard-liner who in contrast to his predecessor in favour of the Annan Plan, won the election.[41] Papadopoulos called for the Greek Cypriots to vote against the plan in the 2004 referendum as he claimed that the plan over-privileged Turkish Cypriots, provided a legal basis for Turkish military in Northern Cyprus and recognised Northern Cyprus as a legal constituent state of the independent nation of the United Cyprus Republic.[42] At the same time, given that the accession of the Republic of Cyprus to the EU was imminent, the Greek Cypriots viewed this move as having the potential to maintain and widen their political and economic advantage over Northern Cyprus, which made them less interested in reaching a compromise in the unification plan.[43]

[36] *Cyprus 2005*, *supra* note 32, at 975–76.

[37] *Id.*

[38] *Id.*

[39] Achilles C Emilianides and Christos Papastylianos, *Citizenship and Nationality: Cyprus*, in Constitutionalism in Context 330, 330–50 (David S Law ed., 2022); *see generally*, Achilles C Emilianides, Constitutional Law in Cyprus (2nd edn, 2019); *see also* Stéphanie Laulhé Shaelou and Andrea Manoli, *A Tale of Two: The COVID-19 Pandemic and the Rule of Law in Cyprus*, Verfassungsblog (Apr 30, 2020). Available at: https://verfassungsblog.de/a-tale-of-two-the-covid-19-pandemic-and-the-rule-of-law-in-cyprus/.

[40] *See* Constitution of the Republic of Cyprus, arts 50(1), 51(1); Constitution of the Turkish Republic of Northern Cyprus, arts 94, 98 and 103.

[41] *Cyprus 2005*, *supra* note 32, at 975–76.

[42] Dinkov, *supra* note 35, at 188–89.

[43] *Id.* at 199.

In the wake of the defeat of the referendum by Greek Cypriots, Annan called for the establishment of technical working groups to address functional issues. Until 2007, little progress was made as the Republic of Cyprus demanded the final solution for Cyprus must be based on UN resolutions, international law and EU policies.[44]

In 2008, the Republic of Cyprus held its presidential election and Demetris Christofias of AKEL, generally considered to be more moderate in terms of its position on the future of Cyprus, was elected. Christofias agreed to set up technical working groups aiming for a bi-zonal and bi-communal federal country as the final solution.[45] In 2014, Nicos Anastasiades of DISY won the election and maintained the moderate position on the fate of Cyprus. The two sides resumed negotiations and explored the possibility of a bi-zonal and bi-communal federal Cyprus.[46]

Table 4.1 Political Orientation of the Leaders of Republic of Cyprus

President	Party	Position
Tassos Papadopoulos (2003–2008)	Democratic Party (DIKO)	Hard-liner
Demetris Christofias (2008–2013)	Progressive Party of Working People (AKEL)	Moderate
Nicos Anastasiades (2013–2023)	Democratic Rally (DISY)	Moderate
Nikos Christodoulides (2023–present)	Independent, formerly Democratic Rally (DISY)	Hard-liner

The TRNC, under the rule of Rauf Denktash of the UBP, had long been against the compromise and pursued independence. However, in the 2003 and 2005 elections, the moderate parties CTP and BDH outperformed and Mehmet Ali Talat was elected first as prime minister in early 2004 and then as president in 2005.[47] The general atmosphere in Northern Cyprus was a willingness to compromise or enter into a new round of negotiations.[48] Until 2008, Talat's aim for the final solution of Cyprus was based on the Annan Plan to establish a bi-zonal and bi communal federal Cyprus. However, in 2010, the UBP won the majority in the assembly; this reflected Turkish Cypriots' intention to adopt a harder position, aiming for a confederation.[49] In 2015, Mustafa Akinci, more moderate compared to his predecessor Derviş Eroğlug, was elected as president.[50]

[44] Hubert Faustmann and Erol Kaymak, *Cyprus*, 47 Eur J Pol Rsch 939 (2008).
[45] Hubert Faustmann et al., *Cyprus*, 53 Eur J Pol Rsch Pol Data YB 78 (2014).
[46] *Id.*
[47] James Ker-Lindsay and Keith Webb, *Cyprus*, 45 Eur J Pol Rsch 1071, 1076–77 (2006).
[48] Dinkov abd Stoyanov, *supra* note 35, at 200.
[49] Erol Kaymak and Hubert Faustmann, *Cyprus*, 49 Eur J Pol Rsch 923, 930 (2010).
[50] Ahmet Sozen and Hubert Faustmann, *Cyprus*, 55 Eur J Pol Rsch Pol Data YB 59, 59 (2016).

Given that both presidents of the Republic of Cyprus and the TRNC belong to the moderate camp, there seemed to be a window of opportunity for the final resolution of Cyprus question. In 2019, a meeting of the two leaders, in the presence of the UN Secretary-General, was held in Berlin to discuss the future of Cyprus. Possible ways of two countries, confederation or a federal country were discussed and the option for a federal country was agreed.[51] However, this window was soon closed in 2020 with the victory of the hard-liner Ersin Tatar, who demanded two countries or confederation.[52] The newly-elected Nikos Christodoulides of the Republic of Cyprus is also considered a hard-liner.

Table 4.2 Political Orientation of the Leaders of TRNC

President	**Party**	**Position**
Rauf Denktash (1983–2005)	National Unity Party (UBP)	Hard-liner
Mehmet Ali Talat (2005–2010)	Republican Turkish Party (CTP)	Moderate
Derviş Eroğlu (2010–2015)	National Unity Party (UBP)	Hard-liner
Mustafa Akinci (2015–2020)	Communal Democracy Party (TDP)	Moderate
Ersin Tatar (2020–present)	National Unity Party (UBP)	Hard-liner

The political climate pre-determines the debate about the future of Cyprus, which in turn shapes, formulates or even constrains the pace and progress of economic cooperation across the island. Given that the Republic of Cyprus does not recognise the TRNC, the presidents of the two sides meet as "leaders", and frequently this unofficial format escapes parliamentary oversight thus undermining democratic legitimacy and accountability. In addition to this high-level political dialogue, where democratic legitimacy and accountability are weak, technical and practical parts of economic cooperation are at times delegated to non-official or semi-official organisations; this further challenges democratic control and accountability mechanisms. Moreover, as the Republic of Cyprus acceded to the EU on May 1, 2004, trade across the island has become an issue of free circulation within the internal market and subject to EU laws and regulations, such that the ownership of policies affecting economic cooperation across the island may be questionable.

[51] Ahmet Sözen and Hubert Faustmann, *Cyprus: Political Developments and Data in 2019*, 59 Eur J Pol Rsch Pol Data YB 82, 82–83 (2020).

[52] Hubert Faustmann and Ahmet Sözen, *Cyprus: Political Developments and Data in 2020*, 60 Eur J Pol Rsch Pol Data YB 84, 92 (2021).

B. The Republic of Cyprus' Non-Recognition of the Turkish Republic of Northern Cyprus and Economic Repercussions

Though the TRNC declared independence in 1983, the UN called for all member states not to recognise it. Therefore, the TRNC is faced with international isolation (with the exception of Turkey). The Republic of Cyprus, which is the sole legitimate government representing the whole island, "has persistently asserted its *de jure* authority over and against the de facto reality of a distinct entity governing [N]orthern Cyprus".[53] The response of the Chargé d'affaires a.i. of the Permanent Mission of Cyprus to the UN concerning a statement of the Turkish Cypriot leader, Mr. Mehmet Ali Talat during an interview by the Turkish newspaper *The New Anatolian* hoping to reopen the ports and airports in the North and to end the economic isolation best illustrated this situation. In a letter dated August 19, 2005 addressed to the Secretary-General of the UN, the Republic of Cyprus maintained:

> following the Turkish military invasion and occupation of the northern part of the island, the Government of the Republic of Cyprus declared all ports of entry into the Republic of Cyprus which are situated in those areas as closed. In particular with regard to airports, it should be noted that the Government of the Republic of Cyprus acted in accordance with the Chicago Convention on International Civil Aviation, which provides that "the contracting States recognize that every State has complete and exclusive sovereignty over the airspace above its territory", including designation of official ports of entry. Moreover, according to International Civil Aviation Organization decisions of 1974, 1975, and 1977, a country not exercising, temporarily, effective control over its territory by reasons of military occupation, does not lose its sovereign rights over its territory and the airspace above it. In that context, the two airports operating in the occupied area of the island – over which the Government of the Republic of Cyprus has temporarily no access or effective control and consequently is not in a position to impose the terms of operation and international safety standards – are illegal and pose potential safety concerns to civil aviation.[54]

For the Republic of Cyprus, the ports and airports are closed; their use by Turkish Cypriots in the North is illegal and poses a threat to civil aviation safety. As international travel to and from ports and airports would implicate the regulatory authority of Northern Cyprus under the TRNC, this is the last thing the Republic of Cyprus wants to see. To this end, its economic engagements with Northern Cyprus are to be guided by this political objective. That being said, before the accession of the Republic of Cyprus into the EU, the political and subsequently economic separation between Northern and Southern Cyrus were imposed mutually and inter-communal trade was virtually non-existent.

[53] Tufan Ekici, The Political and Economic History of North Cypurs: A Discordant Polity 35 (2019).

[54] UN General Assembly Security Council, Letter Dated 19 August 2005 from the Charge D'affaires AI of the Permanent Mission of Cyprus to the United Nations Addressed to the Secretary-General, UN Doc A/59/899–S/2005/537 (Aug 23, 2005).

Inter-communal trade was made possible only after the adoption of the Council Regulation (EC) No 866/2004 (Green Line Regulation)[55] and personal movements crossing the Line took place a bit earlier on 23 April 2003 when then-president of the TRNC, Denktash, unilaterally and unexpectedly eased border travel restrictions and allowed all Cypriots to cross the line. This decision was believed to be a response to the failed UN peace talks and the signing of the EU accession treaty by the Republic of Cyprus. Leaders of the Turkish Cypriots claimed that this easing of travel restrictions was a symbol of good will that contributed to confidence and community building, while Greek Cypriot leaders saw it as a tactic to divert attention from the Turkish Cypriots' negative attitude.[56] Regardless of the hidden motives and divergent perception on this relaxation of travel restrictions, the free movement of persons crossing the line was made possible unilaterally by the TRNC's decision and was subsequently formalised under the Green Line Regulation.

C. The TRNC's Economic Isolation as a Result of the Anastasiou Saga

Since the North–South division of Cyprus in the 1960s, Northern Cyprus, under the governance regimes of the TRNC and its predecessor the TFSC, has relied heavily on trade and investment and aid from Turkey. In addition, the TRNC had relied on Turkish ports and airports to access to European and other foreign market. However, the TRNC's access to the European market was later denied due to a series of decisions, commonly known as the *Anastasiou* saga,[57] handed down by the European Court of Justice (ECJ, now the Court of Justice of the European Union), which resulted in a greater degree of economic isolation for Northern Cyprus. Though these cases involved economic interests, they also implicated recognition of regulatory authority of the TRNC and were thus an extension of the political and diplomatic rivalry between the TRNC and the Republic of Cyprus.

The *Anastasiou* saga started from a legal challenge before the High Court of Justice in the UK by SP Anastasiou (Pissouri) Ltd, twelve Greek-Cypriot producers and exporters of citrus fruit and by the national market board for potatoes in the Republic of Cyprus against the Minister of Agriculture, Fisheries

[55] Corrigendum to Council Regulation (EC) No 866/2004 of 29 April 2004 on a regime under Article 2 of Protocol 10 to the Act of Accession, 2004 OJ (L 206) 51.

[56] Craig Webster and Dallen J Timothy, *Travelling to the 'Other Side': the Occupied Zone and Greek Cypriot Views of Crossing the Green Line*, 8 Tourism Geographies 162, 170 (2006).

[57] On this *Anastasiou* saga, see Maries Cremona, *Case C-432/92 R v* Minister of Agriculture, Fisheries and Food, ex parte S P Anastasiou (Pissouri) LtD and others, *Judgement of 5 July 1994*, 33 Common Mkt L Rev 125 (1996); Panos Koutrakos, *Legal Issues of EC–Cyprus Trade Relations*, 52 Int'l & Compar LQ 489 (2003); Nicholas Emiliou, *Cypriot Import Certificates: Some Hot Potatoes*, 20 Eur L Rev 202 (1995); Stéphanie Laulhé Shaelou, *The European Court of Justice and the* Anastasiou *Saga: Principles of Europeanisation through Economic Governance*, 18 Eur Bus L Rev 619 (2007); Stefan Talmon, *The Cyprus Question before the European Court of Justice*, 12 Eur J Int'l L 727 (2001).

and Food. The complainants alleged that British acceptance of rule of origin and sanitary and phytosanitary certificates from Northern Cyprus, or the TRNC, was not consistent with EU law. The High Court then referred this case to the ECJ. The question that the High Court asked was, essentially, whether the UK could accept rule of origin and sanitary and phytosanitary certificates issued in Northern Cyprus.

The UK and the European Commission argued that in view of the special situation of Cyprus, namely, the impossibility or impracticability for the producers in Northern Cyprus to obtain export certificates issued by anyone other than authorities in that part of Cyprus, the Origin Protocol and Council Directive 77/93/EEC of 21 December 1976 on protective measures against the introduction into the Member States of organisms harmful to plants or plant products (Plant Health Directive) had to be interpreted to the effect that "the authorities of the Member States are bound, with regard to products from the northern part of Cyprus, to accept certificates issued by the entity established in that part of the island and not by officials authorised by the Republic of Cyprus, in order to prevent discrimination between nationals or companies of Cyprus".[58] Emphatically, the UK and the Commission argued that "de facto acceptance of the certificates in question issued by authorities other than the competent authorities of the Republic of Cyprus is certainly not tantamount to recognition of the TRNC as a State, but represents the necessary and justifiable corollary of the need to take the interests of the whole population of Cyprus into account".[59]

This argument nonetheless failed to persuade the ECJ which, fully aware of the political implications of this controversy, undertook a legalistic and technical approach. It started with the direct effect of the Origin Protocol by observing that this regulated the scope of products benefitting from preferential treatment in the EEC market and thus contained "clear, precise and unconditional obligations" to be able to have direct effects in national courts. The acceptance of origin certificates was founded on the "principle of mutual reliance and cooperation between the competent authorities of the exporting State and those of the importing State".[60] In accordance with this principle, the customs authorities in Cyprus and the EEC would cooperate in checking the authenticity of these certificates. In the case of certificates issued by authorities in Northern Cyprus, such a check was not possible. Therefore, the ECJ ruled that the Origin Protocol and Plant Health Directive should be interpreted as precluding member states from accepting rule of origin and sanitary and phytosanitary certificates issued by anyone other than competent authorities of the Republic of Cyprus.[61]

[58] Case C-432/92, *The Queen v Minister of Agric, Fisheries and Food, ex parte SP Anastasiou (Pissouri) Ltd and others*, [1990] ECR I-3087 [hereinafter *Anastasiou I*], para 19.

[59] *Id.* para 34.

[60] *Id.* para 38.

[61] *Id.* para 67.

After *Anastasiou I*, producers in Northern Cyprus signed an agreement with a Turkish company providing that products originating from Northern Cyprus stop at a Turkish port for 24 hours during which Turkish officials would inspect the goods and issue the certificates. The dispute again came before the ECJ through a preliminary ruling from the British Court. The key issue was whether the Origin Protocol and Plant Health Directive should be interpreted as accepting certificates issued by a country other than where the products originated. The ECJ answered affirmatively. According to the Court, the objective of the Plant Health Directive was to safeguard the Community from harmful organisms communicating through plant products. This objective was normally achieved through the task entrusted to the importing country where the products originated. Nonetheless, such objective can also be "attained without requiring plants originating outside the Community to undergo a certification procedure in their country of origin",[62] as long as the products remained in a third country "for such time and under such conditions as to enable the proper checks to be completed".[63]

The rather liberal reading of the Court in *Anastasiou II* on the Origin Protocol and Plant Health Directive temporarily left a door open for products of Northern Cyprus to access to European market; this was soon to be closed. *Anastasiou III* related to a technical requirement in the annex of Plant Health Directive, which provided for an "appropriate origin mark" to be affixed to packaging. The Court stressed that such an origin mark allowed the exporters to furnish official statements in the country of the origin. It would be paradoxical if such an origin mark could be provided by a third country other than where the products originated.[64] Based on this technical requirement, the Court of Justice effectively denied products of Northern Cyprus access to the European market. The Court's decision may have been driven by the imminent accession of Cyprus to the EU and the belief that a comprehensive settlement of the Cyprus issue was possible. As history has shown, the Court's ruling strengthened the need for regulation of the North-South Cyprus trade and subsequently the entry into the European market in consideration of the suspension of the *acquis* in Northern Cyprus as provided in the Accession Protocol.

D. The TRNC's Limited International Engagements

Since the division of Turkish Cypriots in the North and Greek Cypriots in the South, the international community has recognised only the Republic of Cyprus. Since Turkish Cyprus established its administration under the name of TFSC in 1974 and declared the independence of the TRNC in 1983, Turkey has

[62] Case C-219/98, *Regina v Minister of Agric, Fisheries and Food, ex parte SP Anastasiou (Pissouri) Ltd and Others*, [2000] ECR I-05241 [hereinafter *Anastasiou II*], para 32.

[63] *Id* para 36.

[64] Case C140/02, *Regina on the application of SP Anastasiou (Pissouri) Ltd and Others v Minister of Agric, Fisheries and Food*, 2003 ECR I-10635 (*Anastasiou III*), para 60.

been the only country that recognises Northern Cyprus as a state. The UN also issued a number of resolutions denying the legality of the declaration of independence of Northern Cyprus and calling upon its members not to recognise it. For this reason, the TRNC has been excluded from participating in major international institutions, in particular the UN system. Nonetheless, the TRNC has sought participation in international organisations and has made limited progress. Those organisations are mainly those founded by and composed of Islamic countries, such as the Organisation of Islamic Cooperation and the Organisation of Economic Cooperation. In addition, under the framework of the Council of Europe, Northern Cyprus did get its reward after the 2004 referendum. The Parliamentary Assembly of the Council of Europe (PACE) in 2004 adopted Resolution 1376:

> The Assembly considers it unfair for the Turkish Cypriot community, which has expressed clear support for a reunited and European Cyprus, to continue to be denied representation in the European political debate. Such continued isolation may help strengthen the positions of those who are opposing a unified Cyprus. The Assembly therefore decides to associate more closely elected representatives of the Turkish Cypriot community in the work of the Parliamentary Assembly and its committees, beyond the framework of Assembly Resolution 1113 (1997) on the situation in Cyprus and integrate them into the Cypriot delegation.[65]

In accordance with this Resolution, Turkish Cypriots in Northern Cyprus are able to participate in the PACE under the title "elected representatives of the Turkish Cypriot community".[66] Finally, it is worth noting that, since 2014, Turkish Cypriots have been able to vote for the Members of the European Parliament (MEP) even though the elections are held in the Republic of Cyprus and Turkish Cypriots must cross the border to cast their votes. They are also able to run for the position of MEP, as long as they stand on a joint ticket with other Greek-Cypriot candidates. On 26 May 2019, Niyazi Kızılyürek, a Turkish Cypriot who received his high-school education in Northern Cyprus, obtained a degree in Germany but teaches at the University of Cyprus, was elected as an MEP.[67]

III. FORM AND SUBSTANCE OF ECONOMIC COOPERATION

A. The Unexpected Relaxation of the Travel Ban by Northern Cyprus

Travel between North and South Cyprus was made possible on April 23, 2003, which was the first step for economic cooperation across the island.

[65] Eur Parl Ass, *Resolution 1376* (Apr 29, 2004), paras 5–6.

[66] *See Relations with Parliamentary Assembly of Council of Europe*, TRNC Ministry of Foreign Affairs. Available at: https://mfa.gov.ct.tr/foreign-policy/international-organisations/council-of-europe/pace/ (last visited Apr 12, 2024).

[67] *Cyprus elects first Turkish Cypriot as MEP*, France 24 (May 26, 2019). Available at: www.france24.com/en/20190526-cyprus-elects-first-turkish-cypriot-mep.

The unilateral decision to open the border came rather unexpectedly from the northern side. In legal terms, a case handed down by the European Court of Human Rights on February 20, 2003 motivated this move,[68] but, according to James Ker-Lindsay, Rauf Denktash, the leader of Northern Cyprus, decided to open the border with a view to assuaging domestic discontent and political pressure. When the Republic of Cyprus sought accession to the EU, Denktash considered it unlikely as he believed that Turkey would not support this bid. However, the victory of Recep Tayyip Erdogan in November 2002, whose primary goal is that Turkey joins the EU, and his willingness to resolve the Cyprus issue opened a window of opportunity for settlement and narrowed down the policy space of Denktash. The UN Secretary-General Kofi Annan introduced his proposal, but Denktash declined Annan's suggestion to hold simultaneous referenda in both of the Greek and Turkish communities. With the EU's decision to welcome the Republic of Cyprus as a new member state, along with nine other countries, on April 16, 2003, the political pressure overwhelmed Denktash and forced him to relax the travel ban. The Turkish-Cypriot authority announced that Greek Cypriots would be allowed to cross the Green Line as long as they presented a valid passport and filled out a visa form. Within two weeks, it is estimated that a quarter of the population on the island, 200,000 people, had crossed over; the atmosphere was largely positive without any major intercommunal violence reported.[69]

The crossing of the Green Line has been institutionalised since Denktash's decision to allow cross-island travel and the adoption of the Green Line Regulation. Two checkpoints (one on the Turkish Cypriot side, one on the Greek Cypriot side) are to be passed when crossing the Line; the UN buffer zone lies in between. As noted above, the Republic of Cyprus still considers Turkish Cypriots in the north of the island its nationals, and some Turkish Cypriots hold Republic of Cyprus passports. This category of Turkish Cypriots can cross the Line without any problems. Even if Turkish Cypriots use their official documents, i.e., identity cards issued by the authorities of Northern Cyprus, they can easily pass through the Line. A tricky question then relates to third country nationals, which can be distinguished by the following categories: EU nationals, non-EU nationals and third-country immigrants in Northern Cyprus. The first two categories of third-country nationals have no difficulties in crossing the Line with proper documents but third-country immigrants are problematic. Third-country immigrants are, of course, entitled to use their original passports (e.g. from the Philippines) to cross the Line; however, given that the Republic of Cyprus maintains that Northern Cyprus is under illegal military occupation and denies the legality and legitimacy of third-country immigrants in the North,

[68] Djavit An v. Turkey, III Eur. Ct. H.R. 2003. Available at: https://hudoc.echr.coe.int/eng?i=001-60953 (holding by a vote of six to one that by refusing the applicant to cross the Line to participate in a bi-communal meeting, violates Articles 11 and 13 of the Convention).

[69] James Ker-Lindsay, The Cyprus Problem: What Everyone Needs to Know 61–62 (2011).

they cannot cross the Line with their official documents issued by the authorities of Northern Cyprus. Moreover, the legal status of Turkish settlers in the North is denied by the Republic of Cyprus. These Turkish settlers and their offspring, even if one of their parents is Turkish Cypriot, are prevented from crossing the Line.

B. Economic Cooperation Through EU Law: Green Line Regulation

(i) Cyprus's EU Membership Bid and North Cyprus's Economic Isolation

Given that the Republic of Cyprus does not recognise Northern Cyprus and has consistently prevented any measures that would imply such recognition, economic relations involving the crossing of persons, goods and services were reduced to a minimum, if not zero, before the adoption of the Green Line Regulation after Cyprus acceded to the EU in 2004. For the Republic of Cyprus, the ports in Northern Cyprus are all closed; this remains unchanged even after Cyprus's accession. In Cyprus' long march to the EU, two lines of negotiations were taking place: one, of course, the EU accession negotiation; the other being a political solution for the Cyprus issue proposed by the UN Secretary-General Kofi Annan.[70] At the time, there was a great deal of optimism about a comprehensive settlement and it was expected that a united Cyprus would be joining the EU; subsequent developments proved otherwise.

In contrast to the Republic of Cyprus' confident pursuit of EU membership, Northern Cyprus was excluded during the accession negotiation processes, so it was faced with two obstacles in pursuit of its economic relations: one with the Republic of Cyprus in the South and the other with the EU. With regard to the access of Northern Cyprus to the European market, the thorny issue was the certificate of rule of origin and health inspection certificate for sanitary and phytosanitary measures, which would require the recognition of public authorities of Northern Cyprus.[71] As noted above, this recognition issue eventually led to Northern Cyprus's access to the European market being shut down by the ECJ through the series of *Anastasiou* cases.

(ii) Green Line Regulation after Cyprus' Accession to the EU

With the Greek Cypriots' defeat of the Annan Plan, in contrast to Turkish Cypriots' approval, legal and economic relations between Northern Cyprus

[70] See generally, Claire Palley, An International Relations Debacle: the UN Secretary-General's Mission of Good Offices in Cyprus 1999–2004 (2005); Reunifying Cyprus: the Annan Plan and Beyond (Andrekos Varnava and Hubert Faustmann eds, 2009).

[71] Nikos Skoutaris, The Cyprus Issue: the Four Freedoms in a Member States under Siege 126–27 (2011).

and the EU in general and Republic of Cyprus in particular have been carefully arranged. Article 1(1) of Cyprus' accession protocol[72] suspends the application of acquis in Northern Cyprus, i.e. "those areas of the Republic of Cyprus in which the Government of the Republic of Cyprus does not exercise effective control" as the Treaty language puts it. As Article 2(1) of the Cyprus' accession protocol further dictates, "[T]he Council, acting unanimously on the basis of a proposal from the Commission, shall define the terms under which the provisions of EU law shall apply to the line between those areas referred to in Article 1 and the areas in which the Government of the Republic of Cyprus exercises effective control". This lays down the legal basis as well as the obligation for the Union legislature to regulate trade crossing the line and subsequently into the EU market, the end product being the Green Line Regulation. Below, we will examine the regulation on trade, services and free movement of persons as contained in the Green Line Regulation. However, before taking a closer look at the provisions in the Green Line Regulation, it is practical to make some general observations.

To begin with, the Green Line Regulation uses the terminology of "areas" to refer to those areas effectively controlled by the Republic of Cyprus and those that are not. This terminology is politically motivated and tries to downplay the sensitive recognition issue. As the EU recognises the Republic of Cyprus as the only legitimate government, and as the Republic by no means wishes to enhance the political status of Northern Cyprus or recognition of the TRNC, such neutral terminology seems appropriate. The long descriptive phrase "under effective control" is, of course, a concept commonly used in public international law with a view to establishing the international responsibilities of a state or international organisation through the attribution doctrine. The usage of "area" in conjunction with a descriptive clause "under effective control" aims to portray an objective situation of the island of Cyprus. But of course, this de-politicised terminology exposes its political sensitivities. Secondly, given that the Republic of Cyprus does not recognise the TRNC, any formalities related to TRNC that would imply recognition are to be avoided. Therefore, the Green Line Regulation entrusted the Turkish Cypriot Chamber of Commerce (TCCoC) to issue relevant documents for goods destined to cross the line. This designation is, of course, reflective of the *Anastasiou* saga. Interestingly though, Turkish Cypriots, if qualified as "citizens of the Republic", may cross the line by presenting documents issued by the Turkish Cypriot authorities

[72] Act concerning the conditions of accession of the Czech Republic, the Republic of Estonia, the Republic of Cyprus, the Republic of Latvia, the Republic of Lithuania, the Republic of Hungary, the Republic of Malta, the Republic of Poland, the Republic of Slovenia and the Slovak Republic and the adjustments to the Treaties on which the European Union is founded, Protocol No 10 on Cyprus, 2003 OJ (L 236) 955.

(iii) Trade from the North to South and then the EU Market

Free Movement of Goods

As the Republic of Cyprus joined the EU in 2004 and became a Member State of the Union, the line does not constitute an external border of the EU;[73] nonetheless, the free circulation of goods originating from Northern Cyprus is not possible given the suspension of *aquis* thereupon. For goods originating from Northern Cyprus to cross the line and enter into the areas under effective control of the Republic of Cyprus, some requirements must be satisfied: rule of origin documents, sanitary and phytosanitary inspection, and value-added taxes (VAT) if the goods are to enter the territory of other Member States.

Article 4(1) of the Green Line Regulation puts forward two alternate conditions for goods originating from Northern Cyprus to be eligible for the benefits arising thereof: "wholly obtained" or "last substantially economically processed". The first condition is clear. If a good is wholly obtained in Northern Cyprus, it qualifies under the Green Line Regulation. Otherwise, the good has to undergo "its last, substantial, economically justified processing or working in an undertaking equipped" for the purpose of crossing the Line and entering into the Republic of Cyprus. TCCoC is entrusted with the task of ensuring that products crossing the Line fulfil one of these two conditions and are thus eligible for relevant documents. If the goods satisfy either of these conditions, they are not subject to customs duties or charges having equivalent effect.[74]

In addition to the rule of origin, the other contested issue in the *Anastasiou* saga is sanitary and phytosanitary inspection, which must be addressed by independent phytosanitary experts appointed by the European Commission in conjunction with TCCoC. Special emphasis is placed on the inspection of potatoes and citrus fruits, as they constitute the main exports of Northern Cyprus.[75] Finally, if the final destination of the goods is not the Republic of Cyprus but another member state of the EU, the goods must be treated as "an importation of goods" in accordance with the Value Added Tax Directive.[76]

Therefore, the attitude of the Green Line Regulation towards goods originating from North Cyprus is ambivalent. On the one hand, the line does not constitute an external border of the Union; once the rule of origin and sanitary and phytosanitary requirements are fulfilled, customs duties are not to be imposed. On the other hand, if the goods cross the line, enter the Republic and continue to other EU member states, the goods should be treated as an imports and VAT should be imposed.[77]

[73] Council Regulation (EC) 866/2004, 2004 OJ (L 206) 128, 130 [hereinafter Green Line Regulation].

[74] *Id.* art 4(2).

[75] Commission Regulation (EC) No 1480/2004 of 10 August 2004 Laying Down Specific Rules Concerning Goods Arriving from the Areas not under the Effective Control of the Government of Cyprus in the Areas in which the Government Exercises Effective Control, Art. 3, 2004 OJ (L 272) 3.

[76] Council Directive 77/388/EEC, 2006 OJ (L 347) 1 (repealed by Council Directive 2006/112/EC of 28 November 2006 on the common system of value added tax, 2006 OJ (L347) 1).

[77] Skoutaris, *supra* note 71, at 14–41.

Free Provision of Services

The Green Line Regulation touches slightly upon free provision of services and addresses only the VAT issue. When services are supplied across the Line, to and from the areas that are not under effective control of the Republic of Cyprus, by persons established or having their permanent address or usual residence therein, such services should be deemed as received or supplied by persons established or having their permanent address in the areas subject to the effective control of the Republic of Cyprus for the purposes of VAT.[78] Therefore, they are exempt from VAT.

Free Movement of Persons

Regarding the free movement of persons, the Green Line Regulation sets out three categories for persons to cross the line: EU citizens, citizens of the Republic of Cyprus and third-country nationals.[79] In designing the regulatory regime for the free movement of persons within the island of Cyprus, three factors are to be considered: rights of free movement of EU citizens, legitimate concerns of the Republic of Cyprus and the threat public security and public policy.[80] In view of these divergent rights, concerns, and interests, Article 6 of the Green Line Regulation lays down the rules and procedures for effective surveillance of illegal immigrants into the EU after crossed the line. Third-country nationals are only allowed to cross the Line provided they possess the relevant documents and do not present a challenge to either public policy or security. These documents, corresponding to the legal status of third-country nationals, may either be residence permits or travel documents, and a valid visa may be required when applicable.[81]

The critical issue here is how to distinguish citizens of the Republic of Cyprus and third-country nationals, in particular "settlers" from Turkey in Northern Cyprus. Whereas Turkish Cypriots, in accordance with the Citizenship Law of 1967, are entitled to claim nationality from the Republic of Cyprus, the Citizenship Law of 1967 does not extend this privilege to Turkish settlers. Therefore, in crossing the Line, Turkish settlers are to be treated as third-party nationals. Article 1(2) of the Green Line Regulation defines third-country nationals as follows: "any person who is not a citizen of the Union within the meaning of Article 17(1) of the EC Treaty". The condition to be a citizen of the EU is being a national of an EU member state. Without directly addressing the legal status of Turkish settlers, the Green Line Regulation refers to the technical definition provided in the EC Treaty and thus avoids this thorny issue. In effect, the power to define the scope of EU citizens and third-country nationals is left to the Republic of Cyprus. In practice, Turkish settlers and their offspring and immigrants in Northern Cyprus have difficulties in crossing the Line with documents issued by the TRNC.

[78] Green Line Regulation, *supra* note 74, art 7.
[79] *Id*. recital 6; art 2.
[80] *Id*. recital 7; art 2(1).
[81] *Id*. art 2(3).

Trade from the South to the North

For the goods originating from the south entering into the north of Cyprus, or from the areas under effective control of Republic of Cyprus to those that are not, the export formalities are not necessary. This corresponds to the rationale that the Line does not constitute an export border of the Union. Based on this logic, VAT is also exempt. Nonetheless, some sort of documentation is also required.[82] Northern Cyprus maintains a system that mirrors the regulatory regime put forward by the Green Line Regulation: the Charter on limitation of exports from the TRNC region to South Cyprus and of imports from South Cyprus to the TRNC. In accordance with this Charter, goods originating from the Republic of Cyprus are to be accompanied by documents issued by the Greek Cypriot Chamber of Commerce, officially named the Cyprus Chamber of Commerce and Industry (CCCI).[83]

The Implementation of the Green Line Regulation: An Assessment

The Green Line Regulation obliges the European Commission to annually report the implementation of this regulation. As can be seen in the chart below, since 2004, trade from Northern Cyprus to Southern Cyprus grew significantly, reaching its peak in 2008 and then moderating. Since then, the trade volume has been quite stable, around €4 million per year since 2012. Since 2015, the Green Line trade regained its momentum, continued to climb, and reached its second peak in 2019, when the COVID-19 pandemic broke out. The trade volume across the Green Line is illustrated in Table 4.1 below.

Figure 4.1 Trade Volume Across the Green Line

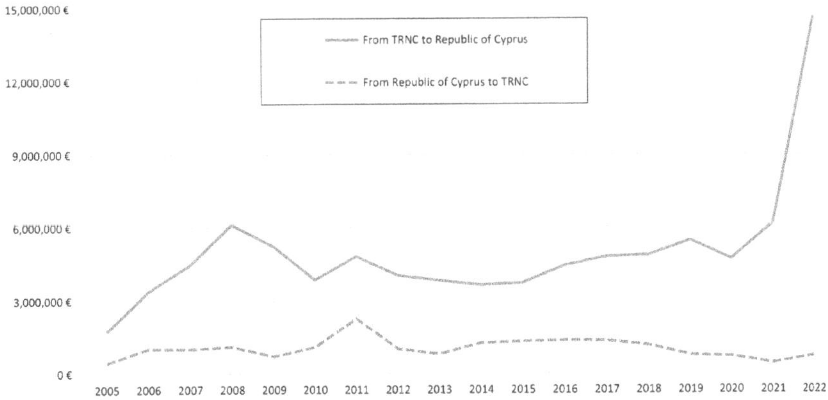

NB: Without taking into account the sale of electricity (€24,096,046) in 2011.

Source: European Commission. Available at: https://eur-lex.europa.eu/legal-content/EN/TXT/PDF/?uri=CELEX:52012DC0251.

[82] Green Line Regulation, *supra* note 73, art 5.
[83] Skoutaris, *supra* note 71, at 143.

During 2019, plastic products were the most traded item, followed by fresh fish, building materials and potatoes.[84] In 2022, building materials were most traded.[85] Potatoes, originally a key trade product, have fallen in importance. An unusual genre of trade is electricity, the demand for which arose from a huge explosion at the Evangelos Florakis military-naval base which subsequently damaged the largest, most important power plant in the Republic of Cyprus.[86] Electricity trade constitutes a peculiar element of North–South trade on the island and will be further discussed below.

Figure 4.2 Total Spread of Values of Sales Through the Green Line: From TRNC to the Republic of Cyprus

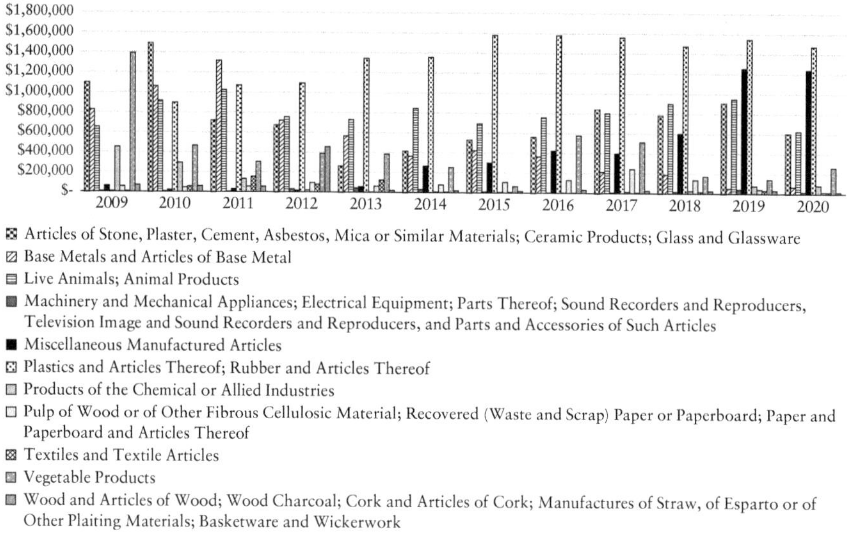

Source: Turkish Cypriot Chamber of Commerce. Available at: www.ktto.net/en/statistics/.

Chronic issues persist in trade across the island, including recognition of the roadworthiness of vehicles and driver's licenses issued by the Turkish Cypriot authorities. As the 2016 Annual Report noted, commercial vehicles above 7.5 tons were not permitted to cross the Line unless they complied with the regulations of South Cyprus. The Republic of Cyprus committed to new rules

[84] *Thirteenth report on the implementation of Council Regulation (EC) No 866/2004 of 29 April 2004 and the situation resulting from its application covering the period 1 January until 31 December 2016*, at 5, COM (2017) 371 final (July 7, 2017) [hereinafter *2017 Implementation Report*]. This issue was already identified in the first Commission report. *See Report on the Implementation of Council Regulation (EC) 866/2004 of 29 April 2004 and the situation resulting from its application*, at 4, COM (2005) 0320 final (July 14, 2005) [hereinafter *2005 Implementation Report*].

[85] *Nineteenth report on the implementation of Council Regulation (EC) No 866/2004 of 29 April 2004 and the situation resulting from its application covering the period 1 January until 31 December 2022*, at 2, COM (2023) 354 final (June 29, 2023) [hereinafter *2022 Implementation Report*].

[86] UN Secretary-General, *Report of the Secretary-General on the United Nations operation in Cyprus*, para 11, UN Doc S/2011/746 (November 30, 2011).

to allow Turkish Cypriots to obtain roadworthiness certificates and professional driving licences, which might significantly boost trade volume.[87] As of 2022, the issue was yet to be resolved.[88] It is also reported that Turkish Cypriot buses carrying EU citizens are not permitted to cross the Line unless they possess *acquis*-compliant documents issued by the authorities of the Republic of Cyprus.[89] Other similar regulatory obstacles linger. Another issue about which North Cyprus complains relates to trade in processed food products and the lack of access to the Republic of Cyprus due to food safety concerns. The European Commission opines that, where the Republic of Cyprus may collect samples of the product for analysis, there is no legal basis in the Green Line Regulation for the authorities of the Republic of Cyprus to check the production process of the premise in the North Cyprus to confirm if producers are complying with relevant EU regulations.[90]

C. Economic Cooperation Through EU Law Resisted and Beyond Trade

The Green Line Regulation is nonetheless still of limited help to Northern Cyprus as goods therefrom are to cross the Line to Southern Cyprus. Direct economic interchange between Northern Cyprus and the outside world is still not possible. As noted above, the Republic of Cyprus aims to prevent anything that may implicate the regulatory authority of the TRNC. For the Republic of Cyprus, the ports and airports in the Northern Cyprus are closed and their use by Turkish Cypriots are illegal. However, Northern Cyprus's need for economic engagement with the wider world is equally compelling, at least from the EU's perspective, and the deadlock must be broken, especially in view of the Turkish-Cypriot approval of the comprehensive settlement of the Cyprus proposal by the UN Secretary-General Kofi Annan at the simultaneous referendum held on April 24, 2004. As the Council of the EU on April 26, 2004 stated,

> The Turkish Cypriot community have expressed their clear desire for a future within the European Union. The Council is determined to put an end to the isolation of the Turkish Cypriot community and to facilitate the reunification of Cyprus by encouraging the economic development of the Turkish Cypriot community. The Council invited the Commission to bring forward comprehensive proposals to this end, with particular emphasis on the economic integration of the island and on improving contact between the two communities and with the EU.[91]

In response, the European Commission soon introduced a proposal to allow direct trade between Northern Cyprus and other EU Member States without

[87] *2017 Implementation Report*, *supra* note 84, at 6–7. This issue was already identified in the *2005 Implementation Report*, *supra* note 85, at 4.

[88] 2022 Implementation Report, *supra* note 85, at 6.

[89] *Id*. at 2.

[90] *2017 Implementation Report*, *supra* note 84, at 6–7.

[91] Council of the European Union, *2576th Council Meeting – General Affairs – Luxembourg*, Press (2004) 115 (Apr 26, 2004).

having to first cross the line to Southern Cyprus[92] but this legislative proposal has not yet been acted upon. The thrust of this proposed regulation is to allow products originated from Northern Cyprus, or those areas of the Republic of Cyprus in which the Government of the Republic of Cyprus does not exercise effective control, to "be released for free circulation into the customs territory of the Community with exemption from customs duties and charges having equivalent effect within the limits of annual tariff quotas".[93]

The main obstacle for the draft regulation to be written into law is the search for appropriate legal basis. The European Commission refers to Article 133 of the Treaty Establishing the European Community (now Treaty on the Functioning of the European Union, TFEU, art. 207) which regulates common commercial policy and is subject to qualified majority rule after the Lisbon Treaty. Cyprus and Greece by contrast insist on the appropriate legal basis for the Draft Regulation to be Article 1(2) of Protocol No 10 annexed to the Treaty of Accession between Cyprus and the EU, signed in April 2003.[94] The Committee of the legal affairs of the European Parliament sided with Greece and Cyprus on this debate.[95] Given that Cyprus joined the EU in 2004 and the North–South Cyprus trade has been transformed into a question of EU law, little progress can be foreseen if the thorny choice of legal basis cannot be sorted out.

Apart from the legal basis, the EU and Republic of Cyprus see the relationship between the economic development of Northern Cyprus and the reunification of Cyprus differently. For the EU, fostering economic development in Northern Cyprus and closing the development gap contribute to peace and community building and thus pave the way for the reunification of Cyprus. By contrast, for the Republic of Cyprus, if Northern Cyprus under the TRNC enjoys similar standards of living, it will reduce the incentive for Turkish Cypriots to unite with the south under the Republic of Cyprus. These divergent beliefs problematise the economic engagement of Northern Cyprus with the wider world.

Finally, economic cooperation under the EU framework may move beyond trade and extends to cultural heritage. Halloumi/Hellim cheese, symbolising the shared heritage of the island of Cyprus and linking the communities living there for centuries, is a case in point. In 2015, then-President of the European Commission Juncker met with the leaders of Turkish and Greek Cypriot communities and reached a common understanding on a temporary solution for Halloumi/Hellim to be implemented pending the reunification of Cyprus, which necessitates the amendment of the Green Line Regulation.

[92] *Proposal for a Council Regulation on special conditions for trade with those areas of the Republic of Cyprus in which the Government of the Republic of Cyprus does not exercise effective control*, COM (2004) 466 final (EC) (Jul 7, 2004) [hereinafter *Draft Direct Trade Regulation*].

[93] *Id.* art 1(1).

[94] Toby Vogel, *MEPs consider allowing EU trade within Northern Cyprus*, Politico (May 19, 2010). Available at: www.politico.eu/article/meps-consider-allowing-eu-trade-with-northern-cyprus/.

[95] *Regulation on direct trade between the EU and occupied Cyprus*, Famagusta Gazette (Oct. 19, 2010), web.archive.org/web/20101027131523/http://famagusta-gazette.com/regulation-on-direct-trade-between-the-eu-and-occupied-cyprus-p10885-69.htm.

The designation of Halloumi/Hellim cheese as protected designation of origin will be applied to the entire island. Given the divide on the island and the fact that the Republic of Cyprus does not effectively control Northern Cyprus and does not recognise its authority, how to conduct quality control under Regulation (EU) No 1151/2012 of the European Parliament and Council of November 21, 2012 on quality schemes for agricultural products and foodstuffs appears challenging. For this reason, it was agreed that Bureau Veritas, an internationally accredited body, will be entrusted with the task of ensuring quality control and compliance with EU standards.[96] Moreover, the reports of Bureau Veritas should be sent to the competent authorities of the Republic of Cyprus and to the Commission while the TCCoC will receive information when deemed appropriate.[97] The case of Halloumi/Hellim cheese shows that, in addition to economic value, cultural heritage also plays a key role in the context of economic cooperation across the island. That said, sovereign concerns may overshadow common cultural heritage. For this reason, Turkish Cypriot authorities are not in a position to produce quality control reports; an international accreditation body will serve this purpose. Further, the semi-official TCCoC plays a supplementary role as it can be informed when appropriate. By doing so, the objective of designating Halloumi/Hellim cheese as one of protected origin may be achieved, and the sensitive sovereignty issues can be sidestepped.

D. Economic Cooperation under the Auspices of the United Nations

The UN has played a critical role in maintaining peace and stability after the ethnical conflict in Cyprus. After Turkey's invasion and occupation of the northern part of Cyprus, the UN is the key actor in brokering and supervising the ceasefire agreement, and the UNICYP is responsible for peacekeeping in the buffer zone. Moreover, various Secretary-Generals of the UN have attempted to mediate or propose a comprehensive settlement of the Cyprus problem. In addition to the political dimension, the UN, especially its special agency the United Nations Development Program (UNDP) and the Secretary-General's "good offices" mission in Cyprus, has also contributed to economic cooperation across the island.

With the divide of Turkish Cypriots in the north and Greek Cypriots in the south since the *coup* followed by the Turkish invasion, various UN

[96] European Commission Press Release IP/15/5448, Cyprus 'Χαλλουμι' (Halloumi)/'Hellim' cheese set to receive Protected Designation of Origin status (Jul 28, 2015). Available at: https://ec.europa.eu/commission/presscorner/detail/en/IP_15_5448). *See also* Kalia Tsiourtou, *Unravelling the Story Behind the Intellectual Property of Halloumi Cheese: A 'State Affair' for Cyprus*, 2 Stockholm Intell Prop L Rev 32 (2019).

[97] Commission Regulation 2021/591, Commission Implementing Regulation (EU) 2021/591 of 12 April 2021 entering a name in the register of protected designations of origin and protected geographical indications ('Χαλλούμι' (Halloumi)/'Hellim' (PDO)), Recital 44, 2021 OJ (L 125) 42.

Secretary-Generals have attempted to facilitate a settlement through good offices. For this to be realised, confidence building across the two communities are necessary for initiating negotiations and concluding agreements. In 1993, in the wake of the failed attempt of "a set of ideas" advanced by the Secretary-General Boutros-Boutros Ghali, the Secretary-General's Deputy Special Representative conducted a series of meetings with the leaders from both communities and presented a package of confidence-building mechanisms,[98] which were gradually implemented and expanded. Currently, 12 technical committees are supervising and resolving differences arising from everyday life across the Green Line.[99] The Technical Committees on Economic and Commercial Matters is of most relevance to this chapter. As the UN mission in Cyprus explains:

> [T]he Technical Committee on economic and commercial matters was established in 2008 by the leaders of the two communities in order to discuss measures and initiatives to promote and facilitate economic contacts and trade between the two sides. The Committee was instrumental in the implementation of several confidence building measures agreed by the two leaders in 2015, including the interconnectivity of the electricity grids and the interoperability of mobile phones.[100]

Before we proceed, one point worthy of reiterating is that the "closure" of ports and airports in the north is a critical issue which has troubled the negotiations since the 1990s. The international community's refusal to recognise Northern Cyprus is the root cause and, at some point, the situations of Taiwan and Northern Cyprus were juxtaposed and compared in parallel. According to the aforementioned 1993 Good Offices report, Denktash, the leader of the Turkish Cypriots, suggested practical ways of opening the Ercan airport (Tymbou) for international travel to destinations in Western Europe without implying recognition of the TRNC. After consulting with the International Civil Aviation Organisation, the Secretary-General concluded that international flights take place in the framework of air service agreements that are concluded exclusively between states, so Denktash's request would be not possible without the recognition of the TRNC. At some point, the air service agreement between Taiwan and the UK was mentioned by Denktash as a point of reference;[101] however, after closer examination of the terms and conditions in that agreement, Northern Cyprus would not accept it as a model because the agreement between Taiwan and the UK may be defined as a commercial agreement in nature.

[98] UN Secretary-General, *Report of the Secretary-General of his Mission on Good Offices in Cyprus*, UN Doc S26026 (July 1, 1993) [hereinafter *1993 Cyprus Good Offices report*].

[99] Mustafa Çıraklı, *Can Confidence Building Measures Help End the Cyprus Deadlock?*, IAI Commentaries (July 7, 2021). Available at: www.iai.it/en/pubblicazioni/can-confidence-building-measures-help-end-cyprus-deadlock.

[100] [*Technical Committee*] *On Economic and Commercial Matters*, UN Cyprus Talks. Available at: https://uncyprustalks.unmissions.org/economic-and-commercial-matters (last visited Mar 25, 2024).

[101] *1993 Cyprus Good Offices report*, *supra* note 98, paras 21–22.

(i) Interconnectivity of Electricity Grids

On July 11, 2011, a huge explosion occurred at the Evangelos Florakis military-naval base in Zygi in Southern Cyprus. Due to this explosion, the most important and largest power plant in the Republic of Cyprus was severely damaged, resulting in electricity problems and widespread power shortages. Thereupon, the leader of the TRNC offered help to the Republic of Cyprus to solve the electricity problem, and this offer of help was accepted. An electricity agreement was signed between the presidents of the Greek Cypriot and Turkish Cypriot Chambers of Commerce.[102] The electricity was thus transmitted to the South from mid-July of 2011. According to this agreement, Northern Cyprus would provide electricity to the Republic of Cyprus until September 2011. Between 100 and 120 megawatts of electricity would be provided during peak hours of electricity demand in the Republic of Cyprus, and between 60 and 70 megawatts of electricity would be sold during low-demand hours.[103] In September 2011, the second private agreement between the two chambers of commerce was signed and both sides agreed to extend the electricity agreement for an additional six months.[104] Electricity sales from the North to the South ended in March 2012. The electricity sales from the Turkish Cypriot side to Greek Cypriot side had a major impact on Green Line trade in 2011 and 2012, resulting in a significant increase in trade volume. According to the European Commission, the electricity sales amounted to €24,085,775 in 2011 and €4,748,881 in 2012.[105]

With the shock of the explosion, the imminent threat of energy insecurity and compelling need for cooperation were felt by both sides of the island. The leaders of the two communities agreed in 2015 to explore possible ways to connect the electricity grids in the North and South, as part of a confidence-building mechanism. On 26 February 2019, under the auspices of Special Representative/Deputy Special Adviser to the Secretary-General on Cyprus, Elizabeth Spehar, the Turkish Cypriot leader, Mr Mustafa Akıncı, and the Greek Cypriot leader, Mr Nicos Anastasiades, announced the completion of the interconnectivity of the two electricity grids. The leaders had decided to make the temporary electricity supply arrangement permanent and without restriction.[106] In other words, the two temporary interconnecting cables, one

[102] UN Secretary-General, *Report of the Secretary-General on the United Nations operation in Cyprus*, para 11, UN Doc S/2011/746 (Nov 30, 2011).

[103] *'Devletsiz' uzlaşı*, Kıbrıs Gazetesi (July 17, 2011). Available at: https://web.archive.org/web/20110719204859/http://www.kibrisgazetesi.com/index.php/cat/2/news/120666/PageName/Ic_Haberler.

[104] *Electricity from TRNC to Greek Cypriots*, Anadolu Agency (Sep 6, 2011). Available at: www.aa.com.tr/en/archive/electricity-from-trnc-to-greek-cypriots/414074.

[105] *Ninth report on the implementation of Council Regulation (EC) 866/2004 of 29 April 2004 and the situation resulting from its application covering the period 1 January until 31 December 2012*, at 6–7, COM (2013) 299 final (May 24, 2013).

[106] *Statement by the United Nations Spokesperson in Cyprus, 26 February 2019*, UN Cyprus Talks (Feb 26, 2019). Available at: https://uncyprustalks.unmissions.org/statement-united-nations-spokesperson-cyprus-26022019.

from Mi Milia to Athalassa and one the Morphou area to Orounta, were to be made permanent, and the transfer of electricity would be provided on an as-needed basis.[107]

Another point worth noting regarding the interconnectivity of electricity grids is that energy security is situated in and closely linked to geopolitics, which policy leaders are painfully aware of in the wake of the Russia-Ukraine war in 2022. Though the two sides of Cyprus agreed to and achieved interconnectivity of electricity grids, they also seek electricity connection with other countries: TRNC with Turkey and Republic of Cyprus with Greece and Israel. On October 11, 2016, the TRNC signed an energy cooperation agreement with Turkey, aiming to connect their electricity grids with a submarine power cable. Though the Economy and Energy Minister of the TRNC Sunat Atun claimed that it was essential for Northern Cyprus to be included in the region's emerging energy picture and be connected to the European grid, some observer cautioned that there is a risk that Turkey is trying to integrate Northern Cyprus into Turkey.[108] In contrast, the Republic of Cyprus pursues a EuroAsia Interconnector, now transformed into the Great Sea Interconnector, linking itself, Greece, and Israel through a high-voltage direct current.[109] This project is, in fact, also supported by the European Commission.[110]

(ii) Interoperability of Mobile Phone and Connectivity 5G Network

As part of a package of confidence-building mechanisms, the leaders of the northern and southern parts of the island agreed to connect the mobile phone networks in 2015; this was finalised in 2019. Prior to this, there was very limited telephone connectivity across the island. The network of the Cyprus Telecommunication Authority (CYTA), the main land-line telephone provider, in Nicosia was connected to the Turkish Cypriot part of Nicosia only by limited telephone lines and the CYTA could not serve other parts of Northern Cyprus.[111]

[107] *CYPRUS: Keeping the power switched on*, Financial Mirror, (Mar 16, 2019). Available at: www.financialmirror.com/2019/03/16/cyprus-keeping-the-power-switched-on/.

[108] Aydin Calik, *The power struggle over the north's electricity*, Cyprus Mail Online (Nov 27, 2016). Available at: https://web.archive.org/web/20171230014020/http://cyprus-mail.com/2016/11/27/power-struggle-norths-electricity/; see also, Mustafa Özge Özden, *Turkey-Cyprus Island Interconnector as an Energy Policy for Turkey*, Transatlantic Policy (Aug 27, 2019). Available at: http://turkishpolicy.com/blog/36/turkey-cyprus-island-interconnector-as-an-energy-policy-for-turkey.

[109] *See generally Ending energy isolation – Project of Common Interest "EuroAsia Interconnector"*, European Commission. Available at: https://commission.europa.eu/projects/ending-energy-isolation-project-common-interest-euroasia-interconnector_en (last accessed May 10, 2024).

[110] *Cyprus to decide on joining Great Sea Interconnector with Israel, Greece*, Philenews (Feb. 2, 2024). Available at: https://in-cyprus.philenews.com/insider/cyprus-to-decide-on-joining-great-sea-interconnector-with-israel-greece/.

[111] *Annual Report 2020*, CYTA. Available at: www.cyta.com.cy/mp/informational/cyta_htmlPages/media_center/annualreports/docs/AnReport_2020_en.pdf (last visited Apr 12, 2024).

Currently, CYTA, Epic, and PrimeTel are the main operators in the Republic of Cyprus and Vodafone/Telsim, and Kibris Mobile Telekomunikasyon Ltd (KKTCELL), a subsidiary of Turkcell, are the main service providers in the TRNC.[112] On February 26, 2019, under the auspices of Special Representative/ Deputy Special Adviser to the Secretary-General on Cyprus, Elizabeth Spehar, "the two leaders decided to implement the confidence-building measure regarding mobile phone interoperability through separate agreements of the operators on both sides with a hub based in Europe, in order to facilitate greater interaction between the two communities".[113]

With the help of roaming services, this problem was partially solved. To be specific, a direct call between the North and South of Cyprus is still not possible, and roaming services with a hub based in Europe is needed. This is considered a legally viable option given that the Republic of Cyprus objected to direct links with Northern Cyprus, which it does not recognise and considers an occupied territory.[114] The first call made as a result of this project was among the leaders of the Turkish and Greek communities.[115] Since then, mobile phones can operate on both sides of the island. Calls can be made by typing the phone number after the code '+90', which is also the dialling code of Turkey, in front of the phone number to call Northern Cyprus, and '+357' to call the Republic of Cyprus. This explains why the Republic of Cyprus is opposed to the idea of direct links between operators across the island.

In addition to mobile phone connection between both sides of island, Greek-Cypriot Negotiator Andreas D Mavroyiannis and the Turkish-Cypriot Special Representative M Ergün Olgun, with the facilitation of the UN Special Representative/Deputy Special Adviser to the Secretary-General on Cyprus Elizabeth Spehar, signed an agreement on the 5G connection across Cyprus in December 2019.[116] According to the agreement, the TV broadcast between the two parties would switch from analogue broadcast to digital broadcast, and the 700 MHz frequency used in TV broadcasts would be allocated to 5G with EU support. The Technical Committee on Broadcasting and Telecommunication plays an important role in the implementation of this Project.

[112] *See generally* Karen Howells and Ebrahim Soujeri, *A Short History and Review of Telecommunications in Cyprus*, 2021 7th IEEE History of Electrotechnology Conference (Nov 10–12, 2021), at 32–37. Available at: https://ieeexplore.ieee.org/document/9787311.

[113] *Statement by the United Nations Spokesperson in Cyprus, 26 February 2019*, *supra* note 106.

[114] *North gears up for mobile link-up with south*, KNEWS (July 2, 2019) Available at: https://knews.kathimerini.com.cy/en/news/north-gears-up-for-mobile-link-up.

[115] Evie Andreou, *Mobile phone links established between two sides*, Cyprus Mail (July 11, 2019). Available at: https://web.archive.org/web/20201127023858/https://cyprus-mail.com/2019/07/11/mobile-phone-links-established-between-two-sides/.

[116] *Statement by the United Nations Spokesperson in Cyprus, 19 November 2021*, UN Cyprus Talks (Nov. 19, 2021). Available at: https://uncyprustalks.unmissions.org/statement-united-nations-spokesperson-cyprus19-november-2021.

E. Bilateral Economic Cooperation Through Chambers of Commerce

Given that the Republic of Cyprus does not recognise the TRNC, and vice versa, official contacts, exchanges or negotiations across the Cyprus island are difficult regardless of the fact that the leaders of both Greek and Turkish Cypriot Communities meet in-person frequently. In addition, the EU does not recognise the TRNC either, though it attempts to foster the economic development of Northern Cyprus through economic cooperation, including trade and investment across the island and the integration of Northern Cyprus into the EU market. In view of these considerations, both economic cooperation between the Republic of Cyprus and the TRNC as well as the EU's engagement with the TRNC must be channelled through indirect means; the two chambers of commerce are key players to this end.

Both the TCCoC and CCCI are private corporate bodies functioning under special laws. The TCCoC was established under the Turkish Cypriot Chamber of Commerce Law, enacted in 1981.[117] However, its troubling history can be dated back to 1958, after the Zurich and London agreements were reached.[118] The CCCI is the Greek Cypriot Chamber of Commerce, officially named the Cyprus Chamber of Commerce and Industry, without limiting itself to Greek Cypriots. It characterises itself as "financially independent, free of any influence by the state",[119] regardless of its status under the special law. Moreover, the TCCoC is authorised by the Turkish Cypriot Chamber of Commerce Law to issue certificates of origin,[120] as the TRNC is not recognised by the international community except Turkey, rendering a certificate of origin issued by the TRNC politically infeasible and impracticable.

Given their status under special laws, these two chambers of commerce play a critical role in advancing and monitoring the progress of economic cooperation across the island when official engagements are infeasible or undesirable. The delegation of authority by their respective governments may not be explicit, but these two chambers on many occasions help to bridge the divide across the island. Overall, the chambers of commerce play the following roles: contracting parties, implementors and collaborators.

In most cases, a formal agreement between public authorities across the island, due to the non-recognition of each other, is not possible, which thus necessitates special arrangements for the *contracting parties*. For this reason, agreements between the North and South of Cyprus are normally signed by

[117] An English translation of the full text of the Turkish Cypriot Chamber of Commerce Law is provided by the Turkish Cypriot Chamber of Commerce itself is available at: https://ktto.net/wp-content/uploads/2020/12/ODA-YASASI_eng.pdf (last visited Apr 12, 2024) [hereinafter Turkish Cypriot Chamber of Commerce Law].

[118] *History of the Chamber*, Turkish Cypriot Chamber of Commerce. Available at: www.ktto.net/en/history-of-the-chamber-2/ (last visited Apr 12, 2024).

[119] *What is the Chamber*, Cyprus Chamber of Commerce and Industry. Available at: https://ccci.org.cy/about-the-ccci/what-is-the-chamber/ (last visited Apr 12, 2024).

[120] Turkish Cypriot Chamber of Commerce Law, *supra* note 117, art 3(1)(e).

these two chambers of commerce. The two electricity purchase agreements in 2011 are cases in point.[121] According to Abboud et al, the president of the CCCI, Manthos Mavrommatis, sent a request to TCCoC with a view to obtaining electricity from the Cyprus Turkish Electricity Authority in the TRNC with the approval of the Republic of Cyprus based on legal advice from the Attorney-General. During the negotiations, technical experts from Electricity Authority of Cyprus also participated. From the perspective of TCCoC, the only question for interconnectivity of electricity was laws and regulations, and in a time of energy crisis necessitating immediate action, this was not a big issue.[122] Informal and formal structures of shared management of the energy crisis driven both by the private sector and government officials on the two sides of the island, led to the conclusion of the electricity purchase agreements with two chambers of commerce being the contracting parties, while the shadow influence of the officials was imminent and the participation of the electricity regulatory authority was indispensable.

The second role played by the two chambers of commerce relates to the *implementation* of the Green Line Regulation on the ground, covering a number of administrative, logistic and statistic matters. There are no "borders" or "customs" across the Green Line, but trade regulatory, supervisory, logistic or statistic issues are necessary. The two chambers of commerce are tasked with these. For example, Article 4 of the Green Line Regulation regulates the treatment of goods originating from the areas not under the effective control of the Government of the Republic of Cyprus; the TCCoC is designated to issue necessary documents for the transportation of goods and keep relevant records to enable the European Commission to monitor Green Line Trade.[123]

Finally, the two chambers of commerce are important *collaborators* for both the UN agencies and the European Commission. For example, the TCCoC collaborated with the UNDP on the UNDP Partnership for the Future,[124] and Action for Cooperation and Trust.[125] Action for Cooperation and Trust is a project aiming to foster economic interdependence, and one of the subject projects is co-implemented by the TCCoC and CCCI. These projects are aimed to enhance the mutual understanding and trust between the two communities. TCCoC also collaborates with the EU on a number of projects, such as Cypriot Civil Society,[126] of which one sub-project (Leading by Example)

[121] Alexander Apostolides et al., *From Conflict to Economic Interdependence in Cyprus*, 24 Peace Rev 430, 434 (2012).

[122] Samer Abboud et al., *Crisis as Impetus Toward Conflict Resolution in Cyprus*, 24 Peace Rev 446, 451 (2012).

[123] Green Line Regulation, *supra* note 73, art 4(3).

[124] *Relations with the United Nations*, Ministry of Foreign Affairs Turkish Republic of Northern Cyprus. Available at: https://mfa.gov.ct.tr/foreign-policy/international-organisations/bm-ile-iliskiler/ (last visited Apr 12, 2024).

[125] Alexander Apostolides et al., *supra* note 121, *at* 431.

[126] *Leading By Example*, Turkish Cypriot Chamber of Commerce. Available at: www.ktto.net/en/leading-by-example-2/ (last visited Apr 12, 2024).

is co-implemented by the two chambers.[127] Similarly, CCCI collaborates with UNDP on such projects as Science and Technology Strategy,[128] aiming to strengthen the technological capacity of developing countries, and the Vienna Program of Action with a view to applying science and technology to resolve fundamental issues facing humankind.[129] CCCI collaborates with the European Commission on a wide array of issues, including EU funding consultancy and advice,[130] talent training,[131] recovery and resilience under the COVID-19 pandemic,[132] and capacity building with a view to taking advantage of the Eastern Mediterranean Regional Network.[133]

IV. EUROPEANISATION OF CYPRUS ECONOMIC RELATIONS OR TAIWANISATION OF NORTHERN CYPRUS? IN SEARCH OF IDENTITY, LEGITIMACY AND ACCOUNTABILITY

Economic cooperation across the Cyprus island has gone through a process of Europeanisation and privatisation, and potentially Northern Cyprus may move toward Taiwanisation. The Europeanisation of economic relations between the North and South of Cyprus results in challenges in democratic legitimacy and accountability mechanism. With the Europeanisation of economic relations across the Cyprus island and the institutionalisation of the Green Line trade, the Cyprus conflict has been transformed into a conformable conflict, which reduces the incentives of Turkish Cypriots to unite with the Republic of Cyprus and may lead to a trend of Taiwanisation of Northern Cyprus. At this point, identity politics play a critical role in determining the limit of economic cooperation across the island. We will unpack these factors below.

Though the EU had repeatedly emphasised its hope of Cyprus' joining the Union as a united country, the political project advanced by the Annan Plan did not work out due to the rejection by Greek Cypriots during the simultaneous referendum. As a result, the Republic of Cyprus, which exercises effective control only over Southern Cyprus, acceded to the EU on behalf of the two Cypriot communities, as the EU recognises the Republic as the sole legitimate government. By virtue of its EU membership, the competence of the Republic

[127] *Id.*

[128] *UNDP in Cyprus*, Permanent Mission of Cyprus to the United Nations. Available at: www.cyprusun.org/?page_id=376 (last visited Apr 12, 2024).

[129] *Id.*

[130] *Business Support Centre – Cyprus*, The European Office of Cyprus. Available at: https://eoc.org.cy/participation-in-european-projects/business-support-centre-cyprus/ (last visited Apr 12, 2024).

[131] *InPluServ*, Cyprus Chamber of Commerce and Industry. Available at: https://ccci.org.cy/inpluserv-2/ (last visited Apr 12, 2024).

[132] *Cluster*, Cyprus Chamber of Commerce and Industry. Available at: https://ccci.org.cy/cluster/ (last visited Apr 12, 2024).

[133] *Sea Of Experience (SoE)*, Cyprus Chamber of Commerce and Industry. Available at: https://ccci.org.cy/sea-of-experience-soe/ (last visited Apr 12, 2024).

of Cyprus in regulating "internally" free circulation of goods, services and free movement of persons and "externally" its economic relations with Northern Cyprus have been transferred to the EU level. The economic relations between North and South of Cyprus island in particular, and the Cyprus conflict in general, are Europeanised.[134]

The Europeanisation of Cyprus's economic relations can be observed at different stages: pre-accession and post-accession.[135] Pre-accession, the EU was able to lay down conditions, in addition to Copenhagen criteria,[136] for Northern and Southern Cyprus to meet. In the context of the regulation of North Cyprus economic relations, the key objective was to ensure the *acquis communautaire* be fully implemented in the Cyprus island, which in turn envisaged a comprehensive settlement of the Cyprus issue in a broader political context. Nonetheless, the incentives introduced by conditionality had their limits as the accession package in 2004 covered ten new member states, and Greece, a key ally of the Republic of Cyprus, threatened to block all other acceding countries if Cyprus was not able to join the EU. As a compromise, Cyprus joined the EU with the suspension of *acquis communautaire* in Northern Cyprus, the area not under the effective control of the Government of the Republic of Cyprus.

After the accession of the EU, the Europeanisation of North–South Cyprus economic relations is manifested by the Green Line Regulation. On the one hand, this Europeanisation process contributes to the stabilisation and institutionalisation of North-South Cyprus trade; on the other hand, it introduces a trap preventing the furtherance of North-South Cyprus trade. The stabilisation

[134] George Kyris, *Europeanisation and Conflict Resolution: The Case of Cyprus* (IBEI Working Papers 2013/39). Available at: https://ssrn.com/abstract=2509894. 'Europeanisation' is a term introduced by academics and policy makers to describe and explain the impact of European integration toward the EU member states, acceding countries or even third countries, including neighbouring countries, association countries and those benefiting from European aid. 'Europeanisation' is widely used but short of clear and precise definition. Broadly speaking, it refers to a process of transformation and two ways of Europeanisation can be observed: at the level of EU institutions and at the level of the domestic politics of Member States or third countries. This paper focuses on the impact of European integration upon domestic politics. *See* Heather Grabbe, *How does Europeanization Affect CEE governance? Conditionality, Diffusion and Diversity*, 8 J Eur Pub Pol'y 1013 (2001); Tanja A Börzel, *Member State Responses to Europeanization*, 40 J Common Mkt Stud 193 (2002); Johan P Olsen, *The Many Faces of Europeanization*, 40 J Common Mkt Stud 921 (2002); Tanja Börzel and Thomas Risse, *When Europe Hits Home: Europeanization and Domestic Change*, 4(15) Eur Integration Online Papers (2000); Claudio Radaelli, *Whither Europeanization? Concept Stretching and Substantive Change*, 4(8) Eur Integration Online Papers (2000).

[135] See Stéphanie Laulhé Shaelou, The EU and Cyprus: Principles and Strategies of Full Integration (2010).

[136] Copenhagen criteria are a set of rules, covering political, economic and legislative dimensions, for candidate country to satisfy to be eligible for the EU membership, which were laid down in the Copenhagen Council in 1993 and reproduced in Article 49 of Maastricht Treaty. See Christophe Hillion, *The Copenhagen Criteria and Their Progeny*, *in* EU Enlargement: A Legal Approach 1 (Christophe Hillion ed., 2004); Tim Haughton, *When Does the EU Make a Difference? Conditionality and the Accession Process in Central and Eastern Europe*, 2007 Pol Stud Rev 233; Dimitry Kochenov, *Behind the Copenhagen Facade. The Meaning and Structure of the Copenhagen Political Criterion of Democracy and the Rule of Law*, 8(10) Eur Integration Online PAPERS (2004).

and institutionalisation of North-South economic relations presents socially and psychologically a "comfortable conflict" within the Cyprus island, in which the two communities have fewer incentives to break up the "status quo".[137] The writing into legal text of the suspension of *acquis communautaire* in Cyprus' accession protocol introduces a political deadlock for North–South economic relations to move forward as the subsequent development of the Draft Direct Trade Regulation reveals.

Ironically, the process of Europeanisation introduces another counter trend which is termed by International Crisis Group as "Taiwanisation", given the greater interaction with outside world. The term Taiwanisation is loosely used and vaguely defined with its core idea of greater economic autonomy without political recognition. As observed by the International Crisis Group, since 2004 the legal status of Northern Cyprus has significantly improved. From the outset, it has been recognised as part of the EU even though the Republic of Cyprus does not exercise effective control over it. Being part of the EU, Northern Cyprus has quasi-diplomatic representation in Brussels and lobbying rights in the European Parliament. Northern Cyprus has elected two representatives in the Parliamentary Assembly of the Council of Europe with the right to speak but not to vote. The administration in Northern Cyprus has been recognised by the European Court of Human Rights as possessing the legal capacity for setting up a local remedy for Greek Cypriots' claim for right of property in Northern Cyprus. The President of North Cyprus has been received by a number of states, including the US Secretary of State and then-President of the European Commission José Manuel Barroso. Moreover, the Organisation of the Islamic Conference, which is composed of 57 member states, upgraded the status of the Turkish Cypriot observer delegation from that of a "community" to "state", based on the Annan Plan. Some countries have established trade offices, and private multinational enterprises have also extended their branches in Northern Cyprus. The elevation of the economic and political status of Northern Cyprus may lead to the partition of North–South Cyprus rather than a comprehensive settlement as envisaged.[138]

Commenting on the potential Taiwanisation of North Cyprus, Nikos Skoutaris, a UK-based Greek scholar, argues that the adoption the Draft Direct Trade Regulation, even in its current form without amendment, will not turn Northern Cyprus into Taiwan, as the Draft Direct Trade Regulation does not address political issues and Northern Cyprus remains a part of the areas over which the Republic of Cyprus does not exercise effective control. Northern Cyprus does not obtain diplomatic recognition by virtue of the adoption of

[137] Constantinos Adamides and Costas M Constantinou, *Comfortable Conflict and (Il)liberal Peace in Cyprus*, *in* Hybrid Forms of Peace: From Everyday Agency to Post-Liberalism 242 (Oliver P Richmond and Audra Mitchell eds, 2012).

[138] *Cyprus: Reversing the Drift to Partition, Crisis Group Europe Report*, International Crisis Group (Jan 10, 2008), at 25–26. Available at: www.crisisgroup.org/sites/default/files/190-cyprus-reversing-the-drift-to-partition.pdf.

the Draft Direct Trade Regulation. Moreover, Northern Cyprus, being part of the Republic of Cyprus and consequently part of the customs territory of the EU, will not be able to join the WTO, just as Taiwan does. Therefore, Taiwanisation in *sensu stricto* does not exist. However, as Skoutaris further elaborates, Taiwanisation "presupposes a rather long process, during which the breakaway State in the North will continue to be internationally unrecognised while the international community will gradually lift the restriction and the isolation on the North, which eventually would Taiwanise the TRNC".[139] The political upgrade of the unrecognised TRNC, the relaxation of the economic isolation of the Turkish Cypriot community, and the potential adoption of the Draft Direct Trade Regulation, albeit a very limited possibility, will contribute to the normalisation of economic relations between the two ethno-religious communities in the Cyprus island and between Northern Cyprus and other EU member states. It may also introduce a danger of absolute stasis or comfortable conflict such that the two sides of the Line have no incentives to pursue comprehensive settlement of the conflict.[140] Seen in this light, Europeanisation may act as a catalyst for Taiwanisation as it institutionalises and stabilises the economic relations between Northern and Southern Cyprus. This process of Europeanisation transforms the Cyprus conflict into one of comfort, which not only reduces the incentives for the two sides of the Line to seek a comprehensive settlement, but also introduces a legal deadlock too difficult for the EU to break through.

The Europeanisation of economic cooperation across the island introduces challenges of democratic legitimacy and accountability. Regardless the controversy of the legal bases of Draft Direct Trade Regulation being Article 207 of the TFEU or Article 1(2) of the Protocol No 10 annexed to the Treaty of Accession, the locus of the debates will centre in Brussels and the European Commission plays a key role. Even though the final result will be adopted in the Council of the EU, the delegates of Cyprus come from the executive branch of the Republic of Cyprus. The legislative branch, namely, the House of Representatives of the Republic of Cyprus, has limited, if any, role in steering the direction and pace of economic cooperation across the island. Democratic legitimacy relies largely on the European Parliament, whose members are directly elected, but the European Parliament has only a complementary role as co-legislator even in the context of ordinary legislative procedure, and Cypriot representation within the Parliament, in terms of seats, is highly diluted. The situation is even worse for Northern Cyprus, which has almost no representatives in the EU institutions and whose voice is hardly heard. The democratic deficit in the context of EU laws and regulations affecting trade relations across the island results in the lack of ownership by Cypriots, Greek and Turkish alike, of the economic cooperation between the two communities.

[139] Skoutaris, *supra* note 71, at 157.
[140] *Id.* at 158.

When it comes to bilateral negotiation between the two communities, two ways of polarisation are observable. In the context of high politics, i.e. regarding the future of Cyprus and a comprehensive settlement, the presidents of the Republic of Cyprus and the TRNC are to meet as "leaders" to avoid political sensitivities and sovereign implications. These high-level political meetings are at times free from parliamentary oversight and lack accountability mechanism. While the final deal will be subject to referendum, just as the Annan Plan was, the Cypriots are faced with a "take it or leave it" choice without opportunities to shape the debates and influence the outcome of negotiations. In the context of low-politics or practical aspects of economic cooperation across the island, most frequently, authority is delegated to semi-official institutions, such as the chambers of commerce, to conclude and implement the agreements, which results in a phenomenon of privatisation of economic cooperation across the island. The two ways of polarisation again pose great challenges to democratic legitimacy and accountability mechanisms. While there is some public involvement in the technical working groups activities, as part of confidence building efforts, under the auspice of the UN Special Representative/Deputy Special Adviser to the Secretary-General on Cyprus, the delegates come dominantly from the executive branches, which share the same democratic deficit and absence of accountability.

As Costas M Constantinou observes, "daily encounters and engagements with the 'other' enhance and intensify the multi-directionality of diplomacy … All kinds of settlements that were not possible before are now an option. Multilevel governance, regional and international, provides a range of new sociolegal parameters within which settlements can be reached across the ethnic divide".[141] He argues that UN resolutions, conventions, laws and regulations as well as decisions by the EU and Council of Europe support and empower individuals and groups of people to take action, negotiate agreements and reach settlements. They term this multi-directionality of diplomacy with the multiplicity of actors as "the privatisation of settlement" – "meaning *à la carte*, cross-ethnic settlements by Cypriots from all communities transgressing the divide, without authorisation or consent by their respective authorities as well as without these authorities having the ability to stop or control them".[142] Constantinou's observation of the multiplicity of actors and his use of the term "empowerment" suggests his positive attitude toward what he calls "the privatisation of settlement". Nonetheless, he also explicitly notes the pitfall that authorities have no abilities to stop or control the process of settlement. This privatisation process is closely related to our concerns about democratic legitimacy and accountability, but it also touches upon the actors who should steer the cooperation process and set the limit. In our view, the answer is quite straightforward: the Cypriots. Nonetheless, identity politics are complex, delicate, ambivalent and far from straightforward.

[141] Costas M Constantinou, *Multidirectional Diplomacy and the Privatization of Settlement*, 24 Peace Rev 454, 460 (2012).

[142] *Id.*

Chronology of Cyprus History in the Latest Century

1925	• *Cyprus island became British Empire crown colony.*
1931	• Civil riots in the island started against British rule.
1954	• Establishment of EOKA (Ethniki Organosis Kyprion Agoniston). • New Constitution was proposed but Greek Cypriots rejected this constitution.
1955	• Tripartite conference was held between Britain, Greece and Turkey about Cyprus issue and negotiations started between Cypriots and British for self-government. • Sir John Harding was selected as a governor of Cyprus with the rising of violence against Turkish Cypriots.
1956	• First major inter-communal clash between Turkish and Greek Cypriots.
1957	• Sir Hugh Foot was selected as a governor of island. • Turkish Resistance Organisation (Türk Mükavemet Teşkilatı, TMT) was established. • Turkish Cypriots started to riot against British rule. • UN Resolution A/RES/1013(XI) on the question of Cyprus.
1958	• Turkish Cypriots established their de facto municipalities. • Macmillan Plan by the British Prime Minister to the House of Commons.
1959	• London conference was held between Britain, Greece and Turkey, which later become as the guarantors of Cyprus. • Cyprus agreements were signed in Zurich and London, based on the principles of independence, partnership of the two communities, autonomy in the social sphere and effective guarantee of a solution by Britain, Greece and Turkey. • Archbishop Makarios was elected as the first president of the Republic of Cyprus, whereas Turkish Cypriot Dr. Fazıl Küçük became the first vice president.
1960	• Republic of Cyprus won its independence.
1963	• President Makarios suggested modification in constitution a total of 13 articles. This created one of the first and biggest tension between two communities. Turkish community in Cyprus left the government. • A 'Peace Keeping Force' consisting of the soldiers of the three guarantor countries, Turkey, Greece and Britain, was formed and placed on the island. Cyprus was divided into two by the green line drawn by the British Joint Force.
1964	• After violence attacks against Turkish Cypriots, Turkish invasion threatened. Acheson Plan was proposed and rejected by Makarios and Greece and a second Acheson Plan was presented. • UN Security Council Resolution S/RES/186 of 4 March 1964 recommended sending peace keeping troops to Cyprus.

(continued)

(Continued)

1968	• Presidential election was held in the Republic of Cyprus and Makarios won the election with 96.26% of the vote. • UN-sponsored negotiations started between two sides of island.
1970	• Assassination attempt against Makarios. • Association Agreement between the EEC and Cyprus came into effect.
1973	• Makarios won the presidential election. • Cyprus signed an association agreement with the European Economic Community.
1974	• Coup d'état supported by Greece in Republic of Cyprus. Junta selected Nicos Sampson, a member of EOKA and right-wing pro-enosis supporter, as president. Sampson declared a Greek Republic in Cyprus. • Military intervention by Turkey in Cyprus. • UN Security Council Resolution 353, demanding the immediate withdrawal of all foreign military personnel in Cyprus. • Sampson was ousted and Glafcos Clerides was elected as interim president. • Geneva Conferences between Turkey, Greece and United Kingdom; at the second Geneva Conference, leaders of Northern and Southern Cyprus also attended. • With the end of armed conflict in 1974, two ceasefire lines were established, separated by a buffer zone stretching from Famagusta in the east to the Gulf of Güzelyurt (Morphou Bay) in the north-west of Cyprus, leading to de facto division of the island. • UN General Assembly Resolution A/RES/3212(XXIX), calling upon all states to respect the sovereignty, independence, territorial integrity of the Republic of Cyprus.
1975	• The Establishment of Turkish Federated State of Cyprus. • Intercommunal talks in Vienna started and an agreement between both sides was reached. Both sides of the island agreed to separate the two parts from each other by a buffer zone (intermediate zone) stretching for 180 km. Turkish Cypriots staying in South were allowed to move to North and Greek Cypriots in the North to the South.
1976	• Presidential election in Turkish Federated State of Cyprus and Rauf Denktash won the election. Rauf Denktash was pro-Turkish Nationalist and supported the independence.
1977	• Meeting was held between both sides. Makarios and Denktash created a framework agreement, which is the first agreement between both sides of island aiming to create a federation with a central administration that is autonomous, bizonal and bicommunal. • Makarios died and Spyros Kyprianou served as president for six months.
1978	• Spyros Kyprianou, a hard-liner and against independence of the Northern Cyprus, was elected as a president. Spyros Kyprianou maintained that the Turkish part should be limited to 20% of the island.

(continued)

(Continued)

1981	• Presidential and multi-party elections in Turkish Federated State of Cyprus. Rauf Denktash won the presidential election and a coalition government was formed among three parties. • Negotiations between both sides of island renewed. Turkish Cypriots offered two separate states and bi-communal federal parliament.
1983	• Turkish Republic of North Cyprus was established. • Republic of Turkey recognised Turkish Republic of North Cyprus and European Community rejected the independence of TRNC. • UN Security Council with S/RES/541 (1983) called upon all States not to recognise any Cypriot State other than the Republic of Cyprus. • Rauf Denktash became the President of the Turkish Republic of North Cyprus. • Kyprianou won the election again with 54.54% of the votes.
1985	• First multi-party and presidential elections after the declaration of Turkish Republic of North Cyprus. Rauf Denktash won presidential election and a coalition among two parties was formed the government. • Kyprianou-Denktash high-level Summit was held in New York. • Turkish Republic of North Cyprus adopted a new constitution. And the independence of Turkish Republic of Northern Cyprus was approved with 70% of the vote in referendum.
1986	• Pérez de Cuéllar prepared "Draft Framework Agreement" for the solution of Cyprus problem. Turkish Cypriots accepted the Draft Framework Agreement and Greek Cypriots rejected it.
1987	• European Community and Republic of Cyprus signed a protocol of the Association Agreement (second stage).
1988	• Vassiliou won the election of Republic of Cyprus and was flexible and ready to meet Denktash for meaningful negotiations.
1989	• Demonstration from Greek Cypriots against the border between South and North.
1990	• Election system was changed in North Cyprus and the President of TRNC, Denktash called for a joint declaration of intent to establish a Greek-Turkish partnership based on political equality, power sharing and equal and effective participation. • Negotiations between both sides of island resumed and intensified in a Camp David marathon summit. • European Community established its official representative office in Nicosia and expressed its support for the unity, independence, sovereignty and territorial integrity of Cyprus. • Republic of Cyprus applied for accession to the European Community.
1992	• UN Secretary General Boutros-Ghali proposed set of ideas for resolution in island. • Meeting between both sides was held in New York. This meeting focused on the core issues of a comprehensive solutions among both sides.

(continued)

(Continued)

1993	• Clerides won the presential election of Republic of Cyprus with 50.31%. Clerides became the fourth President of Cyprus. He served between 1993 and 2003. • Multi-party parliamentary election in the TRNC. Coalition between Democratic Party and Republican Turkish Party came to power.
1994	• The European Court of Justice prohibited the purchase of items offered by Turkish Republic of North Cyprus to the European Economic Community territory (*Anastasiou I*).
1995	• Greece and Republic of Cyprus signed Joint Defence Doctrine.
1996	• Coalition between National Unity Party and Democratic Party came to power in the TRNC. • Violence along buffer zone/ Green Line. Greek Cypriots protested against the Turkish occupation of Cyprus. Two Greek Cypriots died.
1997	• Turkey-TRNC (Turkish Republic of Northern Cyprus) declaration.
1998	• Accession negotiations for the Republic of Cyprus into European Union began.
1999–2000	• Five rounds of talks took place between both sides.
2002	• Leaders of two communities, Clerides and Denktaş met under the UN-sponsorship and started negotiation. • Kofi Annan Plan and its revised version were presented. • European Union invited Republic of Cyprus to be a full member of European Union in 2004.
2003	• Democratic Party and Republican Turkish Party formed a new coalition government. Mehmet Ali Talat was pointed as a prime minister in the TRNC. • Turkish Republic of Northern Cyprus lifted crossing restrictions. • Tassos Papadopoulous, who was against the Annan plan, won the presidential election of the Republic of Cyprus. • Second Revised Version of Kofi Annan Plan was presented and meeting between both sides was held in Hague under UN invitation.
2004	• Referendum for Annan Plan in both sides of Cyprus. Turkish Cypriots accepted the Annan Plan with 64.9% and Greek Cypriots rejected the Plan with 75.8% of the vote. • Republic of Cyprus became a full member of the European Union.
2005	• Mehmet Ali Talat, who supported bi-communal federation, won the presidential election of the TRNC.
2006	• Papadopoulos and Talat agreed on the reunification of Cyprus based on bizonal, bicommunal and politically equal federation.

(continued)

(Continued)

2008	• Dimitris Christofias, in favour of unification of island and supporting peace talks with Turkish Cypriots, was elected as President of Republic of Cyprus. • Christofias and Talat resumed full-fledged negotiations. Leaders of both sides decided to create 6 working groups and seven technical committees about the resolution of issues. • Nicosia's Ledra Street crossing opened.
2010	• Re-unification about the both sides of island talks started. • Limnitis crossing point opened. • Technical Committees on Cultural Heritage emerged from an agreement between the leaders of both sides with support of USAID and UN. • Derviş Eroğlu, a hard-liner and supporter of the independence of Northern Cyprus, was elected as a President of the TRNC.
2011	• TRNC sold electricity to Republic of Cyprus. • Republic of Turkey and TRNC signed a continental shelf delimitation agreement.
2012	• TRNC became an observer member of Economic Cooperation Organisation.
2013	• Banking system collapse in Republic of Cyprus. • Nicos Anastasiades, supporter of Annan Plan, was elected as President of the Republic of Cyprus. • Peace talks negotiations between North and South Cyprus were suspended because of a change of government in the Greek-Cypriot community of Cyprus.
2014	• Joint declaration between North and South Cyprus.
2015	• Mustafa Akıncı, a supporter of reunification and h against the influence of Turkey in TRNC, won the presidential election. • Peace talks started again. However, talks ended without a peace deal. • Presidents of Republic of Cyprus and TRNC agreed on confidence building measures, including mobile telephony network and electricity grids across the island.
2016	• American Vice-President and Turkish Prime Minister stated that they support a solution for the reunification of the Cyprus as bi-communal federation.
2020	• Ersin Tatar, in favour of independence, was elected as President of TRNC.
2022	• President of TRNC, Ersin Tatar, stated that equal international status of the Turkish Cypriot side is non-negotiable.

5

Navigating the Labyrinth: The Complex Interplay of Identity, Democratic Legitimacy, and Changing Geopolitics

I. INTRODUCTION: CLAIMS OVER SOVEREIGNTY IN THE INTERNATIONAL CONTEXT

THE EMERGENCE OF "divided nations" can be traced to the post-Second World War era – a period of the Cold War marked by a significant movement towards self-determination among peoples. "Divided nation" status is transitory, as the partitions may transform into independent states or be reunified, peacefully or by force: the two Germanies and two Vietnams provide respective examples thereof. The duration and nature of these divisions vary significantly, with some nations remaining divided for extensive periods. Economic engagement between "divided nations" differs, with some establishing close ties while others remain aloof. Economic cooperation is often viewed as a crucial means of fostering political integration yet concerns over threats to political independence or sovereignty impose paradoxical limits on such an approach. This dynamic can be particularly pronounced when the national division stems from ideological differences, intensifying the challenge of balancing economic cooperation against political autonomy. A common characteristic of "divided nations" is their contested sovereignty. This chapter seeks to uncover the structures and factors shaping economic cooperation in such nations and, to some extent, delineate their contours. This analysis delves into the economic interactions and foundational reasons behind their similarities and differences based on the above case studies across the Taiwan Strait, the Korean Peninsula, and the Cyprus island.

There are, of course, two dimensions to explore: "internally" the dialectic dynamics between the constituent halves of "divided nations", and "externally" the international frameworks and broad geopolitical contexts in which they are enmeshed. Historical, cultural, and ethnic factors account for much of the root causes of these divisions and, at the same time, present strong potential binding forces. However, one should not overestimate the value of the notion of a "nation-state". A state does not necessarily need to be built on the same nation or people; similarly, the same nation may exist in different states. Furthermore, domestic politics play a critical role in economic cooperation, or the lack thereof, in "divided nations", as some domestic constituencies may favour closer economic cooperation, leading to ultimate political unification, while others adopt a cautious stance to safeguard autonomy or sovereignty.

Externally, the international context plays a pivotal role in setting the institutional framework for economic cooperation. The influence of the United Nations (UN) and the World Trade Organization (WTO) are most significant. UN recognition presupposes sovereign equality between the states and bolsters acceptance of existing partitions, while the WTO governs trade relations and may contribute to trade flows. The UN, for example, played a crucial role in facilitating cease-fire agreements in Cyprus, contributing significantly to peacekeeping efforts on the island. This involvement underscores the UN's function in maintaining peace and security in regions experiencing territorial and political disputes. Concurrently, the WTO provides the foundational framework and essential rules for economic engagement between Taiwan and China. Meanwhile, the European Union (EU), as a regional integration organisation, contributes to fostering economic cooperation across the Cyprus island throughout its accession process and in the eventual Europeanisation of the Cyprus issue. The various degrees of institutionalisation in international organisations helps to explain the predictability and stability of economic cooperation within the three sets of "divided nations" examined in this book.

Finally, geopolitics changes swiftly, and correspondingly, the contours of the economic cooperation in these three "divided nations" continue to evolve. Each "divided nation" emerged and persisted in the context of the rivalry between the US and the Soviet Union, while rivalry between Greece and Turkey played a decisive role in the division of Cyprus. Strategic competition between the US and China is now displacing this dynamic. This shift is likely to influence significantly the nature and essence of economic cooperation in the cases studied in this book, especially concerning economic relations across the Taiwan Strait and within the Korean Peninsula. Finally, this chapter seeks to engage in a normative exploration of the complex, politically charged realm of economic cooperation among "divided nations". It delves into how, amid the fluid dynamics of identity formation and contested sovereignty, mechanisms of accountability and (democratic) legitimacy can be maintained or established in the pursuit of economic collaboration.

II. "INTERNAL" DYNAMICS WITHIN DIVIDED NATIONS

A. Cultural, Ethnic, and Language Proximity but Divergent Political Paths

(i) The Cross-Taiwan Strait

While there are cultural, ethnic, and linguistic connections between both sides of the Strait, Taiwan independently possesses a diverse and intricate cultural identity. This identity is influenced, but not wholly defined, by the history of Han Chinese migration, beginning in the seventeenth century, as a result of which the majority of Taiwan's 23 million inhabitants are of Han Chinese descent.[1] The rich heritage of Taiwan's indigenous peoples, who have long inhabited the island,[2] is intertwined with the genetic lineage of the Taiwanese Han people.[3] Although traditional Han Chinese festivals, such as the Lunar New Year and Qingming, are widely celebrated, Taiwan's indigenous peoples and the island's colonial legacies add significant layers to this cultural tapestry.

Since 1949, when the Republic of China (ROC) under the Nationalist Party retreated to Taiwan, Taiwanese people have gradually carved out a unique contemporary identity – a process particularly evident following Taiwan's transition to a liberal democracy. While Chinese cultural roots remain a major source, surveys indicate a declining number of people in Taiwan identifying as solely "Chinese". Instead, an increasing number, especially among the youth, identify as exclusively "Taiwanese", as discussed in Chapter 2. Beyond its Chinese heritage, Taiwan's culture has been influenced by Japan, particularly during five decades of colonialisation from 1895 to the end of the Second World War.[4]

Taiwanese cultural identity, which is on the rise, is rooted in universal suffrage, competitive elections, and a vibrant civil society. At the same time, while there are shared cultural elements between people on both sides of the Taiwan Strait, the distinct political paths they have taken present notable challenges in fostering further Cross-Strait economic collaboration. In the post-martial law era, Taiwan's journey from an authoritarian government to a fully-fledged constitutional democracy has instilled a deep suspicion of China's authoritarian regime, and a growing recognition of the need for caution in the face of the People's Republic of China (the PRC, or China) overreach and threats to Taiwan's cherished freedoms. Embracing free market economic principles

[1] *About Taiwan*, The Government Portal of the Rep of China (Taiwan). Available at: www.taiwan.gov.tw/about.php (last visited Oct 30, 2023).

[2] Niki Alsford, *Realising Taiwan's Indigenous Potential*, East Asia Forum (Sep 8, 2021). Available at: www.eastasiaforum.org/2021/09/08/realising-taiwans-indigenous-potential.

[3] Notable yet contested research carried out by Dr Marie Lin and her team estimated that around 85 per cent of Taiwanese Han people possess indigenous genetic traits, sparking significant debate. For some, this finding underpins the idea of "Taiwan blood nationalism", supporting Taiwan's independence movement. Others, however, challenge this perspective, criticising the data as manipulated and the conclusions as flawed. This shows the intersection of genetic research with complex political and nationalistic narratives in Taiwan. *See, e.g.*, Yinghong Cheng, *Taiwanese DNA versus Chinese DNA: Genetic Science and Identity Politics Across the Taiwan Strait*, 57 Mod Asian Stud 940, 948 (2023); Yun-Hua Lo et al., *Detecting Genetic Ancestry and Adaption in the Taiwanese Han People*, 38 Molecular Bio & Evolution 4149 (2021) (noting that the Taiwanese people trace much of their ancestry to waves of migrants from China, starting with the Minnan and Hakka people who came across the Taiwan Strait over 400 years ago). Today, over 95 per cent of Taiwanese identify as Han Chinese. However, Taiwan's genetic makeup also reflects a mixture of indigenous Austronesian tribes and other East Asian ancestries over time. *Id.*

[4] *See e.g.*, LIAO Ping-Hui and David Der-Wei Wang, Taiwan Under Japanese Colonial Rule, 1895–1945: History, Culture, Memory (2006); Jean-François Dupré, Culture Politics and Linguistic Recognition in Taiwan: Ethnicity, National Identity, and the Party System 34–37 (2017).

akin to those operative in advanced Western nations, Taiwan has come to prioritise human rights, the rule of law, transparency, and individual freedoms during its democratic evolution. This democratic orientation stands in stark contrast to the authoritarian, one-party communist ideology and the highly regulated political climate prevalent in China. China's unwavering stance on reunification, underscored by its aggressive military posturing and adherence to its self-asserted "One China" principle, is at odds with Taiwan's fervent aspiration to preserve its independent status, even as its official designation remains the "Republic of China". This apprehension towards China could, arguably, be reflected in movements such as the Sunflower Movement, which evidences Taiwan's active civil society and its dedication to safeguarding its democratic values and autonomy from external influence.[5] Hence, despite the cultural and historical bonds between the people on the two sides of the Taiwan Strait, their divergent political trajectories have created significant challenges for Cross-Strait economic cooperation. This complex backdrop sets the stage for intricate economic interactions across the Taiwan Strait.

(ii) The Korean Peninsula

The people of the Korean Peninsula share a long, unified history dating back thousands of years, characterised by shared traditions, customs, and a common language. At the end of the Second World War and during the subsequent Cold War, geopolitics led to the peninsula's division into two states with vastly different political, economic, and social systems. Thus, today, South and North Korea share similar ethnic, linguistic, and, to some extent, cultural contexts despite, as noted in Chapter 3, the division formalised by the Korean Armistice Agreement in 1953.[6]

[5] *See e.g.*, Brian Christopher Jones and Yen-Tu Su, *Confrontational Contestation and Democratic Compromise: The Sunflower Movement and its Aftermath*, 45 Hong Kong LJ 193, 199–200 (2015) (arguing that Critics are concerned that the pact might compromise free speech and national security, particularly in critical areas such as printing and telecommunications). Jones and Su perceive the Movement as a proactive defence against the pact's potential to erode democratic values, reflecting fears that it could lead to a situation in Taiwan similar to that in Hong Kong. *See also* Jiunn-rong Yeh, *Marching towards Civic Constitutionalism with Sunflowers*, 45 Hong Kong LJ 315, 316 (2015) (observing that Sunflower Movement confirms Taiwan's progress towards civic constitutionalism, rather than indicating a decline in its maturing democracy or liberal values). Yeh's analysis emphasises a shift driven by dissatisfaction with existing democratic and constitutional frameworks, further intensified by the challenges posed by ambiguous cross-Strait policies to Taiwan's political and civic structures.

[6] Note that ROK was not a signatory to the 1953 Armistice Agreement, because President Syngman Rhee disagreed with dividing the Korean peninsula at the 38th parallel and refused to sign the document. *See* Balbina Y Hwang, *Reviving the Korean Armistice: Building Future Peace on Historical Precedents*, 6(6) Korea Economic Institute Academic Paper Series, at 3–5 (June 2011). Also, DPRK withdrew from the Armistice Agreement several times (in 1994, 1996, 2003, 2006, 2009, and 2013). *Chronology of Major North Korean Statements on the Korean War Armistice*, Yonhap News (May 28, 2009). Available at: www.en.yna.co.kr/view/AEN20090528004200315. *See also supra* Chapter 3.

After the Second World War, the political evolution of the two Koreas has taken them down divergent paths. South Korea has developed into a full democracy with a strong economy. North Korea, by contrast, remains one of the most isolated and authoritarian states in the world, which focuses on one-man leadership, military spending, and nuclear development over economic welfare and human rights. The regime of the Democratic People's Republic of Korea (DPRK) has strict control over information and economic activities, in stark contrast with South Korea's open and democratic society.

While cultural, ethnic, and language proximity might well facilitate bilateral dialogue and open channels for economic cooperation, divergent political paths have been the strongest factor in raising military tensions and barriers to sustainable economic cooperation.[7] The Korean people, whether of the North or South, share a historical connection that, to some extent, is manifest in their language, traditions, and ethnic identity. Despite over 70 years of separation and various modern developments, traditional aspects of Korean culture – language, cuisine, Hanbok (traditional clothing), and holidays like Chuseok (Korean Thanksgiving) – remain similar across the border.[8] Arguably, in the Korean context there exists greater similarity in terms of cultural, ethnic, and language proximity as opposed to the cross-Taiwan-Strait or Cyprus island context.[9] Nevertheless, the gap between the divergent political systems adopted in the two Koreas has been significant and now constitutes a major source of tension and conflict.

These differences notwithstanding, cultural, economic, and sporting exchanges hint at a shared desire for peace and long-term reunification. Indeed, both Koreas have historically espoused the general aspiration of reunification and a high-level belief in ethnic and national unity, reflecting a common view that they belong to one single Korean nation, albeit with starkly different approaches.[10] The Republic of Korea (ROK) officially supports the idea of reunification, seeing it as a long-term goal to be achieved through peaceful means and dialogue. South Korea's approach to reunification has varied over the years, and it has been influenced by changes in domestic politics, relations

[7] For a contemporary view of the relevant twentieth-century dynamics, *see generally* Robert A Scalapino, *Current Dynamics of the Korean Peninsula*, 30(6) Probs Communism 16 (1981). *See also* Paik Nak-chung, The Division System in Crisis: Essays on Contemporary Korea (2011).

[8] For a more nuanced comparison, *see generally* The Northern Region of Korea: History, Identity, and Culture (Sun Joo Kim ed., 2010); Shang E Ha and Seung-Jin Jang, *National Identity in a Divided Nation: South Koreans' Attitudes toward North Korean Defectors and the Reunification of Two Koreas*, 55 Int'l J Intercultural Rel 109 (2016).

[9] For a discussion of such similarities, *see, e.g.*, Dennis Hart, *Proclaiming Identity, Claiming the Past: National Identity and Modernity in North and South Korean Education*, 24(3) Asian Perspective 135 (2000).

[10] Note North Korea's recent proclamations of war-readiness and stated shift of attitude toward South Korea as enemy rather than part of the same Korean state. *See* Hyunsu Yim, *North Korea's Kim Calls for South to Be Seen as "Primary Foe", Warns of War*, Reuters (Jan 16, 2024). Available at: www.reuters.com/world/asia-pacific/north-koreas-kim-calls-change-status-south-warns-war-2024-01-15/.

with North Korea, and the international situation. The ROK Government has pursued policies to increase engagement and cooperation with the North, such as the Sunshine Policy initiated in the late 1990s resulting from the end of the Cold War. However, the level of engagement has fluctuated depending on the political climate. The DPRK also officially advocates for reunification (the recent, rather dramatic change in North Korea's claims notwithstanding[11]), but under its own terms, which have historically emphasised the leadership of the North and the establishment of a socialist system over the entire peninsula. North Korea's approach to reunification has often been marked by a combination of diplomatic outreach with assertive but unpredictable, sometimes militaristic, actions which reflect the regime's isolationism and core desire to maintain its sovereign security. All in all, such a political divide, underscored by the DPRK totalitarian regime, military and nuclear tensions, and the different interests of global powers, continues to hinder progress toward easing tensions and reducing unpredictability, not to mention reunification. As previously discussed, the divergent political paths have created a complex and often tense relationship, marked by periods of both confrontation and cautious engagement, making the Korean Peninsula one of the most challenging geopolitical issues in East Asia.

(iii) Cyprus

In contrast, at the heart of the division of the island of Cyprus are the ethnic, cultural, and linguistic differences between Greek Cypriots and Turkish Cypriots, who now occupy the south and north, respectively, separated by the UN-negotiated Green Line. The ethnic division of the island was implemented under a UN-mediated cease-fire agreement with the aim of controlling and containing ethnic conflict. Undoubtedly, ethnic diversity contributed to the instability of the bi-communal government of the Republic of Cyprus after the proclamation of independence. Indeed, even before achieving independence, Greek and Turkish Cypriots had different visions of the future. Greek Cypriots sought *enosis* (union) by joining Greece, while Turkish Cypriots desired *taksim* (partition) with a separate state on the island. This explained why, in the decolonisation era, Turkish Cypriots cooperated with the British colonisers to police the independence demonstrations of Greek Cypriots and, in fact, seeded distrust and suspicion between the two communities and within the bi-communal government. In fact, the Republic of Cyprus was established against a backdrop wherein Greek and Turkish patriotism prevailed.[12] During the ethnic conflicts immediately following independence, and before partition, "the Greek Cypriot community was the main point of reference for the Turkish Cypriot identity. The Turkish Cypriot 'we' was structured in a

[11] *See Id.*

[12] Leonard W Doob, *Cypriot Patriotism and Nationalism*, 30 J Conflict Resol 383, 386–89 (1986).

violent conflict with 'them,' the Greek Cypriots".[13] This did much to motivate identification with Turkey.

Paradoxically, definitions of self and other would shift after the partition of the island. Importantly, Turkish Cypriots in the North developed an identity distinct from Turkey and demonstrated a strong inclination to identify themselves as Cypriots rather than Turks, regardless of ethnic traits. Their Cypriot identity may be reinforced when meeting foreigners with little knowledge of the island. In such a scenario, Turkish Cypriots might be wrongly assumed to be Greek or Turk, neither of which is an identity they claim,[14] leading to confusion and frustration and further motivating them to claim a self-defined identity. In other words, the Turkish Cypriot community, while fully aware of their Turkish ethnic, linguistic, and cultural background, identifies itself as Cypriot in terms of political orientation. As Kizilyürek Niyazi observes, Turkish Cypriots today talk about "we the Cypriots" vis-à-vis "they the Turks".[15] This may be a result of resentment towards Turkey's interference in their politics and economy. In fact, it was Turkish Cypriots who voted in favour of the Annan Plan and Greek Cypriots who voted against it, preventing a comprehensive settlement of the Cyprus issue.

Writing in 1986, Leonard Doob observed that "[s]ymptoms of Cypriot patriotism that transcended Turkish and Greek Cypriot patriotism and nationalism remained, even as persons on both sides could and would not forget their heritage as well as the economic and military assistance and encouragement received from the mother countries".[16] Similarly, Neophytos G. Loizides observed that

> [i]n the period following 1974, the general feeling of dissatisfaction with the two motherlands, Greece in particular, led to the formation of such organizations as the New Cyprus Association. ... The members of the association did not deny their ethnic origins and cultural links but asked the Cypriot people to consider themselves as Cypriots first and as Greeks, Turks, or others second.[17]

Arguably, the separation of the two communities weakened the sense of identity each felt for Cyprus without strengthening their loyalty to their home countries. Recently, there has been a tendency to identify themselves as Cypriots qualified

[13] Niyazi Kizilyürek, *The Politics of Identity in the Turkish Cypriot Community: a Response to the Politics of Denial?*, *in* Méditerranée: Ruptures et Continuités. Actes du colloque tenu à Nicosie les 20–22 octobre 2001, Université Lumière-Lyon 2, Université de Chypre 202 (2003). Available at: www.persee.fr/doc/mom_1274-6525_2003_act_37_1_969. *See* Yiannis Papadakis, *Greek Cypriot Narratives of History and Collective Identity: Nationalism as a Contested Process*, 25 Am Ethnologist 149 (1988).

[14] Christos Anagiotos, *Is National Identity Learned? The Case of Turkish-Cypriot Young Adults in Cyprus* 49 (Adult Education Research Conference 2014). Available at: www.newprairiepress.org/aerc/2014/papers/6.

[15] Kizilyürek, *supra* note 13, at 203.

[16] Doob, *supra* note 12, at 390.

[17] Neophytos G Loizides, *Ethnic Nationalism and Adaptation in Cyprus*, 8 Int'l Stud Persp 172, 179 (2007).

by an adjective, especially in the North by "Turkish" while less frequently in the South by "Greek".[18] This phenomenon may be termed as "ethnic Cypriotism". As Neophytos G. Loizides notes,

> Although attachment to one's ethnic community could be considered as a middle ground between "motherland nationalism" and "Cypriotism", in reality, it serves a different function. While it appropriates themes, symbols, and rhetoric both from mainland nationalism and Cypriotism, thereby performing a middle-man role, it pays more attention to the aspirations of the ethnic community in the island than to the interest of the "national centers" or Cyprus as a whole. Thus, Greek Cypriotism and Turkish Cypriotism take ascendancy in two respective frequently oppositional camps.[19]

Whereas this "ethnic Cypriotism" may contribute to Cypriot identity shaping, it may also have disruptive side effects. When leaders of either side of the island promote ethnocentric nationalism, the prospect of Cypriot unity fades. The best example is the failure of the Annan Plan.[20] That said, the two communities do share elements of their cultural heritage capable of contributing to a common identity and shared destiny. Halloumi/Hellim cheese, which symbolises the shared heritage of the island of Cyprus and has linked communities in Cyprus for centuries, is a case in point. For this reason, the European Commission granted Halloumi/Hellim cheese Protected Designation of Origin status with the aim of shaping a common understanding of Cyprus culture and helping to cement Cypriot identity. To make this possible, the Cypriots have to transcend the ethnocentric nationalism that separates the two communities. This tremendous challenge thus defines the boundary of economic cooperation or, more ambitiously, integration across the island.

In terms of political systems, both the North and South of Cyprus have established functional government systems based on regular elections, even though some degree of authoritarianism may be felt, particularly in the North. There is also moderate-to-strong competition between parties for governing power and, in fact, the two sides of the island have experienced regime changes, with one ruling party (coalition) being replaced by another. This feature makes the case for the circumstances in Cyprus being distinct from those prevailing across the Taiwan Strait or in the Korean Peninsula – in the latter two cases, the ruling parties of the PRC and DPRK, respectively, have never changed. For this reason, economic cooperation across Cyprus is subject to stricter parliamentary oversight compared to the other two case studies in this book and enjoys stronger democratic legitimacy, although the oversight and legitimacy remain weak. Moreover, in the case of Cyprus, the resolution of its division

[18] Doob, *supra* note 12, at 393.

[19] Loizides, *supra* note 17, at 179.

[20] Harry Anastasiou, *Nationalism as a Deterrent to Peace and Interethnic Democracy: The Failure of Nationalist Leadership from the Hague Talks to the Cyprus Referendum*, 8 Int'l Stud Persp 190 (2007).

uniquely rests in the hands of its people, who must approve any final settlement through a referendum. This approach starkly contrasts with the situations in the other case studies, where democratic self-governance is not considered by leaders in the PRC or DPRK, who contemplate unification by force of Taiwan with China, or in the two halves of the Korean Peninsula. This highlights a significant divergence in the pursuit of national unity across these three sets of "divided nations".

B. Bilateral Economic Interactions: Forms and Substance

(i) The Cross-Taiwan Strait

Over the past few decades, Cross-Strait trade and investment between Taiwan and China have been significantly transformed. In the late 1970s and early 1980s, following a period of minimal economic interaction due to political tension, both sides began to relax trade and travel restrictions.[21] This shift paved the way for a surge in economic exchange across the Taiwan Strait. Trade and investment ties deepened and evolved following the democratic reforms in Taiwan in the 1990s, and especially following the accession of Taiwan and China to the WTO in the early 2000s. Taiwan emerged as a major source of foreign direct investment for China, initially focusing on labour-intensive industries but later diversifying into high-tech sectors. China, in turn, became Taiwan's largest export market, absorbing around 40 per cent of its exports.[22] Despite political differences, economic interdependence grew, with Taiwan consistently running trade surpluses. Yet this close economic relationship introduced challenges as Taiwan grappled with its increasing reliance on the Chinese market while navigating the complexities of its political stance. The trajectory of Cross-Strait economic ties over these decades reflects a blend of economic pragmatism, political antagonism, and evolution in the global trade landscape. This can be evidenced in the unique way each side engages the other in trade and investment.

Two critical factors largely shape the complex dynamics of Cross-Strait economic relations. Firstly, both sides perceive their interactions with the other not as typical international affairs but through a constitutional lens. China's constitution states that "Taiwan is part of the sacred territory of the People's Republic of China" and enshrines national reunification as a sacred duty of the Chinese people.[23] This constitutional principle guides China's tailored economic approach toward Taiwan across trade in goods, services, intellectual property rights, and investment. In trade, for instance, the "Measures for the Administration of Trade with Taiwan Region" governs economic ties but

[21] *See* Chapter 2, sections I–II.
[22] *Id.*, section II A(i).
[23] *See* Xianfa Preamble, para 9 (1982)(China).

prohibits using words or symbols inconsistent with its "One-China" principle in Cross-Strait commerce.[24] Trade in services similarly reflects regulations, as demonstrated by the "Administrative Regulations for Foreign Law Firms' Representative Organisations in China",[25] which subjects Taiwanese lawyers to separate requirements rather than treating them on par with foreign lawyers under China's WTO/GATS commitments.[26] Such differentiation reflects how the PRC government sees Taiwan as a breakaway province rather than a sovereign state. Overall, China's economic engagement with Taiwan, as a matter of unilateral domestic law, is premised on a constitutionalised "One-China" principle rather than any recognition of the sovereignty of the other side.

On the other side of the Strait, the 1991 amendment to Taiwan's Constitution, known as the "Additional Articles", is introduced by pivotal language concerning Taiwan's future trajectory, as the stated purpose of the amendment is "[t]o meet the requisites of the nation before national unification".[27] Some see this inclusion as keeping open the possibility for future unification with China, indicative of a pragmatic approach to the Cross-Strait relations amidst this island's evolving political climate. Taiwan's Constitution, while retaining the name "Republic of China" and symbolising continuity with its historical roots, acknowledges the governance of the "Republic of China" over both the "Free Area", under its direct jurisdiction, and the "Mainland Area", controlled by China. This dual acknowledgment is mirrored in Taiwan's "Law Governing Relations Between the People of the Taiwan Area and the Mainland Area", as discussed in Chapter 2. However, interpretation of these provisions is politically sensitive and controversial, highlighting the complexity and nuances of Taiwan's constitutional and legal position regarding its sovereignty and its relationship with the PRC.

There is ongoing debate regarding interpreting the Preamble of the amended Constitution of the Republic of China. On one side, some argue that it represents an affirmation of the "One (Republic of) China" concept.[28] Conversely, others

[24] *See* Chapter 2, section IIA(ii).

[25] *Id.*

[26] *Id.*

[27] Preamble, Additional Articles of the Constitution, Republic of China (Taiwan).

[28] For instance, during former President MA Ying-Jeou's recent trip to China, he highlighted that, according to an amendment to the ROC Constitution, "Taiwan and mainland China are both part of China". LIN Liang-sheng, *KMT Defends Ma's 'One China' comments*, Taipei Times (Apr 4, 2023). Available at: www.taipeitimes.com/News/taiwan/archives/2023/04/04/2003797296; 蘇永欽，《尋找共和國》SU Yeong-chin Xuunzhao Gongheguo [Su Yeong-chin, Searching for the Republic] 5–9 (2008). One of Taiwan's leading public law experts and current the President of the Judicial Yuan, Hsu Tzong-li, pointed out that the term "prior to unification" seems to be interpreted as the constitution itself proclaiming the goal of unification. Accordingly, pursuing amalgamation with the other side (Mainland China) could constitute a constitutional obligation for the entire Republic of China (Taiwan); however, he also cautioned that such reading may not be accepted by the Taiwanese people. 許宗力，兩岸關係的法律定位 – 臺灣的角度出發，收於：黃昭元編，《兩國論與台灣國家定位》HSU Tzong-li, The *Legal Status of Cross-Strait Relations – From Taiwan's Perspective*, *in* The Debate on Two States and Taiwan's National Positioning 154 (HUANG Jau-Yuan ed., 2000).

contend that the formal, written (large C) Constitution should not be viewed as the exclusive or definitive source when understanding Taiwan's constitutional norms. In this view, the evolution of Taiwan's unwritten (small-C) constitutional norms, reflecting popular sovereignty and liberal democracy, has largely outpaced the changes in the written Constitution, which is evidenced through electoral politics and socio-political movements.[29]

Therefore, even though Taiwan's Constitutional Court once stated that, from a legal perspective, "Agreements concluded between Taiwan and Mainland China are not regarded as international written agreements",[30] the island's progress towards democratisation and a distinct identity has heightened its vigilance towards economic integration with China, considering the political connotations such integration may entail. For instance, restrictions under the "Regulations Governing Permission of Trade Between Taiwan Area and Mainland Area" and the "Regulations Governing the Approval of Investment or Technical Cooperation in Mainland China" signalled Taiwan's caution despite referring to "Mainland Area" as part of its territory from the constitutional perspective.[31] Influenced by Taiwan's internal political shifts, various administrations, including those led by Lee Teng-hui, Chen Shui-bian, Ma Ying-jeou, and Tsai Ing-wen, have adjusted restrictions to reflect their respective stances towards the PRC. These policy changes mirror the evolving political landscape and attitudes within Taiwan.

To navigate the political sensitivities surrounding "sovereignty", Taiwan and China have engaged each other through "quasi-official" intermediaries. Taiwan's Straits Exchange Foundation (SEF) and China's Association for Relations Across the Taiwan Strait (ARATS) have negotiated agreements under a "white gloves" model.[32] This has yielded over 20 Cross-Strait pacts since the 1990s, despite both sides' refusal to recognise the other formally. For Taiwan, however, concerns over the lack of transparency and democratic oversight of deals seen as ceding too much sovereignty ultimately limited this mechanism, as evidenced by the failure of the Cross-Strait Services Trade Agreement.

The uniqueness of cross-Taiwan-Strait relations likewise manifests in the bilateral agreements between SEF and ARATS. These avoid overt references to sovereignty, unlike traditional inter-state treaties. For instance, the "Cross-Straits Economic Cooperation Framework Agreement" (ECFA) is termed an "agreement" rather than a "treaty".[33] The agreement's provisions notably

[29] *See e.g.*, Yen-tu Su and Chien-Chih Lin, *The Constitutional Law and Politics in Taiwan*, *in* Oxford Handbook of Constitutional Law in Asia (David Law, Alex Schwartz, and Holning Lau eds, forthcoming 2024); Ching-Fu Lin and Chien-Huei Wu, *Is Taiwan a State?*, Verfassungsblog (Oct 18, 2022). Available at: www.verfassungsblog.de/is-taiwan-a-state/.

[30] Judicial Interpretation 329, the Constitutional Court, ROC (Taiwan).

[31] *See* Chapter 2, section IIB(ii).

[32] *See* Chapter 2, section IIB(ii).

[33] *Id.*, section IIB(i).

deviate from the typical language found in conventional FTAs. For instance, while China's CEPA with Hong Kong employs an independent panel for dispute resolution, this agreement entrusts such matters to a Cross-Strait committee. The Cross-Strait Bilateral Investment Protection and Promotion Agreement is likewise crafted carefully to avoid terms like "nations" or "national treatment". Notably, it omits the standard option of international arbitration under the ICSID Convention. Central to Taiwan's strategic linguistic choices is the multifaceted and politically charged "One China" issue, interpreted differently by various administrations and further complicated by debates around the existence and meaning of the so-called "1992 Consensus". These political dynamics inevitably lead to varied approaches and reactions from the other side of the Strait. Therefore, the nuanced crafting of these bilateral agreements reflects the deep political considerations at play. Ultimately, the extent and areas in which the two sides will engage depend heavily on these political dynamics and are particularly influenced by Taiwan's ruling party's stance on the polarising spectrum of independence versus unification.

In conclusion, the asymmetry between China's stance on unification with what it views as a breakaway province, and Taiwan's cautious balancing act, profoundly shapes their unique economic engagements. Despite their close connections, both parties have established distinct legal frameworks and regulations that specifically address economic exchanges across the Taiwan Strait, approaching each other as matters that fall outside the usual scope of international affairs. Further, the two sides cautiously craft bilateral agreements, negotiated through quasi-official intermediaries, that internalise rather than fully normalise economic relations across the Taiwan Strait – at least not in the way they treat and engage with other sovereign states. The activity levels and roles of the Mainland Affairs Council (MAC) and SEF vary with different Taiwan administrations, reflecting the government's Cross-Strait policy. Under presidential administrations favouring closer ties with the PRC, the MAC and SEF engage more actively. Conversely, with presidents advocating for Taiwan's independence or a more cautious approach to relations with China, these institutions might limit or cease contact with their counterparts in China. This variability highlights the influence of Taiwan's domestic politics on its approach to cross-Taiwan-Strait relations.

The variability in the activities of the MAC and SEF under different Taiwanese administrations, as outlined earlier, is intrinsically linked to the differentiated laws, regulations, and arrangements that govern cross-Taiwan-Strait interactions. These variances in approach and policy directly reflect the underlying tensions between China's push for unification and Taiwan's endeavour to strike a balance between economic integration and the preservation of the *status quo*. Managing these intricate and often conflicting dynamics is a continuous challenge and a defining aspect of the evolving nature of Cross-Strait relations.

(ii) The Korean Peninsula

The economic relationship between South and North Korea has been characterised by fluctuating periods of cooperation and tension, reflecting the broader political (and military) dynamics on the Korean Peninsula, as well as global and regional geopolitics. Despite their contrasting economic systems and the ongoing state of conflict since the Korean War, as Chapter 3 shows, there have been a small number of notable attempts at economic cooperation. These have been driven primarily by political motives and peace initiatives; the economic benefits for both sides have not been the core driving factor.

To be sure, there exist vast and salient economic differences between the two Koreas, which must be bridged via *ad hoc, project-based* economic cooperation. South Korea has one of the world's largest and most advanced economies, strongly emphasises technology, innovation, manufacturing, and international trade, and is deeply integrated into the global supply chain. It is a member of the WTO, the Organisation for Economic Co-operation and Development (OECD), and the G20, with significant global economic influence. North Korea operates a centrally planned and tightly controlled economy with agriculture, military spending, and heavy industry as its main components. The economy of the North is much smaller, less developed, and significantly isolated from the global financial system due to international sanctions related to its nuclear weapons program.[34] Until recently, the economic cooperation between the two has been formal but limited, *ad hoc*, project-based, and policy-driven, and the level of institutionalisation has been low, with fluctuating outcomes.[35]

As mentioned in Chapter 3, the Kaesong Industrial Complex (KIC), located just north of the DMZ, was established in 2004 as a symbol of eased tension and economic cooperation. Combining South Korean business investment and technology with North Korean labour to produce a range of consumer products, at its peak, the KIC hosted over 120 South Korean companies and employed around 55,000 North Korean workers.[36] However, due to political changes and military tension, the KIC's operations have been suspended and resumed several times, with the latest suspension by the ROK government in 2016

[34] *See, e.g.*, Yong Suk Lee, *International Isolation and Regional Inequality: Evidence from Sanctions on North Korea*, 103 J Urb Econ 34 (2018); Jihee Kim et al., *The Economic Costs of Trade Sanctions: Evidence from North Korea*, 145 J Int'l Econ Article 103813 (2023).

[35] *See* Chapter 3, section II. *See also* Ralph M Wrobel, *Ten Years of Kaesong Industrial Complex: A Brief History of the Last Economic Cooperation Project of the Korean Peninsula*, 14 Econ & Env't Stud 125 (2014).

[36] For additional detail, *see* Pierce Lee, *Rules of Origin and the Kaesong Industrial Complex: South Korea's Uphill Battle against the Principle of Territoriality*, 39 NC J Int'l L 1 (2013); Mark E Manyin and Dick K Nanto, Congressional Research Service, The Kaesong North-South Korean Industrial Complex (2011).

following a DPRK nuclear test.[37] Another project was the Mount Gumgang Tourist Resort, initiated in 1998 to allow South Korean tourists to visit Mount Kumgang in North Korea. This project provided a point of limited economic exchange between the two Koreas but was, more importantly, symbolic of the potential for peace and reconciliation. The tours were suspended in 2008 after a North Korean guard shot a South Korean tourist, and efforts to restart the programme have been sporadic and largely unsuccessful.[38] The Mount Gumgang Resort has remained closed since 2008, and for South Korean citizens, a glimpse of life in the DPRK is now just a memory.

Beyond these projects, the ROK has been a significant source of humanitarian aid to the DPRK, including food and medical assistance, especially during periods of natural disasters or food shortages in the North. These hardly constitute economic cooperation, however.[39] Three inter-Korean summits in 2000, 2007, and 2018 touched upon some economic cooperation issues, leading to various agreements on reconnecting rail and road links and undertaking joint economic projects on infrastructure and natural resources.[40] However, the implementation of these agreements has often been hampered by escalating tensions related to North Korea's nuclear programme and international sanctions, with the latter limiting the scope of permissible trade and investment activities.

Overall, economic relationships and cooperation between South and North Korea are deeply influenced by the political climate on the Korean Peninsula and broader global geopolitics. The potential for economic cooperation exists, but realising this requires a stable political foundation and institutionalisation, which has been elusive due to the ongoing conflict and differences between the two Koreas. Therefore, economic cooperation between the two Koreas has been extremely limited and fluctuating.[41] The recent tensions have further decreased the possibility of stable dialogue and economic cooperation.

(iii) Cyprus

The division of Cyprus led to the establishment of two distinct political entities, neither of which recognises the other. The Republic of Cyprus views Northern Cyprus as part of its territory under occupation arising from the Turkish

[37] Choe Sang-Hun, *South Korea to Shut Joint Factory Park, Kaesong, Over Nuclear Test and Rocket*, New York Times (10 Feb, 2016). Available at: www.nytimes.com/2016/02/11/world/asia/north-south-korea-kaesong.html.

[38] Jonathan Watts, *South Korean Tourist Shot Dead in North Korea*, Guardian (July 11, 2008), at www.theguardian.com/world/2008/jul/11/korea.

[39] *See* Mika Aaltola, *Emergency Food Aid as a Means of Political Persuasion in the North Korean Famine*, 20 Third World Q 371 (1999).

[40] *See* Chapter 3, section I.

[41] Sabine Burghart and Rudiger Frank, *Inter-Korean Cooperation 2000–2008: Commercial and Non-Commercial Transactions and Human Exchanges* 9 (Vienna Working Papers on East Asian Economy and Society, Working Paper 1(1), 2008).

invasion and declines to recognise the authority and legitimacy of the Turkish Republic of Northern Cyprus (TRNC). In return, the TRNC does not recognise the Republic of Cyprus. Economic engagements across the island were virtually absent until 23 April 2003, when Denktash, then President of the TRNC, unilaterally and unexpectedly eased border travel restrictions and allowed all Cypriots to cross the Green Line. The accession of the Republic of Cyprus to the EU changed the dynamic; initiated the process of economic cooperation across the island; and led to the Europeanisation of the Cyprus issue.[42] Nonetheless, given that neither North nor South recognises the other, economic cooperation activities and negotiations must be channelled through semi-official organisations, notably the Cyprus Chamber of Commerce and Industry (CCCI) and Turkish Cypriot Chamber of Commerce (TCCoC).

The two chambers of commerce work as the key actors in the negotiations and implementations of economic cooperation across the island. The chambers catalysed two electricity purchase agreements after an explosion at a power plant in the Republic of Cyprus and helped to cement an agreement that now permanently links the electricity grid across the island. Officials from both sides of the island had a strong influence over the course of the negotiations, but the two chambers of commerce acted as the contracting parties to these deals. At the implementation phase or on the administrative level, the two chambers of commerce are entrusted with the task of monitoring the implementation of EU regulations, confidence-building mechanisms, and collaborative projects. For example, the two chambers of commerce are responsible for the issuance of the certificate of rule of origin and maintaining a record of trade volume.

The delegation of public authority to these chambers of commerce nonetheless poses challenges to democratic legitimacy and accountability. Democratic oversight and accountability mechanisms for the activities conducted under the framework of the two chambers of commerce remain weak, if not absent. Moreover, as a result of the mutual non-recognition of the island's two governments, the presidents of the Republic of Cyprus and TRNC meet in their capacity of "leaders", rather than as heads of state, when it comes to mattes of high politics, leaving the source and scope of their authority intentionally ambiguous. While the outcome of political negotiations might eventually be subject to a referendum, the populace is essentially given a "take it or leave it" choice, affording them minimal influence over the negotiation process itself.[43] This "leaders" meeting model not only undermines democratic legitimacy and escapes accountability mechanisms, but it also largely subjects the course and progress of economic cooperation to political preference.

[42] Angelos Sepos, The Europeanization of Cyprus: Polity, Policies and Politics (2008); Nikos Skoutaris, The Cyprus Issue: the Four Freedoms in a Member States under Siege (2011); Stéphanie Laulhé Shaelou, The EU and Cyprus: Principles and Strategies of Full Integration (2009); Frank Hoffmeister, Legal Aspects of the Cyprus Problem: Annan Plan and EU Accession (2006).

[43] Nicolas Jarraud et al., *The Cypriot Civil Society Movement: A Legitimate Player in the Peace Process?* 8(1) J Peacebuilding & Dev 45 (2013).

The substance of economic cooperation across the island is largely dominated by the EU, in particular the European Commission. The four fundamental freedoms of the EU internal market are regulated by the EU *acquis*, which is suspended in the context of Northern Cyprus. To remedy this legal vacuum, the EU adopted the Green Line Regulation to regulate trade across the island. For this reason, trade relations across the island are Europeanised, which raises concerns over ownership of the trade policies impacting the island. Such concerns are even more acute for Northern Cyprus, as it does not have official channels to voice its worries and safeguard its interests in the Union. On the one hand, EU membership institutionalises the trade relations across the island; on the other hand, the two sides of the island have lost a degree of agency in this regard.

When economic cooperation extends to matters not covered by the EU *acquis*, the UN may play a role in facilitating the process. Most frequently, cooperation is carried out under the auspices of the Special Representative/Deputy Special Adviser to the Secretary-General on Cyprus to circumvent the potential issue of recognition. Mobile phone roaming services are an illustrative example. Both sides recognise the compelling need for such services, yet they strive to avoid any solution that might imply recognition of their counterparty's authority. For this reason, telecom services on the two sides of the islands must first connect to a third country to enable roaming services. As such, political sensitivity defines the limits of economic cooperation.

III. "EXTERNAL" DYNAMICS FACING THE REST OF THE WORLD

A. Membership in International Organisations

(i) The Cross-Taiwan Strait

Economic engagement between Taiwan and China is intricately linked with broader multilateral dynamics, a relationship that became even more pronounced after both sides acceded to the WTO in 2002. This accession was not straightforward. When Taiwan first applied for General Agreement on Tariffs and Trade (GATT) membership in the early 1990s, China vehemently opposed the bid, arguing that Taiwan could only be admitted after the PRC was "restored" to China's seat in the organisation.[44] Later in the 2000s, China pushed the WTO to categorise Taiwan as a "Separate Customs Territory of China" rather than an independent member, but this move was rejected by the US.[45]

Despite these challenges, joining the WTO offered both sides of the Taiwan Strait a structured platform to interact under global trade rules, transcending their politically charged domestic laws and bilateral arrangements. The WTO

[44] *See* Chapter 2, section I.
[45] *Id.*

accession also empowered Taiwan with recourse to raise trade concerns to the world if faced with discriminatory treatment from China. Yet, even with Taiwan's membership under the name "Separate Customs Territory of Taiwan, Penghu, Kinmen, and Matsu" or "Chinese Taipei", China remains steadfast in not recognising Taiwan as an equal member state, instead viewing it as a domestic matter under its self-asserted "One-China principle". The PRC's approach towards Taiwan within the WTO is evident in its actions, such as its 2003 anti-dumping investigation: Targeting Taiwanese products, among others, China bypassed the required notification process, choosing to inform only industry associations instead of the Taiwan government. For China, this approach aligned with its stance that Taiwan is a province. Through this and other differentiated dealings, China reinforces Taiwan's subordinate status.

Within the WTO dispute settlement system, Taiwan and China have avoided formal trade disputes targeting one another. Though either side may occasionally participate in WTO proceedings as a third party,[46] to date China has not filed any complaints against Taiwan, and Taiwan has also not initiated any disputes against China. However, in recent years, it has not been uncommon for Taiwan to raise specific trade concerns about China's measures before the committees on Technical Barriers to Trade and Sanitary and Phytosanitary Measures.[47] This appears to signal a tentative move towards internationalising Cross-Strait trade disputes by utilising the global trading system, even if it stops short of a formal legal process. It remains uncertain if Taiwan will progress to lodging a formal WTO complaint against China – or the other way around. However, such trends suggest a possible inclination towards addressing Taiwan Strait trade conflicts in a more multilateral context. In essence, although the WTO accession provided a more rules-based engagement mechanism, it did not fundamentally alter the power dynamics of the "One-China" issue. External dimensions have shaped and will continue to shape how the two sides interact within the global trade architecture. This will also be shaped by the changing geopolitical climate, as discussed below.

(ii) The Korean Peninsula

Unlike the economic engagement between Taiwan and China that has been intricately linked with broader multilateral fora and dynamics, the two Koreas

[46] As of this writing, there have been 29 cases where either Taiwan or China has joined an existing dispute as a third party against the other, but neither side has directly initiated legal proceedings against the other.

[47] *See e.g.*, Comm on Technical Barriers to Trade, *Minutes of the Meetings of 21–22 March 2018*, WTO Doc G/TBT/M/74 (May 22, 2018). In this meeting, Taiwan expressed concerns about certain articles in China's Cybersecurity Law. It was claimed, inter alia, that these articles might constitute unnecessary trade barriers due to their vague implementation methods, definitions, and scopes; Taiwan therefore urged China to discuss these issues further to improve transparency and predictability. *See also* Comm on Sanitary and Phytosanitary Measures, *Summary of the Meeting of 12–14 July 2023*, WTO Doc G/SPS/R/110 (Sept 13, 2023). Note, however, that the underlying meeting minutes for this latter SPS meeting are still classified as confidential.

hold equal status in the United Nations and many international organisations as full member states, but not in trade and investment settings – most importantly, the WTO (and the International Monetary Fund). As noted earlier, South Korea has developed into a vibrant democracy with a booming economy and innovative development, deeply integrated into the global economic system. It is known for its technological advancements, democratic governance, and vibrant culture with global appeal. The ROK has been a WTO member since 1995 and a member of the GATT since 1967, and now has over 20 Free Trade Agreements with Association of Southeast Asian Nations (ASEAN), Australia, Canada, Chile, China, India, New Zealand, Singapore, the EU, among others.[48] North Korea, by contrast, remains one of the most isolated and authoritarian states in the world. It is governed by a totalitarian regime that prioritises one-man leadership, military spending, and nuclear development over economic welfare and human rights.[49] The DPRK regime has strict control over information and economic activities, in stark contrast to South Korea's open and democratic society.[50] North Korea is not a member of the WTO, which isolates it from the multilateral trading system and most of the global supply chain. The DPRK's lack of WTO membership means that both Koreas do not have multilateral settings in trade and investment to leverage the international rule-based system and facilitate cooperation that goes beyond bilateral project-based activities. Yet, interestingly, via South Korea's FTAs and membership in the WTO, goods produced in part by the DPRK in the Kaesong Industrial Complex can enjoy access to some free trade channels and bypass many of the trade sanctions placed upon North Korean goods.

Beyond the trade and investment setting, both Koreas are member states of the United Nations. In fact, ROK and DPRK were simultaneously admitted to the United Nations in 1991. More specifically, in 1948, the UN General Assembly officially recognised the ROK under Resolution 195 and allowed it to participate as an observer.[51] The following year, both South and North Korea applied for UN membership, but the Soviet Union blocked South Korea's admission.[52] The situation escalated in 1950 when North Korea invaded South Korea, prompting the UN Security Council to condemn the invasion and call for international support to South Korea under a unified command led by the United States.[53] By 1971, changes in the recognition of PRC's representation

[48] As of November 2023, South Korea has 21 FTAs concluded with 59 countries (effectuated and agreed). *FTA Trend in Korea*, KCS Total Solution YES! FTA Portal (Nov 2023). Available at: www.customs.go.kr/engportal/cm/cntnts/cntntsView.do?mi=7304&cntntsId=2329.

[49] *See* Francis Grice, *The Improbability of Popular Rebellion in Kim Jong-un's North Korea and Policy Alternatives for the USA*, 4 J Asian Sec & Int'l Affs 263 (2017).

[50] *Id.*

[51] GA Res 195 (III), at 228 (Dec 12, 1948).

[52] United Nations Repertory of Practice of United Nations Organs, Articles 1–22 of the Charter 169 (1955).

[53] The Security Council supported South Korea with the following resolutions: The Requestment of the Cessation of Hostilities in Korea, SC Res S/1501 (June 25, 1950); The Creation and Operation

of China to the UN also allowed North Korea to gain observer status in 1973. The end of the Cold War in 1991 saw a shift in dynamics, with South Korea seeking independent UN membership, a move initially opposed by North Korea due to fears of legitimising the division of Korea.[54] However, facing the reality of South Korea's likely admission without facing a veto, North Korea also applied for membership, arguing it was necessary to protect its interests on the global stage. This led to both Koreas being unanimously recommended by the UN Security Council for membership and officially joining the UN on 17 September 1991.[55] With UN membership, North Korea has also joined other international organisations, including the World Health Organization, the United Nations Educational, Scientific and Cultural Organization, the Food and Agriculture Organization, the International Civil Aviation Organization, and the Codex Alimentarius Commission – but, as can be logically envisaged, such memberships have not played an influential role in facilitating inter-Korea economic cooperation. Again, DPRK's absence in the WTO, the most relevant and influential forum of international trade, prevents both Koreas from utilising a multilateral framework for trade and investment. This limitation hinders their ability to engage in and benefit from the international rule-based system, restricting their cooperation to *ad hoc*, project-based bilateral activities rather than broader, more institutionalised or systematic engagements.

(iii) Cyprus

The course and progress of economic cooperation across the island of Cyprus is heavily impacted by the EU and, to a lesser extent, by the UN. When intercommunal conflict broke out in the early 1970s, especially following the *coup d'état* on 15 July 1974 that led to the Turkish invasion, the UN was the key actor brokering the cease-fire agreements that resulted in the North–South divide of the island. The UN continues to recognise the Republic of Cyprus as the sole legitimate government of the country. When Turkish Cypriots in the North declared independence and established the TRNC in 1983, the UN Security Council called upon its members not to recognise it.[56] As a consequence, the TRNC is only recognised by Turkey. The political isolation of the TRNC constitutes the main backdrop for the economic cooperation across the island. This may help to explain why the Turkish Cypriots approved the Annan Plan: they wished to end their political and economic isolation. Indeed, the membership of the Republic of Cyprus and the non-recognition of TRNC by

of the Unified Command, SC ResS/1588 (25 July 1950); and The Relief and Support of the Civilian People of Korea, SS Res S/1655 (July 31, 1950).

[54] For a thorough discussion of important historical events and their implications *see* Chong-Ki Choi, *The Korean Question in the United Nations*, 8 Verfassung und Recht in Übersee [L & Pol Afr, Asia & Latin Am] 395 (1975).

[55] SC Res702 (Aug 8, 1991).

[56] SC Res 541 (Nov 18, 1983).

the UN lend great political capital and leverage to the Republic of Cyprus in negotiating with the TRNC.

In 2004, two lines of negotiations were ongoing: Politically, there was a hope that a political solution to the Cyprus issue would result from the Annan Plan referendum. Economically, Northern Cyprus hoped that its economic isolation would come to an end with the accession to the EU of the island as a whole. Neither hope was realised: Greek Cypriots voted against the Annan Plan, and the Draft Direct Trade Regulation has yet to be adopted due to the unanimity requirement set out in Cyprus' Accession Protocol. That said, the UN mission in Cyprus first helped with peacekeeping across the Line with the establishment of the buffer zone and has subsequently contributed to confidence-building across the island. Various technical committees have been established, with one key achievement being the implementation of mobile phone roaming services. The EU, by contrast, made trade across the island possible by virtue of its Green Line Regulation, as detailed in Chapter 4.

The EU plays a critical role in economic cooperation across the island as trade within Cyprus constitutes trade within the internal market. Europeanisation of trade relations across the Cyprus island has its promises and pitfalls. On the one hand, the Green Line Regulation enables trade across the island. On the other hand, the Republic of Cyprus insists that the ports and airports in the North, or the "occupation area" in its words, are closed, as evidenced in its 19 August 2005 letter to the Secretary-General of the UN.[57] This position remains unchanged even after the Republic of Cyprus acceded to the EU in 2004. For this reason, direct transportation from Northern Cyprus into the internal market of the EU is still not possible. Goods and services or free movement of persons from Northern Cyprus must be conducted via the Republic of Cyprus or, alternatively, via Turkey. Though there is an attempt to legislate a Direct Trade Regulation that would make direct transportation from Northern Cyprus to other EU Member States possible, it has been blocked by Cyprus. The impasse cannot be resolved. Arguably, the UN has introduced peace and stability across the island while the EU has brought about a "comfortable conflict" for Northern Cyprus which makes the comprehensive settlement of the Cyprus issue less attractive. Some even argue that if the TRNC can obtain more economic autonomy, such as the status of "separate customs territory", it may lead to a "Taiwanisation" process.[58]

[57] UN General Assembly Security Council, Letter Dated 19 August 2005 from the Charge D'affaires A.I. of the Permanent Mission of Cyprus to the United Nations Addressed to the Secretary-General, UN Doc A/59/899–S/2005/537 (Aug 23, 2005).

[58] International Crisis Group, Cyprus: Reversing the Drift to Partition 25–26 (2008). Available at: www.crisisgroup.org/europe-central-asia/western-europemediterranean/cyprus/cyprus-reversing-drift-partition.

B. The Role of Geopolitics in Shaping the Bilateral Economic Relations

(i) Cross-Taiwan Strait

Cross-Taiwan-Strait economic relations have been deeply influenced by shifting geopolitical dynamics, especially the strategic interventions of the US globally in the post-war era. In the post-war era, the US adopted two interconnected grand strategies: one realist, focused on containing Soviet power through building alliances and deterrence capabilities, and one liberal, focused on promoting an open economic order among market democracies.[59] These grand strategies were interlinked, as security alliances enabled economic integration that bound democratic countries together.[60] These strategies were deployed in both Western Europe and East Asia. Through the establishment of strategic partnerships, backed by its formidable economic and military prowess, the US reorientated the global economy, laying the groundwork for a new international economic order aimed at fostering prosperity and peace.

In Western Europe, it pursued an ambitious agenda to unite the continent, create a bulwark against communism, and support centrist democratic governments.[61] This led the US to bargain with European countries and agree to institutional constraints on its power, yielding multilateral institutions like the North Atlantic Treaty Organization (NATO) and the Bretton Woods system that integrated Western Europe into an American-led order.[62] In East Asia, on the other hand, the US opted for a bilateral "hub-and-spoke" approach enabling maximum control and freedom of action, binding countries to its preferred order through patron-client relationships;[63] it contributed to East Asia's economic development by providing its partners with security protection and access to American markets and technology within an increasingly open regional order.[64] Its post-war East Asian strategy ultimately fostered stability and prosperity, despite lacking the multilateral constraints present in Europe.

A notable example is Japan. Americans took significant steps to integrate Japan into its preferred global order, emphasising its accession to the GATT 1947 as part of drawing Japan into the Western economic sphere.[65] This integrated

[59] G John Ikenberry, *Power and Liberal Order: America's Postwar World Order in Transition*, 5 Int'l Rel Asia-Pac 133, 137–38 (2005); *see also* Jacques deLisle, *Soft Power in a Hard Place: China, Taiwan, Cross-Strait Relations and US Policy*, 54 Orbis 493, 520–24 (2010).

[60] *See* Ikenberry, *supra* note 59, at 138.

[61] *Id.* at 145–46.

[62] *Id.*

[63] *Id.* at 146.

[64] *Id.* at 137–38.

[65] Petros C Mavroidis and Andre Sapir, China and the WTO: Why Multilateralism Still Matters 22–23 (2021); *see also* Aaron Forsberg, *The Politics of GATT Expansion: Japanese Accession and the Domestic Political Context in Japan and the United States, 1948–1955*, 27 Bus & Econ Hist 185 (1998).

approach was driven by geopolitical considerations, as the US aimed to anchor Japan firmly to the West and distance it from potential regional threats posed by the Soviet bloc amidst the emerging Cold War.[66] Japan's post-war trajectory aligned swiftly with Western economic ideals, culminating in its OECD membership in 1964.[67]

Decades later, the US attempted to facilitate the integration of China, recognising vast opportunities in its massive domestic market. This was a period marked by China's economic reforms under Deng Xiaoping's Open Door Policy in the 1980s.[68] Then, the Clinton administration supported China's accession to the WTO in 2001 after intense negotiations on economic reforms required for membership. For Clinton, there existed the potential trajectory of China and the US–China relationship as an opportunity for both nations to build a better and distinct future within the Asia Pacific community.[69] Likewise, the American business community was optimistic about the economic benefits of normalising trade relations with the PRC. The American business community had long advocated for bolstering trade ties with China; they believed "Permanent Normal Trade Relations" would bring economic and security benefits, encourage China's economic reform, and lead to a more stable geopolitical situation.[70] President Clinton therefore signed the US–China Relations Act of 2000 in October, granting Beijing permanent normal trade relations with the US and paving the way for China's WTO accession in 2001.[71]

However, China's journey post-WTO entry presented a contrasting narrative to Japan's post-WWII development. While many in the US anticipated that China's WTO membership would act as a catalyst for economic and political reforms, the PRC largely retained its state-led socialist market economy ruled by the Chinese Communist Party. This adherence to its distinct economic model, in contrast to Japan's rapid westernisation,[72] has heightened economic tensions with major trade partners.[73] This, in turn, became a major source of US-China trade conflicts.

[66] Mavroidis and Sapir, *supra* note 65, at 141–44.

[67] Fumio Kishida, *Japan: Half a Century of OECD Membership*, 298 OECD Observer 33 (2014). Available at: www.oecd.org/japan/japan-half-a-century-of-oecd-membership.htm.

[68] Mavroidis and Sapir, *supra* note 65, at 209–10.

[69] Jennifer Hillman, *China's Entry into the WTO: A Mistake by the US?*, *in* China and the WTO: A Twenty-Year Assessment 400, 405 (Henry Gao et al eds, 2023).

[70] *Id.* at 406.

[71] For general background, *see, e.g.*, *US–China Relations (1949–2023)*, Council on Foreign Rels. Available at: www.cfr.org/timeline/us-china-relations (last visited Apr 19, 2024).

[72] Mavroidis and Sapir, *supra* note 65, at 132 (noting that while the Allied Occupation of Japan after the Second World War shifted Japan away from militarism toward democracy, economically, Japan already had a market-oriented economy in place when it joined GATT – even if it did not formally qualify as a typical Western economy at that time.).

[73] Hillman, *supra* note 69, at 424–25. As Hillman observes, the Clinton administration initially saw the WTO as a neutral mediator to bolster liberal trade rules with China, a view formed when global trade was seen as strategically beneficial by US strategists. However, this stance has changed, requiring the US to utilise a wider array of tools beyond the WTO to address its concerns and prompting a call for deeper WTO reforms to reconcile differences between market-oriented and

Across the Taiwan Strait, following the defeat of imperial Japan in 1945, the US played a pivotal role in reconstructing Asian capitalism and defining the parameters for East Asia's integration into the global capitalist system. Japan, Taiwan, and South Korea underwent transformations into industrial capitalist developmental economies with an export orientation. Specifically, Taiwan's march towards democratisation in the 1990s was deeply intertwined with its economic metamorphosis and extensive integration into the global trading system.

This evolution was not just an internal progression; it was profoundly influenced by its interactions with trading partners, especially within the framework set by the US. The Korean War and the subsequent Vietnam war further underscored the depth of the US-Taiwan relationship. The US showed its commitment to Taiwan by pledging military assistance against potential communist aggression in 1954.[74] The Vietnam War, much like the Korean War's economic impact on Japan, provided a significant boost to Taiwan's economy.[75] The US made extensive purchases of food and military equipment from Taiwan, which not only bolstered Taiwan's economy but compensated for the termination of US economic aid. As a result of these intertwined economic and security dynamics, Americans gained considerable influence over Taiwan's political and economic decisions. This influence was particularly salient during the Cold War and post-Cold War eras, reflecting patterns evident in other parts of East Asia as Taiwan's economic transformation became deeply intertwined with US strategic interests.[76]

As Taiwan started to democratise in the 1990s, it also embraced economic reforms and trade liberalisation. Privatisation of state-owned enterprises began under the Kuomintang (KMT) and accelerated under the Democratic Progressive Party (DPP) in the 2000s.[77] Parallel to these domestic political and

state-controlled economies. In fact, concerns regarding China's market-oriented economic stance are echoed by numerous WTO Members. During a G-20 trade ministers' meeting in September 2020, for instance, discussions mainly revolved around bolstering the WTO and reaffirming the Marrakesh Agreement's principles and objectives. Yet, China opposed the affirmation of "market-oriented policies" as a WTO principle. This core disagreement has prompted some prominent trade scholars to identify two clashing economic systems: a Western-led, market-driven model rooted in the rule of law, and an authoritarian, state-driven model advocated by China. They proposed forming a "compact" among like-minded developed market economies to devise new strategies against unfair non-market practices, tackle key twenty-first-century economic issues like the digital economy, climate change, and labour, and enhance economic relations in crucial innovative, growth, and national security sectors.

[74] Robert Wade, Governing the Market: Economic Theory and the Role of Government in East Asian Industrialization 138 (2003).

[75] *Id.*

[76] *Id.* 346.

[77] *Id.* 131. Kuotsai Tom Liou, *Privatization Development in Taiwan: Background and Issues*, 34 *Pub Admin Q* 3, 9–10 (2010). Liou notes that, in addition to economic factors, Taiwan's privatisation policy was motivated by its political democratisation movement. Literature references highlight that privatisation decisions are primarily political, with policymakers embracing and executing privatisation policies to further their political ideologies (*e.g.*, minimising the government's role and size)

economic shifts, Taiwan was actively engaging with the US via platforms like the Trade and Investment Framework Agreement (TIFA).[78] Established in 1994, TIFA served as a cornerstone for the US-Taiwan economic dialogue, addressing issues such as intellectual property rights and paving the way for Taiwan's preparations for WTO accession.[79] Across the political spectrum, both the KMT and DPP, despite their ideological divide on cross-Taiwan-Strait ties, have shown a commitment to Western liberal norms facilitated by WTO accession. This stands in stark contrast to China's persistent state capitalism, underscoring Taiwan's alignment with the US-dominated global economic framework. Such economic ties, however, are intrinsically linked with security considerations.

Taiwan's strategic reliance on Americans drove it to integrate with the US economically, binding itself through economic exchanges reinforced vital security ties in the shadow of potential Chinese aggression. Therefore, Taiwan's economic alignment with the US could be viewed as complementing its security needs – though at the expense of autonomy. This interplay of economic and security interests reflects calculations made by US allies during the Cold War. Such security-driven reliance, however, does not exist in the US–China context.[80]

In recent years, intensifying US–China strategic competition has further impacted Cross-Taiwan-Strait economic ties. Security concerns resurfaced. Taiwan, like many others, has faced great pressure from the rivalry between these two major powers. Taiwan is caught between economic relations with the PRC and the need for greater strategic autonomy supported by Americans. The escalating assertiveness of China in the Indo-Pacific region, coupled with the intensive debate surrounding the notion of "One China", further complicates the matter.[81]

and interests (*e.g.*, boosting public approval by reducing government waste). These political motives have shaped Taiwan's privatisation policy development, as the political democratisation movement has shifted traditional political ideology and accelerated the pace of privatisation.

[78] Riley Walters, *A Backgrounder on the History of US–Taiwan Trade and Investment Talks*, Global Taiwan Institute (Jun 30, 2021). Available at: www.globaltaiwan.org/2021/06/a-backgrounder-on-the-history-of-us-taiwan-trade-and-investment-talks/.

[79] *Id.*

[80] Mavroidis and Sapir aptly contextualise this against the trade-security background, noting that while "Japan has been dependent on the United States for its security … China, conversely, has never depended on the United States for its national security". Mavroidis and Sapir, *supra* note 65, at 143. This view would also hold true in the case of Taiwan. Given its dependence on the US for security concerns, the Taiwan government needs to take into account not only the factors vis-à-vis the PRC but also the influence of the US Although the US has no official ties with Taiwan, it sees Taiwan as a key democratic and technological partner in the Indo-Pacific. This support is provided through the American Institute in Taiwan, mandated by the Taiwan Relations Act. Critically, the US makes defence articles and services available to enable Taiwan's self-defence capability, maintaining the capacity to resist coercion that can jeopardise Taiwan's security or socio-economic system. In August 2023, the US approved a military aid package for Taiwan via the Foreign Military Sales (FMS) program amid the escalating tension. Patricia Zengerle, *Biden Approves Military Aid to Taiwan under Program Normally Used for Sovereign States*, Reuters (Aug 31, 2023). Available at: www.reuters.com/world/asia-pacific/biden-approves-military-aid-taiwan-under-program-normally-used-sovereign-states-2023-08-30/.

[81] *See e.g.*, Ankit Panda and Catherine Putz, *The Biden Administration Releases an Indo-Pacific Strategy: Reading Between the Lines*, Diplomat (Feb 18, 2022). Available at:

Of relevance to our analysis is the recurring debate over "One China". As noted in Chapter 2, in 1971, UN Resolution 2758 recognised the PRC as representing "China" in the UN but remain silent on Taiwan's status.[82] Over time, China has incrementally equated this resolution with its asserted "One China" principle and claimed sovereignty over Taiwan. The US and other nations, however, maintain their own versions of what constitutes the "One China" policy that is more ambiguous on Taiwan's status.[83] These debates have, fuelled by changing geopolitics, come to the forefront in recent years. Debates have resurfaced over whether Taiwan should be allowed meaningful participation in the UN and other international organisations. Notably, US lawmakers proposed to amend the 2019 Taiwan Allies International Protection and Enhancement Initiative (TAIPEI) Act of 2019 by passing the "Taiwan International Solidarity Act",

www.thediplomat.com/2022/02/the-biden-administration-releases-an-indo-pacific-strategy-reading-between-the-lines/1; Natasha Kassam, *Australians Worry About China and Muscle-flexing over Taiwan*, Interpreter (June 30, 2022). Available at: www.lowyinstitute.org/the-interpreter/australians-worry-about-china-and-muscle-flexing-over-taiwan.

[82] While the PRC maintains that UN Resolution 2758 is clear and unambiguous on Taiwan's status as part of China, arguably "[i]n legal terms, UN General Assembly Resolution 2758 addresses only UN representation of China and does not touch upon the sovereignty of Taiwan". Chien-Huei Wu and Ching-Fu Lin, *Taiwan and the Myth of UN General Assembly Resolution 2758*, VerfassungsBlog, (Apr 14, 2023). Available at: www.verfassungsblog.de/taiwan-and-the-myth-of-un-general-assembly-resolution-2758/ ("[UN Resolution 2758] addresses only the representation of China in the UN, that is, the question of who is entitled to occupy China's seat in the UN. It does not, in any sense, touch upon the territorial title of Taiwan".); *see, e.g.*, Editorial, *UN Resolution 2758 Clear and Unambiguous on Taiwan's Status as Inalienable Part of China*, China Daily (Aug 1, 2023). Available at: www.chinadaily.com.cn/a/202308/01/WS64c8f608a31035260b819b8a.html; *Foreign Ministry Spokesperson's Remarks on the Government of the Republic of Nauru's Announcement to Break Diplomatic Ties with the Taiwan Region and Seek to Reestablish Diplomatic Ties with China*, Ministry of Foreign Affairs (PRC) (Jan 15, 2024). Available at: www.mfa.gov.cn/eng/xwfw_665399/s2510_665401/202401/t20240115_11223838.html. ("There is but one China in the world, Taiwan is an inalienable part of China's territory, and the government of the People's Republic of China is the sole legal government representing the whole of China. It's what has been affirmed in Resolution 2758 of the UN General Assembly and is a prevailing consensus among the international community".).

[83] *See e.g.*, Jessica Drun and Bonnie Glaser, The German Marshall Fund of the US, The Distortion of UN Resolution 2758 to Limit Taiwan's Access to the United Nations (2022) (examining how the PRC has distorted UN Resolution 2758 to limit Taiwan's international space). This Marshall Fund report notes that the 1971 resolution solely recognised the PRC as holding the "China" seat at the UN; it did not determine Taiwan's status. However, the PRC has since systematically attempted to equate Resolution 2758 with its own "One China" principle asserting sovereignty over Taiwan. Beijing has pressured UN staff, revised records, and enlisted other countries to support its narrative. The Marshall Fund report recommends that the US and like-minded allies push back against the PRC's distortion of Resolution 2758. Proposed actions include directly challenging Beijing's stance at the UN, reversing problematic technical standards, and emphasising differences between the US's "One China" policy and the PRC's political principle. *See also* Madoka Fukuda, *China Is Using a UN Resolution to Further Its Claim Over Taiwan*, Diplomat (Aug 26, 2022). Available at: www.thediplomat.com/2022/08/china-is-using-a-un-resolution-to-further-its-claim-over-taiwan/(noting that the PRC emphasises Resolution 2758 to validate its One China principle amid dwindling global consensus on the issue). According to Fukuda, China relies on the resolution to characterise Taiwan as a PRC province in relation to the UN, contradicting the original intent of the resolution, which does not mention Taiwan. Recent emphasis on Resolution 2758 in the PRC's white papers reflects its diplomatic effort to reshape global perception, which has led to calls for collective opposition against such distortions to preserve the international order.

which clarifies that UNGA Resolution 2758 "did not address the issue of representation of Taiwan and its people in the United Nations or any related organizations".[84] Such an initiative has received harsh criticism from the PRC, which contended that "[o]nce and for all, the Resolution 2758 of the UN General Assembly resolved, politically, legally, and procedurally, the issues of the representation of the whole China, including Taiwan, in the UN and international institutions".[85] On this basis, the PRC urged the US to follow Resolution 2758, the "One-China principle, and … the three China-US joint communiqués", and "stop interfering in China's domestic affairs with Taiwan".[86]

The "One China" debate, a subject of ongoing contention, significantly influences cross-Taiwan-Strait economic dynamics. As discussed in Chapter 2, Taiwan's engagement as a sovereign state globally could, of course, provoke economic retaliation from China, potentially hindering trade and investment. On the other hand, if Taiwan were to expand its international presence, it could diversify its economic partnerships, reducing the risks associated with the weaponization of trade. This ongoing debate about the "One China" policy remains a key factor in shaping the economic interactions across the Strait.

The trajectory of Taiwan's international status, swaying towards broader recognition or enduring constraints because of the PRC's position, will steer the unfolding scenario. Presently, two overarching implications emerge from these evolving dynamics. Firstly, U.S. support does not necessarily aid Taiwan in gaining traction in other trade pacts, be they bilateral or regional, such as the Comprehensive and Progressive Agreement for Trans-Pacific Partnership (CPTPP) or the Regional Comprehensive Economic Partnership (RCEP). Consequently, it appears less likely for both sides of the Taiwan Strait to explore additional venues for economic exchanges beyond the existing frameworks. Second, the US will likely forge even closer ties with Taiwan, both in security and economic terms, reminiscent of its Cold War-era alliances.[87] The tightened

[84] Taiwan International Solidarity Act, HR1176, 118th Congress (2023). Available at: www.congress.gov/bill/118th-congress/house-bill/1176/all-info. Section 2 states that "United Nations General Assembly Resolution 2758 (XXVI) established the representatives of the Government of the People's Republic of China as the only lawful representatives of China to the United Nations. The resolution did not address the issue of representation of Taiwan and its people in the United Nations or any related organisations, nor did the resolution take a position on the relationship between the People's Republic of China and Taiwan or include any statement pertaining to Taiwan's sovereignty", while underscoring that the US "opposes any initiative that seeks to change Taiwan's status without the consent of the people". This bill was passed by the US House of Representatives on July 25, 2023, and is currently awaiting further action in the Senate.

[85] *Spokesperson of the Chinese Mission Speaks on the "Taiwan International Solidarity Act" Passed by the US*, Permanent Mission of The People's Republic of China to The United Nations Office at Geneva and Other International Organizations in Switzerland (Dec 17, 2021). Available at: http://geneva.china-mission.gov.cn/eng/ryrbt/202305/t20230520_11080428.htm.

[86] *Id.*

[87] *See generally* Council on Foreign Relations, US–Taiwan Relations in a New Era: Responding to a More Assertive China (2023) This report depicts the political framework governing relations between Taiwan, China, and the US as increasingly brittle. Prospects for a peaceful resolution between the two sides of the Strait are fading as Taiwanese identity consolidates and China grows

export controls of certain semiconductor products already signal Washington's intent to bind Taiwan into its strategic initiatives vis-à-vis China.[88] This is further evidenced by the US negotiating a bilateral trade deal with Taiwan.[89] While Taiwan gains security assurances, its policy latitude narrows under asymmetric alliances.[90] In this light, it is fair to say that the cross-Taiwan-Strait economic tie is not solely defined by the two sides of the Strait; rather, it is influenced significantly by external powers and their geostrategic interests.

more authoritarian. It also predicts that China will intensify its coercion of Taiwan using military threats, economic sanctions, diplomatic pressure, etc. Although Taiwan's critical role as the top global semiconductor producer acts as a brake on conflict, it has not fundamentally altered China's political goals. The report cautions that war would bring severe economic consequences globally. To respond, the report argues the US must strengthen deterrence and build Taiwan's self-defence capabilities with key recommendations including transforming US–Taiwan military ties, seeking clarity on allied support, reducing economic dependence on China, and making Taiwan contingencies the Pentagon's top priority. In summary, preventing war through resolute deterrence is argued to be an urgent priority, given increasing risks.

[88] While not a member of key multilateral export control regimes, Taiwan aligns its policies with international arrangements. Taiwan's export control system is founded on domestic legislation like the Foreign Trade Act. Among others, Articles 13 and 27 enable restrictions on "Strategic High-Tech Commodities" (SHTC) trades. However, Taiwanese high-tech firms are not only subject to export restrictions under Taiwan's Foreign Trade Act but also restrictions imposed by the US. The US Commerce Department's Bureau of Industry and Security (BIS) has, for instance, issued new rules since October 2022 to restrict China's access to advanced computing chips, components, and manufacturing equipment and software to protect American national security interests. Despite the instigation of these rules and the subsequent amendment to Taiwan's Foreign Trade Law to heighten the penalties, enforcement challenges linger, significantly driven by the close cross-Strait economic interactions. The evolution of Taiwan's strategic export controls is also swayed by the changing geopolitical landscape. This can be evidenced by, for instance, on 4 January 2023, Taiwan aligned its ban with international arrangements by announcing an addition of 52 new export control entries for Russia and Belarus. The 2023 enhancement mirrors the export regulations of the EU and the US *See* Foreign Trade Law [Maoyifa], arts 13 and 27 (貿易法) (as amended 25 Dec 2019). 經濟部國際貿易署，「修正『戰略性高科技貨品種類、特定戰略性高科技貨品種類及輸出管制地區」之「輸往俄羅斯及白俄羅斯高科技貨品清單」(如附件)，並自即日生效」（發文字號：經貿字第11140106300號）(Jing Ji Bu Guo Ji Mao Yi Shu, Xiu zheng "*zhan lue xing gao ke ji huo pin zhong lei, te ding zhan lue xing gao ke ji huo pin zhong lei ji shu chu guan zhi di qu" zhi "shu wang e luo si ji bai e luo si gao ke ji huo pin qing dan" (ru fu jian), bing zi ji ri sheng xiao, Jing mao zi di 11140106300 hao*) [Notice of the International Trade Administration, Ministry of Econ. Aff. (Taiwan), "Amendment to the 'Types of Strategic High-Tech Commodities, Specific Types of Strategic High-Tech Commodities, and Export Control Areas' regarding the 'High-Tech Goods List for Export to Russia and Belarus' (as attached), Effective Immediately" (Jan 4, 2023) (Reference Number: 11140106300)]. Available at: www.trade.gov.tw/Pages/Detail.aspx?nodeID=39&pid=755244.

[89] *United States and Taiwan Announce the Launch of the US-Taiwan Initiative on 21st-Century Trade*, Office of the United States Trade Representative (June 1, 2022). Available at: www.ustr.gov/about-us/policy-offices/press-office/press-releases/2022/june/united-states-and-taiwan-announce-launch-us-taiwan-initiative-21st-century-trade.

[90] *See, e.g.*, Brian Hioe, *TSMC's US Investments Spark Political Controversy in Taiwan*, Diplomat (Jan 18, 2023), Available at: www.thediplomat.com/2023/01/tsmcs-us-investments-spark-political-controversy-in-taiwan/ (reporting that TSMC's plans for new US chip plants stir political debate in Taiwan, raising doubts about the US's commitment to Taiwan's "silicon shield" and its overall interests); Juliana Liu, *As the World Courts TSMC, Taiwan Worries About Losing Its "Silicon Shield"*, CNN (Dec 9, 2022). Available at: www.edition.cnn.com/2022/12/09/tech/taiwan-tsmc-chips-hnk-intl/index.html (noting that Taiwan's TSMC is under pressure from the US and others to expand chip manufacturing abroad, creating unease in Taiwan about losing high-tech jobs and influence even as political leaders fete TSMC's investments).

(ii) The Korean Peninsula

The geopolitical landscape significantly shapes the economic relationship between ROK and DPRK, much like the dynamics observed in the cross-Taiwan-Strait relations. However, the context and key players differ, with the Korean Peninsula being a focal point of strategic interest for major powers such as the US, China, and Russia, among others. These external influences, coupled with the internal politics and policies of the Koreas, create a complex framework within which limited, *ad hoc* economic interactions take place. An overview here on the roles and influences of the US, China, and Russia, while not exhaustive, helps understand how geopolitics has shaped and reshaped the bilateral and troubled economic relation between ROK and DPRK. But before we start, it is practical to recall the link between the Korean Peninsula and cross-Taiwan-strait relations. After Japan's surrender at the end of the Second World War and the Chinese civil war between the Communist and Nationalist in 1945, resulting in the latter's retreat to Taiwan in 1949, the US was ambiguous about the territorial status of Taiwan and hesitant in recognising the Republic of China led by Chiang Kai-shek. At approximately the same time, the Korean Peninsula was divided along the 38th parallel as a temporary measure to disarm Japanese forces, with the Soviet Union occupying the north and the US occupying the south. However, Cold War tensions between the Soviet Union and the US led to the establishment of two separate governments in 1948. It was only until following the outbreak of the Korea war on 25 June 1950 that the US decided to send its seventh fleet to patrol the Taiwan strait, following which it eventually signed a joint defence treaty with the Republic of China in Taiwan in 1954. In this sense, the divide between the Korean Peninsula and the divide across the Taiwan strait share a common historical context; in fact, all three case studies in this book are situated in the context of the spread and containment of communism, the rivalry between the Soviet camp and the democratic camp, and the legacy of the Cold War.

China's role in the dynamics between the two Koreas is highly visible, multifaceted, and rooted in historical, political, and strategic considerations. As North Korea's most significant ally and economic lifeline, China is seen to be able to exert considerable influence over the peninsula's security and diplomatic landscape. For years, China's approach to the DPRK has been driven by a blend of strategic calculus and regional security concerns, aiming to set up a buffer state between itself and the US-allied ROK. Therefore, China's main goal has been to support Pyongyang's survival amidst international isolation by providing economic assistance, investment, and diplomatic backing in international organisations when possible. Yet there has recently been a noticeable shift in North Korea's diplomatic posture to deepening its strategic ties with China in parallel with its move away from reunification dialogues with South Korea. The recalibration and strengthening of China-DPRK relations underscore a major shift in the geopolitical dynamics of the Korean Peninsula that gives

China more weight in the interactions, in terms of economic cooperation and regional security.[91] However, China's relationship with ROK is also significant, characterised by robust economic ties, interdependence in high-tech supply chains, and a largely shared interest in regional stability. Despite occasional tensions, particularly regarding the deployment of the United States' Terminal High Altitude Area Defence (THAAD) missile system in ROK by the US, China and ROK have more or less managed their differences, recognising the mutual benefits of economic cooperation. Beijing's dual role as a supporter of DPRK and a key economic partner to ROK places it in a unique position to influence the inter-Korean relationship, where it advocates for dialogue and stability while carefully managing its strategic interests.

Russia's engagement with the Korean Peninsula, while not as visible as that of China, has also played a non-negligible role in the balance of power at the regional level. Historically, Russia has strategically supported – by way of energy exports, military cooperation, and diplomatic efforts to mediate tensions on the Korean Peninsula – DPRK as part of its broader strategy to assert influence in North-east Asia and counter US dominance. In terms of economic engagement, Russia has recently worked on increased cooperation with both ROK and DPRK with the aim of linking both into broader Eurasian economic projects as well as reasserting its influence on the Korean Peninsula. Such economic cooperation initiatives have included proposals for trilateral cooperation on infrastructure and energy projects that would connect South Korea with Russia through North Korea, offering a vision of economic/infrastructural integration that could provide mutual benefits and reduce tensions. Nevertheless, Moscow's relationship with Seoul has been overshadowed by the North Korean issue. Kim Jong-un visited Russia in September 2023 and met Putin at the Vostochny Spaceport, then made a tour to military aircraft production sites at Komsomolsk-on-Amur, warplanes and hypersonic missile systems, and Russia's Pacific Fleet at Vladivostok.[92] The 2023 Kim-Putin summit focused on military exchange and cooperation, and it was reported that a dramatic increase in rail traffic ensued, which likely indicated North Korea's supply of arms and munitions to Russia and therefore a stronger military alliance between the two.[93] According to a Center for Strategic and International Studies (CSIS) analysis, while "[p]revious talks concerning North Korean-Russian cooperation have centred around arms for food and energy … Kim's

[91] Heather Chen and Yoonjung Seo, *North Korea Says It Will No Longer Seek Reunification with South Korea, Will Launch New Spy Satellites in 2024*, CNN (1 Jan. 2024). Available at: www.edition.cnn.com/2023/12/31/asia/north-korea-reconciliation-south-korea-intl-hnk/index.html.

[92] Guy Faulconbridge and Soo-Hyang Choi, *Putin and North Korea's Kim Discuss Military Matters, Ukraine War and Satellites*, Reuters (13 Sep 2023). Available at: www.reuters.com/world/nkoreas-kim-meets-putin-missiles-launched-pyongyang-2023-09-13/.

[93] Joseph S Bermudez Jr. et al., *Dramatic Increase in DPRK-Russia Border Rail Traffic After Kim-Putin Summit*, Beyond Parallel (6 Oct. 2023). Available at: www.beyondparallel.csis.org/dramatic-increase-in-dprk-russia-border-rail-traffic-after-kim-putin-summit/.

unusual itinerary during the recent summit hints at Russian willingness to assist North Korea with satellite and space-launched vehicle technology, which could include [intercontinental ballistic missile] technology".[94] Increasing military technology transfers and cooperation will likely heighten tensions in the Korean Peninsula and increase barriers to dialogue and economic exchange.

As for the US, Chapter 3 briefly discusses the policy dimensions of the Trump and Biden Administration, underlining the continuing and paramount relevance and influence of the United States in the Korean Peninsula. Prior to Donald Trump's presidency, the United States had attempted to tackle challenges posed by North Korea's nuclear arsenal through enhanced military alliances, extensive sanctions, export restrictions, and diplomatic efforts to halt North Korea's nuclear program in return for economic aid. For instance, the United States had a significant influence on South Korea's Sunshine Policy, particularly under the Clinton and Bush administrations which co-shaped the trajectory and effectiveness of inter-Korean economic cooperation. Under Clinton, there was a more supportive environment for the Sunshine Policy,[95] facilitating engagement with the North to create conditions of stability on the Korean Peninsula.[96] Three months before the end of his term (9-12 October 2000), President Clinton received the special envoy of Kim Jong Il, and the US-DPRK Joint Communiqué was released after the meeting. The Joint Communiqué noted the improved security environment on the Korean Peninsula after the historic inter-Korean summit and subsequent economic cooperation, and declared that "neither government would have hostile intent toward the other … [US-DPRK] relations should be based on the principles of respect for each other's sovereignty".[97] The Clinton administration's policy to explicitly support President Kim Dae-jung's vision of engagement and efforts toward reconciliation with the North was characterised by the idea of a "soft landing" assuming that engagement was the rational option to prevent the deterioration of military security and the potential collapse of North Korea.[98] However, the Bush administration's harder stance on North Korea marked a divergent path from the Clinton administration and presented challenges for South Korea's engagement efforts under the Sunshine Policy. The Bush administration's approach was characterised by a form of "moral absolutism" that did not view North Korea as a rational actor but an evil entity that needed to

[94] *Id.*

[95] *See generally* Haksoon Paik, *Assessment of the Sunshine Policy: A Korean Perspective*, 26 Asian Persp 13 (2002); Jong Kun Choi, *Sunshine over a Barren Soil: The Domestic Politics of Engagement Identity Formation in South Korea*, 34 Asian Persp 115 (2010).

[96] *See generally* Young Chul Cho, *Collective Identity Formation on the Korean Peninsula: United States' Different North Korea Policies, Kim Dae-Jung's Sunshine Policy, and United States–South Korea–North Korea Relations*, 10 Int'l Rels Asia-Pac 93 (2010).

[97] US Department of State, US-DPRK Joint Communique (Oct 12, 2000), 1997–2001.state.gov/regions/eap/001012_usdprk_jointcom.html.

[98] Cho, *supra* note 96, at 99–100; *see also* Selig S Harrison, *Promoting a Soft Landing in Korea*, 106 Foreign Pol'y 56 (1997).

be punished rather than engaged, and this ideological opposition was stark, with the Bush administration seemingly focused on regime change in North Korea, viewing the US-DPRK Joint Communiqué and related policy attempts as insignificant and easily disregarded.[99]

Trump attempted to depart from past administrations' diplomatic techniques by cultivating a personal rapport and summits with Kim Jong Un to build mutual trust in the talks, but such an approach ultimately did not work out with concrete results.[100] Notably, while there seemed to be some progress at the Singapore summit in relation to denuclearisation, the second Trump-Kim summit in Hanoi in February 2019 ended unfruitfully.[101] Four months later, on 30 June 2019, the US and the leaders of the two Koreas came to establish a one-day summit at the DMZ, but the meeting – albeit a milestone for the trilateral relationship since the end of the Korean War – was regarded more as a formalistic handshake rather than a serious negotiation.[102]

Joe Biden's administration has prioritised diplomacy and patience in its approach to the inter-Korean relationship, stressing collaboration with its regional allies like South Korea and Japan to tackle North Korea's nuclear threat and ensure regional security and underscoring the role of multilateralism and global cooperation via the UN and other forums to apply pressure on North Korea with sanctions. Notably, the Biden administration has sanctioned a number of people and entities for their involvement in developing ballistic missile-related programs and weapons of mass destruction, including Russia-based DPRK nationals, China-based chief representatives involved in related procurement, and Russian firms and nationals.[103] Economic sanctions led by the US and supported by the international community have significantly restricted North Korea's ability to engage in formal international economic trade. With sanctions in place, the US stated that it is prepared to negotiate denuclearisation and human rights with the DPRK at any time. Pyongyang, on the other hand, has indicated that it will not engage in discussions with Washington unless such

[99] Cho, *supra* note 96, at 109–10; *see also* Chung-in Moon and Jong-Yun Bae, *The Bush Doctrine and the North Korean Nuclear Crisis*, 27(4) Asian Persp 9 (2003).

[100] *See, e.g.*, Lisa Collins and Sue Mi Terry, *Assessment of the Trump-Kim Hanoi Summit*, Ctr for Strategic and Int'l Stud (28 Feb 2019). Available at: www.csis.org/analysis/assessment-trump-kim-hanoi-summit.

[101] As the world was watching how the United States communicates with North Korea, the United States was optimistic that there would be an impressive improvement in the Hanoi summit compared to. However, North Korea has demanded immediate relaxation from all sanctions in exchange for just partial denuclearisation, putting the two parties at an impasse. Kim Suk Hi, *The Assessment of President Donald Trump's North Korean Policy*, 2(16) N Kor Rev 121, 124 (2020); Congressional Research Service, The February 2019 Trump-Kim Hanoi Summit (2019). Available at: www.crsreports.congress.gov/product/pdf/IN/IN11067.

[102] Peter Baker and Michael Crowley, *Trump Steps into North Korea and Agrees with Kim Jong-un to Resume Talks*, New York. Times (June 30, 2019). Available at: www.nytimes.com/2019/06/30/world/asia/trump-north-korea-dmz.html.

[103] Amanda Macias, *US Sanctions 8 People and Entities Following North Korean Missile Launches*, CNBC (Jan 12, 2022). Available at: www.cnbc.com/2022/01/12/us-sanctions-5-north-koreans-over-weapons-programs-following-missile-launches.html.

sanctions are abandoned.[104] Following a series of recent missile tests and spy satellite launches, the US coordinated with Australia, Japan, and South Korea to impose further sanctions.[105]

Most recently, tensions on the Korean Peninsula, and between North Korea and the US, have increased dramatically, and the inter-Korean relationship has worsened under the Yoon administration.[106] In the midst of an international environment troubled by the Russia-Ukraine war and US-China rivalry, the Yoon administration has moved closer to the US and shown greater support for the latter's Indo-Pacific strategy and regional security efforts, leaving little room for further economic cooperation with the North. These tensions were further heightened when President Yoon recently called for regional peace but emphasised that any cooperation with the DPRK by Russia (or arguably China) on military affairs must cease.[107] In his latest New Year's address, Yoon vowed to "completely block" North Korea's nuclear threat and to strengthen the ROK's military preparedness in hopes of achieving "a true and lasting peace based on strength".[108] For his part, Kim Jong Un condemned US intervention, named South Korea as its principal enemy, and declared that North Korea will no longer seek reconciliation and reunification with South Korea but will further increase its military means – including spy satellites and nuclear weapons – to counter what he called "US-led confrontation" and "South Korea provocation".[109] Kim Jong Un also attempted to bring China closer (or more visibly) to the table by exchanging messages with Xi Jinping on forging closer ties between the two countries. This may increase the risk of instability in the Peninsula and raise barriers to further cooperation.[110]

[104] Hyun-wook Kim, *A Korean Perspective on the Biden Administration's North Korea Policy*, Stimson (Feb 28, 2022). Available at: www.stimson.org/2022/a-korean-perspective-on-the-biden-administrations-north-korea-policy/.

[105] Press Release, US Department of the Treasury, Treasury Targets DPRK's International Agents and Illicit Cyber Intrusion Group (30 Nov. 2023). Available at: www.home.treasury.gov/news/press-releases/jy1938; *US Slaps Sanctions on North Korea with Allies over Spy Satellite*, Kyodo News (Dec 1, 2023). Available at: www.english.kyodonews.net/news/2023/12/4515793768bc-us-slaps-sanctions-on-n-korea-in-response-to-spy-satellite-launch.html; and Chen and Seo, *supra* note 91.

[106] *See e.g.* Ju-min Park, *Military Agreement Fractures as Tensions Rise with North Korea*, Reuters (Nov 23, 2023). Available at: www.reuters.com/world/asia-pacific/military-agreement-fractures-tensions-rise-with-north-korea-2023-11-22; Julian Ryall, *North Korea Ends Military Pact with South Korea – What Next?*, Deutsche Welle (Nov 24, 2023). Available at: www.dw.com/en/north-korea-ends-military-pact-with-south-korea-what-next/a-67541707.

[107] Jack Kim, *South Korea's Yoon Says any Military Cooperation with North Korea Must Stop*, Reuters (Sep 6, 2023). Available at: www.reuters.com/world/asia-pacific/south-koreas-yoon-says-any-attempt-cooperate-militarily-with-north-korea-must-2023-09-06/.

[108] Steven Borowiec, *South Korea's Yoon Vows to "Completely Block" North's Nuclear Threat*, Nikkei Asia (Jan 1, 2024). Available at: www.asia.nikkei.com/Politics/Defense/South-Korea-s-Yoon-vows-to-completely-block-North-s-nuclear-threat.

[109] Hyung-Jin Kim, *North Korea's Kim Vows to Launch 3 More Spy Satellites and Produce More Nuclear Materials in 2024*, AP (Jan 1, 2024). Available at: www.apnews.com/article/north-korea-kim-spy-satellites-nuclear-party-meeting-236fcaee8927d8f69359b45aaa88e2c0.

[110] Jack Kim, *North Korea Kim Jong Un, China's Xi Exchange Message Vowing Closer Ties, Yonhap Reports*, Reuters (Jan 1, 2024). Available at: www.reuters.com/world/asia-pacific/north-korea-kim-jong-un-chinas-xi-exchange-message-vowing-closer-ties-yonhap-2023-12-31/.

All in all, the economic relationship between North and South Korea cannot be viewed in isolation from the global geopolitical context. The strategic interests and agendas of major powers (in particular the US, Russia, and China) on the Korean Peninsula have directly and indirectly influenced the possibilities and limits of economic cooperation. Already fluctuating, limited, and *ad hoc* economic engagements have often been overshadowed by security concerns and the broader geopolitical rivalry/competition between the US, Russia, and China – even more so than in the case of Cyprus, or arguably cross-Taiwan-Strait relations.

(iii) Cyprus

The Cyprus case reflects events in the history of colonisation and decolonisation, from the dissolution of the Ottoman Empire and rise of British Empire, to calls for self-determination. When the British decided to leave Cyprus, the major two resident ethnic communities had different visions of the future. These visions were strongly influenced by regional powers: their "motherlands", Greece and Turkey. Early on, Cold War dynamics strongly influenced the destiny of the island. Later, the UN played a significant role establishing the Green Line that still today divides the island. Following the fall of the Berlin Wall and the expansion of the EU, the conflict was Europeanised. In a word, the division of Cyprus tells the history of geopolitical change, competing interests, and the waxing and waning of great powers and regional players.

British dominion of Cyprus took root at the Berlin Congress of July 1878 in the aftermath of the Russo-Turkish War of 1877–1878. The Ottoman Empire agreed to the Cyprus Convention with the British Empire in exchange for British support during the Berlin Congress on 4 June 1878. Under the Cyprus Convention, the Ottoman Empire retained sovereignty over Cyprus while the British Empire established administration on the island. Cyprus thus became a protectorate of the British Empire. In the First World War, Turkey joined the Central Powers, and Britain annexed the island in 1914. The Crown Colony of Cyprus was proclaimed in 1925. Britain's annexation of Cyprus was ratified in the Treaty of Sèvres in 1920 and reconfirmed in the Treaty of Lausanne in 1923. This was the era of great power competition and still the heyday of colonisation. Acquisition of territory through force was considered legitimate, and the transfer of sovereignty was largely decided by negotiations between great powers; the peoples involved had little to no voice.

Following the Second World War, a new international order emerged, embedded within the UN system, which proclaimed the right of peoples to self-determination. Between 1945 and 1960, there were waves of decolonisation and independence movements, which included Cyprus. The 1960 Treaty of Establishment of the Republic of Cyprus was signed against the background of the Cold War, and in a very different international security environment.

At the end of the Second World War, the Balkans had fallen behind the Iron Curtain, and communism had reached the shores of the Mediterranean. NATO was established in 1949 and admitted Greece and Turkey in 1952. When the British left Cyprus in 1960, the US was concerned with containing communism and ensuring two NATO allies with vested interests in the island would not go to war against each other.[111] Additionally, although the British were leaving, they did not intend to give up their military bases on the island. In fact, the US hoped Britain would retain such strategically advantageous staging points.

The independent Republic of Cyprus was soon troubled by inter-ethnic conflict, but the US was hesitant to intervene as it considered Cyprus a matter for the British.[112] The US objective was to prevent the conflict from growing and destabilising the region. The US further hoped that Cyprus would develop political stable democratic institutions and a pro-Western orientation, and thus could join in forming a solid bulwark against communism.[113] It was only when the conflict between Turkey and Greece threatened to undermine the NATO alliance that the US intervened, albeit ineffectually. Following the failure of other diplomatic efforts, a June 5, 1964 letter from President Johnson to Turkey forbad the use of US-supplied weapons in Cyprus.[114] As Van Coufoudakis wrote, "Johnson's letter to Prime Minister Inonu was not only considered a 'blow' to Turkey's national pride, but also a clear sign of abandonment by the United States after a decade and a half of Turkey's total commitment to the Western alliance. It was also seen as proof of America's 'pro-Greek' tilt".[115]

With a Greek-sponsored *coup* in Cyprus in 1974, and Turkey's subsequent invasion, the position of the US was ambivalent.[116] Interestingly, much of this

[111] TW Adams, *The American Concern in Cyprus*, 401 Annals Am Acad Pol & Soc Sci 95 (1972); *see also* Parker T Hart, Two NATO Allies at the Threshold of War (1990).

[112] Andreas Constandinos, *US–British Policy on Cyprus, 1964–1974*, 23 Cyprus Rev 17 (2011).

[113] Aylin Güney, *The USA's Role in Mediating the Cyprus Conflict: A Story of Success or Failure?*, 35 Sec Dialogue 27, 29 (2004).

[114] *Id.* at 30. To some degree, the worsening of the US-Turkish relations led to the rapprochement between the USSR and Turkey. *See* Ilksoy Aslım, *The Soviet Union and Cyprus in 1974 Events*, 2 Athens J Hist 249 (2016).

[115] Van Coufoudakis, *Turkey and the United States: The Problems and Prospects of a Post-War Alliance*, 9 J Pol & Mil Socio 179, 183 (1981).

[116] Up to this day, it has been rumoured and discussed, though never confirmed without reasonable doubt, that the United States government knew about the Greek junta intentions in advance and did not oppose it at the time, a claim which was backed by some accounts. Geoffrey Warner, *Review Article*: *The United States and the Cyprus Crisis of 1974*, 85 Int'l Affs 129, 135 (2009). According to Warner, two intelligence documents analysed by the United States House of Representatives' Select Committee on Intelligence agree that "… the US government did not apply sufficiently strong pressure on the Greek government to prevent it from making any rash move with regards to Cyprus. This was largely due to the attitude of the US embassy in Athens. As Colby stated, reporting from the embassy in the pre-coup period was 'weak' and 'fairly consistently downplayed the likelihood of serious trouble over Cyprus, even in the face of repeated expressions of great concern from Nicosia and Washington'". The embassy, in fact, opposed

diplomacy was out of the hands of Henry Kissinger, who was simultaneously serving as President Nixon's Secretary of State and National Security Adviser and tasked with handling US–China relations. Again, the primary objective of the US was to prevent "a wider Greco-Turkish confrontation over Cyprus that could lead to a possible Soviet involvement".[117]

As Güney argues, "US restraint *vis-à-vis* the Greek-led *coup d'état* was coupled with a policy of tolerance towards Turkey's landing troops on the island on 20 June 1974".[118] The US chose not to forcefully prevent the invasion as such a move might push Turkey towards the Soviet camp. During the few days between the Greek-backed *coup* and the Turkish invasion, Kissinger scrambled to defuse the situation or contain the conflict to the island and avoid Soviet involvement. According to Geoffrey Warner:

> At the WSAG [Washington Special Actions Group] meeting on 16 July 1974, Kissinger outlined American objectives as: "(1) to prevent the internationalization of the situation, and (2) if civil war develops to conduct ourselves so that the Communists aren't encouraged to exploit the situation. The first thing we have to do is decouple the Greeks and do it today. We also have to get the Turks to stay out of it".[119]

The US failed to convince the Turks not to intervene. On 20 July 1974, Turkish troops landed on the island, after which a contentious period of delicate behind-the-scenes negotiations involving the US, Turkey and Greece followed. Kissinger was determined to balance the US position between Greece and Turkey – the first being a valuable bulwark against communism in the Balkans, and the second housing US military bases and missile launch sites. According to Warner, during the first few days following the invasion, as Turkish forces were deploying on the northern portion of the island and as the Greek military junta was collapsing, there were intense negotiations among NATO members to quickly end the debacle.[120]

Importantly, the Republic of Cyprus was part of the non-aligned movement. The Progressive Party of the Working People (AKEL), Cypriot's communist party, was and still is very influential, and then Archbishop Makarios was believed to have close links with the Soviet Union. The US felt that it could not afford to further agonise Turkey because of the risk that Cyprus might slip from non-aligned into the Soviet camp. In the end, the US Congress "succeeded

confronting Ioannides directly. When the State Department asked the ambassador, Henry Tasca, on 17 May 1974 to warn Ioannides about American concern at developments in Cyprus, Tasca argued against it; the message was not actually delivered until 13 June 1974 – and then only to the Cyprus desk officer in the Greek Foreign Ministry".

[117] Güney, *supra* note 113 at 34; see also Christos Kassimeris, *The Inconsistency of United States Foreign Policy in the Aftermath of the Cyprus Invasion: the Turkish Arm Embargo and its Termination*, J Mod Greek Stud 91, 94–95 (2008).

[118] Güney, *supra* note 113 at 34.

[119] Warner, *supra* note 116, at 135.

[120] *Id.*

in punishing the administration [of Inonu] by cutting off all military aid to Turkey in February 1975, which, in turn, led to the Turkish government depriving the United States of access to its own bases in Turkey (bar one air base), including valuable intelligence-gathering facilities ... this would appear to indicate that Kissinger's policy was a calamitous failure".[121] Christos Kassimeris thus suggested that "Kissinger's tilt, first towards the Greek and then to the Turkish side, meant that American foreign policy formulators were changing tactics from supporting the union of Cyprus with Greece to the partition of the island".[122] Perhaps Washington was only interested in maintaining the *status quo*, which would explain its recognition of the Sampson government and its "welcoming" of the *de facto* partition of the island.[123] The Cold War mindset, supplemented by the UN's intervention establishing the Green Line as a buffer zone, stabilised the island by freezing the conflict.

Cyprus, following the example Greece had set in 1961, signed an association agreement with the European Economic Community (EEC) in 1972, which demonstrated the EEC's influence in that region and over the island. The EEC's stake in the Cyprus issue was amplified by the fall of the Greek junta in 1974, the democratisation of Greece, its efforts to join the EEC and eventual accession in 1981. *Détente* and the fall of the Berlin Wall changed the geopolitical landscape yet again, as manifested by the conclusion of Europe Agreements between the European Community and the Central and Eastern European (CEE) countries, which eventually joined the EU in 2004.

At the insistence of Greece, which strongly supported Cyprus's membership bid and objected to Turkey's candidacy, Cyprus's accession was packaged with that of the CEE countries. With Turkey's candidate status confirmed in the Helsinki summit in 1999 and the landslide victory of the Justice and Development Party led by Recep Tayyip Erdoğan in 2002, Turkey was enthusiastic about the EU accession process in the new millennium. This in turn impacted attitudes in Northern Cyprus regarding the terms of economic cooperation across the island and the goal of reaching a comprehensive political settlement. However, when Turkey grew frustrated by long delays in its accession process and lost its appetite for joining the EU, Northern Cyprus became more aggressive in its pursuit of statehood and recognition.

The accession of Cyprus into the EU in 2004 fundamentally transformed the nature of the Cyprus conflict and turned it into a European matter. Obviously, trade across the island falls into the scope of the internal market and constitutes an exclusive competence of the EU. The accession protocol addresses the divide of the island by suspending the application of *acquis communautaire* in Northern Cyprus while at the same time attempting to redress it through the Green Line Regulation. The Europeanisation of the Cyprus conflict

[121] *Id.* at 140.
[122] Kassimeris, *supra* note 117, at 94.
[123] *Id.* at 95.

effectively sets a limit on economic cooperation across the island because the accession protocol prescribes unanimity for the realisation of direct trade. Turkish Cypriots' approval of the Annan Plan – though they were outvoted by Greek Cypriots – won the Turkish community a greater voice in the Council of Europe and, to a lesser degree, other EU institutions. This helped transform the Cyprus conflict into a more manageable, comfortable condition and reduce the appetite of Turkish Cypriots for political unification. Here, an interesting comparison between Taiwan and Northern Cyprus can be registered. Apart from sharing in the same Cold War legacy and critical role of Kissinger, Northern Cyprus is argued to have undergone a process of "Taiwanisation", signifying its possession of a substantial degree of economic autonomy albeit without full political recognition.

IV. CONCLUDING REMARKS: IN SEARCH OF LEGITIMACY AND ACCOUNTABILITY

The six states identified as pair groups among these three "divided nations" display distinct features characteristic of their differing political regimes. Freedom House categorises four of the states as free, with the following scores out of 100: Taiwan (94), South Korea (83), Republic of Cyprus (92), and Northern Cyprus (76). China (9) and North Korea (3) are identified as not free countries.[124] Given the diverse political systems of these states, assessing the legitimacy and accountability of their government actions in international economic cooperation is complex, especially viewed from the perspective of their citizens. It is natural for democracies to speak about democratic legitimacy, but not authoritarian regimes. Even China differs from North Korea in significant ways. At the risk of oversimplification, the DPRK is a one-person regime while the PRC is a one-party regime, though under Xi Jinping the CCP is cycling back to a one-person regime model. In these case studies, the most challenging intellectual exercise is to conceptualise and critique how one democracy economically engages with its authoritarian counterpart and to assess consequential costs and benefits, as demonstrated in the Taiwan strait and Korean Peninsula cases.

Generally speaking, democratic legitimacy and congressional oversight function in a similar manner in Taiwan, ROK, Republic of Cyprus and the TRNC given their political organisation as democracies. Practically speaking, the path and pace of economic cooperation will be regularly evaluated and assessed by

[124] *Countries and Territories*, Freedom House. Available at: www.freedomhouse.org/ (last visited Apr 19, 2024, data accessible under "Global Freedom Scores"). The Economist Intelligence Unit's 2023 "Democracy Index" lists Taiwan and South Korea as full democracies with scores of 8.92 and 8.09 out of ten respectively. Republic of Cyprus (7.38) is categorised as flawed democracy, whereas China (2.12) and North Korea (1.08) are authoritarian regimes. Economist Intelligence Unit, Democracy Index 2023. Available at: www.eiu.com/n/campaigns/democracy-index-2023/.

the constituencies through elections. Different candidates have different political preferences or policy agendas in terms of economic cooperation in the "divided nations". More often than not, these political preferences and policy agendas are decisive elements in the presidential elections. Therefore, democratic accountability through elections constitutes the main safety valve for economic cooperation.

However, there is a subtle difference between Taiwan, the Republic of Cyprus and the TRNC on the one hand and ROK on the other, as Taiwan and the Republic of Cyprus are in a state of mutual non-recognition with the PRC and the TRNC respectively. Thus, negotiations must take place through different channels with authority delegated to semi-official entities: the SEF for Taiwan, ARATS for China, CCCI for Republic of Cyprus and TCCoC for the TRNC. The question then arises how to hold these organisations accountable and sustain their (democratic) legitimacy. The tasks for the semi-official organisations to conduct negotiations or monitor the implementations may be carried out by virtue of the mechanism of administrative entrustment (*Beleihung*), where the agency holds the ultimate control. This nonetheless gives rise to principal-agent difficulties: e.g., the interests between the principal and agent may vary, the principal may not be well-informed and, at times, the agent may escape the control of the principal. Moreover, this administrative entrustment raises transparency concerns, and the legislature is faced with even greater difficulty in overseeing the economic cooperation activities. A good example is the negotiation process of the Cross-Strait Service Trade Agreement, which eventually led to a massive student protest that storm the Legislative Yuan, the Parliament of Taiwan. The contested "1992 consensus", a term coined by a former Secretary General of Taiwan's National Security Council in 2001, is also a case in point. The KMT argued that, in 1992, through meetings in Hong Kong, the representatives of the SEF and ARATS made a verbal statement regarding the relationship between Taiwan and China and an implicit consensus was reached. Then-President Lee Teng-hui and the DPP nonetheless deny its existence. Given the opacity of the negotiation processes between the SEF and ARATS and the near absence of congressional oversight and accountability mechanisms, the so-called "1992 consensus" has become the most controversial concept in cross-Taiwan-Strait relations. Not only does China keep revising its understanding and interpretation of this questionable "1992 consensus", but it is also hardly justifiable, in Taiwan's democratic constitutional order, that a verbal agreement reached by the representatives of semi-official organisation could decide such a fundamental issue. Such consensus, if it ever existed, was not subject to approval or even endorsement by the Legislative Yuan.

Importantly, given the non-recognition between Taiwan and China and between Republic of Cyprus and the TRNC, the presidents of the pair of "divided nations" meet unofficially as "leaders" rather than as heads of state. Such format poses further challenges to accountability and legitimacy. Do the "leaders" meet *ex officio* or not? Do their statements represent the will of the population or simply reflect their personal preferences? Does a commitment made, or consensus reached, at a meeting in their capacities as "leaders" subsequently bind the countries? These are all thorny issues that demand sober reflection.

The "legitimacy" of authoritarian regimes is derived from different sources than their democratic counterparts. For China, economic growth is the main source of legitimacy for its party-state system. Chinese citizens are largely satisfied with sacrificing political rights for higher economic growth. For this reason, in the age of Deng Xiaoping, how to attract Taiwanese (and Hong Kong's) investments and capital, which constituted one of the main drivers for Chinese economic growth in the aftermath of Tiananmen Square Massacre when economic sanctions were imposed by Western countries, was one of the highest priorities of China's policy agenda. In response, Taiwan's policymakers prioritised preventing the economic hollowing-out of Taiwan. As China's economic growth surged with increased exports, the leadership legitimacy of Jiang Zemin, who facilitated China's WTO entry, and Hu Jintao, was largely based on economic achievements. This context influenced Cross-Strait relations, with China attempting to attract Taiwan using economic incentives, drawing on the "one country, two systems" approach modelled after Hong Kong.

Significant shifts began when Xi Jinping, unsatisfied with merely economic growth, aimed for the great rejuvenation of the Chinese nation. For Xi, the unification of Taiwan, whether through peaceful means or by force, is crucial for maintaining or boosting his leadership legitimacy within the CCP. The legitimacy of the CCP in general and each leader in particular, lies not in democratic election but in China's economic growth and national pride. These dynamics significantly shape China's strategy in engaging economically with Taiwan – and likewise, shape Taiwan's counter-responses – as a way to facilitate political unification. Consequently, China tactically applies economic incentives and, when necessary, implements penalties. Ultimately, the pursuit of political aims underpins the legitimacy of PRC's economic interactions with the other side, and officials may face scrutiny for not securing Taiwan's alignment.

The one-party regime of the PRC and, admittedly, the one-person regime of the DPRK present a challenge for their counterparts in economic cooperation, as their counterparts are still determining the credibility of their commitments. In the future, Kim Jong Un may unilaterally retract his commitments, undermining cooperation efforts. Similarly, the CCP might suspend or revoke its ECFA obligations to penalise the DPP government for not yielding politically. The fragility of these commitments is highlighted by domestic political systems where decisions by individuals or oligarchic elites can alter economic cooperation policies, compounded by the minimal involvement of multilateral frameworks. North Korea, as one of the most isolated nations, shows little interest in joining economic organisations, including the WTO. As for China-Taiwan relations, China has persisted and tried to sidestep the WTO, which can be clearly illustrated by its reluctance to notify the WTO committee on regional trade agreement on the conclusion of the ECFA and the possible suspension of commitments made thereunder. In this sense, it is fair to say that multilateral institutions may play a role in stabilising relations between a pair of "divided nations" and in monitoring or supervising the implementation of economic commitments.

In view of these considerations identified above, the case of China–Taiwan relations, where the authoritarian counterpart is much more powerful, poses the most daunting challenge in terms of conceptualising the legitimacy and accountability and assessing the consequential costs and benefits. The unique nature of the sovereignty disputes between "divided nations" and the existence of a wide range of stakeholders in broader geopolitical contexts often necessitates that negotiations between divided nations are so opaque that effective democratic control and accountability mechanisms are infeasible or inadequate. Besides, whereas a democracy is subject to a number of constraints, be it domestic constitutional order or international law, an authoritarian country enjoys much more "freedom" and manoeuvrability in the process of negotiations. This asymmetry of procedural requirements may give the authoritarian regime undue advantage on the negotiating table as its democratic counterpart is hand-tied. Moreover, such negotiations risk eventually undermining its democratic legitimacy and domestic political support of the democratic halves of the "divided nations". Namely, negotiating and trading with an authoritarian trade giant risks democratic backlash and erosion of the rule of law since the democratic counterpart may be tempted or compelled to sidestep democratic oversight and accountability mechanisms with a view to competing with its negotiating partner. Even worse, the benefits of such negotiations are also limited by the fact that the commitments of an authoritarian regime may not be reliable, as the political leaders within that regime may change or cancel them at will. Therefore, even agreements which are, on their face, mutually economically beneficial are may constitute a source of concern. This is particularly true in the China-Taiwan context.

By contrast, in view of their domestic political regimes, their memberships in international organisations notably in the UN, and potential sovereignty implications, economic cooperation in the Korean Peninsula is conducted through a government-to-government model, which, in the case of the ROK, is subject to democratic control for accountability and legitimacy. By contrast, there is little to no legitimacy or accountability mechanism from the DPRK side. Stated plainly, for the whole DPRK regime, such concepts as legitimacy and accountability do not exist; the maintenance of the Kim family in power is the sole consideration. From the perspective of the ROK, its policies of economic cooperation with the DPRK must be scrutinised by the National Assembly and indirectly approved by universal suffrage when the citizens of the ROK vote in presidential elections. For example, the Sunshine Policy advanced by Kim Dae-jung (1998–2003) and followed by Roh Moon-hyun (2002–2008) came to an end when Lee Myung-bak was elected President in 2008. The Sunshine policy was only again embraced when Moon Jae-in was elected as President in 2017.

It is fair to say that the people of South Korea have a say – perhaps the final say – over the progress of ROK economic cooperation with North Korea.

While the ROK Constitution does not detail procedures for inter-Korean economic cooperation specifically, the National Assembly, which holds electoral legitimacy and represent the ROK citizens, has the general authority to oversee the Ministry of Unification regarding the policies towards and economic cooperation with North Korea.[125] The Inter-Korean Exchange and Cooperation Act, which defines the inter-Korean economic relationship as internal transactions rather than international trade,[126] authorises the Ministry of Unification to issue "executive orders" in relation to certain inter-Korean trade matters through an institutional consultation and coordination framework under the Inter-Korean Exchange and Cooperation Promotion Council.[127] The Development of Inter-Korean Relations Act, which also defines inter-Korean trade as "intranational trade",[128] sets up the Inter-Korean Relations Development Committee under the Ministry of Unification for general matters on the development of inter-Korean relations.[129] The Act provides rules and procedures for the conclusion, ratification, suspension, and termination of inter-Korean agreements (e.g. the President has the general power to act on such agreements with the Minister's assistance after a formal deliberation by the State Council)[130] and for the appointment of representatives of inter-Korean summits.[131] Most importantly, the National Assembly "shall have a right to consent to the conclusion and ratification of South-North Korean agreements which place heavy financial burdens on the State or nationals, or South-North Korean agreements concerning legislative matters", but not when such agreements only "determine simple technical or procedural matters concerning the implementation of South–North Korean agreements already concluded or ratified by the President".[132]

As noted in Chapter 3, while we have limited access to DPRK's legal framework for inter-Korean economic cooperation, we have discussed the relevant

[125] In light of the special relationship between the South and North Korea, the ROK's National Security Act will likely apply where the DPRK works as an illegal group of anti-state movements, and the Inter-Korean Exchange and Cooperation Act will likely apply where the DPRK works towards conversation and cooperation related to peaceful unification with the ROK. Relevant ROK legislations include, inter alia, Development of Inter-Korean Relations Act, Inter-Korean Exchange and Cooperation Act (and its Enforcement Decree), Inter-Korean Cooperation Fund Act (and its Enforcement Decree), and the National Security Act. *See* Chapter 3, *supra*, for more discussion.

[126] Inter-Korean Exchange and Cooperation Act, art 12.

[127] *See e.g.* Inter-Korean Exchange and Cooperation Act, arts 4, 9, 10, 13, and 15.

[128] Development of inter-Korean Relations Act, art 3.

[129] *Id.* art 14.

[130] *Id.* arts 21 and 23.

[131] *Id.* arts 15 and 16.

[132] *Id.* Upon the completion of the due procedure set by Article 21: "South-North Koran agreements, which have been ratified by the National Assembly or have undergone deliberation by the State Council under Article 21 shall be promulgated by the President under the Act on the Promulgation of Statutes." *Id.* art 22.

provisions of the Socialist Constitution of the DPRK[133] and the North-South Economic Cooperation Law. The latter law designates the Central National Economic Cooperation Guidance Agency as the responsible agency[134] and stipulates that all inter-Korean economic cooperation plans shall go through an application and approval process managed by the agency, and that nothing can proceed without prior formal approval.[135] Overall, North Korea has extremely restrictive rules for inter-Korean economic cooperation that allows for only *ad hoc* and pre-approved projects, subject to the ultimate decision of the party leader rather than public deliberation.

Further, it is important to consider the role of membership in the UN, WTO, and the EU in the process of economic cooperation. As elaborated above, the admission of the two Koreas to the UN acknowledges that they have equal footing and suggests that they would not shy away from intergovernmental official meetings, if necessary. The switch of China's seat in the UN from the Republic of China to the PRC and the denial of UN recognition of Northern Cyprus both undermine the relevant sovereignty claims, such that UN membership is a significant source of power asymmetry in inter se relations between the pairs of "divided nations". The coexistence of China and Taiwan in the WTO, and the incorporation of the entire island of Cyprus as part and parcel of the EU's customs territory or internal market, despite *acquis communautaire* being suspended in Northern Cyprus demonstrate that the institutionalisation process in the economic cooperation in these two pairs of "divided nations" introduced by the international organisations has its contribution to economic cooperation across the border but also its limit. The WTO offered an opportunity to normalise trade relations across the Taiwan Strait by way of common trading rules and a forum for dialogue, and indeed neither Taiwan nor China opted for non-application of the WTO rules. Nonetheless, sovereignty concerns and identity politics set a limit there. Similarly, by virtue of EU membership, the Cyprus issue has been Europeanised, and the Green Line Regulation governs trade relations across the Line. Nonetheless, this Europeanisation process cannot push further as, politically, the divergences between the two communities remain significant, and legally, the unanimity requirement set in the Cyprus accession protocol gives the Republic of Cyprus a veto power even if the European Commission intends to pursue the agenda of direct trade between Northern Cyprus and other EU member states.

[133] The DPRK Constitution basically codifies the Juche-orientated ideas of Kim Il Sung and the Kim Jong Il and describes all the specific regulations that the government and the citizens of North Korea should adhere with the immortal Juche mindset. The ultimate goal of reunification is explicitly spelled out in the preamble. For more discussion, *see* Chapter 3, *supra*.

[134] North-South Economic Cooperation Law, art 5.

[135] *Id.* arts 10–12. Further, any inter-Korean economic cooperation that may undermine the "safety of society", the "development of the national economy", the "health and environmental protection of residents", and the "flow of the people" shall be prohibited. *Id.* art 8.

Institutionalising the economic relations within "divided nations" nonetheless may backfire, as seen in the Cyprus case. Sharing the same pitfalls of accountability, transparency, and democracy issues as the case of economic cooperation across the Taiwan Strait, the Europeanisation of Cyprus issue presents a challenge of its own kind. Given that trade across Cyprus island falls within the domain of the internal market and constitutes the exclusive competence of the EU, how to ensure the ownership of North and South Cyprus in steering the progress of economic cooperation across the island reflects a democratic deficit of EU decision making. The problem may plague Northern Cyprus more as it has little to no voice in the EU decision-making processes.

"Internal" and "external" dynamics largely condition the initiative, momentum, trajectory, contour, and limit of the economic cooperation of "divided nations". The current states of the Korean Peninsula, the Taiwan strait and the island of Cyprus are all situated in the broad context after the Second World War decolonisation and the Cold War era, when one of the highest priorities of US foreign policy was to contain communism. This main theme resulted in and to some degree sustains the division of these "divided nations". In addition to great power competition between the US and the Soviet Union, regional powers such as Turkey and Greece, especially in the case of Cyprus, add diversity to the actors who contribute to division or cooperation/reunification. Indeed, the outbreak of the Korean war finally prompted the hesitant Truman administration to side with the Republic of China led by Chiang Kai-shek and sustained Taiwan's capacity to safeguard itself from China's military threat and attack. The fact that both Greece and Turkey are NATO allies of the US led it to prioritise its Cyprus policy to avoid dividing the alliance. International organisations constitute an additional layer of the background scene where these "divided nations" interact, and at times such organisations set the rules of the game for *inter se* economic cooperation. The two Koreas in the UN, China and Taiwan in the WTO, and Cyprus as an EU member are decisive in institutionalising the economic cooperation. The Cold War context has been replaced with the idea of trade liberalisation and economic integration and interdependence, which enabled *détente* and fostered great economic cooperation.

But it has its limits given the new geopolitics dominated by the US–China strategic competition. Internally, the diversity of these three pairs of "divided nations" display different patterns of economic cooperation. In correspondence with their constitutional setting and foreign policy agenda, cooperation is influenced by different models of legitimisation and accountability mechanisms. Democratic legitimacy is pursued by some, but not all, of these "divided nations", which introduces challenges in their economic engagement. At times, commitments may be suspended or cancelled by the leaders of authoritarian regimes, which add more complexities, if not difficulties, for economic cooperation. While historical, cultural, and linguistic proximity act as an impetus to explore economic cooperation, but identity politics set a limit on that cooperation.

6

Conclusion

As the exploration of "divided nations" concludes, we find ourselves at the crossroads of historical legacies, geopolitical trajectories, and contemporary challenges. The three sets of divided nations were born in the tumultuous aftermath of the Second World War and against the background of the Cold War, with some prominent political figures, such as Henry Kissinger, visible in the background. The conclusion of the Second World War and subsequent decolonisation process introduced further complexities to the contexts in which these three sets of divided nations find themselves. While people in Taiwan, the Korean Peninsula, and Cyprus sought self-determination, the sway of geopolitics appeared to wield significant influence in shaping their identities and means of interacting with the world. The future contours of these three sets of divided nations are, in fact, intertwined. The burst of the Korean War finally prompted the Truman administration to side with the government of the Republic of China in Taiwan led by Chiang Kai-shek, which contributed to the persistent divide across the Taiwan Strait. Kissinger's decision to normalise the US relations with the People's Republic of China resulted in a fundamental change in China-Taiwan relations. Similarly, Kissinger's efforts in mediating divergences between two key US allies in the North Atlantic Treaty Organization, Turkey and Greece, demonstrate how geopolitics – or more specifically, the changing interests and agenda of hegemonic powers – shapes the "bilateral" relationship between divided nations. Ironically, anti-communism in the Cypriot context was still the most important policy goal even though Kissinger pursued for the normalisation of US–China relations.

A closer look at the internal dynamics of these divided nations reveals complex tapestries of shared histories, cultures, and languages. Such bonds, in theory, can smooth the way to economic integration, suggesting an easier path to engagement. However, the reality is far more intricate, complicated by ideological divides, changing identities, and sovereignty concerns that cast long shadows over these relationships. The case of Cyprus is even thornier as there exist multiple cultures and identities involving Greek, Turkish, and, most importantly, Cypriot.

Political systems and ideologies introduce significant friction in attempts to integrate economically. Each side perceives the other differently, diverging from the norms of typical international agreements, and employs distinct approaches to engagement. This dynamic complicates negotiations, demanding nuanced understandings of constitutional law and international relations. The dichotomy between democratic and authoritarian regimes, particularly evident across the Taiwan Strait and on the Korean Peninsula, further exacerbates these tensions. Such political landscapes challenge the transparency of economic engagement, legitimacy, and accountability – bringing scrutiny to every move under the vigilant eyes of both domestic and international observers. Indeed, the political sensitivities pose tremendous challenges to the overseeing of economic cooperation activities and accounting for them, in particular when the paired divided nations do not recognise each other. The challenges are two-dimensional. At the low politics level such as trade liberalisation and economic integration, negotiations over economic cooperation agreements and their subsequent implementation and supervision may have to be done through private or semi-official organisations, which may fall outside the scope of governmental oversight or accountability mechanisms. At the high politics level, notably the future of political integration, the pair of divided nations tend to avoid acting in *ex-officio* capacities as this may complicate recognition. The result would be a "leaders' meeting" wherein there is no stipulation of which political entities they are representing. This introduces a thorny issue as regards the nature and effect of the agreement, or consensus reached by these leaders. What is the role of the constituency of the divided nations during this leaders' meeting? How can legitimacy and accountability be assessed at this level of interaction? This issue is particularly acute in both the cross-Taiwan-Strait and in Cyprus.

Moreover, while certain areas of cooperation, like trade in agricultural products, may appear less contentious, the unpredictable nature of political sensitivities can quickly turn these into flashpoints. In regimes with much less robust checks and balances, governments may employ economic relationships as strategic instruments to serve political ends. This approach, though intended to advance the "national interests", may inadvertently erode trust from the other side and undermine the very foundation of economic cooperation and integration. Weaponising economic ties by prioritising strategic manoeuvres over collaborative efforts could lead to further estrangement between two sides, obstructing the journey toward mutual understanding and shared prosperity.

The broader and changing geopolitical context adds another layer of complexity. The geopolitical landscape, deeply influenced by Second World War alliances, significantly shapes the interactions across the Taiwan Strait and on the Korean Peninsula. Taiwan and South Korea's enduring alliances with America have been pivotal in their regional security strategies and in navigating the dynamics of their respective divided nation. The US, through its strategic commitments, directly impacts the course of engagement and the potential for cooperation or discord in these regions. With the US–China rivalry intensifying, these relationships gain additional layers of complexity. This competition does not merely influence global politics; it directly affects the prospects for economic cooperation and conflict resolution between two sides of a "divided nation". In Taiwan, US strategic support plays into the island's calculations around cross-strait relations, often in opposition to China's ambitions. Meanwhile, the Korean Peninsula sees a similar dynamic, with US involvement affecting North–South interactions and the broader security environment. Whereas the European Union (EU) plays a stabilising role in Cyprus, the antagonism between Turkey and Greece remains a source of worry.

Thus, this intricate mesh of alliances and rivalries is crucial in unfolding the potential for cooperation or confrontation. The role of the US, particularly against the backdrop of its rivalry with the PRC, underscores the significant influence of external powers on the dynamics of two sides of a "divided nation". This context is crucial for comprehensively grasping these regions' unique challenges and opportunities in striving for economic integration and peaceful coexistence.

While the US has significantly influenced the dynamics of the Taiwan Strait and Korean Peninsula, Cyprus has been influenced first by the great powers of the US and UK, and regional powers Greece and Turkey, and later by the EU, which introduced a distinctive set of dynamics that shapes the cooperation between the North and South. When the British decided to leave the island, the Americans were thinking about how to prevent Cyprus from siding with the Soviet Union and how to prevent its two key NATO allies, Turkey and Greece, from going to war. Later on the democratisation of Greece and its subsequent entry into the EU (then European Economic Community) helped to stabilise the region. Cyprus's entry into the EU in 2004 significantly transformed the Cyprus issue and turned it into a "comfortable conflict". These international frameworks and geopolitical considerations underscore the unpredictable nature of inter se relations between the "divided nations", making a straightforward path to integration elusive.

As this book reflects upon the divided nations in the era after the Second World War, it becomes clear that their legacies are as diverse as the challenges they face. Our investigation would, nevertheless, offer insights into the key features defining these unique relationships amid this complexity. Understanding the complex interplay between the two sides of a "divided nation" involves recognising the historical ties, political ideologies, sovereignty concerns, and the unique legal frameworks that govern these entities. This comprehension is essential for policymakers to navigate the nuanced relations with greater clarity and purpose. Acknowledging that these interactions extend beyond typical international relations, influenced by deep-rooted legal and sovereign nuances, enables a tailored approach to fostering cooperation and addressing the challenges posed by contested sovereignty.

As the global landscape has been transformed, insights from studying divided nations have become crucial for reducing tensions, enhancing trade, and promoting peace. This book sheds new light on these complex dynamics, offering a comprehensive perspective that informs and inspires future strategies, and will hopefully build bridges in our increasingly fragmented world, fostering hope for reconciliation and cooperative progress.

Bibliography

Aaltola, M, "Emergency Food Aid as a Means of Political Persuasion in the North Korean Famine", *Third World Quarterly*, 20(2) (1999), 371–86.

Abboud, S. et al., "Crisis as Impetus Toward Conflict Resolution in Cyprus", *Peace Review*, 24(4), (2012), 446–53.

ABC News, "South Korean court rejects former president Park Geun-hye's appeal against corruption conviction." (Jan 14, 2021). Available at:: www.abc.net.au/news/2021-01-14/former-south-korea-president-park-guen-hye-final-appeal-fails/13058974.

Adamides, C and Constantinou, CM, *Comfortable Conflict and (Il)liberal Peace in Cyprus*, in Richmond, O P and Mitchell, A *Hybrid Forms of Peace: From Everyday Agency to Post-Liberalism.* (Palgrave Macmillan, 2012), pp. 242–59.

Adams, T W, "The American Concern in Cyprus", *The Annals of the American Academy of Political and Social Science*, 401 (1972), 95–105.

Agence France-Presse (AFP), "Cyprus elects first Turkish Cypriot as MEP." (May 26, 2019). Available at: www.france24.com/en/20190526-cyprus-elects-first-turkish-cypriot-mep.

Agence France-Presse (AFP), "North and South Korea hold fifth round of Kaesong industrial zone talks", *The Telegraph*, (July 22, 2013). Available at: www.telegraph.co.uk/news/worldnews/asia/northkorea/10194327/North-and-South-Korea-hold-fifth-round-of-Kaesong-industrial-zone-talks.html.

Ahn, D, *Legal Issues for Korea's "Internal Trade" in the WTO System*, in Lim, W and Torrent, R *Multilateral and Regional Frameworks for Globalization: WTO And Free Trade Agreements.* (World Scientific, 2016), pp. 345–59.

Alsford, N, "Realising Taiwan's Indigenous Potential", East Asia Forum, (Sep 8, 2021). Available at: https://eastasiaforum.org/2021/09/08/realising-taiwans-indigenous-potential/.

Alvik, I, *Contracting with Sovereignty: State Contracts and International Arbitration.* (Hart Publishing, 2011).

Anadolu Agency, "Electricity from TRNC to Greek Cypriots." (Sept 6, 2011). Available at: www.aa.com.tr/en/archive/electricity-from-trnc-to-greek-cypriots/414074#.

Anagiotos, C, "Is National Identity Learned? The Case of Turkish-Cypriot Young Adults in Cyprus", Adult Education Research Conference, (2014). Available at: https://newprairiepress.org/aerc/2014/papers/6/.

Anastasiou, H, "Nationalism as a Deterrent to Peace and Interethnic Democracy: The Failure of Nationalist Leadership from the Hague Talks to the Cyprus Referendum", *International Studies Perspectives*, 8(2) (2007), 190–205.

Andreou, E, "Mobile phone links established between two sides (Updated)", *Cyprus Mail*, (July 11, 2019). Available at: https://web.archive.org/web/20201127023858/https:/cyprus-mail.com/2019/07/11/mobile-phone-links-established-between-two-sides/.

Apostolides, A et al., "From Conflict to Economic Interdependence in Cyprus", *Peace Review*, 24(4) (2012), 430–37.

Ash, R F and Kueh, Y Y, "Economic Integration within Greater China: Trade and Investment Flows between China, Hong Kong and Taiwan", *The China Quarterly*, 136 (1993), 711–45.

Aslım, I, "The Soviet Union and Cyprus in 1974 Events", *Athens Journal of History*, 2(4) (2016), 249–62.

Atkinson, J, "Taiwan's Sunflower Movement Chooses Democracy Over China Trade Pact", *World Politics Review*, (Apr 9, 2014). Available at: www.worldpoliticsreview.com/taiwan-s-sunflower-movement-chooses-democracy-over-china-trade-pact/.

Baker, P and Crowley, M, "Trump Steps into North Korea and Agrees with Kim Jong-un to Resume Talks", *New York Times*, (June 30, 2019). Available at: www.nytimes.com/2019/06/30/world/asia/trump-north-korea-dmz.html.

Barkin, JS and Cronin, B, "The State and the Nation: Changing Norms and the Rules of Sovereignty in International Relations", *International Organization*, 48(1) (1994), 107–30.

Bartelson, J, "The Concept of Sovereignty Revisited", *European Journal of International Law*, 17(2) (2006), 463–74.

BBC News, "Historic Taiwan-China trade deal takes effect." (Sept 12, 2010). Available at: www.bbc.com/news/world-asia-pacific-11275274.

BBC News, "Park Geun-hye: South Korea's First Female President." (Apr 6, 2018). Available at: www.bbc.com/news/world-asia-20787271.

Berman, PS, "From International Law to Law and Globalization", *Columbia Journal of Transnational Law*, 43 (2005), 485–556.

Bermudez, JS, Jr et al., "Dramatic Increase in DPRK-Russia Border Rail Traffic After Kim-Putin Summit", *Beyond Parallel*, (Oct 6, 2023). Available at: https://beyondparallel.csis.org/dramatic-increase-in-dprk-russia-border-rail-traffic-after-kim-putin-summit/.

Besson, S, "Sovereignty" in *Max Planck Encyclopedia of Public International Law* (2011, April). Available at: https://opil.ouplaw.com/display/10.1093/law:epil/9780199231690/law-9780199231690-e1472?prd=MPIL.

Bodin, J, *On Sovereignty: Four Chapters from the Six Books of the Commonwealth* (Julian Franklin, ed. and trans.). (Cambridge University Press, 1992).

Borowiec, S, "South Korea's Yoon Vows to "Completely Block" North's Nuclear Threat", *Nikkei Asia*, (Jan 1, 2024). Available at: https://asia.nikkei.com/Politics/Defense/South-Korea-s-Yoon-vows-to-completely-block-North-s-nuclear-threat.

Börzel, TA, "Member State Responses to Europeanization", *Journal of Common Market Studies*, 40(2) (2002), 193–214.

Börzel, and Risse, T, "When Europe Hits Home: Europeanization and Domestic Change", *European Integration online Papers*, 4(15) (2000), 1–23.

Brand, RA, "External Sovereignty and International Law", *Fordham International Law Journal*, 18 (1995), 1685–97.

Brazinsky, GA, *Democratization in South Korea*, in Seth, M. J. Routledge *Handbook of Modern Korean History*, 1st edn (Routledge, 2016).

Bridges, B, *Japan and Korea in the 1990s: From Antagonism to Adjustment.* (Edward Elgar, 1993).

Brown, R, "The Fruits of Diplomacy", *Foreign Policy*, (Aug 15, 2011). Available at: https://foreignpolicy.com/2011/08/15/the-fruits-of-diplomacy/.

Bureau of Industry and Security, "Commerce Implements New Export Controls on Advanced Computing and Semiconductor Manufacturing Items to the People's Republic of China (PRC)", (Oct 7, 2022). Available at: www.bis.doc.gov/index.php/documents/about-bis/newsroom/press-releases/3158-2022-10-07-bis-press-release-advanced-computing-and-semiconductor-manufacturing-controls-final/file.

Burghart, S and Frank, R, "Inter-Korean Cooperation 2000–2008: Commercial and Non-Commercial Transactions and Human Exchanges", *Vienna Working Papers on East Asian Economy and Society*, Working Paper 1(1) (2008).

Burke, J, *Britain and the Cyprus Crisis of 1974: Conflict, Colonialism and the Politics of Remembrance in Greek Cypriot Society*, 1st edn (Routledge, 2018).

Buzo, A, *Routledge Handbook of Contemporary North Korea*, 1st edn (Routledge, 2021).

Calik, A, "The power struggle over the north's electricity", *Cyprus Mails Online*, (Nov 27, 2016). Available at: https://web.archive.org/web/20171230014020/http://cyprus-mail.com/2016/11/27/power-struggle-norths-electricity/.

Caspersen, N, *Unrecognized States: The Struggle for Sovereignty in the Modern International System.* (John Wiley and Sons, InC, 2011).

Chae, GJ, *The Korean War and its Politics*, in Seth, M. J. *Routledge Handbook of Modern Korean History*, 1st edn (Routledge, 2016).

CHAN, M-J et al. (詹滿容等), *WTO架構下兩岸互動之研究WTO Jiagouxia Liangan Hudong Zhi Yanjiu [Studies on the Cross-Strait Interaction under the WTO Framework]*. (行政院研究發展考核委員會[Research, Development and Evaluation Commission, Executive Yuan], 2003).

Chang, J and Goldstein, SM, *Introduction: The WTO and Cross-Strait Economic Relations*, in *Economic Reform and Cross-Strait Relations: Taiwan and China in the WTO*. (World Scientific Publishing Co., 2007), pp. 1–42.

Chang, P and Lim, K-U, "Taiwan's Case for United Nations Membership", *UCLA Journal of International Law and Foreign Affairs*, 1(2) (1996), 393–430.

Chao, C-M and Dickson, BJ, *Introduction: Assessing the Lee Teng-hui Legacy*, in *Assessing the Lee Teng-hui Legacy in Taiwan's Politics: Democratic Consolidation and External Relations* 1st edn (Routledge, 2002), pp. 1–24.

Chao, VY, "So-Called '1992 Consensus' A Fabrication: Lee Teng-Hui", *Taipei Times*, (Dec 28, 2010). Available at: www.taipeitimes.com/News/front/archives/2010/12/28/2003492047.

Charney, JI. and Prescott JRV, "Resolving Cross-Strait Relations between China and Taiwan", *The American Journal of International Law*, 94(3) (2000), 453–77.

Charnovitz, S, "Taiwan's WTO Membership and Its International Implications", *Asian Journal of WTO and International Health Law and Policy*, 1(2) (2002), 401–32.

Chen, H-P, (陈辉萍), ECFA 框架下海峡两岸投资协议的法律思考 "ECFA kuangjiaxia haixialiangan touzixieyi de falü sikao" [Some Legal Reflections on the Investment Agreement Between Mainland China and Taiwan under the ECFA Framework], 《時代法学》*Presentday Law Science*, 43 10(3) (2012), 43–49.

Chen P-H, "A Fake Right of Priority under the Cross-Strait Agreement on Intellectual Property Right Protection and Cooperation", *Marquette Intellectual Property Law Review*, 20(2) (2016), 214–39.

Chen, C, "Taiwan's Application to the GATT: A New Urgency with the Conclusion of the Uruguay Round", *Indiana Journal of Global Legal Studies*, 2(1) (1994), 275–99.

Chen, H. and Seo, Y, "North Korea Says It Will No Longer Seek Reunification with South Korea, Will Launch New Spy Satellites in 2024," *CNN*, (Jan 1, 2024). Available at: https://edition.cnn.com/2023/12/31/asia/north-korea-reconciliation-south-korea-intl-hnk/index.html.

Chen, L-c and Reisman, WM, "Who Owns Taiwan: A Search for International Title", *The Yale Law Journal*, 81(4) (1972), 599–671.

Chen, T-C, *The International Law of Recognition*. (Frederick A Praeger, Inc, 1951).

Chen, Y-J and Cohen, AJ, "China-Taiwan Relations Re-examined: The "1992 Consensus" and Cross-Strait Agreements", *University of Pennsylvania Asian Law Review*, 14 (2019), 1–40.

Chen, Y-J, "One China Contention in China–Taiwan Relations: Law, Politics and Identity", *The China Quarterly*, 252 (2022), 1025–44.

Cheng, Y, "Taiwanese DNA versus Chinese DNA: Genetic Science and Identity Politics Across the Taiwan Straits", *Modern Asian Studies*, 57(3) (2023), 1–26.

Cheung, E et al., "Taiwan Voters Dismiss China Warnings and Hand Ruling Party a Historic Third Consecutive Presidential Win", *CNN*, (Jan 13, 2024). Available at: https://edition.cnn.com/2024/01/13/asia/taiwan-presidential-election-results-intl-hnk/index.html.

Chevalérias, P, "The Taiwanese Economy After the Miracle: An Industry in Restructuration, Structural Weaknesses and the Challenge of China", *China Perspectives*, 3 (2010), 35–44.

Chiang, F, *The One-China Policy: State, Sovereignty, and Taiwan's International Legal Status* 1st edn (Elsevier, 2017).

Chiang, M-H, *China-Taiwan Rapprochement: The Political Economy of Cross-Straits Relations*, 1st edn (Routledge, 2016).

Chiang, Y. F, "One-China Policy and Taiwan", *Fordham International Law Journal*, 28(1) (2004), 1–87.

Chiang, Y. F, "State, Sovereignty, and Taiwan", *Fordham International Law Journal*, 23(4) (1999), 959–1004.

China Daily, "UN Resolution 2758 Clear and Unambiguous on Taiwan's Status as Inalienable Part of China" (Editorial), (Aug 1, 2023). Available at: www.chinadaily.com.cn/a/202308/01/WS64c8f608a31035260b819b8a.html.

Chiu, H, "The International Legal Status of the Republic of China (Revised Version)" *Occasional Papers/Reprints Series in Contemporary Asian Studies*, 1 (1992), 2–37.

Cho, Y. C, "Collective Identity Formation on the Korean Peninsula: United States' Different North Korea Policies, Kim Dae-Jung's Sunshine Policy, and United States–South Korea–North Korea Relations", *International Relations of the Asia-Pacific*, 10(1) (2010), 93–128.

Choe, S-H, "Park Geun-hye, Ex-South Korean Leader, Gets 25 Years in Prison", *New York Times*, (Aug 24, 2018). Available at: www.nytimes.com/2018/08/24/world/asia/park-geun-hye-sentenced-south-korea.html?smid=url-share.

Choe, S-H, "South Korea to Shut Joint Factory Park, Kaesong, Over Nuclear Test and Rocket", *New York Times*, (Feb 10, 2016). Available at: www.nytimes.com/2016/02/11/world/asia/north-south-korea-kaesong.html.

Choi, C-K, "The Korean Question in the United Nations", *Verfassung und Recht in Übersee [Law and Politics in Africa, Asia and Latin America]*, 8(3/4) (1975), 395–406.

Choi, J. K, "Sunshine over a Barren Soil: The Domestic Politics of Engagement Identity Formation in South Korea", *Asian Perspective*, 34(4) (2010), 115–38.

Chu, H, *The International Legal Status of Taiwan*, in Henckaerts, J-M, *The International Status of Taiwan in the New World Order: Legal and Political Considerations.* (Martinus Nijhoff Publishers, 1996).

Chu, Y-H, "Taiwan's National Identity Politics and the Prospect of Cross-Strait Relations", *Asian Survey*, 44(4) (2004), 484–512.

Çıraklı, M, "Can Confidence Building Measures Help End the Cyprus Deadlock?", *Istituto Affari Internazionali*, (July 7, 2021). Available at: www.iai.it/en/pubblicazioni/can-confidence-building-measures-help-end-cyprus-deadlock.

Clapham, A, *Brierly's Law of Nations*, 7th edn (Oxford University Press, 2012).

Collins, L and Terry, SM, "Assessment of the Trump-Kim Hanoi Summit", *Center for Strategic and International Studies (CSIS)*, (Feb 28, 2019). Available at: www.csis.org/analysis/assessment-trump-kim-hanoi-summit.

Congressional Research Service, "The February 2019 Trump-Kim Hanoi Summit", RCS Reports IN11067, (Mar 6, 2019). Available at: https://crsreports.congress.gov/product/pdf/IN/IN11067.

Constandinos, A, "US–British Policy on Cyprus, 1964–1974", *Cyprus Review*, 23(1) (2011), 17–48.

Constantinou, CM. and Papadakis, Y, *The Cypriot State(s) in situ: Cross-Ethnic Contact and the Discourse of Recognition*, in Diez, T. *The European Union and The Cyprus Conflict: Modern Conflict, Postmodern Union.* (Manchester University Press, 2002), pp. 73–97.

Constantinou, C. M, "Multidirectional Diplomacy and the Privatization of Settlement", *Peace Review*, 24(4) (2012), 454–61.

Coufoudakis, V, "Turkey and the United States: the Problems and Prospects of a Post-War Alliance", *Journal of Political and Military Sociology*, 9(2) (1981), 179–96.

Council on Foreign Relations, "U.S.–China Relations (1949–2023)." Available at: www.cfr.org/timeline/us-china-relations.

Crawford, JR, *The Creation of States in International Law*, 2nd edn (Oxford University Press, 2007).

Cyprus Chamber of Commerce and Industry (CCCI), "Cluster." Available at: https://ccci.org.cy/cluster/.

Cyprus Chamber of Commerce and Industry (CCCI), "InPluServ." Available at: https://ccci.org.cy/inpluserv-2/.

Cyprus Chamber of Commerce and Industry (CCCI), "Sea of Experience (SoE)." Available at: https://ccci.org.cy/sea-of-experience-soe/.

Cyprus Telecommunications Authority (Howellswells), "Annual Report 2020", (2020). Available at: www.cyta.com.cy/mp/informational/cyta_htmlPages/media_center/annualreports/docs/AnReport_2020_en.pdf.

Davidson, H and Hawkins, A, "China's Muted Reaction to Taiwan's Election Result May Signal a Waiting Game", *The Guardian*, (Jan 18, 2024). Available at: www.theguardian.com/world/2024/jan/18/china-response-taiwan-election-democratic-progressive-party?ref=upstract.com.

De Bear, A, "From Sunshine to Storm Clouds: An Examination of South Korea's Policy on North Korea", *Michigan State International Law Review*, 23(3) (2015), 824–84.

DeLisle, J, "Soft Power in a Hard Place: China, Taiwan, Cross-Strait Relations and U.S. Policy", *Orbis*, 54(4) (2010), 493–524.

DeLisle, J, "Trump, Tsai, and the Three Communiques: Prospects for Stability in US–China-Taiwan Relations", *Foreign Policy Research Institute*, (Mar 9, 2017). Available at: www.fpri.org/2017/03/trump-tsai-three-communiques-prospects-stability-us-china-taiwan-relations/.

Demetriou, O, Catalysis, "Catachresis: The EU's Impact on the Cyprus Conflict", in Diez, T. et al. *The European Union and Border Conflicts: The Power of Integration and Association*. (Cambridge University Press, 2008), pp. 64–93.

Democratic Progressive Party, "Resolution on Taiwan's Future" (ratified at the 2nd Session of the 8th DPP National Congress on May 8 and 9, 1999). Available at: www.dpp.org.tw/en/upload/download/Resolutions.pdf.

Diez, T, *The European Union and the Cyprus Conflict: Modern Conflict, Postmodern Union*. (Manchester University Press, 2002).

Dinkov, D and Stoyanov, S, "The Cyprus Problem: International Politics Simulation", *Managerial Law*, 47(3–4) (2005), 171–216.

Dobb, LW, "Cypriot Patriotism and Nationalism", *The Journal of Conflict Resolution*, 30(2) (1986), 383–96.

Dodd, C, *The History and Politics of the Cyprus Conflict*. (Palgrave Macmillan, 2010).

Dong, W, *The Two Koreas and the United States: Issues of Peace, Security and Economic Cooperation*, 1st edn (Routledge, 2000).

Drun, J and Glaser, B, *The Distortion of UN Resolution 2758 to Limit Taiwan's Access to the United Nations*. (German Marshall Fund of the United States, 2022).

Duncan, EM (ed.), *Foreign Relations of the United States, 1969–1976, Volume V, United Nations, 1969–1972*. (United States Government Printing Office Washington, 2004).

Dupre, J-F, *Culture Politics and Linguistic Recognition in Taiwan: Ethnicity, National Identity, and the Party System*, 1st edn (Routledge, 2017).

Eckholm, E, "Taiwan's New Leader Ends Decades of Nationalist Rule", *New York Times*, (May 20, 2020). Available at: www.nytimes.com/2000/05/20/world/taiwan-s-new-leader-ends-decades-of-nationalist-rule.html.

Economic Cooperation Framework Agreement (ECFA), 海峽兩岸經濟合作架構協議(ECFA)執行情形 "Haixia liangan jingji hezuo jiagou xieyi (ECFA) zhi hang qingxing" [Implementation of the Economic Cooperation Framework Agreement (ECFA) Across the Taiwan Strait]. Available at: www.ecfa.org.tw/ShowDetail.aspx?nid=1121&pid=1044.

Economist Intelligence Unit, "Democracy Index 2023." Available at: www.eiu.com/n/campaigns/democracy-index-2023/.

Ekıcı, T, *The Political and Economic History of North Cyprus: A Discordant Polity*. (Palgrave Macmillan, 2019).

Election Study Center, National Chengchi University, "Taiwanese / Chinese Identity (1992/06~2023/12)" (Feb 22, 2024). Available at: https://esc.nccu.edu.tw/PageDoc/Detail?fid=7800&id=6961.

Emilianides, AC and Papastylianos, C, *Citizenship and Nationality: Cyprus*, in Law, D S *Constitutionalism in Context*. (Cambridge University Press, 2019), pp. 330–50.

Emiliou, N, "Cypriot Import Certificates: Some Hot Potatoes", *European Law Review*, 20 (1995), 202–10.

European Commission, "Cyprus 'Χαλλουμι' (Halloumi)/'Hellim' cheese set to receive Protected Designation of Origin status" (Press Release IP/15/5448), (Jul. 28, 2015). Available at: https://ec.europa.eu/commission/presscorner/detail/en/IP_15_5448.

Falk, RA, *A Study of Future Worlds*. (The Free Press, 1975).

Famagusta Gazette, "Regulation on direct trade between the EU and occupied Cyprus." (Oct 19, 2010). Available at: https://web.archive.org/web/20101027131523/http://famagusta-gazette.com/regulation-on-direct-trade-between-the-eu-and-occupied-cyprus-p10885-69.htm.

Fan, J, "The Economics of the Cross-Strait Services Agreement", *Brookings*, (Apr 18, 2014). Available at: www.brookings.edu/articles/the-economics-of-the-cross-strait-services-agreement/.

Faulconbridge, G and Choi, S-H, "Putin and North Korea's Kim Discuss Military Matters, Ukraine War and Satellites", *Reuters*, (Sep 13, 2023). Available at: www.reuters.com/world/nkoreas-kim-meets-putin-missiles-launched-pyongyang-2023-09-13/.

Faustmann, H and Kaymak, E, "Cyprus", *European Journal of Political Research*, 47 (2008), 939–46.

Faustmann, H and Kaymak, E, "Cyprus", *European Journal of Political Research Political Data Yearbook*, 49 (2010), 923–38.

Faustmann, H and Sözen, A, "Cyprus: Political Developments and Data in 2020", *European Journal of Political Research Political Data Yearbook*, 60 (2021), 84–102.

Faustmann, H et al., "Cyprus", *European Journal of Political Research Political Data Yearbook*, 53(1) (2014), 78–91.

Financial Mirror, "CYPRUS: Keeping the power switched on." (Mar 16, 2019). Available at: www.financialmirror.com/2019/03/16/cyprus-keeping-the-power-switched-on/.

Fischer-Lescano, A and Teubner, G, "Regime-Collisions: The Vain Search for Legal Unity in the Fragmentation of Global Law", *Michigan Journal of International Law*, 25(4) 2004, 999–1046.

Ford, RT, "Law's Territory (A History of Jurisdiction)", *Michigan Law Review*, 97(4) (1999), 843–930.

Forsberg, A, "The Politics of GATT Expansion: Japanese Accession and the Domestic Political Content in Japan and the United States, 1948-1955", *Business and Economic History*, 27(1) (1998), 185–95.

Foster-Carter, A, "North Korea-South Korea Relations: Summit Success?", *Comparative Connections*, 9(3) (2007), 93–108.

Freedom House, "Countries and Territories." Available at: https://freedomhouse.org/countries/freedom-world/scores.

French, D, *Fighting EOKA: The British Counter-Insurgency Campaign on Cyprus, 1955–1959.* (Academic, 2015).

Fukuda, M, "China Is Using a UN Resolution to Further Its Claim Over Taiwan", *The Diplomat*, (Aug 26, 2022). Available at: https://thediplomat.com/2022/08/china-is-using-a-un-resolution-to-further-its-claim-over-taiwan/.

Galtung, J, "Divided Nations as a Process: One State, Two States, and In-Between: The Case of Korea", *Journal of Peace Research*, 9(4) (1972), 345–60.

Geldenhuys, D, *Contested States in World Politics*. (Palgrave Macmillan, 2009).

General Administration of Customs of the People's Republic of China, 海关总署：3日起暂停台湾地区柑橘类水果、冰鲜白带鱼、冻竹荚鱼输入大陆 "Haiguan zong shu: 3 ri qi zanting Taiwan diqu ganju lei shuiguo, bing xian bai daiyu, dong zhu jia yu shuru dalu" [General Administration of Customs: Suspension of imports of citrus fruits, chilled beltfish, and frozen bamboo pod fish from the Taiwan region to the mainland starting from the 3rd day] (Aug 3, 2022). Available at: www.gwytb.gov.cn/bmst/202208/t20220803_12457969.htm.

Georgiou, GC, "Cyprus: Economic Consequences of Reunification", *Mediterranean Quarterly*, 20(3) (1999), 51–62

Gerdes, LI, *North Korea and South Korea*. (Greenhaven Press, 2007).

Glaser, BS and Mark, J, "Taiwan and China are Locked in Economic Co-Dependence: Both Sides Have Leverage but Have Been Reluctant to Use It", *Foreign Policy*, (Apr 14, 2021). Available at: https://foreignpolicy.com/2021/04/14/taiwan-china-econonomic-codependence/.

Global Times, "Chinese Mainland to End Tariff Concessions for 12 Taiwan-produced Products", (Dec 21, 2023). Available at: www.globaltimes.cn/page/202312/1304048.shtml.

Gordon, SM et al., "U.S.–Taiwan Relations in a New Era: Responding to a More Assertive China", *Council of Foreign Relations*, Independent Task Force Report No. 81, (June 2023). Available at: www.cfr.org/task-force-report/us-taiwan-Relations-in-a-new-era.

Government Information Office of The Executive Yuan, *The Republic of China Yearbook 2010 (Taiwan)*. (光華畫報 [Sinorama Magazine], 2010).

Government Portal of the Republic of China (Taiwan), "About Taiwan." Available at: www.taiwan.gov.tw/about.php.

Grabbe, H, "How does Europeanization affect CEE governance? Conditionality, diffusion and diversity", *Journal of European Public Policy*, 8(6) (2001), 1013–31.

Grice, F, "The Improbability of Popular Rebellion in Kim Jong-un's North Korea and Policy Alternatives for the USA", *Journal of Asian Security and International Affairs*, 4(3) (2017), 263–93.

Gu, W, *Conflicts of Divided Nations: The Cases of China and Korea*, Vol. I of *Ams Studies in Religious Tradition*. (Frederick A. Praeger, InC, 1995).

Guichard, J, "In the Name of the People: Disagreeing over Peoplehood in the North and South Korean Constitutions", *Asian Journal of Law and Society*, 4(2) (2017), 405–45.

Güney, A, "The USA's Role in Mediating the Cyprus Conflict: A Story of Success or Failure?", *Security Dialogue*, 35(1) (2004), 27–42.

Guzman, A, *How International Law Works: A Rational Choice Theory*. (Oxford University Press, 2008).

Ha, SE. and Jang, S-J, "National identity in a divided nation: South Koreans' attitudes toward North Korean defectors and the reunification of two Koreas", *International Journal of Intercultural Relations*, 55 (2016), 109–19.

Harding, H, "The Impact of Tiananmen on China's Foreign Policy", *NBR Analysis*, 1(3) (1990). Available at: www.nbr.org/publication/the-impact-of-tiananmen-on-chinas-foreign-policy/.

Harrington, J, "Scrutiny and Approval: The Role for Westminster-Style Parliaments in Treaty-Making", *The International and Comparative Law Quarterly*, 55(1) (2002), 121–59.

Harris, T et al., "Prospects for Diplomacy with North Korea", *Center for American Progress*, (Nov 3, 2021). Available at: www.americanprogress.org/article/prospects-diplomacy-north-korea/.

Harrison, M, "Australia's One-China Policy and Why It Matters", *The Interpreter*, (Oct 11, 2017). Available at: www.lowyinstitute.org/the-interpreter/australia-s-one-china-policy-why-it-matters.

Harrison, SS, "Promoting a Soft Landing in Korea", *Foreign Policy*, 106 (Spring, 2017), 56–75.

Hart, D, "Proclaiming Identity, Claiming the Past: National Identity and Modernity in North and South Korean Education", *Asian Perspective*, 24(3) (2000), 135–58.

Hart, PT, *Two NATO Allies at the Threshold of War*. (Duke University Press Books, 1990).

Haughton, T, "When does the EU Make a Difference? Conditionality and the Accession Process in Central and Eastern Europe", *Political Studies Review*, 5(2) (2007), 233–46.

Hernández, JC, "China Suspends Diplomatic Contact with Taiwan", *New York Times*, (June 25, 2016). Available at: www.nytimes.com/2016/06/26/world/asia/china-suspends-diplomatic-contact-with-taiwan.html.

Herscovitch, B and Harrison, M, "Enhancing Australia's Taiwan ties", *Lowy Institute*, (Dec 6, 2023). Available at: www.lowyinstitute.org/publications/enhancing-australia-s-taiwan-ties.

Herz, JH, "Korea and Germany as Divided Nations: The Systemic Impact", *Asian Survey*, 15(11) (1975), 957–70.

Herzog, D, *Sovereignty, RIP*. (Yale University Press, 2000).

Hickey, DV, *Foreign Policy Making in Taiwan: From Principle to Pragmatism*, 1st edn (Routledge, 2007).

Hilf, M, *Divided States*, in Bernhardt, R. *Encyclopaedia of Public International Law*, Vol. X. (Elsevier Science Publishers, 1987), pp. 126–30.

Hillion, C, *The Copenhagen Criteria and Their Progeny*, in *EU Enlargement: A Legal Approach*. (Hart Publishing, 2004), pp. 1–22.

Hillman, J, *China's Entry into the WTO: A Mistake by the US?*, in Gao, H et al. *China and the WTO: A Twenty-Year Assessment*. (Cambridge University Press, 2023), pp. 400–23.

Hinsley, FH, *Sovereignty*, 2nd edn (Cambridge University Press, 1986).

Hioe, B, "TSMC's US Investments Spark Political Controversy in Taiwan", *The Diplomat*, (Jan 18, 2023). Available at: https://thediplomat.com/2023/01/tsmcs-us-investments-spark-political-controversy-in-taiwan/.

Ho, M-S, "Occupy Congress in Taiwan: Political Opportunity, Threat, and the Sunflower Movement", *Journal of East Asian Studies*, 15(1) (2015), 69–97.

Hoffmeister, F, *Legal Aspects of the Cyprus Problem: Annan Plan and EU Accession.* (Martinus Nijhoff Publishers, 2006).

Holland, B, "Sovereignty as Dominium? Reconstructing the Constructivist Roman Law Thesis", *International Studies Quarterly*, 54(2) (2010), 449–80.

Hong, TL and Yang, TH, "The Economic Cooperation Framework Agreement between China and Taiwan, Understanding Its Economics and Politics", *Asian Economic Papers*, 10(3) (2011), 79–96.

Hornby, L, "Taiwan and China Sign Trade Pact", *Reuters*, (June 29, 2010). Available at: www.reuters.com/article/us-china-taiwan-signing/taiwan-and-china-sign-trade-pact-idUSTRE65S17Z20100629/.

Howells, K and Soujeri, E, "A Short History and Review of Telecommunications in Cyprus", 2021 7th IEEE History of Electrotechnology Conference, (Nov 10–12, 2021). Available at: https://ieeexplore.ieee.org/document/9787311.

Hsieh, PL, "*China-Taiwan Trade Relations: Implications of the WTO and Asian Regionalism*", in Davidson, PJ *Trading Arrangements in the Pacific Rim: ASEAN and APEC* (Oceana, 2008), pp. 1–18.

Hsieh, PL, "Facing China: Taiwan's Status as a Separate Customs Territory in the World Trade Organization", *Journal of World Trade*, 39(6) (2005), 1195–221.

Hsieh, PL, "Legitimacy of Taiwan's Trade Negotiations with China: Demystifying Political Challenges", *Political Science*, 68(1) (2016), 3–21.

Hsieh, PL, "The China-Taiwan ECFA, Geopolitical Dimensions and WTO Law", *Journal of International Economic Law*, 14 (2011), 121–56.

Hsieh, PL, "The Taiwan Question and the One-China Policy: Legal Challenges with Renewed Momentum", *Die Friedens-Warte*, 84(3) (2009), 59–81.

Hsu, T-L (許宗力), 兩岸關係法律定位百年來的演變與最新發展 "Liangan guanxi falü dingwei bainianlai de yanbian yu zuixin fazhan" [The Evolution and Latest Development of the Legal Positioning of Cross-Strait Relations over the Past Century], 《月旦法學雜誌》 *The Taiwan Law Review*, 12 (1996), 40–47.

Hsu, T-L (許宗力), 兩岸關係的法律定位 – 臺灣的角度出發 *Liangan guanxi de falü dingweiFF – Taiwan de jiaodu chufa [The Legal Status of Cross-Strait Relations – From Taiwan's Perspective]*, in Hwang, J-Y. (黃昭元) 《兩國論與台灣國家定位》*Liangguolun yu taiwan guojia dingwei [The Debate on Two States and Taiwan's National Positioning]*. (學林出版社[Sharing Culture Enterprise Co.], 2000), pp. 39–47.

Huan, G, "China's Open Door Policy, 1978–1984", *Journal of International Affairs*, 39(2) (1986), 1–18.

Huang, ET-L, "Taiwan's Status in a Changing World: United Nations Representation and Membership for Taiwan", *Annual Survey of International and Comparative Law*, 9(1) (2003), 55–99.

Huang, J, "Negotiating the First Bilateral Investment Agreement between Mainland China and Taiwan: Difficulties and Solutions", *Hong Kong Law Journal*, 42 (2012), 971–1000.

Hwang, BY, "Reviving the Korean Armistice: Building Future Peace on Historical Precedents", *Korea Economic Institute Academic Paper Series*, 6(6) (2011), 1–8.

Hwang, EG, *The Search for a Unified Korea: Political and Economic Implications.* (Springer, 2010).

Ian, CJ, "The Many 'One Chinas': Multiple Approaches to Taiwan and China", *Carnegie Endowment for International Peace*, (Feb 9, 2023). Available at: https://carnegieendowment.org/2023/02/09/many-one-chinas-multiple-approaches-to-taiwan-and-china-pub-89003.

Ikenberry, GJ, "Power and Liberal Order: America's Postwar World Order in Transition", *International Relations of the Asia-Pacific*, 5(2) (2005), 133–52.

International Crisis Group, "Cyprus: Reversing the Drift to Partition, Crisis Group Europe Report." (Jan 10, 2008). Available at: www.crisisgroup.org/sites/default/files/190-cyprus-reversing-the-drift-to-partition.pdf.

International Crisis Group, "The Case for Kaesong: Fostering Korean Peace through Economic Ties." (June 24, 2019). Available at: www.crisisgroup.org/asia/north-east-asia/korean-peninsula/300-case-kaesong-fostering-korean-peace-through-economic-ties.

International Trade Administration of the Republic of China (Taiwan), 修正「戰略性高科技貨品種類、特定戰略性高科技貨品種類及輸出管制地區」之「輸往俄羅斯及白俄羅斯高科技貨品清單」(如附件)，並自即日生效 "Xiuzheng zhanlue xing gao keji huopin zhonglei, teding zhanlue xing gao keji huopin zhonglei ji shuchu guanzhi diquzhi shu wang eluosi ji baieluosi gao keji huopin qingdan'(ru fujian), bing zi jiri shengxiao" [The "List of High-Tech Goods for Export to Russia and Belarus" under the "Types of Strategic High-Tech Goods, Specific Types of Strategic High-Tech Goods, and Export Control Areas" has been amended (as attached) and is effective immediately], (Jan 4, 2023). Available at: www.trade.gov.tw/Pages/Detail.aspx?nodeID=39&pid=755244.

Isachenko, D, *The Making of Informal States: Statebuilding in Northern Cyprus and Transdniestria*. (Palgrave Macmillan, 2012).

Jacobs, JB and Liu, I-H B, "Lee Teng-hui and the Idea of "Taiwan"", *The China Quarterly*, 190 (2007), 375–93.

Jain, JP, "The Legal Status of Formosa: A Study of British, Chinese and Indian Views", *The American Journal of International Law*, 57(1) (1963), 25–45.

James, A, *Sovereign Statehood: The Basis of International Society*, Vol. II of *Key Concepts in International Relations*. (Allen and Unwin, 1986).

Janow, ME, "Assessing APEC's Role in Economic Integration in the Asia-Pacific Region", *Northwestern Journal of International Law and Business*, 17(1) (1997), 947–1013.

Jarraud, N et al., "The Cypriot Civil Society Movement: A Legitimate Player in the Peace Process?", *Journal of Peacebuilding and Development*, 8(1) (2013), 45–59.

Jing, B-J, "Taiwan Holds All the Chips in US-China Tech Showdown", *East Asia Forum*, (Dec 3, 2022). Available at: https://eastasiaforum.org/2022/12/03/taiwan-holds-all-the-chips-in-us-china-tech-showdown/#:~:text=China%E2%80%99s%20trade%20flow%20data%20for,of%20which%20came%20from%20Taiwan.

Jones, BC and Su, YT, "Confrontational Contestation and Democratic Compromise: The Sunflower Movement and Its Aftermath", *Hong Kong Law Journal*, 45(1) (2015), 193–210.

Jones, BC. and Su, Y-T, *The Sunflower Movement and Its Aftermath*, in Jones, B. C. *Law and Politics of Taiwan Sunflower and Hong Kong Umbrella Movements*. (Routledge, 2017).

Joseph, J, Cyprus: *Ethnic Conflict and International Politics: From Independence to the Threshold of the European Union*. (Palgrave Macmillan, 1997).

Kao, C (高長),「兩岸經貿交流30週年之回顧與前瞻」 "Liangan jingmao jiaoliu 30 zhounian zhi huigu yu qianzhan" [Retrospect and Prospect on the 30th Anniversary of Cross-Strait Economic Exchanges], 《展望與指南》 *Prospect and Exploration*, 15(11) (2017), 8–15.

Kassam, N, "Australians Worry About China and Muscle-flexing over Taiwan", *The Interpreter*, (June 30, 2022). Available at: www.lowyinstitute.org/the-interpreter/australians-worry-about-china-and-muscle-flexing-over-taiwan.

Kassimeris, C, "The Inconsistency of United States Foreign Policy in the Aftermath of the Cyprus Invasion: The Turkish Arms Embargo and its Termination", *Journal of Modern Greek Studies*, 26(1) (2008), 91–114.

KCS Total Solution Yes! FTA Portal, "FTA Trend in Korea." (Nov 2023). Available at: www.customs.go.kr/engportal/cm/cntnts/cntntsView.do?mi=7304&cntntsId=2329.

Kelsen, H, "Recognition in International Law: Theoretical Observations", *The American Journal of International Law*, 35(4) (1941), 605–17.

Ker-Lindsay, J and Webb, K, "Cyprus", *European Journal of Political Research*, 44 (2005), 975–82.

Ker-Lindsay, J and Webb, K, "Cyprus", *European Journal of Political Research*, 45(7–8) (2006), 1071–77.

Ker-Lindsay, J, "Cyprus", *European Journal of Political Research*, 43(7–8) (2004), 969–79.

Ker-Lindsay, J, *EU Accession and UN Peacemaking in Cyprus*. (Palgrave Macmillan, 2005).

Ker-Lindsay, J, *The Cyprus Problem: What Everyone Needs to Know*. (Oxford University Press, 2011).

Khamidov, A, "The Lee Myung-bak Revolution: Explaining Continuity and Change in South Korea's Foreign Policy", *SAIS U.S.-KOR. Year Book*, (2008), 23–38.

Kim, B and Kim, H, "Analysis and Proposals to the Laws in the Kaesong Industrial Complex: For Better Regulations under New Environments on the Korean Peninsula", *Korea Journal*, 54(4) (2014), 80–105.

Kim, CN, "The Roh Moo Hyun Government's Policy Toward North Korea", *East-West Center*, Working Paper 11 (2005).

Kim, HC, "Does Annex 22-B of the Proposed United States-Korea Free Trade Agreement Contemplate and Allow for Trade with Respect to North Korea", *Georgetown Journal of International Law*, 40(1) (2008), 67–98.

Kim, H-J, "North Korea recalls 53,000 workers, suspends operations at North-South factory complex", *Toronto Star*, (Apr 8, 2013). Available at: www.thestar.com/news/world/north-korea-recalls-53-000-workers-suspends-operations-at-north-south-factory-complex/article_a64904a0-53bb-5779-83c5-a85162295fb2.html.

Kim, H-J, "North Korea's Kim Vows to Launch 3 More Spy Satellites and Produce More Nuclear Materials in 2024", *AP*, (Jan 1, 2024). Available at: https://apnews.com/article/north-korea-kim-spy-satellites-nuclear-party-meeting-236fcaee8927d8f69359b45aaa88e2c0.

Kim, H-K, "South Korea's Sunshine Policy, Reciprocity and Nationhood", *Perspectives on Global Development and Technology*, 11(1) (2012), 99–111.

Kim, H-W, "A Korean Perspective on the Biden Administration's North Korea Policy", *The Stimson Center*, (Feb 28, 2022). Available at: www.stimson.org/2022/a-korean-perspective-on-the-biden-administrations-north-korea-policy/.

Kim, J et al., "The economic costs of trade sanctions: Evidence from North Korea", CESifo Working Paper No. 10630, (2023). Available at: https://papers.ssrn.com/sol3/papers.cfm?abstract_id=4564442.

Kim, J, "North Korea Kim Jong Un, China's Xi Exchange Message Vowing Closer Ties, Yonhap Reports", *Reuters*, (Jan 1, 2024). Available at: www.reuters.com/world/asia-pacific/north-korea-kim-jong-un-chinas-xi-exchange-message-vowing-closer-ties-yonhap-2023-12-31/.

Kim, J, "South Korea's Yoon Says any Military Cooperation with North Korea Must Stop", *Reuters*, (Sep. 6, 2023). Available at: www.reuters.com/world/asia-pacific/south-koreas-yoon-says-any-attempt-cooperate-militarily-with-north-korea-must-2023-09-06/.

Kim, PS, "Who's Preparing for the Pecuniary Downside of the Merger? Economy: The Imperative in the Reunification of North and South Korea", *The Journal of Business, Entrepreneurship and the Law*, 9(2) (2016), 296–315.

Kim, S. H, "The Assessment of President Donald Trump's North Korean Policy", *North Korean Review*, 16(2) (2020), 121–8.

Kim, SJ (ed.), *The Northern Region of Korea: History, Identity, and Culture*. (University of Washington Press, 2010).

Kim, SS, *The Rivalry Between the Two Koreas*, in Ganguly, S. and Thompson, W. R. *Asian Rivalries: Conflict, Escalation, and Limitations on Two-Level Games*. (Stanford University Press, 2011), pp. 145–75.

Kim, YS, "Building a Two-Fold Structure in Resolving Political Disputes on the Korean Peninsula: Case Study on the Kaesong Industrial Complex", *Southwestern Journal of International Law*, 21 (2014), 375–405.

Kirk, D, "South Korean Leader Assailed on Funds Transfer to North", *New York Times*, (Jan 31, 2003). Available at: www.nytimes.com/2003/01/31/international/asia/south-korean-leader-assailed-on-funds-transfer-to-north.html.

Kishida, F, "Japan: Half a Century of OECD Membership", OECD Observer, (2012). Available at: www.oecd.org/japan/japan-half-a-century-of-oecd-membership.htm.

Kizilyürek, N, "The Politics of Identity in the Turkish Cypriot Communit: A Response to the Politics of Denial?", *MOM Éditions*, 37 (2003), 197–204.

KNEWS, "North gears up for mobile link-up with south." (July 2, 2019). Available at: https://knews.kathimerini.com.cy/en/news/north-gears-up-for-mobile-link-up.

Kochenov, D, "Behind the Copenhagen Facade. The Meaning and Structure of the Copenhagen Political Criterion of Democracy and the Rule of Law", *European Integration Online Papers*, 8(10) (2004), 1–24.

Koh, HH, "The 1994 Roscoe Pound Lecture: Transnational Legal Process", *Nebraska Law Review*, 75(1) (1996), 181–207.

Kohn, H, *The Idea of Nationalism: A Study in Its Origins and Background*, 1st edn (Macmillan Publishers, 1944).

Kong, Q, "Cross-Taiwan Strait Relations: What Are the Legitimate Expectations from the WTO?", *Minnesota Journal of International Law*, 14(1) (2005), 91–110.

Koremenos, B et al., "The Rational Design of International Institutions", *International Organization*, 55(4) (2001), 761–99.

Krasner, SD, *Sovereignty: Organized Hypocrisy*. (Princeton University Press, 1999).

Kratochwil, F, "*Sovereignty as* Dominium*: Is There a Right of Humanitarian Intervention?*", in Lyons, G. M. and Mastanduno, M. *Beyond Westphalia? National Sovereignty and International Intervention* (Johns Hopkins University Press, 1995), pp. 21–42.

Ku, Y, Lee, I and Woo, J, *Politics in North and South Korea Political Development, Economy, and Foreign Relations*, 1st edn (Routledge, 2018).

Kuomintang (中國國民黨), 中國國民黨聲明 "zhongguo guomindang shengming" [The Statement of the KMT], (Jan 3, 2019). Available at: www.kmt.org.tw/2019/01/blog-post_3.html.

Kyodo News, "U.S. Slaps Sanctions on North Korea with Allies over Spy Satellite", (Dec 1, 2023). Available at: https://english.kyodonews.net/news/2023/12/4515793768bc-us-slaps-sanctions-on-n-korea-in-response-to-spy-satellite-launch.html.

Kyris, G, "Europeanisation and Conflict Resolution: The Case of Cyprus", IBEI Working Papers 2013/39, (2013). Available at: www.ibei.org/europeanisation-and-conflict-resolution-the-case-of-cyprus_20622.pdf.

Lake, DA, "Domination, Authority, and the Forms of Chinese Power", *The Chinese Journal of International Politics*, 10(4) (2017), 357–82.

Lankov, A, *A Dynastic Polity in Economic Stagnation and Decline*, in Seth, M. J. Routledge *Handbook of Modern Korean History*, 1st edn (Routledge, 2016), pp. 220–33.

Lauterpacht, H, "Recognition of States in International Law", *The Yale Law Journal*, 53(3) (1944), 385–458.

Lee, E, "Operation Denucleunification: A Proposal for the Reunification and Denuclearization of the Korean Peninsula", *Hastings International and Comparative Law Review*, 33(1) (2010), 245–84.

Lee, H-W, "The Current State and Required Modifications of the Inter-Korean Exchange and Cooperation Act", *Journal of Korean Law*, 11 (2011), 55–76.

Lee, J, *The Division of Korea and the Rise of Two Koreas, 1945–1948*, in Seth, M. J. *Routledge Handbook of Modern Korean History* 1st edn (Routledge, 2016), pp. 168–77.

Lee, J-K. and Nam, J-W, *North Korea's External Trade Relations*, in Kim, J. J. and Minjeong, H. *Outside Looking In: A View into the North Korean Economy*. (The Asian Institute for Policy Studies, 2014), pp. 96–111.

Lee, P, "Rules of Origin and the Kaesong Industrial Complex: South Korea's Uphill Battle against the Principle of Territoriality", *North Carolina Journal of International Law*, 39(1) (2013), 1–41.

Lee, R, "Taiwan's China Dependency is a Double-Edged Sword", *East Asia Forum*, (July 6, 2021). Available at: https://eastasiaforum.org/2021/07/06/taiwans-china-dependency-is-a-double-edged-sword/.

Lee, S-H, "Dispute Settlement in Cross-Border Public-Private Partnerships with Diplomatic Agendas: Learning from the Kaesong Industrial Complex", *Journal of International and Area Studies*, 23(2) (2016), 61–76.

Lee, T-H, "Inaugural Address, Lee Teng-hui President Republic of China", *New Congress*, (May 20, 1996). Available at: http://newcongress.yam.org.tw/taiwan_sino/leespeec.html.

Lee, YH. and Kim, MJ, "What You Need to Know about South Korea's President-Elect, Yoon Suk-yeol", *Washington Post*, (Mar 9, 2022). Available at: www.washingtonpost.com/world/2022/03/09/south-korea-yoon-suk-yeol-president/.

Lee, YS, "International Isolation and Regional Inequality: Evidence from Sanctions on North Korea", *Journal of Urban Economics*, 103 (2018), 34–51.

Leifer, M, "Taiwan and South-East Asia: The Limits to Pragmatic Diplomacy", *The China Quarterly*, 165 (2001), 173–85.

Liao, P-H. and Wang, D-W, *Taiwan Under Japanese Colonial Rule, 1895–1945: History, Culture, Memory.* (Columbia University Press, 2006).

Liberty Times, "Change Course Now on Strait Policy", *Taipei Times*, (Sep. 12, 2004). Available at: www.taipeitimes.com/News/editorials/archives/2004/09/12/2003202613.

Lim, E-C, *Kaesong Industrial Complex: History, Pending Issues, and Outlook.* (Haenam Publishing Co., 2007).

Lin, C-C (林建志), 給臺灣制憲的備忘錄－以程序面為中心 "Gei taiwan zhixian de beiwanglu – yi chengxumian wei zhongxin" [Memorandum to Taiwan's Constitution Makers: The Procedural Dimension], 《中研院法學期刊》 *Academia Sinica Law Journal*, 33 (2023), 145–222.

Lin, C-F and Wu, C-H, "Is Taiwan a State?", *Verfassungsblog*. (Oct 18, 2022). Available at: https://verfassungsblog.de/is-taiwan-a-state/.

Lin, SS, *Taiwan's China Dilemma: Contested Identities and Multiple Interests in Taiwan's Cross-Strait Economic Policy*. (Stanford University Press, 2016).

Lin, Y-C (林詠青), 柯文哲喊重啟服貿 嗆綠營不做兩岸監督條例 "Ko Wen-Zhe han chongqi fu mao qiang luying bu zuo liangan jiandu tiaoli" [Ko Wen-je Called for the Restart of Trade in Services, Choking the Green Camp and Not Implementing Cross-Strait Supervision Regulations] *Radio Taiwan INTL*, (June 20, 2023). Available at: www.rti.org.tw/news/view/id/2171289.

Lin, Y-J, "Taiwan's Trade Imbalance with China: The Factors and the Trend", *American Journal of Chinese Studies*, 12(2) (2005), 139–58.

Liu, H-W, "A Missing Part in International Investment Law: The Effectiveness of Investment Protection of Taiwan's Bits vis-à-vis ASEAN States", *University of California Davis Journal of International Law and Policy*, 16 (2010), 130–69.

Liu, J, "As the World Courts TSMC, Taiwan Worries About Losing Its 'Silicon Shield'", *CNN*, (Dec 9, 2022). Available at: https://edition.cnn.com/2022/12/09/tech/taiwan-tsmc-chips-hnk-intl/index.html.

Liu, J, "In Taiwan, the Tiananmen Tragedy Has a Special Resonance." *The Diplomat*. (June 8, 2019). Available at: https://thediplomat.com/2019/06/in-taiwan-the-tiananmen-tragedy-has-a-special-resonance/.

Lo, Y-H, "Detecting Genetic Ancestry and Adaptation in the Taiwanese Han People", *Molecular Biology and Evolution*, 38(10) (2021), 4149–65.

Locke, J, *Locke: Two Treatises of Government*, in *Cambridge Texts in the History of Political Thought*, 3rd edn (Cambridge University Press, 1960).

Loizides, NG, "Ethnic Nationalism and Adaptation in Cyprus", *International Studies Perspectives*, 8(2) (2007), 172–89.

Loizides, NG, "Greek – Turkish Dilemmas and the Cyprus EU Accession Process", *Security Dialogue*, 33(4) (2002), 429–42.

Loizides, N, *Designing Peace: Cyprus and Institutional Innovations in Divided Societies*. (University of Pennsylvania Press, 2016).

Lyu, Z. and Zhou, H, "Contesting Master Narratives: Renderings of National History by Mainland China and Taiwan", *The China Quarterly*, 255 (2023), 768–84.

Macias, A, "North Korea says it won't restart nuclear discussions until U.S. drops its 'hostile policies'", *CNBC*, (March 17, 2021). Available at: www.cnbc.com/2021/03/17/north-korea-says-wont-restart-talks-until-us-drops-its-hostile-policies.html.

Macias, A, "U.S. Sanctions 8 People and Entities following North Korean Missile Launches", *CNBC*, (Jan 12, 2022). Available at: www.cnbc.com/2022/01/12/us-sanctions-5-north-koreans-over-weapons-programs-following-missile-launches.html.

Maehara, S, *Lee Teng-hui and the Formation of Taiwanese Identity*, in Jocobs, J. B. and Kang, P. *Changing Taiwanese Identities*. (Routledge, 2017), pp. 87–92.

Mainland Affairs Council Republic of China (Taiwan) et al., "Supporting Mechanisms for "Active Management, Effective Opening" in Cross-Strait Economic and Trade Relations." (Mar 22, 2006). Available at: https://ws.mac.gov.tw/001/Upload/OldFile/public/data/97716221671.pdf.

Mainland Affairs Council Republic of China (Taiwan), "Allowing RMB-NTD conversion business to be implemented in the Taiwan Area." Available at: www.mac.gov.tw/en/cp.aspx?n=7EAA16F21B02FD43&s=7A3354652CAE6AEA.

Mainland Affairs Council Republic of China (Taiwan), "Expanding the 'Mini-Three-Links.'" Available at: www.mac.gov.tw/en/cp.aspx?n=7EAA16F21B02FD43&s=EE6922E9CFA19138.

Mainland Affairs Council Republic of China (Taiwan), "Facilitating visits by Mainland professionals to Taiwan." Available a:t www.mac.gov.tw/en/cp.aspx?n=7EAA16F21B02FD43&s=670812630439EA8C.

Mainland Affairs Council Republic of China (Taiwan), "The Government's Mainland Policy and Related Important Measures Since May 20, 2008." Available at: www.mac.gov.tw/en/News_Content.aspx?n=C62A6E4BD490D38E&sms=F56AA93EEC16ECD5&s=C0DAD6AE6B654676.

Mainland Affairs Council Republic of China (Taiwan), 大陸政策與工作 "Dalu zhengce yu gongzuo" [Mainland China Policy and Work]. Available at: www.mac.gov.tw/News_Content.aspx?n=9223A12B5B31CB37&sms=35FA2C4073CF4DFB&s=1EBF54814FF20ABD.

Mainland Affairs Council Republic of China (Taiwan), 行政院院會通過「臺灣地區與大陸地區人民關係條例第五條之三」修正草案 "Xingzheng yuan yuan hui tongguo Taiwan diqu yu dalu diqu renmin guanxi tiaoli di wu tiao zhi sanxiuzheng caoan" [The Executive Yuan Council approves the amendment draft of "Article 5-3 of the Act Governing Relations between the People of the Taiwan Area and the Mainland Area], (Mar 28, 2019). Available at: www.mac.gov.tw/News_Content.aspx?n=B383123AEADAEE52&s=912E9F6266E55408.

Mainland Affairs Council Republic of China (Taiwan), 兩岸協議 "Liangan Xieyi" [Cross-Strait Agreements]. Available at: www.mac.gov.tw/cp.aspx?n=1494D59CE74DF095.

Mainland Affairs Council Republic of China (Taiwan), 兩岸經濟交流統計速報九十一年十二月份 "liangan jingji jiaoliu tongji subao jiushiyi nian shier yuefen" [Brief of Cross-strait Economic Exchanges, December 2002], (Dec 2002). Available at: www.mac.gov.tw/001/Upload/OldFile/public/data/97116484171.gif.

Mainland Affairs Council Republic of China (Taiwan), 兩岸經濟統計月報 (283期) "liang anjing jitong jiyue bao (283 qi)" [Cross-Strait Economic Statistics Monthly Report, No. 283]. Available at: www.mac.gov.tw/News_Content.aspx?n=2C28D363038C300F&sms=231F60B3498BBB19&s=098983FEC0388D55.

Mainland Affairs Council Republic of China (Taiwan), 陸委會與海基會關係 "Lu wei hui yu hai ji hui guanxi" [The relationship between the Mainland Affairs Council and the SEF]. Available at: www.mac.gov.tw/cp.aspx?n=0984A85A3A9A6677.

Mainland Affairs Council Republic of China (Taiwan), 落實大陸投資「積極開放、有效管理」政策說明"Luoshi dalu touzi 'Jīji kaifang, youxiao guanli' zhengce shuoming" [Explanations of "Active Openness, Effective Management" Policy], (Nov 7, 2001). Available at: www.mac.gov.tw/News_Content.aspx?n=C07A4E0160AC69CE&sms=B69F3267D6C0F22D&s=B39520BC69B9114C.

Maizland, L, "Why China-Taiwan Relations Are So Tense?", *Council on Foreign Relations*, (Feb 8, 2024). Available at: www.cfr.org/backgrounder/china-taiwan-relations.

Manyan, ME and Nanto, DK, "The Kaesong North-South Korean Industrial Complex." CRS Report for Congress RL34093. (Apr 18, 2011). Available at: www.fas.org/sgp/crs/row/RL34093.pdf.

Maritain, J, "The Concept of Sovereignty", *The American Political Science Review*, 44(2) (1950), 343–57.

Mavroidis, PC, *China and the WTO: Why Multilateralism Still Matters*. (Princeton University Press, 2021).

McCurry, J, "South Korea to Withdraw Last Workers from Kaesong Joint-Venture with North", *The Guardian*, (Apr 29, 2013). Available at: www.theguardian.com/world/2013/apr/29/south-korea-workers-venture-north.

McDonald, T, "China and Taiwan Face Off in Pineapple War." *BBC News*. (Mar 20, 2021). Available at: www.bbc.com/news/business-56353963.

Mendez, M, "Constitutional Review of Treaties: Lessons for Comparative Constitutional Design and Practice", *International Journal of Constitutional Law*, 15(1) (2017), 84–109.

Ministry of Commerce of People's Republic of China Bureau of Industry Injury Investigation, 我国对原产于俄罗斯、韩国、乌克兰、哈萨克斯坦、台湾地区的冷轧板卷进行反倾销立案调查 "Woguo dui yuanchanyu eluosi, hanguo, wukelan, hasakesitan, taiwan diqu de lengyabanjuan jinxing fanqingxiao lian tiaocha" [China's Anti-Dumping Investigation Against Cold-Rolled Coils Originating in Russia, South Korea, Ukraine, Kazakhstan, and Taiwan] (Mar 20, 2002). Available at: http://dcj.mofcom.gov.cn/article/date/ckzcfg/200507/20050700199760.shtml

Ministry of Commerce of the People's Republic of China (中华人民共和国商务部), 商务部关于就台湾地区对大陆贸易限制措施进行贸易壁垒调查的公告 "shang wubujiutaiwandi quduida lumao yixian zhicuo shi jin xingmao yibi leidiao chadegong gao" [Announcement on the Final Conclusion of the Trade Barrier Investigation Regarding Trade Restriction Measures by the Taiwan Region Against the Mainland, Announcement No. 54 of 2023], No. 11, (Dec 15, 2023). Available at: www.mofcom.gov.cn/article/zwgk/gkzcfb/202304/20230403403369.shtml.

Ministry of Economic Affairs, Republic of China (Taiwan), 兩岸洽簽服務貿易協議對我總體經濟及產業之影響評估 "Liangan qiaqian fuwu maoyi xieyi dui wo zongti jingji ji chanye zhi yingxiang pinggu" [Cross-strait Negotiation for Service Trade Agreement Impact on the Overall Economic and Industrial Impact Assessment] (July 17, 2013). Available at: /www.ecfa.org.tw/Download.aspx?No=40&strT=ECFADoc.

Ministry of Foreign Affairs of the People's Republic of China, "China and Nauru Resume Diplomatic Relations", (Jan 24, 2024). Available at: www.mfa.gov.cn/eng/zxxx_662805/202401/t20240124_11232061.html.

Ministry of Foreign Affairs, People's Republic of China, "Foreign Ministry Spokesperson's Remarks on the Government of the Republic of Nauru's Announcement to Break Diplomatic Ties with the Taiwan Region and Seek to Reestablish Diplomatic Ties with China", (Jan 15, 2024). Available at: www.mfa.gov.cn/eng/xwfw_665399/s2510_665401/202401/t20240115_11223838.html.

Ministry of Foreign Affairs, Turkish Republic of Northern Cyprus, "Relations with the United Nations." Available at: https://mfa.gov.ct.tr/foreign-policy/international-organisations/bm-ile-iliskiler/.

Ministry of Unification of South Korea, "Inter-Korean Exchanges and Cooperation", Data and Statistics. Available at: www.unikorea.go.kr/eng_unikorea/relations/statistics/exchanges/.

Ministry of Unification of South Korea, "Weekly Report on North Korea from March 27 to April 2, 2021 (No. 1563)." (Apr 2, 2021). Available at: www.unikorea.go.kr/eng_unikorea/relations/infoNK/weekly/?boardId=bbs_0000000000000040&mode=view&cntId=54352&category=&pageIdx=10.

Ministry of Unification of South Korea, "White Paper on Korean Unification 2010." Available at: www.unikorea.go.kr/eng_unikorea/news/Publications/whitepaper/.

Ministry of Unification of South Korea, *White Paper on Korean Unification 2021*. (Ministry of Unification of South Korea, 2021).

Moon, C-I. and Bae, J-Y, "The Bush Doctrine and the North Korean Nuclear Crisis", *Asian Perspective*, 27(4) (2003), 9–45.

Movsesian, ML, "The Persistent Nation State and the Foreign Sovereign Immunities Act", *Cardozo Law Review*, 18(3) (1996), 1083–110.

Nanto, DK, "The Rise of China and Its Effect on Taiwan, Japan, and South Korea: U.S. Policy Choices." CRS Report for Congress RL32882, (Jan 13, 2006). Available at: https://sgp.fas.org/crs/row/RL32882.pdf.

National Archives and Records Services of Democratic People's Republic of Korea, "The Committee for the Peaceful Reunification of the Fatherland (in Korean)", (archived Nov 23, 2011). Available at: https://web.archive.org/web/20111123120534/http://contents.archives.go.kr/next/content/listSubjectDescription.do?id=007131.

Naughton, B, *The China Circle: Economics and Technology in the PRC, Taiwan, and Hong Kong*. (Brookings Institution Press, 1997).

Ng, K, "Nauru Cuts Diplomatic Ties with Taiwan in Favour of China", *BBC News*, (Jan 15, 2024). Available at: www.bbc.com/news/world-asia-67978185.

Ng, N, "China Has Banned Taiwan's Pineapples. Taiwan Says It's Not Fair Play", *CNBC*, (Mar 4, 2021). Available at: www.cnbc.com/2021/03/04/taiwan-chinas-ban-on-pineapples-not-in-line-with-global-trade-rules.html.

Nicholson, R, *Statehood and the State-Like in International Law*. (Oxford University Press, 2019).

Noland, M, "Are North and South Korea Back in Business? (Interview)", *Council on Foreign Relations*, (Aug 14, 2013). Available at: www.cfr.org/interview/are-north-and-south-korea-back-business.

Noland, M, *The North Korean Famine*, in Seth, M. J. Routledge *Handbook of Modern Korean History*, 1st edn (Routledge, 2016).

Novo, AR, *EOKA Cause, The: Nationalism and the Failure of Cypriot Enosis*. (Bloomsbury Academic, 2021).

Nugent, N, "EU Enlargement and 'The Cyprus Problem'", *Journal of Common Market Studies*, 38(1) (2000), 131–50.

Oberdorfer, D and Carlin, R, *The Two Koreas: A Contemporary History*. (Basic Books, 2013).

Office of the President Republic of China (Taiwan), "President Chen's Concluding Remarks at National Security Conference", (Feb 27, 2006). Available at: https://english.president.gov.tw/NEWS/2180.

Office of the President, Republic of China (Taiwan), "Inaugural address of ROC 14th-term President Tsai Ing-wen", (May 20, 2016). Available at: https://english.president.gov.tw/News/4893.

Office of the President, Republic of China (Taiwan), "Inaugural address of ROC 15th-term President Tsai Ing-wen", (May 20, 2020). Available at: https://english.president.gov.tw/NEWS/6004.

Office of the President, Republic of China (Taiwan), "President Lee Addresses National Assembly", (Dec 8, 1992). Available at: https://english.president.gov.tw/NEWS/1205.

Office of the United States Trade Representative, "United States and Taiwan Announce the Launch of the U.S.-Taiwan Initiative on 21st-Century Trade", (June 1, 2022). Available at: https://ustr.gov/about-us/policy-offices/press-office/press-releases/2022/june/united-states-and-taiwan-announce-launch-us-taiwan-initiative-21st-century-trade.

Oh, I and Jun, H, *Economic Miracle: From Post-War Reconstruction to Post-Crisis Affluence*, in Seth, MJ Routledge *Handbook of Modern Korean History*, 1st edn (Routledge, 2016), pp. 292–311.

Oh, K (ed.) and Hassig, R. C. (ed.), *Korea Briefing 2000–2001: First Steps Toward Reconciliation and Reunification*, 3rd edn (Routledge, 2002).

Olsen, JP, "The Many Faces of Europeanization", *Journal of Common Market Studies*, 40(5) (2002), 921–52.

Oppenheim, LF, *International Law: A Treatise*, Vol. II of *War and Neutrality*. (Longmans, Green and Co., 1906).

Özden, MÖ, "Turkey-Cyprus Island Interconnector as an Energy Policy for Turkey", Transatlantic Policy, (Aug 27, 2019). Available at: http://turkishpolicy.com/blog/36/turkey-cyprus-island-interconnector-as-an-energy-policy-for-turkey.

Paik, H, "Assessment of the Sunshine Policy: A Korean Perspective", *Asian Perspective*, 26(3) (2002), 13–35.

Paik, N-C, *The Division System in Crisis: Essays on Contemporary Korea*. (University of California Press, 2011).

Pak, C. Y, *Korea and the United Nations*. (Martinus Nijhoff Publishers, 2000).

Palley, C, *An International Relations Debacle: The UN Secretary-General's Mission of Good Offices in Cyprus 1999–2004*. (Hart Publishing, 2005).

Panagides, SS, "Communal Conflict and Economic Considerations: The Case of Cyprus", *Journal of Peace Research*, 5(2) (1968), 133–45.

Panda, A and Putz, C, "The Biden Administration Releases an Indo-Pacific Strategy: Reading Between the Lines", *The Diplomat*, (Feb 18, 2022). Available at: https://thediplomat.com/2022/02/the-biden-administration-releases-an-indo-pacific-strategy-reading-between-the-lines/.

Papadakis, Y, "Greek Cypriot Narratives of History and Collective Identity: Nationalism as a Contested Process", *American Ethnologist*, 25(2) (1998), 149–65.

Park, G-H, "A New Kind of Korea: Building Trust Between Pyongyang and Seoul", *Foreign Affairs*, 90(5) (2011). Available at: www.foreignaffairs.com/articles/northeast-asia/2011-09-01/new-kind-korea.

Park, HS, "North Korean Perceptions of Self and Others: Implications for Policy Choices", *Pacific Affairs*, 73(4) (2014), 503–16.

Park, J-M, "Military Agreement Fractures as Tensions Rise with North Korea", *Reuters*, (Nov 23, 2023). Available at: www.reuters.com/world/asia-pacific/military-agreement-fractures-tensions-rise-with-north-korea-2023-11-22.

Permanent Mission of Cyprus to The United Nations, "UNDP in Cyprus." Available at: www.cyprusun.org/?page_id=376.

Permanent Mission of The People's Republic of China to The United Nations Office at Geneva and Other International Organizations in Switzerland, "Spokesperson of the Chinese Mission Speaks on the "Taiwan International Solidarity Act" Passed by the U.S.", (Dec 17, 2021). Available at: http://geneva.china-mission.gov.cn/eng/ryrbt/202305/t20230520_11080428.htm.

Petersmann, EU, *Multilevel Constitutionalism for Multilevel Governance of Public Goods: Methodology Problems in International Law*. (Hart Publishing, 2017).

Philenews, "Cyprus to decide on joining Great Sea Interconnector with Israel, Greece", (Feb 2, 2024). Available at: https://in-cyprus.philenews.com/insider/cyprus-to-decide-on-joining-great-sea-interconnector-with-israel-greece/.

Phillips, CS Jr, "The International Legal Status of Formosa", *The Western Political Quarterly*, 10(2) (1957), 276–89.

Philpott, D, "Sovereignty: An Introduction and Brief History", *Journal of International Affairs*, 48(2) (1995), 353–68.

Qian, M (钱明雅), 广州60条惠及台胞措施 "Guangzhou 60 tiao huiji tai bao cuoshi" [Guangzhou releases 60 measures benefiting Taiwan compatriots; Taiwanese enterprises recognized as "high-tech enterprises" can receive millions in subsidies], 南方日報 *[Nanfang Daily]*, (Feb 8, 2023). Available at: https://news.southcn.com/node_54a44f01a2/cb0c90e606.shtml.

Qing, W, '"One Country, Two Systems': The Best Way to Peaceful Reunification", *Beijing Review*, 33 (1990). Available at: www.bjreview.com.cn/nation/txt/2009-05/26/content_197568.htm.

Radaelli, CM, "Whither Europeanization? Concept Stretching and Substantive Change", *European Integration Online Papers*, 4(8) (2000), 1–27.

Richmond, OP, *Mediating in Cyprus: The Cypriot Communities and the United Nations* 1st edn (Routledge, 1998).

Roh, J-H, *The Legal and Institutional Approach to Inter-Korean Relations*, in Kim, S. S. *Inter-Korean Relations: Problems and Prospects*. (Palgrave Macmillan, 2004), pp. 159–74.

Rosen, DH and Wang, Z, *The Implications of China-Taiwan Economic Liberalization*. (Columbia University Press, 2010).

Roth, B, *Sovereign Equality and Moral Disagreement*. (Oxford University Press, 2011).

Roy, D, *Taiwan. A Political History*. (Cornell University Press, 2003).

Ruan, LY, "The Chinese Communist Party and Legitimacy: What is the Chinese Communist Party's official discourse on legitimacy?", *The Diplomat*, (Sept 2015). Available at: https://thediplomat.com/2015/09/the-chinese-communist-party-and-legitimacy/.

Ruggiero, A and Zweiz, M, "Biden's North Korea Policy Needs Rebooting", *Foreign Policy*, (Jan 24, 2022). Available at: https://foreignpolicy.com/2022/01/24/biden-north-korea-missiles-sanctions/.

Ryall, J, "North Korea Ends Military Pact with South Korea – What Next?", *Deutsche Welle*, (Nov 24, 2023). Available at: www.dw.com/en/north-korea-ends-military-pact-with-south-korea-what-next/a-67541707.

Sanger, DE, "North Korea Reluctantly Seeks U.N. Seat", *New York Times*, (May 29, 1991). Available at: www.nytimes.com/1991/05/29/world/north-korea-reluctantly-seeks-un-seat.html.

Scalapino, RA, "Current Dynamics of the Korean Peninsula", En Problems of Communism [Problems Communism], 30(6) (1981), 16–31.

Schütze, R, "Parliamentary Democracy and International Treaties", *Global Policy*, 8(6) (2017), 7–13.

Select Committee on Foreign Affairs, "Written Evidence: How Many Turkish Cypriots Remain in Cyprus", UK Parliament, (Feb 22, 2005). Available at: https://publications.parliament.uk/pa/cm200405/cmselect/cmfaff/113/113we33.htm.

Sepos, A, *The Europeanization of Cyprus: Polity, Policies and Politics*. (Palgrave Macmillan, 2008).

Serdy, A, "Bringing Taiwan into the International Fisheries Fold: The Legal Personality of a Fishing Entity", *British Yearbook of International Law*, 75(1) (2005), 183–221.

Shaelou, SL and Manoli, A, "A Tale of Two: The COVID-19 Pandemic and the Rule of Law in Cyprus", *Verfassungsblog*, (Apr 30, 2020). Available at: https://verfassungsblog.de/a-tale-of-two-the-covid-19-pandemic-and-the-rule-of-law-in-cyprus/.

Shaelou, SL, "The European Court of Justice and the Anastasiou Saga: Principles of Europeanisation through Economic Governance", *European Business Law Review*, 18(3) (2007), 619–39.

Shaelou, SL, *The EU and Cyprus: Principles and Strategies of Full Integration*. (Martinus Nijhoff Publishers, 2010).

Shan, J, "Cross-Strait Trade and Investment and the Role of Hong Kong", *Wisconsin International Law Journal*, 16 (1998), 661–86.

Sharma, D, "Taiwan Has Lost Ground Because of Pelosi's Visit: Chinese Military Exercises Have Changed the Status Quo in Its Favor", *Nikkei Asia*, (Aug 14, 2022). Available at: https://asia.nikkei.com/Opinion/Taiwan-has-lost-ground-because-of-Pelosi-s-visit.

Shaw, MN, *International Law* 8th edn (Cambridge University Press, 2018).

Shin, G-W and Straub, D, "Jang Song-taek Purge Further Undermines North Korea's Foreign Relations", *East Asia Forum*, (Feb 12, 2014). Available at: https://eastasiaforum.org/2014/02/12/jang-song-taek-purge-further-undermines-north-koreas-foreign-relations/.

Shin, J, *North Korean State-Making: Process and Characteristics*, in Seth, M. J. Routledge *Handbook of Modern Korean History* 1st edn (Routledge, 2016), pp. 195–210.

Shin, M, "Yoon Suk-yeol Becomes South Korea's President-Elect", *The Diplomat*, (Mar 10, 2022). Available at: https://thediplomat.com/2022/03/yoon-suk-yeol-becomes-south-koreas-president-elect/.

Shirk, SL, *China: Fragile Superpower*, 1st edn (Oxford University Press, 2008).

Simonovic, I, "State Sovereignty and Globalization: Are Some States More Equal?", *Georgia Journal of International and Comparative Law*, 28(3) (2000), 381–404.

Skoutaris, N, "The Application of the acquis communautaire in the Areas Not under the Effective Control of the Republic of Cyprus: The Green Line Regulation", *Common Market Law Review*, 45(3) (2008), 727–55.

Skoutaris, N, *The Cyprus Issue: The Four Freedoms in a Member State Under Siege*. (Hart Publishing, 2011).

Slaughter, AM, *A New World Order*. (Princeton University Press, 2004).

Smith, G, "Taiwan's Sunflower Movement", *Foreign Policy in Focus*, (May 29, 2014). Available at: https://fpif.org/taiwans-sunflower-movement/.

Smith, H, *North Korea: Markets and Military Rule*, 1st edn (Cambridge University Press, 2015).

Snyder, S and Byung, S-W, "Cheonan and Yeonpyeong: The Northeast Asian Response to North Korea's Provocations", *The RUSI Journal*, 156(2) (2011), 74–81.

Snyder, S, "South Korean President-Elect Yoon Suk-Yeol's Early Foreign Policy Challenges", *Forbes*, (Mar 24, 2022). Available at: www.forbes.com/sites/scottasnyder/2022/03/24/south-korean-president-elect-yoon-suk-yeols-early-foreign-policy-challenges/?sh=6ff57658656d.

Son, K-Y, *South Korean Engagement Policies and North Korea: Identities, Norms and the Sunshine Policy*, 1st edn (Routledge, 2006).

Sonyel, SR, *Cyprus: The Destruction of a Republic and its Aftermath. British Documents, 1960–1974.* (CYREP, 2003).

Sözen, A and Faustmann, H, "Cyprus: Political Developments and Data in 2019", *European Journal of Political Research Political Data Yearbook*, 59 (2020), 82–97.

Sozen, A and Faustmann, H, "Cyprus", *European Journal of Political Research Political Data Yearbook*, 55(1) (2016), 59–68.

Statista, "Breakdown of the Gross domestic product (GDP) of Taiwan from 2013 to 2023, by economic sector", (Feb 2024). Available at: www.statista.com/statistics/321366/taiwan-gdp-breakdown-by-sector/.

Statista, "China's Leading Import Partners in 2022, by import value", (Feb 2024). Available at: www.statista.com/statistics/257042/chinas-main-import-partners-by-import-value/.

Statista, "Distribution of Chinese Exports in 2022, by Trade Partner", (Feb 2024). Available at: www.statista.com/statistics/270326/main-export-partners-for-china/.

Statista, "Merchandise Trade Balance of Taiwan with Mainland China and Hong Kong from 2013 to 2023 (in billion U.S. dollars)", (Feb 2024). Available at: www.statista.com/statistics/320608/taiwan-trade-balance-with-china-and-hong-kong/.

Statista, "Share of Taiwan's exports in 2023, by major trade partner", (Feb 2024). Available at: www.statista.com/statistics/1266748/main-export-partners-for-taiwan/.

Stern, RE and Liu, RJ, "The Good Lawyer: State-Led Professional Socialization in Contemporary China", *Law and Social Inquiry*, 45(1) (2020), 226–48.

Stern, RE, "Political Reliability and the Chinese Bar Exam", *Journal of Law and Society*, 43(4) (2016), 506–33.

Su, C (蘇起, ed.) and Cheng, A-K (鄭安國, ed.), 一個中國各自表述共識的史實 *"'Yige Zhongguo Gezi Biaoshu' Gongshi De Shishi" [One China, With Respective Interpretations" – A Historical Account of The Consensus Of 1992], Vol. I-VIII.* (國家政策研究基金會 [National Policy Foundation], 2002).

Su, C, *Taiwan's Relations with Mainland China: A Tail Wagging Two Dogs* 1st edn (Routledge, 2010).

Su, Y-C (蘇永欽), 尋找共和國 *"Xuunzhao Gongheguo" [Searching for The Republic].* (元照出版公司 [Angle Publishing Co.], 2008).

Suksi, M, "Divided States" in *Max Planck Encyclopedia of Public International Law* (2013). Available at https://opil.ouplaw.com/display/10.1093/law:epil/9780199231690/law-9780199231690-e1031?rskey=ppzjJM&result=1&prd=MPIL.

Sun, G (孙国平), 论ECFA争端解决机制模式之构建 "Lun ECFA zhengduan jiejuejizhi moshi zhi goujian" [The Construction of DSM Mode of ECFA], 《国际经济法学刊》 *Journal of International Economic Law*, 18(3) (2011), 239–58.

Sun, WS, *A comparison between the CEPA and the ECFA*, in Chow, C. Y. Economic Integration Across the Taiwan Strait: Global Perspectives. (Edward Elgar, 2013), pp. 30–55.

Sung, P-F (宋佩芬) and Chang, W-H. (張韡曦), 臺灣史的詮釋轉變：國族歷史與國家認同教育的省思 "Taiwanshi de quanshizhuanbian: Guozulishi yu guojiarentong jiaoyu de xingsi" [Taiwanese History: Reflections on National History and the Education of National Identity], 《教育科學研究期刊》 *Journal of Research in Education Science*, 55(3) (2010), 123–50.

Taiwan Today, "EU chamber's Position Papers push direct links agenda." (Nov 3, 2006). Available at: https://taiwantoday.tw/news.php?unit=6,23,45,6,6&post=8119.

Talmon, S, "The Cyprus Question before the European Court of Justice", *European Journal of International Law*, 12(4) (2001), 727–50.

Tan, TW, "Comments on Implications of the U.S.–China Trade War for Taiwan", *Asian Economic Papers*, 19(1) (2020), 84–91.

Tanner, MS, *Chinese Economic Coercion Against Taiwan: A Tricky Weapon to Use.* (RAND Corporation, 2007).

The Committee for the Peaceful Reunification of Korea (CPRK), "Important Measures to Defend Nation's Sovereignty, Dignity and Country's Supreme Interests: CPRK", *Korean Central News Agency (KCNA)*, (Mar 8, 2013). Available at: www.kcna.co.jp/item/2013/201303/news08/20130308-01ee.html.

The European Office of Cyprus, "Business Support Centre – Cyprus." Available at: https://eoc.org.cy/participation-in-european-projects/business-support-centre-cyprus/.

The Guardian, "North Korea withdraws from nuclear treaty" (Jan 10, 2003). Available at: www.theguardian.com/world/2003/jan/10/northkorea1.

The Guardian, "US and allies condemn North Korea over missile test 'provocations.'" (Feb 13, 2022). Available at: www.theguardian.com/world/2022/feb/13/us-and-allies-condemn-north-korea-over-missile-test-provocations.

The Taiwan Affairs Office of The State Council and The State Council Information Office, "The Taiwan Question and China's Reunification in the New Era." (Aug, 2022). Available at: http://gm.china-embassy.gov.cn/eng/sgxw/202208/P020220810850182763063.pdf.

Tocci, N, *The EU and Conflict Resolution: Promoting Peace in the Backyard*, 1st edn (Routledge, 2007).

TRNC Ministry of Foreign Affairs, "Relations with Parliamentary Assembly of Council of Europe." Available at: https://mfa.gov.ct.tr/foreign-policy/international-organisations/council-of-europe/pace/.

Tsai, C-H, "Exit, Voice and International Jurisdictional Competition: A Case Study of the Evolution of Taiwan's Regulatory Regime for Outward Investment in Mainland China, 1997–2008", *Syracuse Journal of International Law and Commerce*, 39(2) (2012), 303–55.

Tsai, S, *Lee Teng-hui and Taiwan's Quest for Identity*. (Palgrave MacMillan, 2005).

Tsai, W. (蔡學儀), 兩岸三通之發展與分析 "Liangan santong zhi fazhan yu fenxi" [The Dynamics and Analyses of Direct Trading Relationships between Taiwan and China], 《展望與探索》 *Prospect and Exploration*, 2(2) (2004), 34–50.

Tsiourtou, K, "Unravelling the story behind the Intellectual property of Halloumi Cheese; a 'State Affair' for Cyprus", *Stockholm Intellectual Property Law Review*, 2(2) (2019), 32–47.

Turkish Cypriot Chamber of Commerce (TCCoC), "History of the Chamber." Available at: www.ktto.net/en/history-of-the-chamber-2/.

Turkish Cypriot Chamber of Commerce (TCCoC), "Leading by Example." Available at: www.ktto.net/en/leading-by-example-2/.

US Department of State, "U.S.-D.P.R.K. Joint Communique", (Oct 12, 2000). Available at: https://1997-2001.state.gov/regions/eap/001012_usdprk_jointcom.html.

US Department of the Treasury, "Treasury Targets DPRK's International Agents and Illicit Cyber Intrusion Group" (Press Release), (Nov 30, 2023). Available at: https://home.treasury.gov/news/press-releases/jy1938.

Ulusoy, K, *Europeanization's Time Constraint: The Case of Cyprus*, in Akçay, B and Yilmaz, B *Turkey's Accession to The European Union: Political and Economic Challenges*. (Lexington Books, 2012), pp. 227–300.

UN Cyprus Talks, "Statement by the United Nations Spokesperson in Cyprus, 26 February 2019." (Feb 26, 2019). Available at: https://uncyprustalks.unmissions.org/statement-united-nations-spokesperson-cyprus-26022019.

UN Cyprus Talks, "Statement by the United Nations Spokesperson in Cyprus, 19 November 2021." (Nov 19, 2021). Available at: https://uncyprustalks.unmissions.org/statement-united-nations-spokesperson-cyprus19-november-2021.

United Nations Repertory of Practice of United Nations Organs, "Articles 1–22 of the Charter", (1955). Available at: https://legal.un.org/repertory/.

Van der Vyver, JD, "Sovereignty and Human Rights in Constitutional and International Law", Emory International Law Review, 5(2) (1991), 321–444.

Varnava, A (ed.) and Faustmann, H (ed.), *Reunifying Cyprus: The Annan Plan and Beyond*. (I.B. Tauris, 2009).

Varnava, M, *Cyprus Before 1974: The Prelude to Crisis*. (I.B. Tauris, 2020).

Vogel, T, "MEPs consider allowing EU trade within Northern Cyprus", *Politico*, (May 19, 2010). Available at: www.politico.eu/article/meps-consider-allowing-eu-trade-with-northern-cyprus/.

Voice of America, "South Korea Formally Declares End to Sunshine Policy." (Nov 17, 2010). Available at: www.voanews.com/a/south-korea-formally-declares-end-to-sunshine-policy--108904544/130750.html.

Wade, R, *Governing the Market: Economic Theory and the Role of Government in East Asian Industrialization*. (Princeton University Press, 1990).

Walters, R, "A Backgrounder on the History of US-Taiwan Trade and Investment Talks", *Global Taiwan Institute*, (Jun. 30, 2021). Available at: https://globaltaiwan.org/2021/06/a-backgrounder-on-the-history-of-us-taiwan-trade-and-investment-talks/.

Wang, J (王建民), 「30年两岸交流与两岸关系发展回望(上)」 "30 nian liangan jiaoliu yu liangan guanxi fazhan huiwang (shang), tongyiluntan zazhi" [Looking Back at 30 years of Cross-Strait Exchanges and the Development of Cross-Strait Relations (Part 1)], 《统一论坛》杂志*Unity Forum Magazine* (Dec 26, 2017).

Wang, TY, "Lifting the 'No Haste, Be Patient' Policy: Implications for Cross-Strait Relations", *Cambridge Review of International Affairs*, 15(1) (2010), 131–9.

Wang, T-S, "The Emergence of Modern Constitutional Culture in Taiwan", *National Taiwan University Law Review*, 5(1) (2010), 1–38.

Wang, C-K (王照坤), 時空背景不同 陸委會：現無談判服貿需求 "Shikong beijing butong lu wei hui: Xian wu tanpan fu mao xuqiu" [Different Contexts, Mainland Affairs Council: There is Currently No Need to Negotiate the Service Trade Agreement] *Radio Taiwan INTL*, (June 29, 2023). Available at: www.rti.org.tw/news/view/id/2172118.

Warner, G, "Review Article: The United States and the Cyprus Crisis of 1974", *International Affairs*, 85(1) (2009), 129–43.

Watanabe, RN, "Foreign Exchange and Capital Movement Controls in Taiwan", *UCLA Pacific Basin Law Journal*, 16(1) (1997), 1–37.

Watts, J, "South Korean Tourist Shot Dead in North Korea", *The Guardian*, (July 11, 2018). Available at: www.theguardian.com/world/2008/jul/11/korea.

Webster, C. and Timothy, DJ, "Travelling to the 'Other Side': the Occupied Zone and Greek Cypriot Views of Crossing the Green Line", *Tourism Geographies*, 8(2) (2006), 162–81.

Wertz, D, "The U.S, North Korea, and Nuclear Diplomacy", *The National Committee of North Korea (NCNK)*, (Oct, 2018). Available at: www.ncnk.org/resources/briefing-papers/all-briefing-papers/history-u.s.-dprk-relations.

Wessel, RA, "Informal International Law-Making as a New Form of World Legislation?", *International Organizations Law Review*, 8(1) (2011), 253–65.

Wheaton, H, *Elements of International Law*, 2nd edn (Steven and Sons, Ltd., 1880).

Wheaton, H, *Elements of International Law*, 4th edn (Steven and Sons, Ltd., 1904).

World Bank, "Population Total – Cyprus" (Dataset). Available at: https://data.worldbank.org/indicator/SP.POP.TOTL?locations=CY.

Wrobel, RM, "Ten years of Kaesong Industrial Complex: A brief history of the last economic cooperation project of the Korean peninsula", *Economic and Environmental Studies*, 14(2) (2014), 125–47.

Wu, C-H, "Dance with the Dragon: Closer Economic Integration with China and Deteriorating Democracy and Rule of Law in Taiwan and Hong Kong?", *Hong Kong Law Journal*, 45(1) (2015), 275–94.

Wu, C-H. and Lin, C-F, "Taiwan and the Myth of UN General Assembly Resolution 2758", *Verfassungsblog*, (Apr 14, 2023). Available at: https://verfassungsblog.de/taiwan-and-the-myth-of-un-general-assembly-resolution-2758/.

Wyeth, G, "Time to Reopen the Kaesong Industrial Complex? A Conversation with Jin-hyang Kim", *The Diplomat*, (Feb 27, 2020). Available at: https://thediplomat.com/2020/02/time-to-reopen-the-kaesong-industrial-complex-a-conversation-with-jin-hyang-kim/.

Xanthaki, H, *The Route to EU Accession*, in Stefanou, C. *Cyprus and the EU: The Road to Accession*, 1st edn (Routledge, 2005), pp. 25–60.

Xiao, P (肖平) and Zeng, L (曾丽凌), 论《海峡两岸经济合作框架协议》之法律性质与效果 "Lun haixialiangan jingjihezuo kuangjia xieyi zhi falü xingzhi yu xiaoguo" [On the Legal Nature and Effects of the Economic Cooperation Framework Agreement], 《海峡法学》*Cross-Strait Legal Science*, 1 (2011), 30–4.

Xinhua she (新华社), 15种台湾水果8月1日起正式实施零关税措施"15 zhong Taiwan shuiguo 8 yue 1 ri qi zhengshi shishi lingguanshui cuoshi" [15 Types of Taiwan Fruits Formally Implement Zero-Tariff Measures from 1 August], *Xinhua News Agency*, (Aug 2, 2005). Available at: www.gov.cn/jrzg/2005-08/02/content_19516.htm.

Xinhua she (新华社), 习近平出席《告台湾同胞书》发表40周年纪念会并发表重要讲话 "Xijinping chuxi "gao taiwan tongbao shu" fabiao 40 zhounian jinian hui bing fabiao zhongyao jianghua" [Xi Jinping Attends the 40th Anniversary Commemoration of the "Message to Compatriots in Taiwan" and Delivers an Important Speech], *Xinhua News Agency*, (Jan 2, 2019). Available at: www.gov.cn/xinwen/2019-01/02/content_5354209.htm.

Xinhua she (新华社), 国台办：大陆暂停进口台湾菠萝是正常生物安全防范举措 "Guo tai ban: Dalu zanting jinkou Taiwan boluo shi zhengchang shengwu anquan fangfan jucuo" [The Taiwan Affairs Office of the State Council: The mainland's suspension of imports of Taiwan pineapples is a normal biosecurity precaution], *Xinhua News Agency*, (Feb 26, 2021). Available at: https://tinyurl.com/2v82c6w2.

Xinhua she (新华社), 国台办：台湾地区两项选举结果改变不了两岸关系基本格局和发展方向" Guo tai ban: Taiwan diqu liangxiang xuanju jieguo gaibian bu liao liangan guanxi jiben geju he fazhan fangxiang" [The Results of Two Elections in the Taiwan Region Cannot Change the Basic Pattern and Development Direction of Cross-Strait Relations], *Xinhua News Agency*, (Jan 17, 2024). Available at: www.gwytb.gov.cn/xwdt/xwfb/wyly/202401/t20240117_12594378.htm.

Xinhua she (新华社), 国台办：暂停输入台湾地区番荔枝和莲雾科学合理、完全正当 "Guo tai ban: Zanting shuru Taiwan diqu fan lizhi he lian wu kexue heli, wanquan zhengdang" [Taiwan Affairs Office of the State Council: The Suspension of the Import of Custard Apples and Lotus Mist from Taiwan is Scientifically Reasonable and Completely Justified], *Xinhua News Agency*, (Sept 22, 2021). Available at: www.gov.cn/xinwen/2021-09/22/content_5638743.htm.

Yakinthou, C, *The EU's Role in the Cyprus Conflict: System Failure or Structural Metamorphosis?* in Hughes, J. *EU Conflict Management*. (Routledge, 2010), pp. 32–49.

Yang, C and Hung, S-W, "Taiwan's Dilemma Across the Strait: Lifting the Ban on Semiconductor Investment in China", *Asian Survey*, 43(4) (2003), 681–96.

Yeh, J-R, "Marching Towards Civic Constitutionalism with Sunflowers", *Hong Kong Law Journal*, 45(1) (2015), 315–30.

Yeh, J-R, *The Constitution of Taiwan – A Contextual Analysis*. (Hart Publishing, 2016).

Yeung, J and Bae, G, "South Korea's new President Yoon Suk Yeol Urges North Korean Denuclearization in Inauguration Address", *CNN*, (May 10, 2022). Available at: https://edition.cnn.com/2022/05/10/asia/yoon-suk-yeol-south-korea-president-inauguration-intl-hnk/index.html.

Yeung, J et al, "How South Korea's New President Could Shake up the Region", *CNN*, (Mar 11, 2022). Available at: https://edition.cnn.com/2022/03/10/asia/yoon-suk-yeol-new-south-korean-president-stance-intl-hnk/index.html.

Yilmaz, ME, "The Cyprus conflict and the question of identity", *Uluslararası Hukuk ve Politika [Review of International Law and Politics]*, 4 (2005), 74–90.

Yim, S, "North Korea's Kim calls for South to be seen as 'primary foe', warns of war", *Reuters*, (Jan 16, 2024). Available at: www.reuters.com/world/asia-pacific/north-koreas-kim-calls-change-status-south-warns-war-2024-01-15/.

Yin, Y-R (殷英珈) and Tsai, T-H (蔡宗顯), 111 年我國出進口貿易概況 "111 Nian woguo chu jinkou maoyi gaikuang" [Overview of the Nation's Import and Export Trade for 2022], *Ministry the Interior Department of Statistics*, (Feb 24, 2023). Available at: https://service.mof.gov.tw/public/Data/statistic/bulletin/112/111%E5%B9%B4%E6%88%91%E5%9C%8B%E5%87%BA%E9%80%B2%E5%8F%A3%E8%B2%BF%E6%98%93%E6%A6%82%E6%B3%81.pdf.

Yonhap News, "Chronology of Major North Korean Statements on the Korean War Armistice." (May 28, 2009). Available at: https://en.yna.co.kr/view/AEN20090528004200315.

Yoo, JT, *The Koreas: The Birth of Two Nations Divided* 1st edn (University of California Press, 2020).

Zengerle, P, "Biden Approves Military Aid to Taiwan under Program Normally Used for Sovereign States", *Reuters*, (Aug 31, 2023). Available at: www.reuters.com/world/asia-pacific/biden-approves-military-aid-taiwan-under-program-normally-used-sovereign-states-2023-08-30/.

Zhang, Y (张业遂), 张业遂：进一步为港澳台投资提供更加开放、便利的营商和发展环境 "Jinyibu wei gangao tai touzi tigong gengjia kaifang, bianli de ying shang he fazhan huanjing" [Zhang Yesui, Further provide a more open and convenient business and development environment for investment in Hong Kong, Macao and Taiwan], Xinhua News Agency, (Mar 4, 2019). Available at: http://www.xinhuanet.com/politics/2019lh/2019-03/04/c_1210072714.htm.

Zhao, S, "Economic Interdependence and Political Divergence: The Emerging Pattern of Relations across the Taiwan Strait", *Journal of Contemporary China*, 6(15) (1997), 177–97.

Zheng, Y, "China's New Foreign Investment Law and Its Contribution Towards the Country's Development Goals", *The Journal of World Investment and Trade*, 22 (2021), 388–428.

Zhou, W and Laurenceson, J, "Demystifying Australia – China Trade Tensions", *Journal of World Trade*, 56(1) (2000), 21–36.

Index

NB: Page numbers in *italics* denote information in figures and those in **bold** denote information in tables

www.ingramcontent.com/pod-product-compliance
Lightning Source LLC
LaVergne TN
LVHW020409270125
802249LV00003B/36